How to Do Everything with

Windows Mobile®

Frank McPherson

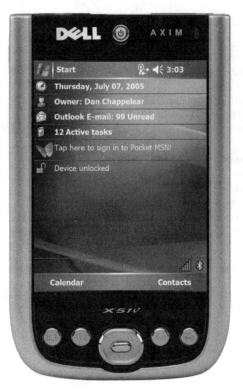

McGraw-Hill

New York   Chicago   San Francisco   Lisbon
London   Madrid   Mexico City   Milan   New Delhi
San Juan   Seoul   Singapore   Sydney   Toronto

The McGraw-Hill Companies

McGraw-Hill books are available at special quantity discounts to use as premiums and sales promotions, or for use in corporate training programs. For more information, please write to the Director of Special Sales, Professional Publishing, McGraw-Hill, Two Penn Plaza, New York, NY 10121-2298. Or contact your local bookstore.

How to Do Everything with Windows Mobile®

1234567890 DOC DOC 019876

ISBN 0-07-226250-8

Acquisitions Editor	Megg Morin
Project Editor	Janet Walden
Acquisitions Coordinator	Agatha Kim
Production Supervisor	James Kussow
Technical Editor	Todd Ogasawara
Copy Editor	William McManus
Proofreader	Francesca Ferrie
Indexer	Claire Splan
Composition	International Typesetting and Composition
Illustration	International Typesetting and Composition
Series Design	Mickey Galicia
Cover Series Design	Dodie Shoemaker

This book was composed with Adobe® InDesign®

Bill Weber was the best boss that anyone could wish for. He treated with me with respect, allowed me to take risks, kept my ego in check when things went well, and supported me without hesitation when things went bad. It is no surprise that Bill became a good friend and mentor. In some of the most important moments of my life—when I got married and when I first started writing these books—Bill provided encouragement that carried me through anxiety and doubt.

All of us who called Bill a friend feel he passed away too soon. Few days go by when I don't remember something that he said. Nothing pleases me more than to share my memories of Bill with you, and this book that you are about to read and which Bill helped me write.

About the Author

Frank McPherson is an avid user of handheld computers, starting with the Newton MessagePad in 1993 and all versions of Microsoft Pocket PCs, Pocket PC Phones, and Smartphones. He developed and maintains the Pocket PC Hints and Tips web site (www.pocketpchow2.com), which is visited by Pocket PC users around the world seeking help using their Pocket PCs.

Frank has been a sports columnist and reporter for the *Norway Current*, a weekly newspaper in Norway, Michigan, and has also covered high school sports for the *Iron Mountain Daily News* in Iron Mountain, Michigan. Articles written by Frank about Pocket PCs have appeared in *Pocket PC Magazine*, *Brighthand.com*, and *PocketPC.com*.

He is a 1989 graduate of Michigan Technological University with a B.S. degree in computer science. Frank is a senior information specialist at EDS, where he has been employed for over fifteen years. Originally from Norway, Michigan, located in Michigan's beautiful Upper Peninsula, this Yooper now lives in West Bloomfield, Michigan with his wife, Ruth.

About the Technical Editor   Todd Ogasawara is currently the eGovernment Team Leader for the State of Hawaii Information & Communication Services Division. Previous to that, he was at GTE/Verizon as an advanced technology engineer. During that same period, he simultaneously worked as a contractor for the Microsoft Network (MSN), and later ZDNet (when MSN Technology Forums moved to ZDNet) as the online forum manager for both the Telephony and the Windows CE Forums. At ZDNet, these forums were renamed the Communications & Messaging Forum and the Handhelds Forum.

Todd was privileged to have been the co-manager of the Communications & Messaging Forum with the legendary Don Watkins while at ZDNet. He served as an editor for the Microsoft Uplink web site that focused on the Palm-size PC, and authored dozens of articles for the Microsoft PocketPC.com web site. He has been awarded the Microsoft Most Valuable Professional in the Mobile Devices category for the past several years. You can find his mobile device commentary, reviews, and how-to articles at www.MobileViews.com.

Contents at a Glance

Contents

Acknowledgments

Although the title does not indicate it, this is now the fourth edition of my book on handheld computers that run Microsoft software. Over the years since the first edition of this book became available, I have received many kind e-mails from readers complimenting my work. This book that you are holding would not exist if not for those who bought the previous editions. So first, and foremost, I want to thank all of you for buying this book.

It has been a pleasure to work again with the entire crew at McGraw-Hill. While my name is on the cover, many more have worked behind the scenes to produce this book. Special thanks to Megg Morin, Janet Walden, and Agatha Kim.

Writing this book was a collaborative effort with my technical editor, Todd Ogasawara. Todd's many suggestions in each chapter have made this book better, and you and I have benefited from his work. Thank you, Todd.

Thanks also go to John Starkweather and Andrew Brown at Microsoft for providing information and answering questions about the Windows Mobile.

For securing the images seen on this book's cover, thanks go out to Amy Thompson at Dell, Melinda Neely at HTC America, and Lyndsay LaGree at Motorola. Thanks to Michael Boone at Biomobility, LLC. for providing permission to include screen shots of their products in this book. Their quick turnaround and efforts are much appreciated.

Thanks to my friends, mentors, and co-workers including: Ray Anderson, Scott Van Wolvelaere, Amy Dulan, Bob Naglich, Brad Gee, Shirley Myrick, Saverio Rinaldi, Keith Muir, Dawn Pfaff, and Rhonda Belinc. I appreciate your friendship and support.

Thanks to my niece, Carley Lindquist, for helping with the screen shots in this book. Thanks to my grandmother, Dorothy McPherson, and my mother, Sharon McPherson, for their love and support. And last but not least, thanks to my wife Ruth. Your love, patience, understanding, and support are what made this book happen.

Introduction

What's in a name? Over the years since it first released software for handheld devices, Microsoft has changed the software name three times. First it was Windows CE, then Windows Powered, and now Windows Mobile Software.

Regardless of the names, the software remains true to its Windows heritage, enabling us to use handheld computers in much the same way that we use desktop computers. Critics claim that the Windows user interface was never designed for, and therefore not appropriate for, handheld computers. What the critics overlook is the power of familiarity that enables one to pick up a Pocket PC and Smartphone and use it right away.

Windows Mobile devices help you interact in different ways with a variety of information. Think about all of the information that is important to you. It might be appointments, addresses, bank account balances, or documents. It might even be voice recordings, web pages, video clips, or music.

Many people have turned to personal computers to help them keep track of all this different information. But, there is a problem with personal computers. Most sit on tables and desks at home, yet we might need the information they contain when we are sitting in a meeting or out shopping. With a Windows Mobile device, that information can be taken out of the computer so it's with you at any time and anywhere. And when you return home, that information can be easily updated to your personal computer.

Pocket PCs, Pocket PC Phones, and Smartphones are part of a series of hardware devices that run the Microsoft Windows CE .NET operating system and application software. Also in the series are the Handheld PC, Auto PC, and embedded devices. Microsoft calls the series Windows Mobile devices. The combination of Windows CE .NET and application software is known as Windows Mobile Software for Pocket PCs, Pocket PC Phones, and Smartphones.

These are incredibly powerful little devices that you can use for work and play. In *How to Do Everything with Windows Mobile*, I show you how to use the latest Windows Mobile Software to create documents and spreadsheets, check off those items on your task list, and then relax to the sounds of your favorite music. If there is something that you want to do with a Pocket PC or Smartphone, this book will show you how to do it.

Part I provides the information that you need to get started with Windows Mobile. Chapter 1 provides an overview of the devices that make up the Windows Mobile platform to help you decide which is right for you. Then starting in Chapter 2, I walk you through setting up your Pocket PC, personalizing your Pocket PC, changing Pocket PC settings, and setting up Smartphones.

Part II, "Connect with PCs," provides instructions for moving information from your personal computer into the device. Chapter 6 shows you how to connect Windows Mobile devices with personal computers, and in Chapter 7 you learn how to use the ActiveSync software to synchronize data so that what is stored in Microsoft Outlook on your PC also appears in Outlook Mobile on your device. As that information changes, synchronization ensures that it is the same on both the PC and Pocket PC or Smartphone.

The Internet has become a very important tool for retrieving and exchanging information, and Part III, "Get Connected with Windows Mobile," provides all the instructions you need to connect to and use the Internet. Windows Mobile devices can connect to the Internet using landline and wireless modems, mobile phones, and wired or wireless local area networks. Once the connection is made, you can send and receive e-mail, chat with friends using instant messaging, and browse any web site.

Part IV, "Make the Most Out of Windows Mobile," focuses on how you will use your Windows Mobile device every day. You will use Outlook Mobile to manage your appointments, addresses, and tasks, and Office Mobile to create documents and spreadsheets. I also provide tips for using your device at the office and when you are traveling. And when you are ready for a break, you can install and play one of the many games available for Windows Mobile. In Chapter 19, you learn how to expand the functionality of your Pocket PC or Smartphone with software and hardware.

A number of special elements have been added to help you get the most out of this book:

- ■ **How to...**   These special boxes explain, in a nutshell, how to accomplish certain tasks that use the skills that you learn in this book.
- ■ **Did You Know...**   These boxes provide additional information about topics relating to Windows Mobile.
- ■ **Notes**   These provide extra information or important things that you need to watch out for in certain situations.
- ■ **Tips**   These tell you how to do something better, faster, or in a smarter way.

Within the text you will find words in special formatting. New or defined terms are in *italic*. If there is a hyphen between two different keys, such as CTRL-B, that's a keyboard combination, and you should press each key while holding down the others, then release them simultaneously. Some instructions involve tapping or pressing different buttons or menu items in sequence. Each step in the sequence is separated by an I-beam, for example File | Open means tap or press the File and then Open menu options.

Technology changes at a breakneck pace, and undoubtedly you will have a question or encounter a problem not covered in this book. One good source for information is the microsoft .public.pocketpc Internet newsgroup, which is monitored by Microsoft Mobile Device MVPs. You can also reach me through my web site, Pocket PC Hints and Tips, at www.pocketpchow2 .com, or via the e-mail address, feedback@fmcpherson.com.

Part I

Get Started with Windows Mobile

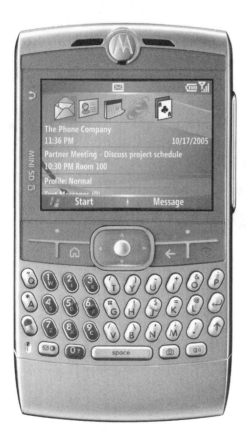

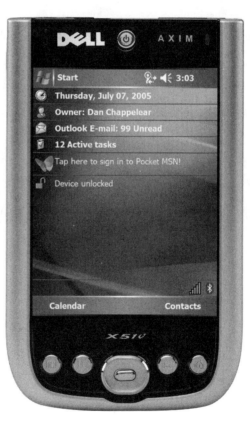

Chapter 1

Welcome to Windows Mobile

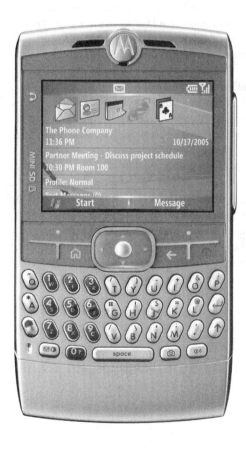

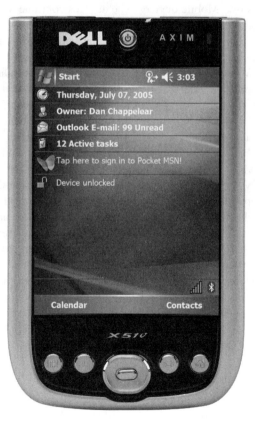

How to...

■ Recognize the different Windows Mobile platforms

■ Know what Windows Mobile devices include

■ Know the different parts of the Windows Mobile software

In 1996, several companies, including Hewlett-Packard, Casio, Sharp, and Compaq, began selling new devices that complied with the Handheld PC platform created by Microsoft. Handheld PCs run Microsoft software, including the Windows CE operating system and other programs for managing personal information and creating documents and spreadsheets.

The Handheld PC was only the first of a variety of types of what Microsoft now calls Windows Mobile devices. The devices continue to evolve and include the Pocket PC, Pocket PC Phone Edition, and Smartphone, which are the subjects of this book. Each device is designed so that you can work with the information that's important to you, wherever it is needed and in the manner you find most comfortable.

Windows Mobile devices do more than just manage appointments, addresses, and task lists, although they do those tasks very well. With a Windows Mobile device, you can read your e-mail and surf the Web. You can write a letter, balance your checkbook, make voice recordings, read books, and listen to music. In the case of the Pocket PC, all these things are possible in a device that can rest in your hand and fit in your pocket.

Everyone's information needs are different, and the software for Pocket PCs and Smartphones provides unique tools to meet your needs. Smartphones, while not the greatest devices for data entry, are designed for easy operation with one hand. Pocket PCs, which usually require two hands to operate, provide more functionality and several ways to enter data. This book is about how to use the Windows Mobile software to get the most out of your Pocket PC or Smartphone.

Each component of Windows Mobile is covered in depth in the chapters of this book, which focuses on the current versions of the software that run on Pocket PCs and Smartphones. While older versions continue to exist, and much of what is contained in this book applies to those versions, the focus is on the newest software for these platforms.

I'll begin by providing a history of the information appliances that inspire Windows Mobile. Next, I describe all the hardware platforms that, when combined, comprise the Windows Mobile devices. And I'll conclude with an introduction to the Windows Mobile software, all the details of which are explained in more depth in the remaining chapters of this book.

Information Appliances

In the 70 years since it was introduced, the television set has undergone a number of changes. From black-and-white to color images, and from simple 19-inch round displays to 35-inch flat panels, the television set has been improved and reinvented. Through it all, one thing has remained constant: Each television set has a power button, and when you press that button the screen springs to life to display what we commonly call TV.

It is true of all consumer electronic devices that we expect them to work the instant we turn them on. Radios and CD/DVD players immediately start playing music, and Game Boys start games. What about your personal computer? What happened the last time you turned it on? Did it spring to life and start computing?

In offices all around the world, the following ritual is played out every morning (you might even find yourself doing it): After fighting through traffic and dragging yourself and the work you brought home into your cube or office, you hang up your coat, turn on your computer, grab your coffee mug, and head for the coffee machine. Sound familiar? This ritual has come about because of what is known as the *booting process* of personal computers. The booting process includes all steps that a computer takes from when it is first turned on until it is ready for you to use, and this typically takes more time than turning on consumer electronic devices.

Wouldn't it be great if your computer were as easy to use as a television set and functioned from the moment you turned it on? That is the promise of information appliances. In his book *The Invisible Computer* (MIT Press, 1998), Donald A. Norman defines the information appliance as "an appliance specializing in information: knowledge, facts, graphics, images, video, or sound. An information appliance is designed to perform a specific activity, such as music, photography, or writing. A distinguishing feature of information appliances is the ability to share information among themselves."

Apple Newton MessagePad

A form of an information appliance is the *personal digital assistant (PDA)*. During a speech at the 1992 Consumer Electronics Show in Las Vegas, former Apple Computer CEO John Sculley defined the PDA and announced Apple's intention to develop such a device. PDAs are information appliances that use computer technology to help manage personal information and assist with mundane tasks. Later that same year, Sculley introduced Apple's PDA, the Newton MessagePad, at the Spring Consumer Electronics Show (CES) in Chicago.

From the time of its introduction in 1992 to its launch at the 1993 MacWorld Expo in Boston, a tremendous amount of hype was generated about the Newton MessagePad. Unfortunately, the hype was short-lived; and during the lifespan of the Newton MessagePad from 1993 to 1998, sales never reached Apple's projected levels. Sadly, despite the technology of the Newton MessagePad, it may be best known in computing history for a series of *Doonesbury* comic strips that made fun of the results of Newton's handwriting recognition.

With the benefit of hindsight, one can look back at the Newton MessagePad and see its shortcomings. The handwriting recognition was not complete when it was first released, which resulted in the PDA being branded a failure. During its five years, Newton MessagePad grew larger in size and increased in price, conflicting with a market that wanted smaller devices at a lower cost. Finally, exchanging information between a MessagePad and a desktop computer was too difficult.

Despite these shortcomings, the Newton MessagePad leaves a legacy of creating the PDA market and furthering the cause of information appliances. Lessons learned from the Newton MessagePad were applied to both Palm Computing devices and Microsoft PC Companions.

Microsoft PC Companions

During the summer of 1992, Microsoft began its version of the Newton MessagePad, which it called WinPad. At the same time another Microsoft project, Pulsar, was underway to develop a pager-like device. In 1994, senior management at Microsoft reviewed both projects and decided to combine the two into a new project that was given the code name Pegasus, which became Windows CE.

WinPad was designed to be a companion for Windows desktop computers and was based on Windows 3.1. Pulsar was to include an entirely new object-oriented operating system, completely unlike any other Microsoft product. In the end, Pegasus did not include the technology from either of these projects, but it did inherit the WinPad vision of being a companion for Windows desktop computers. That vision was initially known as the *PC Companion,* and lives on in *Windows Mobile* devices.

Windows Mobile Devices and Platforms

A Windows Mobile device is small enough to fit in the palm of your hand and is designed to exchange information with programs running on personal computers. The device enables you to carry all of the information you create on a personal computer, wherever it may be needed. And, equally important as its size and ability to communicate with personal computers, a Windows Mobile device uses an operating system stored on a computer chip that runs continuously, eliminating the booting process. The device functions immediately when it is turned on, just like a television set.

Here is how you use a Windows Mobile device. Enter information on a notebook computer using a program like Microsoft Outlook, and then download the information to a device. If all you need is the information contained in Outlook, you can leave the notebook computer behind and pack only the device when you're traveling.

Now, when your boss calls to ask if you can attend a meeting, all you need to do is take out your device, turn it on, and look up the information—in no more time than it takes to retrieve and look up the same information in a planner. After you determine that you are available on the date and time of the meeting, you create the appointment on the device. When you return to the office, you connect the Windows Mobile device to the notebook computer; the new appointment uploads to Outlook, eliminating the need to re-enter information, as might be the case if you were using a planner and Outlook together.

The process of exchanging information between a Windows Mobile device and a desktop computer is called *synchronization*. Synchronization is actually a bit more sophisticated than simply uploading and downloading information, because it has the ability to determine what has been added to both devices and to ensure that the information is the same on both, all in one step.

One can debate whether or not a Windows Mobile device is an information appliance. It specializes in information, yet it can perform multiple activities. Because information can be expressed and used in many different ways, a Windows Mobile device manages not only personal information, such as your appointments and addresses, but also documents, spreadsheets, web pages, voice recordings, and music.

Nor is information the only variable; how each person wishes to interact with that information is also variable. Some people prefer using small devices with small keyboards, while others are comfortable with a stylus and handwriting recognition. Others prefer a larger device, closer in size to a notebook computer, and some prefer to have that information available in their cars, which they can retrieve by using voice commands.

Over the years since 1996, when the first PC Companion was introduced, Microsoft has continually made changes to the Windows CE operating system and the software that it includes to support a wide range of information types. At the same time, new hardware has been introduced by a variety of third-party companies, targeted at the variety of different ways users want to interact with the device. Today three different types of Windows Mobile devices are available: Pocket PCs, Pocket PC Phone Editions, and Smartphones.

Since Microsoft launched the first device, several original equipment manufacturers (OEMs), such as Asus, Hewlett-Packard, and Dell, have made the hardware while Microsoft has created the software. The software includes an operating system and mobile versions of some Microsoft desktop software, such as Outlook Mobile (Calendar, Contacts, Tasks, and Messaging) and Mobile Office (Word Mobile, Excel Mobile, and PowerPoint Mobile).

Unlike the software of a personal computer, the software of Windows Mobile devices is stored on a computer chip. Windows Mobile software for Pocket PCs, Pocket PC Phone Editions, and Smartphones is available only on a read-only memory (ROM) chip. Using a ROM chip enables Microsoft to store all of the software in a very small amount of space and to eliminate the booting process. In the beginning, the combination of the operating system, the user interface, Pocket Outlook, and Pocket Office became known as Windows CE, even though Windows CE is really just the operating system. Today, Microsoft calls this combination of software on a ROM chip Windows Mobile Software for Pocket PCs or Smartphones.

Microsoft has released several versions of Windows Mobile software over the years. The initial releases were Pocket PC 2000 and 2002, after which came Windows Mobile 2003 and 2003 Second Edition. The current software is Windows Mobile Version 5.

The Handheld PC was the first Windows Mobile hardware platform, and since 1996 Microsoft has introduced six additional platforms: Palm-size PC, Auto PC, Handheld PC Professional, Pocket PC, Smartphone, and Portable Media Center.

Portable Media Center provides only music and video playback, and is an extension to Windows XP Media Center Edition. Portable Media Center is not covered in this book.

Handheld PC

Handheld PC was the result of the Pegasus project, which began in 1994. The platform included the first versions of the Windows CE operating system, Pocket Outlook, and Pocket Office. The first version of Pocket Office included only Word and Excel. Microsoft also included a copy of its first Personal Information Manager (PIM), Schedule +, and Handheld PC Explorer, which provided synchronization between Schedule + and the Handheld PC.

Along with the software, the following hardware specifications were typical for Handheld PCs:

- *Clamshell* design, approximately 3.5×7 inches and weighing 13 ounces
- Powered by alkaline batteries
- 480×240-resolution monochrome display
- Keyboard for data input and a stylus instead of a mouse
- One serial port and cable to connect the Handheld PC to desktop computers
- An IrDA (Infrared Data Association)-compliant infrared port to exchange information with other Handheld PCs

Devices based on the Handheld PC platform are no longer made, and Microsoft no longer supports this platform.

Palm-Size PC

In 1998, Microsoft introduced two more Windows Powered platforms: Palm-size PC and Auto PC. A Palm-size PC device, which is the predecessor to Pocket PC, is approximately 3×5 inches and weighs around 6 ounces. The Palm-size PC screen uses a portrait layout, and the device does not include a keyboard. Instead, to input data you use a stylus either to write on the screen using a character recognizer or to tap on an onscreen keyboard.

 *Originally Microsoft wanted to call these devices Palm PCs, but Palm Computing filed a lawsuit against Microsoft. In an agreement with Palm Computing, Microsoft changed the name to Palm-size PC, which is a mouthful and is often abbreviated as P/PC.*

Significant changes were made to the software that Microsoft included with the P/PC. Pocket Outlook remained, as did Inbox and Solitaire, but Pocket Office, Windows Explorer, and Pocket Internet Explorer were not included.

 *Examples of the first P/PCs include the Casio E-11, the Philips Nino 320, and the Everex Freestyle Associate.*

In February 1999, Microsoft released the specification for a color version of the P/PC. Other than support for color screens, little else of Windows CE was changed, except a version number change to 2.11. The hardware for these devices retained basically the same physical size, but some included faster processors and more RAM.

Microsoft no longer supports the Palm-size PC platform.

Auto PC

At the same time that Microsoft announced the P/PC, it also announced the Auto PC. An Auto PC replaces your car radio with a Windows Powered information appliance. The device is voice-activated, enabling you to retrieve information, such as driving directions, using spoken commands.

Addresses that you have in the Contacts program on other Windows Powered devices can be transferred to the Auto PC by using infrared.

An optional component of the Auto PC is a wireless receiver with which you can receive traffic conditions, weather, news, stock quotes, and e-mail. The Auto PC voice synthesizer reads all of that information to you.

At the heart of the Auto PC is the Windows CE operating system—the same operating system that runs all other Windows Mobile devices. The Auto PC demonstrates the modular design of Windows CE, which allows Microsoft to remove components, such as the Pocket PC user interface, and replace it with other interfaces, such as the Auto PC voice recognizer.

The Auto PC has evolved to what is now known as Windows Automotive, which is not covered in this book. If you wish to read more information about Windows Automotive you can find information on the Internet at http://www.microsoft.com/windows/embedded/windowsautomotive/default.mspx.

Handheld PC Professional

In the fall of 1998, Microsoft released the Handheld PC Professional. This platform retains the screen and keyboard combination introduced with the Handheld PC but in a larger size. In the fall of 2000, Microsoft updated the platform, and called the new version Handheld PC 2000. The largest Handheld PC Pro device is 10×8 inches, and the smallest is about 4×7 inches.

NOTE   *Shortly after Handheld PC Professional devices became available, Microsoft realized the name confused the market and reverted to calling the platform Handheld PC.*

Handheld PCs were first sold to consumers, but they never sold as successfully as originally anticipated. Today Microsoft and the manufacturers of Handheld PCs target the devices at the corporate market, where they have had great success. Companies use Handheld PCs for specific functions, such as inventory control or customer relationship management. Such functions require the larger screens and keyboards that are part of Handheld PCs. Consumers can still buy Handheld PCs from online sources such as MobilePlanet at http://mobileplanet.com, though there is minimal availability and the devices may be discontinued.

Pocket PC

In April 2000, Microsoft released the first version of the Pocket PC platform, which is now called Pocket PC 2000. Since then, Microsoft has released four additional versions: Pocket PC 2002, Windows Mobile 2003, Windows Mobile 2003SE, and the current Windows Mobile Version 5. Windows Mobile Version 5 includes the CE .NET operating system, Outlook Mobile, and Mobile Office.

Some of the companies that sell Pocket PCs include: Hewlett-Packard, Dell, Asus, and i-Mate. The following hardware features are common to Pocket PCs:

- Intel StrongARM or X-Scale processors
- A Flash ROM chip for storing the Windows Mobile software

What's New in Windows Mobile Version 5

All the improvements available in Windows Mobile Version 5 are covered in detail throughout this book. Here is a summary of the major enhancements:

- User interface improvements that make it easier to use Pocket PCs and Smartphones with one hand
- Persistent data storage
- New PowerPoint Mobile
- New Pocket MSN Client
- Improvements with Internet Explorer Mobile, Word Mobile, and Excel Mobile

- A minimum of 32MB of RAM
- A color touchscreen display
- An infrared port for transferring information between devices
- At least one, and in some cases multiple, storage card slot

Pocket PC Phone Edition

During the summer of 2002, Microsoft released Pocket PC Phone Edition, which is Windows Mobile for Pocket PCs plus additional software to support wireless voice and data communications. The first release of Pocket PC Phone Edition supported only the Global System for Mobile (GSM) telecommunications standard for voice communication and the General Packet Radio Service (GPRS) for data communication used by T-Mobile and Cingular Wireless in the United States.

The Phone Edition version of Windows Mobile 2003 added support for Code Division Multiple Access (CDMA) and its data counterpart CDMA2000 or 1xRTT used by Verizon Wireless and Sprint PCS in the United States. In addition to these two widely used U.S. standards, the 2003 version of the Phone Edition software includes several enhancements, such as the ability to mute and unmute a call, a new speakerphone menu, and a separate volume control for the ringer.

With the release of Windows Mobile Version 5, Microsoft no longer makes a distinction between Phone Editions and Pocket PCs. Regardless of whether or not a Pocket PC includes a phone, the software is simply Windows Mobile Version 5.

Smartphone

The Microsoft vision for mobile computing is that no one device will be the best fit for every person. As you have seen in this chapter, Handheld PCs meet the needs for vertical applications requiring larger screens and keyboards, while Pocket PCs meet the needs for people who want a portable information appliance.

The goal of the Smartphone platform is to provide some of the functionality of the Pocket PC platform in a device that can be easily operated with one hand. While Smartphones have an e-mail client and a version of Internet Explorer, along with Outlook Mobile, they do not have Mobile Office and they do not support stylus input as do Pocket PCs.

Windows Mobile

Windows Mobile includes the Windows CE .NET operating system and application software (such as Outlook Mobile and Mobile Office) that run on Pocket PCs and Smartphones. All Windows Mobile devices include the Windows CE .NET operating system, but some may have different combinations of the application software. For example, some devices may include all the software, while others may include only Outlook Mobile.

This section provides an introduction to the components that make up Windows Mobile.

NOTE   *Pocket PC 2002 runs on the Windows CE 3.0 operating system.*

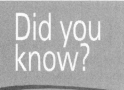

Differences Between Pocket PCs and Smartphones

While Pocket PCs and Smartphones are similar, there are currently two significant differences that you should be aware of. Pocket PCs have touch screens that support stylus input and the Mobile Office applications, while Smartphones do not have touch screens or Mobile Office.

The primary method of operating a Pocket PC is to hold the device in one hand and tap the stylus on the screen using your other hand. You operate Smartphones by holding a device in a hand and pressing buttons with your fingers.

In this book you will find instructions for operating both devices. Operations that you perform only on a Pocket PC will be prefixed with the word "tap"; for example, "tap Start | Settings | System | Screen." Operations that you perform on a Smartphone only will be prefixed with the word "press"; for example, "press Start | Settings | Phone." Operations that have the same steps on Pocket PCs and Smartphones will be prefixed with the word "select," such as "select Menu | Delete."

Windows CE Stands for Nothing

Windows CE .NET

In the simplest of terms, an *operating system* manages the interaction between application software and the hardware on which it runs. As a user, you should not be concerned with how the operating system works, only that it can run software at acceptable performance levels and remain stable.

One may be tempted to look at Windows CE .NET and decide that Microsoft simply transferred Windows 95 to handheld devices. The truth is that Windows CE .NET is a completely new 32-bit operating system, built from the ground up to run on embedded devices.

The following aspects of Windows CE .NET can affect you as a user:

- It implements a subset of the Win32 API, which was completely rewritten for embedded devices. This makes it easier for software developers to write programs using familiar tools, which speeds up the software development process.

- It is portable and can run on a variety of different processor types. That means that OEMs can choose from among a variety of processor manufacturers, enabling them to implement the latest processor technology at a lower price.

- It is a real-time operating system, which means that certain actions performed by the operating system occur within bounded times. To you, this means that the operating system should run faster.

- It is modular, so a system can be built using only the components needed for a particular platform. This means that a variety of different devices, such as the Pocket PC and the Smartphone, can be built from the same core operating system, decreasing product development life cycles.

The Windows CE .NET user interface, called the *shell,* is also a separate component. As such, Microsoft can create a separate shell for each hardware platform that runs the operating system. Separate shells have been created for the Pocket PC and Smartphone platforms, resulting in a slightly different look between the two devices.

The Windows CE .NET modular design means that it can be used in a wide range of devices. In fact, you might be surprised to know that Windows CE .NET is also used in devices such as gas pumps and point-of-sale terminals.

.NET Compact Framework

Included in ROM on all Windows Mobile devices is the .NET Compact Framework. Programmers can leverage their existing skills in C# and Visual Basic .NET to create applications for Windows Mobile. Programs can be quickly developed by providing native web services support and by allowing developers to focus on application development rather than on low-level infrastructure items such as memory management.

ActiveSync

It is important that information appliances easily exchange information with other devices; otherwise, the information is on a virtual island and not accessible everywhere it is needed. All Windows Mobile devices come with infrared ports that can be used to exchange information with other devices, but they also communicate with PCs running ActiveSync.

ActiveSync runs on PCs that use the Windows 2000, Windows Server 2003, or Windows XP operating systems. It synchronizes information between Windows Mobile devices and Outlook 2000 or newer. During synchronization, the software compares information on the device and on the PC, determining what has been added to both. Then, it updates the two so that the information is consistent on both devices.

The primary purpose for ActiveSync is to synchronize appointments, contacts, and tasks, but it also synchronizes Outlook Notes, Mobile Favorites, and Media content. Synchronization can be done using infrared, serial, USB, and Bluetooth. You also use ActiveSync to install programs on the device. Chapters 6, 7, and 8 provide all the details for using this important program.

Outlook Mobile

You can make a Windows Mobile device your personal information appliance in many ways, but chances are you will start by using the Outlook Mobile programs to manage your personal information. You'll use the Calendar program to schedule appointments and all-day events; you'll use Contacts to store addresses; you'll use Tasks to manage your projects; and you'll use Messaging to send and receive e-mail.

ActiveSync synchronizes the information in each of these programs with their counterpart folders in Outlook. When you read Chapter 13, you will learn how to use Calendar, Contacts, and Tasks. Chapter 11 shows you how to use Messaging.

Mobile Office

When you are traveling about with your Pocket PC, you may need to write a letter, read a report, determine how much it will cost to remodel your kitchen, or give a presentation. Chapter 14 shows you how to create documents using Word Mobile. In Chapter 15, you learn how to use Excel Mobile to crunch numbers and how to use the Calculator program to make quick calculations. Finally, in Chapter 16 you learn how to use PowerPoint Mobile to view presentations.

NOTE   *Mobile Office is not available on Smartphone.*

Windows Media Player and Solitaire

The Internet is becoming a popular way for distributing music in the MP3 (MPEG Audio Layer 3) or WMA (Windows Media Audio) file format. You can download these files to a Windows Mobile device and play them using the Windows Media Player introduced in Chapter 18.

A beautiful color display and stereo sound make Windows Mobile devices great for playing games. Included with all Windows Mobile devices is that hallmark of Microsoft game software, Solitaire. Information about games for Windows Powered devices is also provided in Chapter 18.

Internet Explorer and MSN Messenger

Pocket PCs and Smartphones include the software needed to connect to the Internet. Once online, you can use Internet Explorer Mobile to view your favorite web site, use Messaging to send and receive e-mail, and use MSN Messenger to send and receive instant messages. You will find information about MSN Messenger in Chapter 11, and Internet Explorer is covered in Chapter 12.

Wrapping Up

Windows Mobile devices provide a fast and simple way to manage all types of information. Over the course of nine years, Microsoft has improved its software for Windows Mobile devices, resulting in products with many features and integration with Windows desktop software. Today the Microsoft mobile device strategy recognizes that no one device will meet all the needs for handheld computing: Companies need devices with larger screens and keyboards, which Handheld PCs provide. Consumers want devices for storing personal information, for entertainment, and for connecting to the Internet, which Pocket PCs provide. Yet others want some of their personal information in a mobile phone, which Smartphones provide. The remaining chapters of this book provide all that you need to make the most of your Pocket PC or Smartphone. In the next chapter, you'll learn more about Pocket PCs.

Chapter 2

Get Acquainted with Your Pocket PC

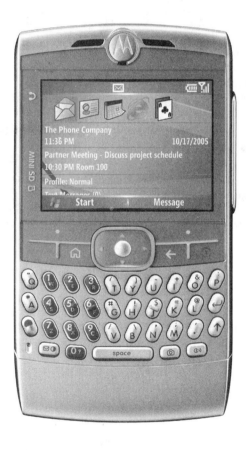

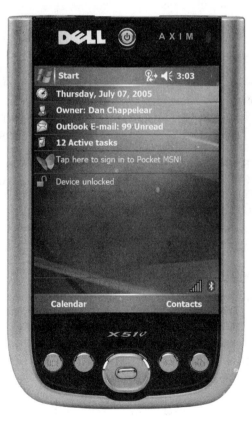

How to...

- Identify hardware components
- Set up your Pocket PC
- Find information
- Use the Start menu
- Use common program elements
- Use Online Help
- Configure storage and program memory
- Organize files and folders

All great athletes master the fundamentals of their sport. Their tremendous physical and mental gifts set them apart, but if you analyze their performances, you often find that the fundamentals are performed flawlessly. This mastery does not come by chance; it is the result of years of practice and coaching. By the time an athlete becomes a professional, the fundamentals have become habit.

To master your Pocket PC, you need to learn the fundamentals of how it works. This chapter provides coaching that can help you understand these fundamentals and polish your skills to become a master.

Following a review of the hardware components that come with the Pocket PC, I'll review the setup procedure. After you set up the device, you'll see the Today screen, which I cover before moving on to the Start menu, common application components, organization of files, and Online Help. This chapter finishes with an overview of an important part of your device—the memory used for storing files and running programs.

Meet Your Pocket PC

Your Pocket PC is a powerful little device that is capable of meeting your needs for an information appliance in a number of different ways. Throughout this book, you'll learn how to make a Pocket PC your own appointment book or checkbook, but to use the device in the best way possible, you need first to understand its fundamental parts.

Each Pocket PC looks slightly different, but several options are found on every device. The Today screen is the closest thing to a PC desktop on the Pocket PC; it provides a summary for appointments, e-mail, and tasks. You enter information using either the onscreen keyboard, character recognizer, or handwriting recognition, which lets you write anywhere on the screen. Like your desktop computer, information is stored in files, which you manage using File Explorer.

If you have difficulty using any of these items, Online Help is available by tapping Start | Help.

Review the Pocket PC

Let's take a tour of a typical Pocket PC, starting with the front of the device. You'll learn the function of parts commonly found on the Pocket PC, but keep in mind that slight variations may exist among various Pocket PC brands. You'll use some parts more often than others, but knowing *how* to use all of them is important.

Review the Front

The largest part of the Pocket PC is its screen. The LCD (liquid crystal display) touch screen has a portrait layout and is used for viewing and entering information.

 *To help you understand the difference between portrait and landscape layouts, think of a standard 8.5×11-inch sheet of paper. The portrait layout of that sheet is oriented vertically, with the 8.5-inch sides at the top and bottom, and a landscape layout is oriented horizontally, with the 11-inch sides at the top and bottom.*

As you can see in Figure 2-1, the buttons below the screen are assigned to various programs or functions. If the Pocket PC is turned off, you can press one of these buttons to turn it on and start the assigned program in one step, unless this feature is disabled.

FIGURE 2-1 The Dell Axim Pocket PC (other Pocket PCs look different but have many of the same parts)

 **Clean Your Pocket PC Screen**

The Pocket PC LCD screen can get dirty quickly through daily use, and some dirt particles can even scratch the screen when they come in contact with the stylus. In my experience, products designed to clean the lenses of glasses work well.

Fellowes sells a PDA Screen Clean kit that includes a soft leather cloth for cleaning the screen throughout the day and packets of wet-dry cleaning cloths for more intensive cleaning. It also sells the WriteRight screen protector, which is a clear plastic overlay that covers the Pocket PC screen. You can find more information about both products at www .fellowes.com.

New with Windows Mobile 5 on the Pocket PC are the left and right softkeys. These hardware buttons are associated to menus or commonly used functions, and make it easier to operate a Pocket PC with one hand. In most Windows Mobile 5 programs the right softkey opens a menu, while the left softkey is assigned to a specific function. For example, in Internet Explorer, pressing the left softkey causes the program to go back one page.

Usually, two of the buttons are assigned to Calendar and Contacts, with third and fourth buttons assigned to Tasks, Inbox, or other programs provided by the hardware manufacturer. The button assignments of each of these programs can be changed using the Buttons icon in the Pocket PC settings; Chapter 3 provides instructions.

 Unlike many of the other hardware buttons on Pocket PCs, you cannot reassign the softkeys to different functions.

Casio was the first company to place a Navigation button on the front of its Pocket PC, and since then, all Pocket PC brands include this feature. The Navigation button provides a way for you to scroll through screens and menu options without using a stylus.

Some Pocket PCs have the Power button and microphone on the front. It is important that you know the location of the microphone on your Pocket PC to make the best voice recordings. When you make a recording, the microphone should be placed as close to the source as possible.

Review the Bottom

At the bottom of the Pocket PC is the accessory port. This port does not look like the ports that you find on desktop computers, and, unfortunately, each Pocket PC brand uses a different port style. Because the ports are variable, you cannot share peripherals, such as cradles and keyboards, among Pocket PC brands.

The accessory port is designed to plug the Pocket PC into a cable that connects to the Universal Serial Bus (USB) port of a desktop computer. The port may also be used to provide power to the Pocket PC and recharge the battery. Some Pocket PCs come with cradles with cables for power and connecting to PCs.

2

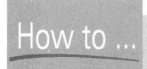 **Connect Your Pocket PC to Devices Using a Serial Cable**

The serial cable that works with your Pocket PC is a special version of what's sometimes called a *null modem cable*. These cables are designed to communicate with other personal computers rather than peripherals, such as modems. To use the serial cable to connect to a serial peripheral device such as a modem, you need a *null modem adapter*. The adapter converts the cable into a standard RS-232 cable that provides communication with serial devices.

You can find null modem adapters at your local RadioShack (you will need a female-to-male DB9 adapter, part number 26-264). Most peripherals have female ports, so if the peripheral to which you are connecting has a 9-pin female port, you will also need a male-to-male DB9 serial gender changer (RadioShack part number 26-231).

Review the Left Side

After the front, the left side of the Pocket PC may be the most important location on your device. Here, you may find Scroll Wheel and Voice Recorder buttons, designed for using the Pocket PC with one hand.

The Scroll Wheel button is used in two ways: Rotating the wheel up or down performs operations similar to pressing the up and down arrows on a computer keyboard. Pressing the button performs an operation similar to pressing ENTER on a computer keyboard. You can scroll through the Start menu items by rotating the wheel up or down, and then press the wheel button to start the program that you select.

 Newer Pocket PCs only have a Navigation button, while some older Pocket PCs have a Scroll Wheel on the left side and a Navigation button on the front. You can use both to scroll up and down on these devices.

To make voice recordings on your Pocket PC, press-and-hold Voice Recorder and begin speaking after the device beeps. Use the Notes program, explained in Chapter 14, to play back and manage voice recordings. You can configure Voice Recorder in Notes either to switch to the Notes program and start recording or to stay in the current program and start recording.

Review the Top

At the top of the Pocket PC you will find the alarm notification LED, headphone jack, and either a CompactFlash (CF) or Secure Digital (SD) card slot. If you have a Pocket PC Phone Edition or a Pocket PC with built-in wireless, your device may have an antenna. The LED will flash whenever an alarm occurs, unless you turn off the LED notification in the Pocket PC settings. This same LED may be used to indicate that the device is charging. (The user manual includes more information about how the LED is used.)

All Pocket PCs have a headphone jack, though the jack may be located somewhere other than at the top. You can plug in a 3.5-millimeter headphone into the jack to listen to voice recordings, music, or videos. Most Pocket PC Phone Editions have a 2.5-millimeter jack, which is the common size found on mobile phones.

Some Pocket PCs have slots that support Type II CompactFlash cards. Type II cards are made a little thicker than Type I cards so that they can support additional functions. The newest Pocket PCs have Secure Digital card slots. Secure Digital cards are significantly smaller and thinner than CompactFlash cards and have built-in support for encryption.

The final item that you will find at the top of some Pocket PCs is an infrared port compliant with the Infrared Data Association (IrDA) standard. Infrared is a form of light, or radiation, beyond red light that cannot be seen by human eyes. An infrared transmitter sends data to a receiver using pulses of infrared light. Every Pocket PC has software that is capable of using the infrared port as either a transmitter or a receiver; and for communication to work, the sending and receiving ports must be lined up with each other. As Chapter 6 shows, the infrared port can also be used with a desktop computer for synchronization.

Some Pocket PCs may have mini-Secure Digital card slots rather than Secure Digital or CompactFlash slots.

Review the Right Side

On the right side of a Pocket PC is the stylus, which you use to interact with the Pocket PC. Some Pocket PCs also place a speaker along this side of the device.

Review the Back

The most important item on the back of the device is the Soft Reset button, which is recessed so that it is not accidentally pressed. A soft reset is similar to rebooting a desktop computer, because it restarts the operating system, and data in the program memory is lost. However, any data in storage memory and all settings are retained. An explanation of program and storage memory is provided in the "File Storage and Program Memory" section later in this chapter.

Be sure to check the user manual for your Pocket PC to verify the location of the Soft Reset button. The location on your Pocket PC may be somewhere other than the back of the device.

The back of some Pocket PCs may include covers for the main and backup batteries and possibly for a memory expansion slot. Because the options on the back of each device vary according to manufacturer, consult your user manual for details about your Pocket PC.

Set Up Your Pocket PC

When you turn on your Pocket PC for the first time, a series of steps are initiated to set up your device, which Microsoft calls the Welcome wizard.

Resetting Pocket PCs

You can reset a Pocket PC two different ways. A soft reset shuts down running programs, clears data from program memory, and restarts the Pocket PC. A hard reset disconnects power from the Pocket PC, which deletes all programs and data that you add to the Pocket PC. The soft and hard reset processes are different for each device and are provided in the Pocket PC user manual.

Windows Mobile 5 treats hard resets differently than previous versions of Windows Mobile. Because Windows Mobile 5 stores all data in ROM, the data remains even when power is unavailable. Most Pocket PC manufacturers include a utility to delete all data and programs from the device to restore the device to the state it was in when it shipped from the factory.

After a hard reset, Windows Mobile 2003SE and older Pocket PCs work as they do when taken out of the box and turned on for the first time. The software that came preloaded remains, but any software that you installed is removed. You will need to either reinstall the software or restore a backup that you have previously created using a backup program on the device. Chapter 8 provides instructions for backing up and restoring Pocket PCs.

Before turning on your Pocket PC, it is important that you charge its main battery so that settings and data are not lost. When you charge the batteries on most Pocket PCs, an LED either blinks or illuminates a certain color. The Pocket PC is fully charged when the light stops blinking or stops changing colors. The first charge of the Pocket PC battery may take several hours. Consult the user manual for specific instructions on charging the battery.

The first screen that you see is the Welcome screen. Tap anywhere on the screen to continue. Next, you align the touch screen so that it properly recognizes any text or taps that you enter. Use the stylus to tap the center of the cross as it moves around the screen.

You can align the screen at any time by tapping Start | Settings. Tap the System tab and then tap the Screen icon. Some Pocket PCs also provide a series of hardware buttons that you can press to start the Align Screen program; consult the user manual for instructions.

Tap Next to move on to the Location screen (shown on the following page). Here, you specify your local time zone by selecting a time zone or location in the drop-down list. If you are in the United States, select a time zone; otherwise, select a city. If the city that you live in is not in the list, select the name of a city in the same time zone.

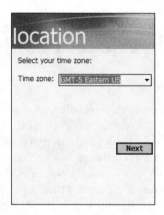

The next two screens that appear introduce you to the *tap-and-hold* process. Tap-and-hold is used throughout the Pocket PC user interface and is similar to right-clicking a Windows desktop, in that it causes a pop-up list of commands to open, which can be executed on the object you select with tap-and-hold.

On the first screen, you are instructed on how to use tap-and-hold. Tap Next to move on. The second screen, shown here, provides an opportunity for you to try out the tap-and-hold procedure—tap Cut, then tap-and-hold the 11 A.M. time slot, and then tap Paste on the pop-up list.

After you've successfully completed the tap-and-hold procedure, a Congratulations screen appears. When you tap Next, you see a screen instructing you to set up a password for your device; tap Next to open the Password settings screen or tap Skip to complete the Welcome wizard.

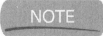 *The instructions for creating passwords on a Pocket PC are provided in Chapter 3.*

More Settings

The Welcome wizard sets the basic information for your Pocket PC, but you should perform some additional steps to complete the setup of your device. To set the date and time, tap Start |

Settings, tap the System tab, and then tap the Clock & Alarms icon. Follow the instructions provided in Chapter 4 for changing the date and time using the Clock & Alarms settings.

If you synchronize multiple Windows Mobile 2003SE or older devices with the same desktop computer, each device must have a unique name. To change the name of your Pocket PC, tap Start | Settings, tap the System tab, and then tap the About icon to display the About Settings dialog box. Tap the Device ID tab, enter a name and description for the device, and tap OK.

 *ActiveSync 4 and Windows Mobile 5 automatically create unique device names for every Pocket PC when it creates a synchronization relationship with a PC.*

Each Pocket PC can store information about you, such as your name and address, which you enter on the Owner Information screen. To open the Owner Information screen, tap Start | Personal | Owner Information. If you want the information to be displayed every time the Pocket PC turns on, tap Identification Information on the Options tab. You can store additional information on the Notes tab.

One of the first things you'll want to do after becoming familiar with your Pocket PC is synchronize it with your desktop computer. During the first synchronization, you establish a synchronization relationship between the device and the desktop computer and you download data in Outlook to the Pocket PC. The entire synchronization process is explained in Chapter 7.

Meet the Today Screen

When the Welcome wizard completes, you end up at the Today screen:

Configure network connections ————————————Mute

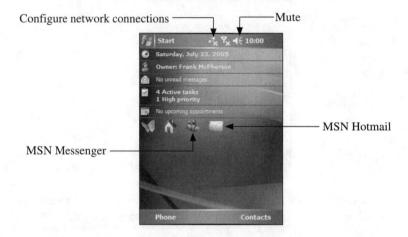

MSN Messenger ————

———— MSN Hotmail

The Today screen serves a purpose similar to the Outlook Today page on the PC. It provides the date, a summary overview of personal information, including the owner's name and telephone number, upcoming appointments, the number of unread and unsent e-mail messages, and the number of active tasks.

New to Windows Mobile 5 is the Pocket MSN launch bar on the Today screen, which provides quick access to MSN Hotmail, MSN Messenger, and the MSN Mobile home page. You will need to configure each of these by using the MSN Options setting as instructed in Chapter 3.

When you tap a section of the Today screen, the associated program starts. For example, tap the appointments section to start the Calendar program. The Owner Information settings display when you tap the owner name. You can also start Inbox and Tasks from the Today screen by tapping the appropriate spots.

To change the date and time from the Today screen, tap the date to open the Clock Settings dialog box.

The bottom of the Today screen may display program icons; the Today screen is the only part of the Pocket PC that displays these icons. Tap an icon to execute a particular function or start a program.

You can select themes that change the appearance of the Today screen, as well as select which items should display on the screen, by changing the Today screen settings. Chapter 3 provides the instructions for changing these settings.

Use the Pocket PC Start Menu

One difference between the Pocket PC user interface and Windows is the location of the Start button. The Start button is located on the upper-left corner of the screen, and the title changes on the Navigation bar to display the name of the current program visible on the screen. When you tap the Start button, the menu expands from the top down, as shown here.

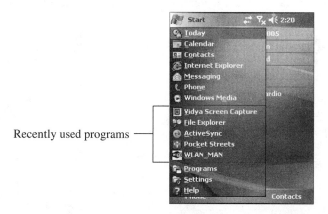

Recently used programs

Another item on the Pocket PC Start menu is the recently used programs section of the menu. Each time you run a program on the Pocket PC, it's added to the recently used section, which displays the last five programs you started. Programs on the Start menu are not added to the recently used section.

When you change the screen orientation to landscape, the recently used programs section is replaced by a shortcut bar of icons at the top of the Start menu.

Another change made to the Start menu is that the Programs and Settings menus do not cascade as they do in Windows XP. Instead, when you tap either item, a separate program window displays—such as the Programs window, shown here. If a program shortcut does not appear on the Start menu, it will be found in the Programs window. Start a program by tapping its icon.

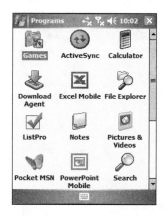

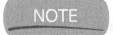 *You can have only seven program shortcuts in the Start menu.*

To indicate whether a shortcut will appear on the Start menu or in the Programs window, tap Start | Settings | Menus to display the Menus Settings dialog box. Tap the check box next to the items that you want to appear on the Start menu. The items not selected will appear in the Programs window.

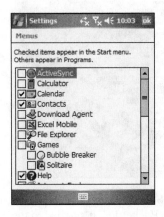

 *To add a program shortcut to the Start menu or Programs window, tap-and-hold a filename in File Explorer and tap Copy. Next, open the Start menu or the Programs subfolder in File Explorer and tap Edit | Paste Shortcut.*

Launching a program from the Start menu on a Pocket PC involves the same process as on all other versions of Windows. Tap Start and then tap the shortcut of the program that you want to run.

Search for Information

On a Pocket PC, you can perform a search on a word or phrase that is stored in any of the Pocket Outlook and Pocket Office data files, as well as in Notes. To search for information, tap Start | Programs | Search to open the Search dialog box.

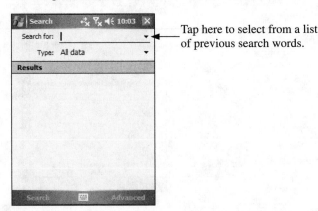

Tap here to select from a list of previous search words.

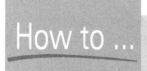

Search for Files

The Pocket PC search functionality is designed to search for information stored in Pocket Outlook, Online Help, Notes, Word Mobile, and Excel Mobile. It does not search for other file types or for files on storage cards. If you want to expand searches to include files on storage cards, you need to download and install a third-party program. One program that provides this functionality is Kilmist FileQuest, at www.kilmist.com.

NOTE *Windows Mobile 2003 and older devices have a Find option at the bottom of the Start menu.*

Enter the word or phrase in the Search For field, and select the type of search from the Type drop-down list. Previous search words or phrases are saved and available in the Search For drop-down list.

You can narrow the search to a specific program by selecting the program name from the Type drop-down list. The default is All Data, which will search through all Pocket Outlook, Pocket Office, and Notes files on the device.

After you enter the search item and select the Type, tap Search or press the left softkey to begin the search. The search results display on the middle of the screen. You can tap any entry in the Results list to open it. When you tap OK to close the item, you return to the results listed in Search For.

Work with Applications

The Pocket PC user interface has a flat design that is simple and easy to navigate. At the top of the screen is the Navigation bar, which displays the title of the active program and the current time. Tap the Start icon, which is immediately to the left of the program title on the bar, to expand the Start menu.

Pocket PC programs display on the entire screen, and they do not appear in separate windows as on desktop computers. At the top-right corner, you'll see a square button labeled with OK (as shown here) or an *X*. OK appears within dialog boxes or screens of a program. For example, when you start Contacts and display a contact, you see an OK button. When you tap OK, the Contacts screen closes, but you remain within the Contacts program at the Contacts List view.

From the Contacts List view, you see an *X* instead of an OK. When you tap *X*, the Contacts program disappears, and you see the

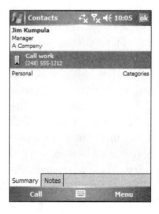

program started prior to running Contacts. Tapping the *X* button allows you to close the current program screen, but the program is still running in memory, which makes it faster to switch among programs as you work.

> **NOTE** *The operating system manages the memory on Pocket PCs and automatically shuts down programs if it starts to run out of program memory. You may prefer to shut down programs manually as you do on a personal computer. To do this, you use the Memory setting on your Pocket PC or use a program task manager. Chapter 3 has instructions for using program task managers to shut down programs.*

At the bottom of the screen is the Command bar, which has menus and buttons that provide commands for programs. The Command bar is where you also see what is assigned to the left and right softkeys in Windows Mobile 5. The Command bar in this image shows that the left softkey is assigned to New and the right softkey is assigned to Menu. In this example, you press the left softkey or tap New to create a new document. Press the right softkey or tap Menu to open the menu for Word Mobile.

When you are in the List view for most Windows Mobile 5 programs, the left softkey will be assigned to New. To create a new item, tap New or press the left softkey.

The Program menu of most Windows Mobile 5 programs contains commonly used functions, such as Undo, Redo, Cut, Copy, Paste, Clear, and Select All, plus submenus. The submenus cascade in a similar manner as they do in Windows.

Windows Mobile 2003SE and older programs contain multiple menus that appear along the Command bar. The Edit menu provides commands used to edit data that you enter on the Pocket PC. It usually includes commands such as Undo, Redo, Cut, Copy, Paste, Clear, and Select All.

The View menu provides commands that change the appearance of the screen. This may include different input modes, such as the Writing and Drawing modes found in Notes, as well as Zoom, found in many programs and used for magnifying the display.

The Tools menu provides additional commands available in the program, such as Insert Date and Beam Document, which you find in Word Mobile. If a program includes an Options dialog box, which is used to configure the program settings, open it by tapping Tools | Options.

View List Views

Programs that create files, such as Notes and Word Mobile, use a List view to display all the files you created using the program. When you start the program, the first screen displayed is the List view, such as that shown in this image for Notes.

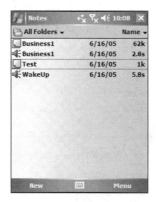

From the List view, you can tap All Folders to navigate through various folders and tap Name to sort the items in the list. Tap an item name in the list to open that item in the program, or tap New to create a new file.

 *The List view displays only when a file associated with the starting program is found on the device. If no file is found, the Program window opens, rather than the List view.*

View Pop-Up Menus

The Pocket PC has a feature that provides the same function as right-clicking an object in Windows on desktop computers. When you tap-and-hold the stylus on an item on the screen, a pop-up menu appears with commands appropriate to the active program.

After the menu appears on the screen, lift the stylus and tap the command that you want to perform. For example, to create a copy of a note, tap-and-hold the stylus on the item to be copied in the Notes List view to open the pop-up list. Then tap Create Copy to create a new copy of the note you selected.

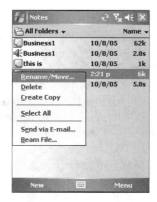

Get Help

Online Help is available directly on your Pocket PC; to open Online Help, tap Start | Help. The information that appears on the screen, an example of which is shown here, will relate to the program window currently open. Tap Contents to open the Online Help contents, and then use the arrows to move backward or forward one page. Some help pages include hyperlinks that you can tap to open another page of information. When you're done, tap the *X* to close Online Help.

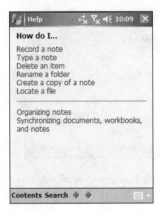

Receive Help on the Internet

Online Help is a great source of information on your device, but it may not provide an answer to your particular question. While this book provides enough information to answer most questions, technology changes at a blinding rate and only the Internet seems able to keep up.

On the Internet you can find pages of frequently asked questions (FAQs) that provide answers for a variety of topics. During the last four years, I have created and maintained the PocketPCHow2 web site at www.pocketpchow2.com, which provides hundreds of links to information that answers many questions about Windows CE and Pocket PCs.

My web site is only one of several web sites on the Internet that are dedicated to Pocket PCs. Included on my web site are several pages of links to other web sites that provide FAQs, news, forums, reviews, and software.

Print Documents

Windows Mobile does not let you print documents. Field Software Products' PrintPocketCE works with all Pocket PC 2002 and 2003 devices. It prints Word Mobile, Excel Mobile, and e-mail documents, and it supports Hewlett-Packard, Canon, Epson, Pentax, Brother, and several other printers. You will find this program at www.fieldsoftware.com.

Pocket Watch Software's ActivePrint provides the ability to print from Windows Mobile 5 devices. To print a document with ActivePrint, you need to connect the Pocket PC to a desktop computer running ActiveSync. You queue up documents to be printed while away from your desk and then, when you synchronize the Pocket PC, the queued documents print. You will find this program at http://activeprint.pocketwatchsoftware.com/.

File Storage and Program Memory

Unlike desktop computers, Pocket PCs do not have built-in hard drives. Instead, they use memory chips for built-in file storage. One of the significant changes between Windows Mobile 5 and previous versions is how it uses Random Access Memory (RAM) and Flash Read Only Memory (ROM). Windows Mobile 5 uses RAM only for program memory, and uses Flash ROM for storing all files and data.

Windows Mobile 2003SE and earlier devices use RAM for both program memory and built-in storage, and use Flash ROM only to provide extra file storage. Pocket Outlook data and all of the Pocket PC settings are stored in RAM. When these devices lose power, all Pocket Outlook data, Pocket PC settings, and any other programs or files stored in RAM are lost.

> **NOTE** *The operating system and all of the Windows Mobile software that comes on Pocket PCs are also stored in a section of Flash ROM, but they are secured so that you cannot accidentally erase the files.*

Flash ROM retains files and data even when there is no power supplied to the chips, which means that data on Windows Mobile 5 devices will not be erased when the batteries drain completely, or during a hard reset. By changing the way it uses Flash ROM, Windows Mobile 5 has significantly improved the way it protects your data.

> **TIP** *Several Windows Mobile 2003 and older devices have Flash ROM chips with extra storage space that you can use to safely store files. Unfortunately, Pocket PC manufacturers do not agree on what to call this special storage. For example, HP refers to it as a File Store, while Dell refers to it as Built-in Storage. Regardless, this storage is ideal for storing your most important files.*

Increase Storage Space

The amount of storage available with Windows Mobile 5 devices is limited by its size of flash memory. Using storage cards can increase the total storage space of a device. Storage cards are available in the CompactFlash, Multimedia Card, Secure Digital, mini-Secure Digital, and PC Card formats, and they come in a variety of sizes.

 **Add More Program Memory**

Storage cards cannot increase program memory; until recently, program memory could not be increased at all. However, Pocket PC Techs at www.pocketpctechs.com now sells internal memory upgrades for several brands of Pocket PCs. Pocket PC Techs can install 64MB and 128MB upgrades. Be aware that this upgrade voids your Pocket PC's warranty, however.

You can add storage space to Pocket PCs by using CF or Secure Digital Flash ROM storage cards. *Flash ROM* is a type of constantly powered, nonvolatile memory that can be erased and reprogrammed in units called *blocks*. Nonvolatile memory has a continuous source of power so that the contents are not lost when the memory is removed from a computing device. Flash ROM gets its name from the fact that the chip is organized in such a manner that the memory cells can be erased in a single action, or a *flash*.

Because flash memory stores information in blocks, it cannot be used for program memory, like RAM, which needs to access information in bytes. Flash storage cards use the same specifications used to access hard disks and therefore are treated like hard disks by computer operating systems.

If you are trying to decide which storage card to buy for your Pocket PC, consider two items. First, what type of card you should buy depends on the type of slot in your Pocket PC. Many newer Pocket PCs only have a Secure Digital slot. The second consideration is cost. Several brands of storage cards are available, and all work equally well, so price is what distinguishes between storage card brands. As a rule, larger capacity storage cards are more expensive.

Another consideration in the future may be speed, as SanDisk recently announced the Ultra CompactFlash format that allows transfer speeds up to 2.8MB per second.

CF storage cards are popular, and they can be used in some digital cameras as well as Pocket PCs. Adapters are available to plug CF cards into Type II PC Card slots, enabling them to be used with notebook computers and desktop computers that have PC Card readers.

Configure Memory

Storage and program memory in Windows Mobile 5 devices is fixed by the amount of Flash ROM and RAM in the device and cannot be adjusted. However, for Windows Mobile 2003SE and older devices, you can adjust the amount of RAM used for storage or programs. To configure memory, tap Start | Settings, tap the System tab, and then tap the Memory icon to open the Memory Settings dialog box.

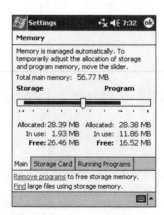

How to ...   Conserve Storage Space

Internal storage in Pocket PCs is finite, and therefore it can be important to use a strategy that conserves internal storage space while installing programs. It helps, therefore, to know what must be stored internally and what can be placed on storage cards.

All data in Calendar, Contacts, Tasks, and Messaging is in databases in internal storage. Over time, you'll want to remove items in these programs, and the best way is to configure Outlook on your PC to archive data automatically. The auto-archive process removes items from the main Outlook folders, and during the next synchronization those items will be removed from the Pocket PC.

Data files, such as Word Mobile documents and Excel Mobile spreadsheets, can be easily stored on storage cards or internally. Both programs automatically check the storage cards for files to display in the File List view. However, files on storage cards are not backed up by ActiveSync or by any of the backup programs provided with Pocket PCs. You may want to store only noncritical files on storage cards, or use Windows Explorer to copy files manually from storage cards to the hard drive on a PC.

You can install most Pocket PC programs on storage cards. The instructions for installing software to storage cards are discussed in Chapter 8. Some programs execute immediately when the Pocket PC turns on, and you may have problems running those programs from storage cards. This is because cards are not available during a slight period of time when the Pocket PC first turns on. Most programs include README files that specify whether the program must be installed to internal storage.

I recommend installing system files to internal storage. If your Pocket PC has only one slot, you need to install programs internally that you would use while peripherals, such as modems, are in the slot.

The left side of the slider represents internal storage memory, and the right side represents program memory. To adjust the amount of memory allocated to either, move the slider left or right.

At the middle of the screen you can see the amount of memory Allocated, In Use, and Free for storage and program memory. Tap the Storage Card tab of the Memory Settings dialog box to see the size of the storage card and the amount of space in use and free.

Manage Files with File Explorer

With File Explorer, you can browse the contents of folders on the Pocket PC to locate, open, copy, move, and delete files. You also use this program to create new folders and to transfer files to other devices using infrared.

The My Documents folder is particularly important on Pocket PCs because it is the storage location for data files. If you synchronize files between a Pocket PC and a desktop computer, the entire contents of the My Documents folder will appear on the desktop computer. Most Pocket PC programs, such as Word Mobile and Excel Mobile, work only with the My Documents folder or its subfolders, while files stored in any other folder on the device will not appear in the program List view.

If you create a My Documents folder on a storage card, the contents of that folder are combined with the contents of the My Documents folder on the device by programs that have a List view. This feature is particularly important for Windows Media Player, which plays music stored in large files that you will want to keep on storage cards. Chapter 18 provides instructions for playing music using Windows Media Player.

Locate Files

To start File Explorer, tap Start | Programs | File Explorer, and the program will open. When File Explorer starts, it opens the My Documents folder and lists the files and subfolders stored therein. The contents of a Folder view can be sorted by Name, Date, Size, or Type by tapping an option in the drop-down list located at the upper-right of the Folder view. Expand the drop-down list at the upper-left of the Folder view to open a parent folder. The Pocket PC root folder is called My Device and contains the My Documents, Program Files, Temp, Storage Card, and Windows folders, among others. If a storage card is in the device, it appears in the My Device Folder view, as shown here.

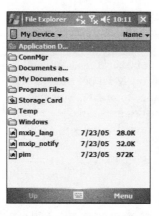

To quickly open a storage card, tap the drop-down list at the upper-left of the Folder view and then tap Storage Card.

Network shares are storage locations on file servers or workstations that share files among users on a network. To open a network share in File Explorer, tap Menu | Open Path | New Path, and the Open dialog box appears.

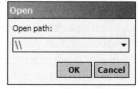

Enter the full path to the network share using the Universal Naming Convention (UNC), which has the form *[server name]* *[share name]*. For example, to open a share with the name *Music* on a computer named *Fred,* you would enter \\Fred\Music.

2

You cannot directly open a file on a network share. Instead, you must first copy the file to the Pocket PC and then open it. However, you can create a shortcut to a file on a network share and paste it on a Pocket PC. This does not actually copy the entire file to the Pocket PC. Because shortcuts only point to files, when you open the shortcut you actually open the file across the network. To create a shortcut, tap-and-hold on a filename and then tap Copy. Switch to the destination location on the Pocket PC and tap Menu | Edit | Paste Shortcut. The only way to open a shortcut is by using File Explorer. You will not see shortcuts in the various program List views.

The process is the same for opening a file or folder in the Folder view; you tap the item, and it opens in its associated program on the Pocket PC. File Explorer does not display file extensions, but an icon appears with each filename to indicate the file type.

Organize Files with Folders

Typically, you will not use File Explorer to open a file; instead, you will start a program, such as Word Mobile, and then open a file from its List view. You will, however, use File Explorer to move files among folders and to create new folders.

A folder can be created in two ways: you can tap-and-hold the stylus on an open space in the Folder view and tap New Folder on the pop-up list, or you can tap Menu | New Folder. A new folder appears with its name selected so that you can enter a new name, as shown here.

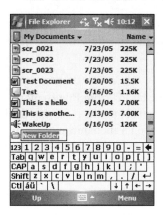

To move or copy a file into a folder, you use tap-and-hold to choose Cut, Copy, and Paste. File Explorer does not support drag-and-drop, but tap-and-hold makes the process easy. To move a file to another folder, tap-and-hold the stylus on the filename, tap Cut on the pop-up list, open the destination folder, tap-and-hold the stylus on the folder, and then tap Paste on the pop-up list.

Copy a file by using the same process, except tap Copy on the pop-up list instead of Cut. If you paste a copy of a file into the same folder, File Explorer will automatically change the filename by adding *Copy of* to the beginning of the name.

To delete a file, tap-and-hold the filename and then tap Delete on the pop-up list. To change the name of a file, tap Rename on the pop-up list, and then enter the new filename.

Send Files with E-mail

You can send any file as an e-mail attachment from File Explorer. Tap-and-hold a filename and then tap Send Via E-mail on the pop-up list. Inbox starts and creates a new e-mail message with the file attached, as shown in this image. Complete and send the e-mail message as instructed in Chapter 11.

 *If you have Messaging configured for multiple e-mail accounts, you will be prompted to select one when sending an attachment from File Explorer.*

Beam Files with Infrared

Files can be transferred to another Pocket PC from File Explorer by using *infrared*. Line up the infrared ports of the two devices and set up the receiving device. To send a file from File Explorer on a Pocket PC, tap-and-hold on a filename and then tap Beam File on the pop-up list. A message box appears on the screen of both devices to indicate that the file was transmitted.

Wrapping Up

Pocket PCs have features that are similar to Windows running on desktop computers. You use the Start menu to start programs and to switch between running programs. Files are stored in folders in a hierarchical manner, and you use File Explorer to browse and manage files and folders. The Today screen on Pocket PCs is the closest thing to the Windows desktop, but the purpose of the Today screen is to provide an overview for your information rather than to display program shortcuts. The Today screen also provides a way for you to personalize your Pocket PC by selecting different themes, which display pictures on the screen and change the colors of the Navigation and Command bars. In the next chapter, you'll learn how to personalize your Pocket PC for your preferences and tastes.

Chapter 3

Personalize Your Pocket PC

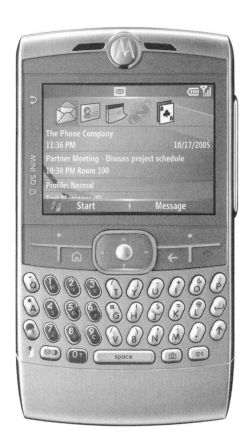
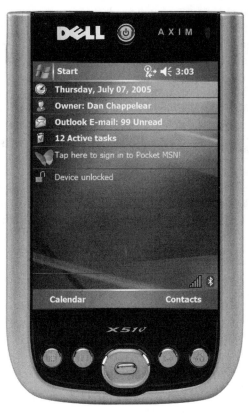

How to...

- Change the Pocket PC personal settings
- Use the Pocket PC input methods to enter information
- Manage running programs using a program task manager
- Change the Pocket PC appearance

It is easy to overlook the second *P* in Pocket PC, which stands for *personal*. Yet of all the computers made, Pocket PCs may be the most personal of all. The information they store—appointments, addresses, and tasks—is personal for most people, as rarely will more than one person share a Pocket PC. So it makes sense for you to want to configure your Pocket PC to conform to your personal needs and tastes.

The Pocket PC software provides several ways to personalize your device, including settings for entering owner information, setting passwords, programming hardware buttons, and configuring input methods. In fact, you can choose among four input methods to use the one that works best for you. If the input methods included with your Pocket PC do not work well for you, others are provided by third-party companies.

Many people find it cumbersome to use the Start menu and the methods for starting and closing programs. Several programs are available to help you manage the programs running on your Pocket PC. If you prefer to use a simple menu of icons to launch programs, you can use one of the many Today screen plug-ins that provide such a menu. In fact, the Today screen is one of the most customizable parts of the Pocket PC, and a variety of plug-ins exist that change the appearance of the screen as well as add functionality.

You can personalize your Pocket PC to make it reflect you, its owner. In this chapter I'll go over the personal settings in detail and show you how to enter data into your Pocket PC. I also take a look at the program task managers and Today screen plug-ins available for the Pocket PC.

Change the Personal Settings

The Personal tab is where you personalize the Pocket PC by changing settings to accommodate the way you work. To access the Personal tab, tap Start | Settings. Table 3-1 contains a summary of what you can do with each icon.

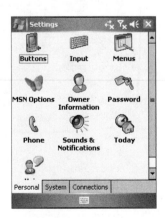

Program Hardware Buttons

In Chapter 2 you learned that hardware buttons may be located in different areas on the Pocket PC. These buttons make it easier for you to navigate within the device and start applications; you can program most buttons to start any application and perform certain functions. The following lists some specifics of hardware buttons.

Icon	Name	Description
	Buttons	Specify which application a button will start.
	Input	Configure options for character recognition and the onscreen keyboard. Also configure word completion and voice record formats.
	Menus	Specify the program shortcuts that appear in the Start menu.
	MSN Options	Configure options for Microsoft Hotmail, MSN Messenger, and SMS.
	Owner Information	Enter personal information, such as address and phone number. A Notes field enables you to enter additional information not included with the owner information. Both sets of information can be configured to display when you turn on your device.
	Password	Create or change the password on your device and specify whether you want to enable password protection for the device.
	Phone	Change Phone settings on Pocket PC Phone Editions.
	Sounds & Notifications	Change the volume of your device as well as the type of sound that is made for particular events.
	Today	Change the appearance of the Today screen with themes and plug-ins.

TABLE 3-1 Icons of the Personal Tab in Pocket PC Settings

- To open the Buttons properties dialog box, shown here, tap the Buttons icon on the Personal tab.

- To change the program associated with a button, first select a button in the list. Then tap the triangle to the right of the Assign A Program field and select the program or function you want from the drop-down menu. Functions are bracketed by greater than and less than signs (< >). You will see the assigned program change in Assignment column of the Button list. When you're finished, tap OK.

- The Up/Down Control tab is used to configure the Action button. The Action button is either a wheel, a rocker, or a navigation pad (a flat button on the front of the device) that is used to move the cursor up or down. This button is particularly useful to use when you're reading documents, because you can scroll through a document while holding the device in one hand.

- Within the Up/Down Control tab, you change how quickly the cursor starts scrolling and how fast it scrolls.
- Move the Delay Before First Repeat slider left or right to control how soon scrolling starts. To control the scrolling speed, move the Repeat Rate slider left or right.

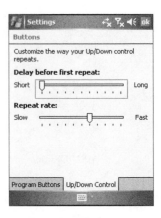

 *Three button assignments are designed to make it easier to operate a Pocket PC with one hand. You can program hardware buttons to open and close the Start menu and the pop-up menu, which normally appears when you tap-and-hold. You can also program a button that you can push rather than having to tap OK or Close.*

Configure the Input Methods

Windows Mobile has four methods of input. The Block and Letter Recognizers recognize characters that you write with the stylus in the Input Panel on the screen. (The Input Panel is discussed in the section "Use the Software Input Panel" later in this chapter.) Microsoft Transcriber is a natural handwriting recognizer that translates to text what you write with the stylus on the Pocket PC screen. Finally, you can use the onscreen keyboard to tap characters. Settings for each method are configured in the Input Settings dialog box, which you open by tapping Start | Settings | Input.

The Input Settings dialog box has three tabs: Input Method, Word Completion, and Options. Use the Input Method tab to configure settings for each method. To make a change to an input method, select it from the drop-down list and then tap Options. (Note that there are no Block Recognizer options.) When you select the Keyboard input method, the Input Settings dialog box looks like the image shown here.

Change the size of the keys on the keyboard by selecting either the Large Keys or Small Keys radio button. When you select Large Keys, you then have the option to use gestures for Space, Backspace, Shift + key, and Enter, which are made on the keyboard.

When you select the Letter Recognizer input method and tap Options, the screen shown on the following page displays. If you select the Quick Stroke option, you must write all letters in one stroke for the Pocket PC to translate. A single stroke enables you to write faster, but it requires that you first learn new ways to write certain letters. The Right To Left Crossbar option specifies whether you write crossbars for *t, f,* and the plus symbol (+) from right to left. If you need to write accented characters, be sure to check the Allow Accented Characters option.

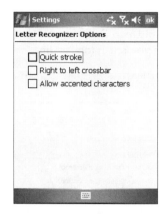

 *Pocket PC Online Help contains demonstrations of how to write characters. To see the demonstration while the Letter Recognizer Options dialog box is displayed, tap Start | Help, and then tap Demo. You can also display help by tapping the Information button on the Input Panel any time that the panel is open.*

As you enter characters in the Input Panel, the Pocket PC will suggest words that you may be writing. If you tap the word that is displayed, that word will be placed wherever the cursor is located. By using this word completion feature, you can speed up data entry on your device. Use the Word Completion tab, shown here, to turn on or off word completion and to specify how many words display. This feature can display one to four words at a time. You can specify how many characters you must enter before a word is suggested in this tab, as well as specify whether you want a space automatically inserted after the word.

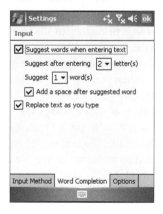

Use the Options tab to configure options wherever writing or recording is supported. Specify the default Voice Recording Format by selecting an option from the drop-down list. Selecting percentages from the Default Zoom drop-down lists specifies the default zoom levels for writing and typing. The Pocket PC automatically capitalizes the first letter of sentences if you select that option in this dialog box. Choose Scroll Upon Reaching The Last Line and the Pocket PC will automatically scroll the window when you reach the last line.

Each of the voice recording options affects the quality and the size of the audio file. Mobile Voice (GSM) is the recommended format because it provides good recording quality and takes far less storage than Pulse Code Modulation (PCM). PCM provides slightly better sound quality, but it can take up to 50 times more storage.

Change the Start Menu

One of the first things you need to do with a new Pocket PC is edit the Start menu so that shortcuts to the programs you use most frequently are listed there. By placing application shortcuts in the Start menu, you decrease the number of taps necessary to start these programs. Change the contents of the Start menu by tapping the Menus icon in the Personal tab of the Settings screen. (To access the Settings screen, tap Start | Settings.) When you tap the Menus icon, the Menus Settings dialog box displays.

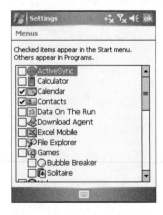

This box lists all the programs installed on your Pocket PC. Items that are checked appear in the Start menu, while the remaining items are available by selecting Start | Programs. To add an item to the Start menu, simply check the box next to its name; to remove an item from the Start menu, deselect the check box next to the name of the program.

NOTE *Windows Mobile 2003SE and older has a New Button menu, which is a pop-up menu that appears on the Command bar. You turn this menu on or off on the New Menu tab of the Menus setting on these devices.*

Configure MSN Options

Windows Mobile 5 is the first version to include Pocket MSN, a subscription-based service that provides access to MSN Hotmail, Messenger, and MSN Mobile web content. If you own a Windows Mobile 2003 or 2003 Second Edition device, you can install the Pocket MSN software for your Pocket PC from http://mobile.msn.com. When you install Pocket MSN, the MSN Options icon is added to the Personal Settings tab.

NOTE *You may be able to access Pocket MSN services even if you have not subscribed, but Microsoft may eventually restrict Pocket MSN to only those who have subscribed.*

The MSN Options setting has five tabs: General, Hotmail, Messenger, SMS, and Switch User. If you have saved your Pocket MSN password on your Pocket PC, you can remove it by tapping Clear Saved Password on the General tab.

The Hotmail tab, shown here, has options for controlling what e-mail is sent to your device. You can turn off e-mail delivery, use filters, or have all new e-mail sent to your device by selecting an option from the E-mail Delivery Options drop-down list. Configure junk mail filtering by selecting an option from the Junk Mail Filter drop-down list.

The Messenger tab configures whether the information for all contacts is updated automatically. If your wireless provider supports it, you can have e-mail and messages sent to you via Simple Message Service (SMS) when your device is not connected to a wireless data network. Open http://mobile.msn.com/getsms on your device to determine whether the service is available, which you can turn on from the SMS tab.

To configure Pocket MSN for a different user ID and password, tap the Switch User button on the Switch User tab of the MSN Options dialog box.

Edit Owner Information

With the Owner Information icon, you can enter your name and address and have this information display whenever you turn on your Pocket PC. Enter this information by following these steps:

1. Tap the Owner Information icon in the Personal tab of the Settings dialog box. The resulting dialog box, shown here, has three tabs: Identification, Notes, and Options.

2. Enter your name, company, address, telephone number, and e-mail address in the Identification tab.

3. Use the Notes tab to add information that is not on the Identification tab. One way to use this tab is to provide a message in case your device is lost. When the device

3

is turned on, you can have the message display along with the owner information by checking the box next to Notes on the Options tab.

4. To have identification information or notes display every time the device is turned on, check the appropriate boxes on the Options tab. With these options checked, the information will display every time the device is turned on, and it continues to display until you tap the screen.

Turn On Password Protection

You can protect the data in your device by requiring a password every time the device turns on. Tap the Password icon on the Personal tab to open the dialog box shown here.

Windows Mobile supports a four-digit password or a strong alphanumeric password. Strong alphanumeric passwords combine letters, numbers, and mixed case characters and are considered to be more secure because they make it more difficult for someone to guess your password.

Sign-On, from Communication Intelligence Corporation, is a password security utility that uses your signature for authentication. Find more information about this program at www.cic.com.

Tap the Prompt If Device Unused For check box to turn on password protection, and configure how often you enter the device password by selecting a time from the drop-down list. Selecting 0 Minutes forces you to enter the password every time you turn on your Pocket PC. Selecting 30 Minutes forces you to enter the password only after the device has not been used for 30 minutes. Thus, if the device is turned off and turned right back on again, you won't have to enter the password.

After you select either Simple 4 Digit or Strong Alphanumeric options, enter the password in the Password field. If you enter a four-digit password, a numeric keypad displays for you to enter the password when you turn on the Pocket PC. Enter the password by tapping the buttons on the screen using either the stylus or your finger.

TIP *Use the onscreen keyboard to enter passwords to ensure that no translation errors occur.*

Strong alphanumeric passwords provide greater security. When you select the Strong Alphanumeric password, two fields display for you to enter a password. The password must be at least seven characters long, and it must contain a combination of uppercase and lowercase letters, numbers, or punctuation.

NOTE *Strong alphanumeric passwords are case sensitive.*

3

It is crucial that you remember your password, because without it you will not be able to retrieve your data. If you forget your password, the only way to access your device is to perform a hard reset, which deletes all data. (The process varies for a hard reset with each manufacturer's device; consult your user manual for details. The process usually involves removing your backup and main batteries so that your device has no power; when you do this, all of your data will be lost.)

To help remember your password, tap the Hint tab and enter a word or phrase that will remind you of the password. The Pocket PC will display the hint after the wrong password is entered five times. Remember that the hint may be visible to others, so make it something that reminds you, yet remains difficult for others to guess.

Change Sounds & Notifications

Using a Pocket PC is both a visual and audible experience. Sound plays an important role in providing feedback. For example, when you tap a button using a stylus, you not only see the button being tapped, but you also hear a sound. In most cases, this sound lets you know that the Pocket PC has recognized your request.

Sounds and their volumes are controlled by using the Sounds & Notifications Settings dialog box. To open this dialog box, shown here, tap the Sounds & Notifications icon on the Personal tab.

You will notice two tabs in the Sounds & Notifications Settings dialog box. The Sounds tab allows you to enable sounds for events or applications. (An *event* is something generated by the operating system, such as opening or closing a program or emptying the recycle bin.) The Notifications tab allows you to specify what you hear when you want to be reminded of appointments and tasks.

Sounds can be enabled for the following by checking their boxes on the Sounds tab:

- ■ **Events**   Such as warnings and system events.

- ■ **Programs and notifications**   Such as alarms and reminders.

- ■ **Screen taps**   Specify Soft or Loud by selecting the appropriate radio button.

- ■ **Hardware buttons**   Specify Soft or Loud by selecting the appropriate radio button.

On the Notifications tab, you specify what sound plays when an event occurs. First, select an event from the drop-down list, and then tap the Play Sound check box and select a sound. To preview the sound, tap the Play button.

Certain events have additional options that appear on the Notifications tab. For example, when you select Beam: Autoreceive from the drop-down list, Display Message On Screen and Flash Light For options appear. When you select the Flash Light For option, you can specify how long the light flashes by selecting a number of minutes from the drop-down list.

Change the Today Screen

The Pocket PC Today screen is similar to the Windows desktop. The Today screen can contain owner information, appointments, e-mail messages, and tasks. Tap the Today icon on the Personal tab to open the Today Settings dialog box and configure the appearance of this screen.

You can tap each item of the Today screen to start the associated application. Tap the Date icon to open the Pocket PC clock settings; tap the Owner icon to open the Owner Information settings; tap the Appointments, Unread Messages, or Tasks icon to open the Calendar, Inbox, or Tasks.

Themes change the look of the Today screen, Start menu, and Navigation bar. Select which theme to use on the Appearance tab of the Today Settings dialog box, shown here. To change the current theme, tap the new theme you want to use from the list box and then tap OK.

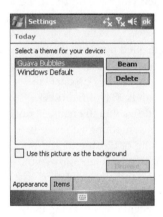

Several programs have been developed for Pocket PCs that change the appearance of the Today screen. An overview of several of these programs is provided later in this chapter in the section "Enhance the Today Screen."

To add a theme to your Pocket PC, copy the theme file, which has a .tsk extension, to either the Windows or My Documents folder on the Pocket PC. Themes can also be stored in a My Documents folder on storage cards, but they should not be in subfolders of My Documents. Chapter 4 shows you how to use ActiveSync to copy files to the Pocket PC, or you can use File Explorer to copy themes from a network share. If you want to share a theme with another Pocket PC, tap the theme, tap Beam, and align the infrared ports. To delete a theme, first tap the theme name, and then tap Delete.

If you don't want to change the appearance of the Start menu or Navigation bar, but you want to change the Today screen background image, tap the Use This Picture As The Background check box, and then tap Browse to select an image. Background images can be either JPEG or GIF files and must be stored in the My Documents folder or a subfolder of My Documents.

You can combine themes and background images to further customize the Today screen appearance to your personal preferences.

The items that can appear on the Today screen are listed on the Items tab of the Today Settings dialog box. To add or remove items from the screen, tap the check box next to the item name. Owner Info, Messaging, Tasks, Calendar, and Pocket MSN can be moved up or down in the list by selecting the item and then tapping the Move Up or Move Down button.

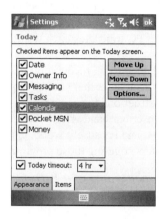

 *Pocket MSN is new with Windows Mobile 5. It adds four buttons to the Today screen for configuring MSN options, opening the MSN Mobile web site, starting MSN Messenger, and viewing Hotmail.*

Options that control what displays on the Today screen can be set for the Calendar and Tasks items. Select either and then tap the Options button. The Today screen can display the next appointment, upcoming appointments, as well as all-day events. Task options include the number of high-priority tasks, the number of tasks due today, and the number of overdue tasks. You can also restrict the task information to a specific category.

 *After the last appointment time for the current day, Windows Mobile will display the first appointment of the next day. If the Show All option is selected, then you will see all of the next day's appointments after the last appointment for the current day.*

The best time for the Today screen to be displayed is when you turn on the device for the first time each day. You might also want to have the screen display after a specified period of time has elapsed, which will happen if you tap the Today Timeout: [ ] check box on the Today Settings dialog box. Specify the number of hours that must elapse before the screen displays from the drop-down list on the dialog box.

Enter Information on Pocket PCs

Handwriting recognition is one of the most intimate ways you can interact with computers. Writing on a computer screen with your own hand, and seeing the writing translated to text, makes the computer more personal than just a machine. It is no wonder that handwriting recognition has captured the imagination of computer users.

Your Pocket PC provides several ways of translating what you write to text. The Block and Letter Recognizers instantly translate a letter that you write on the Pocket PC Software Input Panel to a character inserted at the cursor location. You can also write on the screen as you write on paper and see the results displayed on the screen in digital ink. After you finish writing, either store what was written in the digital ink form or have the Pocket PC translate the digital ink into a text font. Finally, you can write anywhere on the Pocket PC screen in your own handwriting, and after you finish writing, the Pocket PC translates each written word and inserts it at the cursor location.

If you prefer not to use any of the handwriting recognition methods, you can use the stylus to tap letters from an onscreen keyboard. Each letter that you tap appears on the screen at the cursor location. In this section, you'll find instructions for using the onscreen keyboard, the Pocket PC Block and Letter Recognizers, and Transcriber handwriting recognition. The process of translating digital ink is called *deferred recognition,* and because it works in many of the Pocket PC programs, instructions for using it are in the chapters covering those programs.

 *The fastest way to enter information into your Pocket PC is by using ActiveSync to synchronize data between the device and Microsoft Outlook. Chapter 7 provides instructions for using ActiveSync.*

Use the Software Input Panel

The Software Input Panel (SIP) is a window on the Pocket PC screen that provides a location for writing characters or displays the onscreen keyboard. To open the window, tap the SIP button located at the bottom of the application screen:

SIP button

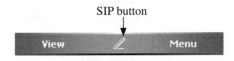

 *If you run a program on a Windows Mobile 5 Pocket PC that was designed to run on earlier versions of Windows Mobile, the SIP button will appear at the bottom-right of the application screen.*

The button image changes to indicate which of the three modes are in use. A keyboard indicates the onscreen keyboard, a pencil indicates the Block or Letter Recognizers, and a hand and pencil indicates the Transcriber.

Once the SIP is open, an arrow appears next to the icon. Tap the arrow to open the pop-up menu shown here.

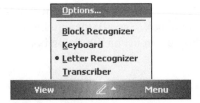

Tap the name of the input method that you want to use; if you select Keyboard, Block Recognizer, or Letter Recognizer, the menu closes and the panel switches to the mode that you select. If you select Transcriber, the panel closes and the icon switches to the hand and pencil.

Included at the top of the pop-up menu is Options, which you can tap to open the Input Settings dialog box, shown here.

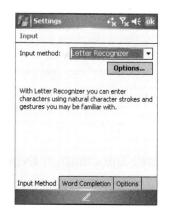

 *You can also open the Input Settings dialog box by tapping Start | Settings | Input.*

Enter Information Using the Onscreen Keyboard

The standard onscreen keyboard displays in the Software Input Panel:

Tap here to switch to the numeric keypad. ➡

Tap here to switch to the special character keyboard.

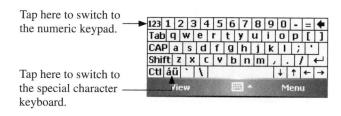

To use the onscreen keyboard to enter information, do the following:

■ To enter text, tap the letters on the keyboard using the stylus. The keyboard has three different modes: Standard, Numeric, and Special Character.

■ To switch to the numeric or special character keyboard, both shown in Figure 3-1, tap the 123 and áü button, respectively, on the standard keyboard.

FIGURE 3-1   On the left is the numeric keyboard; on the right is the special character keyboard.

■ Tap SHIFT to switch the keyboard buttons to their uppercase equivalents, and the number row displays the symbols that normally display above the number row on a standard keyboard. After you enter an uppercase letter by tapping SHIFT and then tapping a letter, the keyboard switches back to lowercase, but tapping CAP locks the keyboard in CAPS LOCK.

■ The standard onscreen keyboard displays small keys, but you can switch to large keys by opening the Input Settings dialog box and selecting the Keyboard Input Method option, as shown earlier in the chapter.

Enter Information Using the Letter Recognizer

To use the Letter Recognizer to enter text, tap Letter Recognizer on the Software Input Panel pop-up menu, which changes the panel, as shown here.

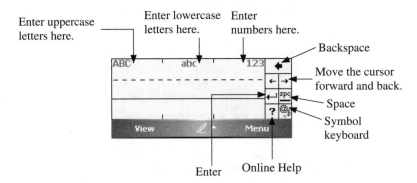

The Letter Recognizer has four areas for entering uppercase letters, lowercase letters, numbers, and keyboard commands, such as BACKSPACE and ENTER.

Drag the stylus across the panel horizontally from left to right to insert a space, and drag from right to left to delete a character or space.

The Letter Recognizer translates letters written in lowercase, but you have the option of using a single stroke to enter certain letters of the alphabet. To enter characters in a single stroke, select the Quick Stroke option on the Letter Recognizer Options screen, which you open by tapping the Options button in the Input Settings dialog box. To see demos for writing all characters, open the Letter Recognizer Online Help, and tap Demo.

The dotted middle line and the solid bottom line on the panel help the Letter Recognizer translate shorter letters and letters with descenders or ascenders. Write letters such as *o* and *c* between the midline (dotted) and baseline (solid). Write letters with descenders, such as *p,* with the top of the letter between the midline and baseline and the descender below the baseline. Letters with ascenders, such as *b,* should be written with the ascender above the midline and the bottom portion between the midline and baseline.

The Letter Recognizer also translates accented and special characters. Open Online Help to see demonstrations of how to enter these characters on the Input Panel.

Enter Information Using the Block Recognizer

If you switch to a Pocket PC from a Palm OS Version 5 or older device, you may prefer using the Block Recognizer because it translates the Palm Graffiti-like character strokes to text. To use the Block Recognizer to enter text, tap Block Recognizer on the Software Input Panel pop-up menu, which changes the panel, as shown here.

Indicates lowercase, Shift, and Caps Lock modes.   Enter letters here.   Enter numbers here.

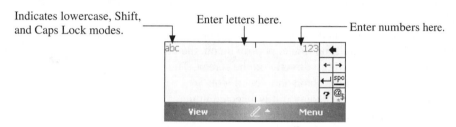

The Block Recognizer has three areas for entering letters, numbers, and keyboard commands such as BACKSPACE and ENTER.

The first word of each sentence is automatically capitalized; otherwise, all other letters translate in lowercase. To capitalize other words, switch to Shift mode by drawing a straight line from the bottom up for at least half the length of the Input Panel. The *abc* label at the upper-left corner of the Input Panel changes to *Abc,* indicating Shift mode. To activate CAPS LOCK, draw two lines from the bottom up. You will know that CAPS LOCK is active by the *ABC* label on the Input Panel.

To see a demonstration of how to enter characters using Graffiti, tap Online Help on the Input Panel, and then tap Demo.

You enter punctuation and symbols anywhere on the Input Panel. To enter punctuation, tap once on the panel, and then write the punctuation mark. A circle appears in the upper-left corner of the Input Panel, indicating punctuation mode. Enter extended characters by first drawing a slash in the Input Panel and then writing the character. A slash appears in the upper-left corner of the Input Panel, indicating Extended Character mode.

Punctuation and symbols can also be entered by tapping the Symbol Keyboard button on the Input Panel, and then by tapping an item on the keyboard.

The Block Recognizer also translates accented characters, special characters, and mathematical symbols. See Online Help for demonstrations on how to enter these characters on the Input Panel.

Word Completion

As you enter letters using the onscreen keyboard or Recognizers, the Pocket PC suggests words in a pop-up window that appears above the Input Panel. Tap the word to enter it at the insertion point.

On the Input Settings dialog box, tap the Word Completion tab to configure options for word completion. When the Pocket PC suggests more words, a greater amount of space is taken up above the Input Panel, which covers up other information in the dialog box where you enter text.

Enter Information Using Transcriber

Transcriber is a natural-handwriting recognition translator for the Pocket PC. It recognizes words written in cursive, print, or mixed handwriting by using an integrated dictionary. When you select Transcriber from the Software Input Panel pop-up menu, the panel closes and you enter text by writing directly on the screen. The Input Panel button changes to the Hand and Pencil icon.

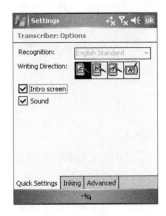

An introductory screen will display if it is selected in the Transcriber Options dialog box, shown here. To open this dialog box, tap the Options button under the Transcriber input method on the Input Settings dialog box. The Quick Settings tab includes options for specifying what language Transcriber uses and the writing direction. Tap the picture that represents the angle at which you write on the screen.

Move the Recognition Delay slider on the Inking tab of the Transcriber Options dialog box to control how quickly writing is translated to text, and tap the Add Space After check box to have a space automatically added after every translated word. You also specify the width and color of the digital ink that Transcriber uses on this tab. Tap Match Letter Shapes To Your Writing to configure Transcriber for your handwriting.

Tap each shape shown on the screen and then tap the Often, Rarely, or Never radio button to specify whether you write the letter in that shape. It's worth taking some time to go through each letter and symbol to increase translation accuracy.

The Advanced tab of the Transcriber Options dialog box configures shorthand, which you can use to create quick shortcuts for words or to launch programs, and dictionaries. Use the Dictionaries option to select what dictionaries Transcriber uses for recognition. Dictionaries have the *.dct extension and are in the Dictionaries folder on the Pocket PC.

Tap the Shorthand Settings button to open the following dialog box, where you can create shortcuts. To create a shortcut, tap Add, select Text Expansion, Function, or Run Program, then tap Next. Use text expansion to define abbreviations that Transcriber expands to full words. Select Functions to create shortcuts that insert the current date or your e-mail address. With Run Program, you can create shortcuts for launching programs on your Pocket PC.

The Transcriber icon bar, shown here, appears at the bottom of the screen when Transcriber is active:

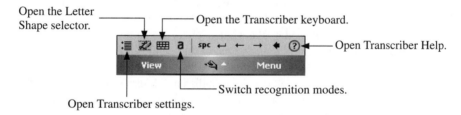

Transcriber has three recognition modes: Unrestricted, Uppercase, and Numeric. Unrestricted mode allows all symbols and words and is indicated by an *a* on the icon bar. Uppercase mode converts everything to uppercase and is indicated by an *A* on the icon bar. Numeric mode converts numbers and some letters and is indicated by a *123* on the icon bar.

The Transcriber keyboard provides an easy way to enter punctuation or symbols. It remains visible until you tap the keyboard button a second time.

You can use several gestures to direct Transcriber to perform certain actions, such as enter a Return or Backspace character. You will find these gestures in Online Help, which you can open by tapping Help (the question mark) on the toolbar or by tapping Start | Help.

To make corrections, first double-tap to select a word and then either rewrite a word or make a short up/down motion to open the Alternates menu. From the Alternates menu, you can select an alternative word from those provided.

Try Alternative Recognizers

Each Recognizer that comes with the Pocket PC might require that you make slight changes to how you write. If the Recognizers have difficulty translating your handwriting, you may want to try one of several alternative Recognizers available for the Pocket PC, such as PenReader or CalliGrapher. Many of these Recognizers come in trial versions so that you can try the software before purchasing it.

 **Use the Transcriber Calculator**

Transcriber has a built-in calculator that can complete simple mathematical equations. Write the equation as you would text, such as $2 + 2 =$. Transcriber recognizes this equation, performs the calculation, and translates what you wrote to $2 + 2 = 4$.

Transcriber supports only the English, French, and German languages. If you write in a language other than these, you may want to consider PenReader from Paragon Software, because it supports 28 languages. It recognizes all national alphabets based on the standard Latin ABC, and additional recognition engines are adjusted for Cyrillic and Greek alphabets. You will find more information about PenReader at www.penreader.com.

CalliGrapher is the big brother of Transcriber. It was developed by ParaGraph, from whom Microsoft licenses code used in Transcriber. ParaGraph is also the company that developed the handwriting recognition software used by the Apple Newton operating system. PhatWare Corporation distributes and supports CalliGrapher. One of the features that sets CalliGrapher apart is PenCommander, which launches user-defined commands that you create using a scripting language. It also includes an integrated spell checker. English and International versions of this program are available, and you will find more information about it at www.phatware.com.

Following are other applications that perform similar functions:

■ **MyScript from Vision Objects** Adds a new Software Input Panel to Pocket PCs that enables you to write across the entire width of the panel. English and French versions are available. Find more information about MyScript at www.visionobjects.com.

■ **Fitaly from Textware Solution** An alternative to the onscreen keyboard. The keys are arranged for optimal input using a stylus, with 84 percent of the keystrokes clustered in a central area. People who are proficient with Fitaly have been able to enter text as fast as 50 words per minute. You will find this program at www.fitaly.com.

■ **Spb Full Screen Keyboard** Provides a full-screen keyboard displayed in landscape, making the keys large enough to enable you to use your fingers to type. You will find this program at www.spbsoftwarehouse.com.

■ **Resco Keyboard Pro** Enhances the onscreen keyboard by adding three numeric layouts, including a calculator for typing numbers or numerical expressions. Another keyboard from Resco stores phrases, which you can insert by simply tapping a button. This program can be found at www.resco-net.com/resco/en/default.asp.

■ **AccessPanel from DeveloperOne** An additional Software Input Panel that speeds data entry by storing phrases that you can insert into documents or e-mail. It also automatically inserts information from the Pocket PC Contacts program into documents. More information about this program can be found at www.developerone.com.

Use External Keyboards

Even though the Pocket PC's handwriting recognizers do a good job, typing remains the fastest way to enter information. Some Pocket PCs have built-in keyboards, while external keyboards are available that connect to most Pocket PCs using either infrared, Bluetooth, or a cable.

One of the popular third-party keyboards is the Stowaway from Think Outside. (www .thinkoutside.com/). When open, the Stowaway keyboard is nearly as large as a full-size keyboard, but it folds up to about the same size a Pocket PC. The keyboards sold by Pocket PC manufacturers also fold up, making them easy to carry.

Enhancements in Windows Mobile make it easier to navigate in programs using keyboards. These enhancements include four new navigation and application keys, menu keyboard accelerators, auto-correct, and auto-suggest.

Manage Running Programs

One of the most hotly debated topics between Microsoft and Pocket PC users is about exiting programs. Microsoft believes it is better to have all programs open and to jump between them, because it is much faster to switch between running programs than it is to start a program. Because of this, Microsoft does not provide a way to exit programs. Pocket PC users prefer to start, exit, and switch between programs on their devices just as they do on their personal computers.

Most Pocket PC users prefer to have more control over what programs run on their Pocket PC. Furthermore, Windows CE does not do a good enough job of managing memory, so when too many programs are running, the Pocket PC slows down. Consequently, software developers have written programs that provide users with the ability to shut down running programs.

While several program task managers exist for Pocket PCs, they all work in a similar way. Additional buttons are added to the Pocket PC Navigation bar at the top of the screen, and the default OK button is replaced with a button that automatically switches between Exit and OK. Tapping Exit shuts down the program.

X Marks the Spot

Windows Mobile has an *X* button that appears to exit programs but does not. When you tap the *X*, the window closes and the previously opened program appears on the screen. However, tapping the *X* really just closes the window and does not exit the program. If you tap Start | Settings | System | Memory, and then tap the Running Programs tab, you will see the program still listed as running. Consequently, it is best to think of the *X* as a minimize button, and use a program task manager to shut down programs.

The choice of which program task manager to install is based on how many features you want. For example, SPB Pocket Plus changes the *X* button so that it exits programs. If you tap-and-hold the *X* button, a pop-up menu displays all the currently running programs. SPB Pocket Plus also includes features that enhance the Today screen, File Manager, and Internet Explorer Mobile. You will find SPB Pocket Plus at www.spbsoftwarehouse.com.

You will find additional task manager programs for Windows Mobile 5 and older in the Encyclopedia of Software and Accessories at www.pocketpcmag.com.

Enhance the Today Screen

The Pocket PC Today screen supports plug-ins, which provide software developers the ability to enhance the Today screen by adding more functions or changing its appearance. You can select from several programs to tailor the Today screen to your personal needs.

Perhaps the most widely used Today screen enhancement is DashBoard from SnoopSoft. DashBoard replaces all the default parts of the Today screen with its own agenda, mail, and task viewers, and it adds a program launcher. You will find more information about this program at www.snoopsoft.com/.

ScaryBear Software provides a number of Today screen plug-ins. QuickCalendar displays the current week, and if you tap the QuickCalendar window, it expands to display two months. QuickAgenda provides an overview for several days of appointments. QuickQuotes displays quotes on the Today screen, and PowerLevel displays meters for power level and memory. You will find these plug-ins at www.scarybearsoftware.com/.

Change the Overall Appearance of the Pocket PC

The skinning capabilities of DashBoard significantly changes the appearance of a Pocket PC. However, DashBoard cannot change some parts of the Pocket PC software, but you can use other software to make these changes.

Stardock has brought the features of its popular WindowBlinds program to the Pocket PC. PocketBlinds changes the appearance of the Navigation bar and allows you to add and place as many buttons on the Navigation bar as you want. You will find this program at www.stardock.com/products/pocketblinds/.

You can use CETuner from Paragon Software to change the color schemes and system fonts on Pocket PCs running Windows Mobile 2003. By decreasing the font size, more information will display on the screen, or you can make the fonts bolder so that they are easier to see. This program is available from www.penreader.com/PocketPC/CETuner.html.

PocketBreeze by SBSH Mobile Software (www.sbsh.net/products/pocketbreeze/) supports skins and can display up to 30 days of appointments and tasks on the Today screen. It also provides viewing of e-mail messages. The same company also provides ContactBreeze, which enables you to work with contacts from within PocketBreeze.

The BirthdayBoy plug-in from Gigabyte Solutions Ltd. displays birthdays and anniversaries up to 31 days in advance. One version of the plug-in works with the Today screen, and another version is available for DashBoard. You can download this plug-in from www.gigabytesol.com.

If you like to quickly see local weather information on your Pocket PC, there are several plug-ins that display weather information on the Today screen. One such program is Spb Weather, which has four different views and several weather sources. It can be found at www.spbsoftwarehouse.com.

Another use for Today screen plug-ins is to provide a quick way for launching programs. Battery Pack Pro adds multiple bars to the Today screen to directly access Pocket PC settings, launch programs, see how much life remains in the Pocket PC's batteries, or see how much memory is being used. You will find Battery Pack Pro at www.omegaone.com.

Wrapping Up

As you have seen, you can emphasize the personal part of the Pocket PC in several ways. Each setting and program discussed in this chapter has the purpose of tailoring the Pocket PC to your tastes and preferences. You now know well that the second *P* stands for personal; in the next chapter you'll understand the importance of the second *C* in Pocket PC, which stands for *computer*. A number of system settings control how the Pocket PC operates, and we'll take a closer look at these settings next.

Chapter 4

Change Your Pocket PC System Settings

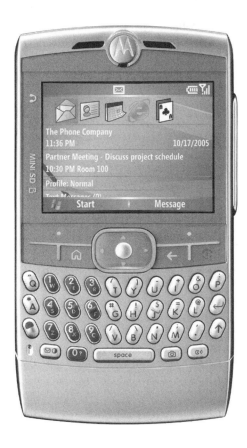

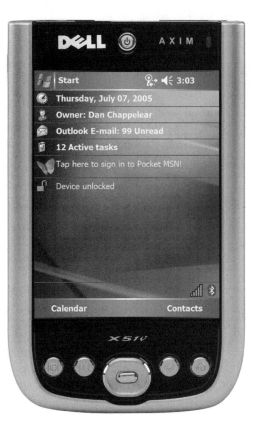

How to...

- Conserve battery power by adjusting the screen brightness
- Change the date and time on your Pocket PC
- Monitor and manage the amount of storage space available in Pocket PCs and storage cards
- Change regional settings

It may not look it, but your Pocket PC is a powerful computer. The Electronic Numerical Integrator And Computer (ENIAC) was the world's first electronic computer, built by the Army during World War II to compute ballistic firing tables. ENIAC weighed more than 30 tons, calculated 5000 additions per second, and stored 200 digits. A Pocket PC weighing 6.1 ounces calculates more than 300 million additions per second and can store more than 16 million digits.

One of the most powerful features of Pocket PCs is that they are designed so that you shouldn't have to change how they operate. However, on occasion you will need to make changes, and for that you use the System tab of the Settings screen.

Some examples of the type of system changes you may need to make include adjusting the date and time on your Pocket PC; managing battery power by adjusting the Backlight and Power settings; and using the Screen setting to fix screen problems (e.g., if taps on the screen do not properly register). In this chapter, you'll learn how to change these and other system settings on your Pocket PC.

Change the System Settings

You use the System tab to change hardware settings. To access the System tab, tap Start | Settings, and then tap the System tab to open it.

Table 4-1 contains a summary of the icons in the System tab. In this chapter, you'll learn how to use each of these.

Change the Device Name Using About

The Windows CE operating system runs on several different types of processors, though Windows Mobile 2003 and Windows Mobile 5 run only on Intel StrongARM and X-Scale processors. Pocket PC 2000 runs on SH3, MIPS, and StrongARM processors, which means that you may need to determine what processor is in these Pocket PCs to install the correct version of a program. The About icon in the System tab displays this information and more. When you tap the About icon, the About Settings dialog box displays.

Icon	Name	Description
	About	Provides information about the Pocket PC version, the processor, and the amount of memory. Specifies the name of the device that is used with ActiveSync.
	Backlight	Configures the screen backlighting to conserve battery power.
	Certificates	Manages personal and root certificates.
	Clock & Alarms	Sets the current date and time on the Pocket PC. Enables the Pocket PC to act like an alarm clock, and provides an option to turn the clock display on or off.
	Error Reporting	Turns error reporting on or off. Error reporting sends information to Microsoft's technical support groups to diagnose program errors.
	GPS	Configures how programs communicate with Global Positioning Satellite (GPS) receivers that may be in the Pocket PC.
	Memory	Displays the amount of internal memory allocated for storage and program memory. Displays the amount of space available on storage cards. Shows the programs that are running and enables you to stop them.
	Power	Shows the amount of main and backup battery power available and configures power saving features. Configures wireless modes to conserve power.
	Regional Settings	Enables your Pocket PC to support international settings that can be used by some programs. Also changes the way numbers, currency, time, and dates display.
	Remove Programs	Uninstalls any applications that you have installed on your device.
	Screen	Changes the way the stylus works with the touch screen. Use this icon if you have problems getting the touch screen to recognize the exact location of the stylus. You also use this icon to change the screen orientation and text size, and to turn ClearType on or off.

TABLE 4-1   The Pocket PC System Settings

As you can see, the dialog box has three tabs: Version, Device ID, and Copyrights. The Version tab, shown here, displays the current version of the Pocket PC, the processor type, the amount of internal memory, and whether the expansion slot is in use. The Copyrights tab displays all the copyright information for the software that is installed on the Pocket PC.

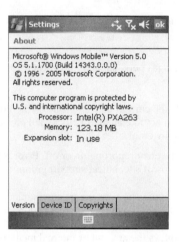

Use the Device ID tab, shown next, to specify a name for the Pocket PC. This name is used to identify the device to other computers on a network. It is also used by ActiveSync to store partnership information. (See Chapter 7 for information about ActiveSync and partnerships.) Enter a name in the Device Name field. If you wish, enter information in the Description field. The Description field can contain up to 50 characters and can be used to display any information.

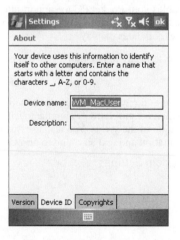

ActiveSync 4 and newer automatically creates unique device names for Windows Mobile 5 or newer devices. The name is based on the user ID logged in to the Windows desktop computer at the time the synchronization relationship is created.

Align the Screen

When you turned on your Pocket PC for the first time, you aligned the touch screen. The process involves tapping the center of a target as it moves across the screen. You will need to realign the screen if you start to have difficulty getting the Pocket PC to respond exactly as you expect when you tap the screen.

To realign the touch screen, tap the Screen icon on the System tab to open the Screen Settings dialog box. Begin the process by tapping Align Screen. Tap the target as it moves around the screen, and the Pocket PC stores the information and returns to this dialog box. Close the dialog box by tapping OK.

4

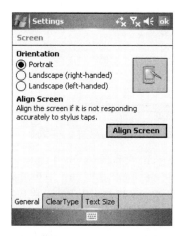

Many Pocket PCs have button sequences you can use to align the screen. For example, on an HP iPAQ, pressing the Navigation and Calendar buttons at the same time opens the Align Screen dialog box. Check the user manual of your Pocket PC to determine whether it has a similar button sequence.

Windows Mobile 2003SE and Windows Mobile 5 can switch the screen orientation from portrait, which is the default orientation, to landscape. Tap one of the orientation radio buttons and then tap OK to change how the screen displays.

You can program a hardware button to switch the screen between portrait and landscape by using the Buttons setting on the Personal tab of your Pocket PC's settings. Assign <Rotate Screen> to a hardware button.

ClearType is a font-smoothing technology originally available only with Microsoft Reader. ClearType is now available for all programs when you select the Enable ClearType check box on the ClearType tab of the Screen Settings dialog box.

To see more text on your Pocket PC's screen, you can adjust the text size on the Text Size tab of the Screen Settings dialog box. As you adjust the slider between Smallest and Largest, the size of the example text will change. This setting does not change the size of text used for menu items.

Adjust the Backlight or Brightness

With this setting, you specify that backlighting be turned off when the device is on battery power and idle for a specified period of time, or when it's on external power and idle for a specified period of time. To configure these settings, tap the Backlight icon in the System tab to open the Backlight Settings dialog box.

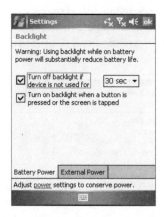

Both Power tabs have the same two check boxes—one to turn off the backlight if the device is not used for a specified amount of time and another to turn on the backlight when a button is pressed or the screen is tapped. Check the appropriate boxes to configure the backlight settings. If you select Turn Off Backlight, you can then select the amount of time to wait from the drop-down list.

Some Pocket PCs also have a Brightness tab on the Backlight Settings dialog box that you use to adjust the brightness level of the display when on battery and external power. Remember that a brighter display will drain the batteries faster than a dimmer display.

Set the Clock and Alarms

When you tap the Clock icon in the System tab, the Clock & Alarms Settings dialog box opens. The Time tab is used to set the date and time of the Pocket PC, and the Alarms tab is used to create alarms.

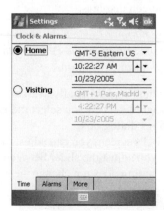

The top half of the dialog box contains the settings for the Home location, and the bottom half contains the settings for a Visiting location. Use either the Home or Visiting settings to change the date and time. Tapping the radio button next to Home or Visiting makes it available for changes.

The Home and Visiting settings are handy for travelers, allowing you to change the date and time between two locations. However, be aware that when you switch between the two, appointment times in Calendar will change to correspond with the new time zone.

To change the date, tap the down arrow to the right of the date to open the date picker, and then follow these steps:

4

1. To change the month, tap the month that is currently displayed, and then select the desired month from the list. Or, tap the left or right arrow to move forward or back one month at a time.

2. To change the year, tap the year that is currently displayed. Use the spinner buttons to increase or decrease the year setting.

3. To change the date, tap the date on the calendar.

To change the time, tap any part of the digital clock to select it, and then tap the up or down arrow to the right of the clock to change the value. Change the time zone for the Home or Visiting location by tapping the current time zone and selecting one from the drop-down list.

When you tap OK after making any change to the clock settings, a dialog box will display asking if you want to save the changes. Tap Yes, and the dialog box will close with the changes in effect. Tap No, and the dialog box will close without saving the changes. Tap Cancel, and you return to the Clock & Alarm Settings dialog box without saving any changes.

To turn off the time display at the top of Pocket PCs running Windows Mobile 5, clear the check box on the More tab of the Clock & Alarms Settings dialog box.

Set Alarms

You can also use the clock to set alarms. Three alarms are available to go off at specified times throughout the day. Tap the Alarms tab to open the dialog box shown here.

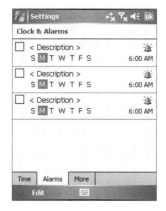

To set alarms, follow these steps:

1. Tap the field that contains <Description> and enter a description of the alarm.

2. Select the day of the week for the alarm from the date abbreviations located below the description. More than one day can be selected by tapping each day of the week.

3. Tap the time to open a window that displays an analog and digital clock. Use either clock to set the alarm time and then tap OK.

Once you have set the alarms, activate them by selecting the check boxes to the left of the alarm descriptions. The alarms you create stay in the Alarms tab, and they stay active even after they go off for the first time. Unless you clear the check boxes, the alarms that you create will go off when the designated times occur every day you selected.

The dialog box shown here appears when you tap the Bell icon (located above the time setting) and enables you to control what happens when an alarm goes off. In this dialog box, you specify whether a sound should be made, whether that sound will repeat, and whether the alarm light should flash when the alarm goes off.

While Windows Mobile 5 provides repeating alarms and the ability to snooze alarms, Pocket PC 2002, Windows Mobile 2003, and Windows Mobile 2003 Second Edition do not. Spb Software House's Pocket Plus provides repeating alarms for 2002 and 2003 devices. You can download it from www.spbsoftwarehouse.com/.

You can change the sound that the alarm plays by using the drop-down list next to the Play Sound option. Tap the down arrow button to expand the list and select the sound that you want. The sound plays after it is selected.

An alarm can be any WAV file stored in the Windows folder. You can also make your own alarms using the Notes voice recording function.

Stop Running Programs

In Chapter 2, you learned how Windows Mobile 5 uses RAM for program execution and Flash ROM for storage. Windows Mobile 2003SE and older devices divide memory between storage space and program execution. Use the Memory Settings dialog box on these devices to change how much memory is allocated for each.

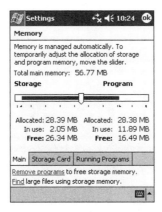

To open the Memory Settings dialog box, tap the Memory icon in the System tab. To adjust the allocation of internal memory between storage and program memory, tap-and-hold the stylus on the slider, and then drag it left or right. After the slider moves, the numbers next to Allocated, In Use, and Free change to reflect the new settings.

 *The Main tab of the Memory Settings dialog box of Windows Mobile 5 displays the total amount of storage space and program memory in the device, how much is in use, and how much is free.*

The Storage Card tab tells you the total amount of storage card memory, how much is in use, and how much is free.

The Running Programs tab, shown here, displays the programs that are currently running. You can switch from one program to another, stop a particular program, or stop all the programs from this tab.

 **Manage Storage Space**

Several programs and Today screen plug-ins are available that show you how much storage space is available without having to use Pocket PC memory settings. Other programs are available for compressing files and searching for large files so that you can free-up storage space. You might consider installing one of the following programs to monitor and manage the amount of space available in your Pocket PC and on your storage cards:

- PowerLevel from ScaryBear Software is a Today screen plug-in that displays battery power and memory information. You will find this program at www .scarybearsoftware.com.

- SpaceLeft, free from Tillanosoft, shows you the amount of storage space remaining in the Pocket PC and on storage cards. You can download this program from http:// tillanosoft.com/ce/sleft.html.

- Compress files using the PC-compatible Zip/Unzip functionality in Resco Explorer, available at www.resco-net.com. Another compression program is HandyZip from CNetX. You will find this program at www.cnetx.com/HandyZIP.

- Repair and format storage cards using Flash Format from CNetX, which is available at www.cnetx.com/format.

- Find out which files take up the most storage space by using Where Is My RAM? (WIMR?) from Rolf Olsen. You will find this free program at http://mypaq.net/ mobilesoft/wimr/.

- Remove temporary files written by Internet Explorer and other programs by using MemMaid by DinarSoft. You will find this program at www.pocketgear.com.

To switch to a program, select it from the Running Programs List and then tap Activate. To stop a program, select it from the Running Programs List and then tap Stop. To stop all the programs that are running, tap Stop All.

 *Chapter 3 provides information about third-party programs that help you manage running programs.*

Manage Power

Most of the time, your Pocket PC will run on battery power. Managing that power so that it lasts as long as possible is important. Tap the Power icon in the System tab to open the Power Settings dialog box. This dialog box provides information about the status of your main and backup batteries.

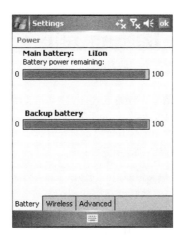

4

    The Power Settings screen is often unique among Pocket PC brands. Your screens may look different from the one shown here.

Tap the Wireless tab to conserve battery power by turning off wireless signals. Tap the Advanced tab to configure the amount of time your Pocket PC is inactive before being turned off. Tap the check boxes to have the Pocket PC turn off after a specified amount of time lapses, and select the amount of time from the drop-down lists.

Change the Regional Settings

Although English may be spoken around the world, how it is spoken differs, and writing numbers, currency, time, and dates can vary from country to country. You can customize your Pocket PC so that these items display in a manner consistent with various locations. The Regional Settings dialog box, shown here, is used to make these changes. To open the Regional Settings dialog box, tap the Regional Settings icon in the System tab.

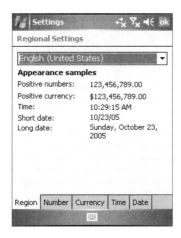

 **Manage Battery Life**

All Pocket PCs use batteries for power. After a period of time, the batteries need to be replaced or recharged. The trick is to extend the life of the batteries, because Murphy's Law dictates that the time to change the batteries is when you need your device the most. Following is some advice to help prolong battery life:

- Use the Backlight settings to adjust the brightness of the display on your device. The brighter the display, the more power is consumed.

- Configure the battery power portion of the Backlight settings so that the backlight automatically turns off after a short period of time.

- Configure the Power settings so that the Pocket PC automatically turns off if it is not in use after a short period of time.

- Turn off sounds.

- Use peripherals that have low power ratings. Most cards that have the *Made for Windows Mobile* logo are designed for low power consumption.

- Remove microdrives and wireless cards that are not being used. If a card is inserted in your device, it may draw power.

- Program a button in Windows Media Player to toggle the screen on and off, and program other buttons to control playback. Turn the screen off when playing music.

- Play music from CompactFlash cards rather than from microdrives. Microdrives have moving parts and thus consume more power than CompactFlash storage cards.

- Keep your Pocket PC in its cradle and charging whenever possible. The lithium ion battery technology used in Pocket PCs does not have the same memory problems that exist with other battery technologies.

- Use a power level monitor plug-in for the Today screen that easily shows you how much battery power is left. (An example is PowerLevel from ScaryBear Software at www.scarybearsoftware.com.) If you use a program task manager such as WIS Bar or GigaBar, you can configure it to display the power level at the top of the screen.

- If you have a Pocket PC that uses an X-Scale processor and includes software to adjust the processor speed, switch the processor to the PowerSave setting.

Some Pocket PC brands drain batteries faster than others. If battery life is a concern, you may want to check message boards or newsgroups on the Internet to find out which device has the longest battery life. Most Pocket PC devices have removable batteries, which you can replace with a spare battery when necessary.

As you can see, five tabs are available in this dialog box: Region, Number, Currency, Time, and Date. The Region tab displays a drop-down list that contains preconfigured settings for different parts of the world. Selecting one of these configurations will automatically configure the appropriate settings in the other four tabs. If you wish to further customize any of these settings, tap a tab and select an item from any of the drop-down lists.

Remove Programs

Chapter 8 shows you how to manage programs using ActiveSync, which is used to install and remove programs on your device. However, you might need to remove a program while you are away from your desktop. Tap the Remove Programs icon in the System tab to open the Remove Programs dialog box, which displays all the programs that have been installed.

To remove a program, simply tap it and then tap the Remove button. A warning message dialog box will display asking if you are sure that you want to remove the program. If you tap Yes, the program is deleted and irretrievable, so be judicious in your use of this feature!

Sometimes, when uninstalling an application, you will see a message saying that a file is in use and the application cannot be uninstalled. If that happens, soft reset the Pocket PC and then uninstall the application.

Manage Certificates

Security certificates are files that help identify computers or users and allow computers to send and receive encrypted data. To use some secure web sites, a computer's browser must be able to accept certificates. Windows Mobile supports security certificates, which you manage by tapping the Certificates icon on the System tab.

You can store two types of certificates on your Pocket PC. Personal certificates, which you manage on the Personal tab, establish your identity. Root certificates, which you manage on the Root tab, establish the identity of the servers with which you connect. To view more information about a certificate, type its name in the Root tab. To delete a certificate, tap-and-hold the certificate name and then tap Delete.

Turn Off Error Reporting

Error reporting sends information to Microsoft that helps them diagnose errors with programs running under Windows Mobile. When an error occurs, a text file is created that contains data about the state of the program and your Pocket PC when the error occurred. The data is transmitted using a secure connection and is kept anonymous in a secured database.

If you prefer to not have your Pocket PC send error reports to Microsoft, tap Start | Settings | System | Error Reporting, tap the Disable Error Reporting radio button, and then tap OK.

Configure GPS

One of the most popular ways for using Pocket PCs is to display maps and location information from Global Positioning Satellite receivers connected to the Pocket PC. Some Pocket PCs have a built-in receiver; if yours does not, you can connect a receiver by using a cable or Bluetooth. The GPS Settings dialog box in Windows Mobile 5 is used to configure how programs communicate with GPS receivers.

You need to specify what communications port programs use to receive GPS data. Tap Start | Settings | System | GPS to open the dialog box shown here. Select a COM port from the GPS Program Port drop-down list. You should find information about the COM port you need to use in the GPS receiver user manual.

Windows Mobile may automatically detect your GPS receiver and configure the hardware settings, but if it doesn't, tap the Hardware tab and select a COM port from the GPS Hardware Port drop-down list. This COM port must be different from the one you select on the Programs tab.

Windows Mobile 5's GPS support enables multiple programs to communicate with a GPS receiver at the same time. By default Windows Mobile is configured to manage access with GPS receivers, but if your GPS software does not work, you may need to turn this feature off. Clear the Manage GPS Automatically check box on the Access tab of the GPS Settings dialog box.

Wrapping Up

The system settings shown in this chapter are available on all Pocket PCs, but each brand of Pocket PC may include additional settings that are unique to that device. You will find more information about these settings in the user manual that comes with your Pocket PC.

Now that you know the basic functions of your Pocket PC and how to change its settings, you will learn the basic functions of Smartphones.

Chapter 5

Get Acquainted with Your Smartphone

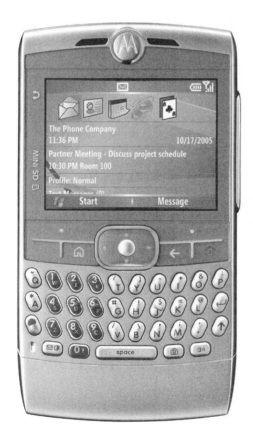

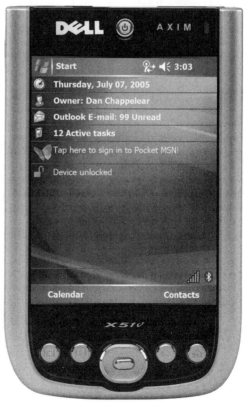

How to...

- Identify hardware components
- Input information
- Set up your Smartphone
- Make phone calls
- Use the Start menu
- Personalize your Smartphone

Before you can begin to take full advantage of all the features that your Smartphone has to offer, you need a good understanding of the basic components that make up the phone. If all you do is use your Smartphone to send and receive calls, you will be missing out on all that it has to offer. In this chapter you will learn the basics for using your phone, while the remaining chapters in this book show how to use all the software that it includes.

Following a review of the hardware components of the Smartphone, I'll show how to use the Navigation button to interact with the software on the phone. I will discuss the Home Screen, which is the "command center" for all Smartphone operations, and then review the Smartphone settings, which you can change to configure the Smartphone to meet your preferences.

Meet Your Smartphone

Microsoft worked with several hardware companies for many years to develop Windows Mobile for Smartphones. Smartphones are intended to be first and foremost a great mobile phone, with additional functionality for managing personal information. Therefore, Smartphones have all the features, like speed dialing and speakerphone, that you expect to find on mobile phones.

Unlike Pocket PCs, which in many cases require two hands to operate, Smartphones are designed for one-hand operation. A key difference between Pocket PCs and Smartphones is that Smartphones do not have touch screens, and therefore you do not use a stylus to input information. Instead, you use one of the several buttons on the front of the device to navigate through its many options and to input information.

Another significant difference from Pocket PCs is that Smartphones do not include the Office Mobile applications.

Review the Smartphone

Let's take a tour of a typical Smartphone, starting with the front of the device. You'll learn the function of parts commonly found on the Smartphone, but keep in mind that slight variations exist among various Smartphone brands. You'll use some parts more often than others, but knowing *how* to use all of them is important.

Review the Front

The largest part of the Smartphone is its screen. The LCD (liquid crystal display) screen is used for viewing and entering information, and it may vary in size depending on the overall size of the Smartphone. Newer Smartphones have Quarter VGA (QVGA) displays with higher resolution for vivid pictures and crisp text.

As you can see in Figure 5-1, the buttons below the screen are assigned to various programs or functions. Push the Navigation button up, down, left, or right to move the cursor, and press the Navigation button to select items on the screen.

5

FIGURE 5-1 The front of a Smartphone (other Smartphones look different but have many of the same parts)

The notification LED provides a variety of information to indicate the phone's status, and may be different between Smartphone brands. Typically the LED will be flashing green, indicating that it is attached to a network. If you are charging the phone, then the LED indicates the charging status; for example, solid amber may indicate that the phone is charging, while solid green indicates the phone is fully charged. A flashing blue LED may indicate that the Bluetooth radio is on, while flashing red may indicate that the battery is very low. Check the user manual that came with your Smartphone for the exact functions of the LED.

The functions of the left and right softkeys change to correspond to commands or menus of the program currently displaying on the screen. Immediately above the softkeys, at the bottom of the screen, you see the name of the function each key executes. For example, on the Home Screen, pressing the left softkey opens the Start menu, and pressing the right softkey opens Contacts.

The Home button always returns to the Home Screen, and the Back button returns you to the previous screen, or backspaces one character in a text field. Talk and End are buttons commonly found on mobile phones. Press Talk to start a call or receive an incoming call; press End to end a call. The Talk and End buttons have these additional functions:

- Press and hold Talk to turn the speakerphone on or off during a phone conversation.
- If you have a call on hold, press and hold Talk to switch between the active call and the call on hold.
- Press Talk on the Home Screen to view the Call History.
- Press and hold End to lock the keypad.
- Pressing End often returns you to the Home Screen.

Most Smartphones have the same numeric keypad layout that you find on telephones and other mobile phones. To make a call, press the numbers on the keypad and then press Talk. As you enter numbers, they display on the screen. The "Use Your Smartphone" section later in this chapter shows you how to use the keypad to enter text.

Some Smartphones may include a QWERTY keyboard, but rather than having a separate number row, numbers are also assigned to the same keys as some letters. Windows Mobile will automatically switch those keys between numbers and letters, depending on what you are doing with your Smartphone.

Review the Sides

The top, bottom, left, and right sides of Smartphones will vary between brands. The items you typically find on the sides of Smartphones are as follows:

- **Power button**   Press this button to turn on the Smartphone. When the Smartphone is on, press this button to display the Quick List to turn Flight mode on or off, lock the Smartphone, or select a profile.

- ■ **Infrared port**   Enables the Smartphone to send and receive data with other devices by using infrared beaming.

- ■ **Volume button**   Press this button to increase or decrease the earpiece volume.

- ■ **Camera button**   If the Smartphone has a built-in camera, it usually has a button that opens the Pictures & Videos program, and is used for taking pictures.

- ■ **Earphone jack**   Enables you to plug in a phone headset for hands-free operation of the Smartphone, and to listen to audio.

- ■ **Mini-USB port**   Most Smartphones have a mini-USB port to plug in a cable that can plug into a computer or an AC adapter. The cable is used to charge the phone and to synchronize data between a computer and the phone. Check the user manual for your Smartphone to see how you use the cable. If your Smartphone does not have a mini-USB port, it will have a different port for a power adapter.

Review the Back

If your Smartphone has a built-in camera, you will normally find the camera lens on the back of the phone. Some phones may also have a tiny mirror on the back to help with taking self-portraits. You will also find a latch for opening the phone's battery compartment.

Depending on the type of phone, the battery compartment may have two important components in addition to the battery. If you have a phone that uses the Global System for Mobile Communications (GSM) protocol, you may have a slot for a Subscriber Identity Module (SIM) card.

How to ... **Use SIM Cards with GSM Phones**

Before you can operate a GSM phone, you must insert the SIM card into the phone. SIM cards store information about your mobile service, and may include an address book for storing phone numbers. To switch GSM phones, all you need to do is transfer the SIM card from one phone to another phone. The mobile service provider provides the SIM cards that work with its service, and in some cases GSM phones are locked to only work with a specific provider. You can buy GSM phones that are "SIM-lock free," which means that you can use any provider's SIM card with the phone. Most GSM phones have a code that unlocks the phone, and there are companies on the Internet that provide a service to enter the code and unlock phones.

The SIM card must be inserted in this slot in order to operate the phone. You may also find a mini–Secure Digital (miniSD) card slot, which you can use to increase storage in your Smartphone by inserting miniSD cards.

Meet the Home Screen

When you turn on a Smartphone, two screens display while the Smartphone is starting up; one displays the Windows Mobile logo, the second displays the mobile service provider's logo. During that time, all of the phone's settings are being loaded and the phone is connecting to a mobile network. Finally, you see the Home Screen, which looks like Figure 5-2.

The layout that you see in Figure 5-2 is one of five layouts that come preinstalled. The section "Personalize Your Smartphone" later in the chapter shows you how to change the Home Screen. At the top of the screen you see a number of different status indicators, as shown in Table 5-1. The status indicator bar at the top of the screen remains no matter what Home Screen layout you use.

As Figure 5-2 shows, the Home Screen may have several parts that display different information. In most cases you can move the cursor to a part and launch a different program. For example, if you select an appointment, the Calendar program runs and displays the appointment. Push the Navigation button up or down to move the cursor through the parts, and press the Navigation button to start the program associated with the part.

The Shortcut bar shows icons for the last ten programs that ran on the device. Push the Navigation button right to scroll through the additional icons that are not displaying on the screen. To open a program, press the Navigation button left or right to move the cursor over the icon of the program and then press the Navigation button to select the program.

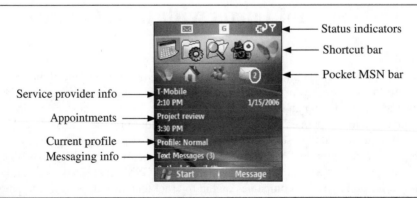

FIGURE 5-2   The Smartphone Home Screen

Indicator	Description
	New e-mail or text message
	New voice mail
	New instant message
	Voice call active
	Data connection active
	GPRS available
	GPRS in use
	Bluetooth is turned on
	Call forwarding
	Call on hold
	Missed call
	Speakerphone is on
	Battery full
	Phone is plugged in
	Signal strength
	Radio off (Flight mode is on)
	Ringer off
	Vibrate mode is on

TABLE 5-1   Windows Mobile Smartphone Status Indicators

The Pocket MSN bar is part of the MSN Default Home Screen layout, which is the initial layout that displays on Windows Mobile 5 Smartphones. The Pocket MSN bar works like the Shortcut bar; use the Navigation button to move the cursor over the icon of the program you want to run, and press the Navigation button to select the program.

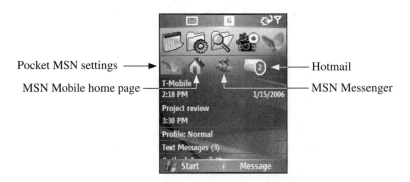

Pocket MSN settings ⟶
MSN Mobile home page ⟶
⟵ Hotmail
⟵ MSN Messenger

Most layouts include the service provider information, which you cannot select or remove from the screen. The Appointments section shows the current or upcoming appointments in the Smartphone Calendar. Chapter 13 shows you how to add appointments to the Calendar.

Profiles specify how Smartphones notify you of different events such as incoming calls, text messages, or e-mail. The Home Screen may show you which profile is currently in use, and if you press the Navigation button on the profile, the Profiles list, shown here, displays. Push the Navigation button up or down to move the cursor and press the Navigation button to select a profile. See the "Personalize Your Smartphone" section later in this chapter for information about each profile.

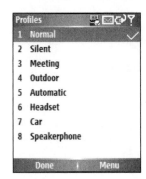

The Messaging section of the Home Screen shows the number of unread messages for each Messaging account. Messaging is the program you use to send and receive text messages and e-mail; Chapter 11 shows you how to use this program. Select one of the Messaging accounts on the Home Screen to open the Messaging program and read the messages.

Use Your Smartphone

As stated at the beginning of this chapter, Windows Mobile Smartphones are designed to be operated with one hand, and you use buttons to operate and input information into the Smartphone. In the previous section you saw how to use the Navigation button to move the cursor and select items on the screen.

Throughout this book you will see instructions for operating your Smartphone, written as follows, "from the Home Screen press Start | More | Games | Solitaire," which instructs you to start the Solitaire program. To execute the instructions, you press a combination of the left or right softkeys and Navigation buttons. A breakdown of the previous instructions, starting from the Home Screen, is as follows:

1. Press the Left softkey, currently assigned to Start.
2. Press the Left softkey, currently assigned to More.
3. Push the Navigation button to select the Games folder, and press the Navigation button.
4. Push the Navigation button to select the Solitaire icon, and press the Navigation button.

As you can tell, it could take a significant amount of writing to explicitly tell you which buttons to press, so I will use the shortcut notation previously described.

NOTE   *You use different methods for performing operations on Pocket PCs and Smartphones. You tap the stylus on the Pocket PC touch screen to execute commands, while you press buttons on Smartphones. For instances in this book where you need to perform the same operation on both devices, I'll prefix the operation string with the word "select." If an operation is just for Pocket PCs, the string will be prefixed with the word "tap," while Smartphone operations will be prefixed with the word "press."*

If at any point you want to back up to the previous screen press the Back button. To return to the Home Screen, press the Home button.

5

Input Text

Some Smartphones may have a QWERTY keyboard, and for these models entering text is a straightforward process of typing on the keyboard. However, usually Smartphones have a numeric keypad, which you use to dial phone numbers and to enter text. Each button on the numeric keypad has multiple functions, with some buttons capable of entering as many as four different letters in either upper- or lowercase, in addition to numbers.

Smartphones with numeric keypads have two text input modes: Multipress and T9. Whenever the cursor is in a text field, you will see one of the indicators in Table 5-2 at the top of the screen, indicating which text mode is currently in effect. To switch modes when the cursor is in a text field, hold down the asterisk (*) button and select the mode you want from the pop-up menu.

In Multipress mode you enter characters by pressing the button of the letter that you want to type. Since buttons have more than one letter, you may need to press the button multiple times to enter the correct character. For example, to enter the word "dog," you would press 3, 66, 4.

If a button contains two letters that you need to enter in succession you must pause after entering the first letter and wait until the underline disappears before entering the next letter. For example, to enter the word "cat," you would press 222, pause, press 2, and then press 8. If you need to backspace, press Back, and to enter a space, press #. To enter punctuation, press 1 until the correct punctuation mark displays.

Input Mode	Description
abc	Multipress, lowercase
ABC	Multipress, uppercase
t9	T9, lowercase
T9	T9, uppercase
123	Numeric

TABLE 5-2   Smartphone Input Modes

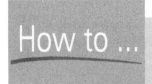

Change the Multipress Time Out

To change the length of time that you have to wait before entering two letters on the same button in Multipress mode, press Start | Settings | More | Accessibility. Move the cursor to the Multipress Timeout field and press the Navigation button, select an option from the list, and press Done. Press Done to return to the Settings menu, or press Home to return to the Home Screen.

Press and hold # to display a table of symbols, then use the Navigation button to select the symbol that you want to insert.

T9 mode provides predictive text entry. You only need to press the button containing the letter of a word once, and as you press the button, the software determines what word you want to enter. If there are multiple possible words, a pop-up menu appears showing each of the words. Push the Navigation button up or down to move through the list, and press the Navigation button to select the correct word. If the word is at the beginning of a sentence, it will be automatically capitalized, and a space is entered after each word.

If T9 mode accurately determines each word that you are entering, typing becomes a process of pressing a series of buttons and then pressing the Navigation button. T9 mode also attempts to determine the next word you are going to enter, and automatically displays that word. If the word is correct, press the Navigation button to move on to the next word, or begin pressing buttons to enter a different word.

In some cases T9 mode will not have the word you are entering in its dictionary. To enter the word, you need to switch to Multipress mode. After you enter the word in Multipress mode, the word will be added to the T9 mode dictionary.

To enter punctuation in T9 mode, press 1, and a pop-up menu displays with punctuation marks that you can select. To enter symbols in either Multipress or T9 mode, press and hold the

button, and the Symbols screen shown here will display. Use the Navigation button to select the symbol that you want to insert, or press Cancel to exit the screen without inserting a symbol.

Some additional input actions are

- **Start a new line**   Press the Navigation button.
- **Switch between lowercase, uppercase, and CAPS LOCK**   Press the * button.
- **Enter a number, asterisk (*), or pound sign (#)**   Press and hold the * button, then select "123" for Numeric mode in the pop-up list.
- **Enter a plus (+) sign**   Press and hold 0.

Make Phone Calls

You can dial phone numbers on a Smartphone just as you do with a mobile telephone, by pressing the number buttons and then pressing Talk. However, Windows Mobile Smartphones provide a number of different ways to quickly place calls, depending on what program is running.

If you want to dial a number, the Home Screen must be displaying. If you are in the Start menu, or running a program, first press Home to return to the Home Screen. As you press the buttons of the numbers on the keypad, the screen changes as shown here. At the top you see the numbers that you have entered, and at the bottom you see a list containing items from either the Call History or Contacts that contain the same number.

If the list contains the number or contact name that you are calling, you can use the Navigation button to select the item in the list. Either the Call History record displays, showing the date, time, and duration of the call, or the Contacts record displays. To dial the number in the Call History, press the Navigation button. Because a contact may have multiple phone numbers, use the Navigation button to select the number you want to call, and press the button to dial the number.

Make Phone Calls from Call History

To quickly display the Call History, press Talk while at the Home Screen, to display the screen shown here. This is the same screen that displays when you dial numbers from the Home Screen, except that you don't see a number populated at the top of the screen. Push the Navigation button up or down to scroll through the list, press the Navigation button to display a Call History record, and press the Navigation button a second time to dial the phone number.

You can also open the Call History from the Start menu. Press Start | Call History, to display the following screen. Use the Navigation button to scroll through the list and display a record. The Call History Menu button has several options, as shown in Table 5-3.

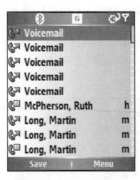

Make Phone Calls from Contacts

Most mobile phones have a built-in address book for storing phone numbers, but the process of entering numbers may be tedious, because you manually enter the name and phone number

Command	Function
Find Contact	Searches Contacts for the phone number of the Call History record, and displays the contact information.
E-mail	Searches Contacts for the phone number of the Call History record and, if an e-mail address is found, creates a new e-mail message.
View Timers	Displays the call duration and the durations for all calls, all incoming calls, outgoing calls, roaming calls, and data calls. To reset the call timers, press Menu | Reset Timers.
Delete	Deletes the selected Call History record.
Delete List	Deletes all the entries in the Call History.
Save To Contacts	Saves the phone number in the Call History to a contact that you select. The left softkey is also assigned to this function.
Filter	Provides options for filtering entries in the Call History so that you only see missed, incoming, or outgoing calls.

TABLE 5-3   The Call History Menu Options

for each contact using the phone's keypad. However, with Windows Mobile, it is simple to add phone numbers by using ActiveSync to synchronize your Outlook contacts with your Smartphone.

Chapter 7 provides instructions for synchronizing Outlook contacts with Windows Mobile devices. See Chapter 13 to learn more about using Outlook Mobile.

The right softkey is assigned to Contacts at the Home Screen. You can also press Start \| Contacts to open the Contacts application, shown here:

To call a person in Contacts, open the contact record, as shown here, use the Navigation button to select the phone number, and then press the Navigation button to dial the number:

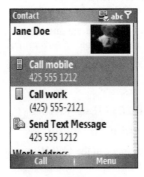

Push the Navigation button up or down to scroll through the Contacts list. To quickly navigate to a contact, start pressing the buttons associated to that contact's name, and the contacts containing the letters you press will be filtered on the screen. For example, to display John Doe, press 36, which displays as shown here:

Use Speed Dial to Make Phone Calls

The fastest way to dial frequently used phone numbers is to assign them to a button to speed dial. To speed dial a number assigned to a button, press and hold the button, and you will hear a short beep indicating that the number is dialing. For example, most Smartphones assign 1 to voice mail, so to check voice mail press and hold 1.

It is possible to create 99 different speed dials. To use a speed dial assigned to a two-digit number, press and hold the second digit. For example, to call a number assigned to 14, press 1 and then press and hold 4.

You can only assign phone numbers that are in Contacts to speed dial. To create a speed dial, open a contact, use the Navigation button to select a phone number, and then press Menu | Add To Speed Dial, which opens the screen shown on the following page. Press the Navigation button on the Key Assignment field to display a list of available speed dials, and use the Navigation button to select the speed dial that you want to use.

 *I sometimes forget what numbers I use for my speed dials, so I try to assign phone numbers to buttons containing the letters of the contact. For example, I assign my home phone number to 4, which is also the H button.*

To see a list of your speed dials, press Start | More | Speed Dial, which displays a list of the speed dials and the associated contact numbers. To place a call from the list, use the Navigation button to highlight an entry and then press Go. To edit a speed dial, use the Navigation button to select the speed dial and then press Edit; to delete a highlighted speed dial, press Menu | Delete.

 To view the entire contact record assigned to a speed dial, press Menu | Find Contact.

Make Phone Calls from Text Messages and E-mail

As you will see in Chapter 11, you can send text messages and e-mail using the Windows Mobile messaging application. Windows Mobile automatically turns phone numbers in text messages and e-mail into links, as shown on the next page. Press the Navigation button up or down to move the cursor over the phone number, and then press the Navigation button to dial the number.

Make Phone Calls Using Voice Commands

Microsoft's Voice Command software provides a way to make phone calls by speaking a command, but it only runs on Pocket PCs. Some Smartphone manufacturers include voice tags, which you can use to record a command to dial select phone numbers. Check the user manual that came with your Smartphone to configure this software if it is included.

You can use VITO VoiceDialer to create voice commands to dial numbers, and it works with Bluetooth headsets. You will find VITO VoiceDialer at http://vitotechnology.com/en/index.php. Another program that enables you to make phone calls using voice commands is Fonix VoiceDial, available at www.fonixspeech.com.

5

If you receive an e-mail or text message from someone that is in the Contacts list, the message header will display the contact's name, as shown here. Press the Navigation button to open the contact information, and then to place a call select one of the contact's phone numbers. If you receive a text message from someone that is not in Contacts, you can press the Navigation button to create a new contact for the phone number.

Use the Start Menu

Like Windows, you launch programs on Windows Mobile Smartphones by selecting them in the Start menu. To accommodate the small screen, nine application icons appear on the screen.

Press Start from the Home Screen to display the Start menu. You can push the Navigation button up, down, left, or right to scroll through the icons on the screen. The icons also correspond to buttons on the numeric keypad. For example, with the Start menu open, press 1 to start Internet Explorer, or press 9 to open Settings. Buttons are associated with an icon's position on the screen, so pressing 1 on the screen shown here opens the Games folder. Button assignments are in numerical order, starting with 1 being assigned to the top-left icon on the screen.

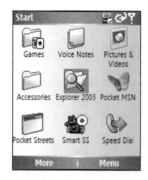

Press More to move through each screen, and press Back to return to the previous screen. You can assign speed dials to quickly launch programs without having to open the Start menu. Use the Navigation button to highlight an icon, then press Menu | Add Speed Dial, and assign a speed dial in the same way as you assign speed dials to phone numbers.

Personalize Your Smartphone

Smartphones have several settings for you to configure how you want your Smartphone to work. To open Settings from the Home Screen, press Start | Settings, which displays the first Settings screen.

Press More to display the second Settings screen, as shown on the following page.

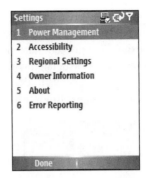

In this section we'll cover the options available for each of these Settings screens.

 Each setting is preceded by a number that you can press to open that setting's screen.

Change Phone Network Settings

Smartphones are available for all of the different mobile phone networks around the world, and there are a number of settings for configuring how your phone works with the network. You do not want to change these settings unless you know what you are doing, because otherwise the phone may not work with your mobile service. When you select the Phone option on the first Settings screen, you see a screen that looks like the one shown here.

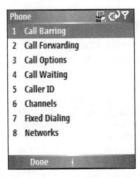

Table 5-4 provides a summary for the settings that you see in the illustration.

Change Ring Tones

One popular way that people personalize their phone is with ring tones. Smartphones can play ring tones in WAV, WMA, and MIDI audio files. To change the ring tone on your Smartphone, select the Sounds option in Settings, to display the screen shown on the following page. Press the Navigation button on the Ring Tone field to display a list of the available audio files on the

Setting	Function
Call Barring	Provides options for blocking incoming and outgoing calls.
Call Forwarding	Provides options for forwarding calls for the following conditions: No Reply, Busy, Unavailable, and Unconditional. By default, No Reply, Busy, and Unavailable are configured to forward calls to voice mail. If you want to forward all incoming calls to another number, enter that number for the Unconditional option.
Call Options	In this screen you configure the phone numbers for voice mail and text messaging, which are provided by your mobile service. You can also specify whether a call can be answered by pressing any key and whether SIM contacts display.
Call Waiting	Provides an option for notifying you while you are on a call that there is another incoming call.
Caller ID	Provides an option to control whether your phone number displays on caller ID. You can specify that everyone sees your number, no one sees your number, or only those people in Contacts can see your number.
Channels	Configures cell broadcast channels.
Fixed Dialing	Limits your calling area to one or more specific phone numbers and/or area codes.
Networks	Displays the current mobile service network that you are connected to, and provides options for automatically connecting to any network, or manually specifying the network the phone connects to.

TABLE 5-4   Windows Mobile Smartphone Phone Settings

phone that you can use as a ring tone. After you select a file, the ring tone will play and return to the Sounds screen. To play a tone again, press Menu | Play.

You can specify what sounds play for several other events such as reminders and new e-mail. Push the Navigation button up or down to scroll through the fields on the screen and press the Navigation button to change an option.

To delete sound files on your Smartphone, press Menu | Delete Sounds. You cannot delete the sound files that come with the Smartphone. If you want to cancel the changes that you made on the Sounds screen, press Menu | Cancel, and press Done to save changes.

Download Ring Tones to Your Smartphone

ActiveSync does not synchronize files with Smartphones as it does with Pocket PCs. Therefore, to download ring tones to your Smartphone, you need to manually copy them from a PC to the phone using Windows Explorer. Connect the Smartphone to a PC running ActiveSync and then start Windows Explorer. Copy the ring tone files from the PC to the Mobile Device icon that you will find under My Computer. After the files copy to the device, you can select the new ring tone using the Sounds setting on the Smartphone.

Edit Profiles

Profiles specify how Smartphones respond to events such as incoming calls. To change profiles, you can either select the Profile item on the Home Screen or press the power button to display the Quick List. There are eight different profiles on Smartphones, which you can edit by selecting the Profiles setting to display the screen shown here. To edit a profile, use the Navigation button to highlight the profile and then press Menu | Edit. Use the Navigation button to change the settings and then press Done to save your settings, or press Cancel to return to the previous screen.

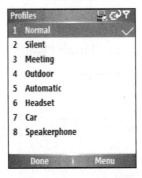

Table 5-5 provides a summary of the default settings for the Smartphone profiles. The volume range is from Off (0) to Loud (5). Each profile also specifies settings for Alarms, Notifications, and System sounds. The Headset and Car profiles include a setting to automatically answer the phone within a specified amount of time. To reset the profiles to their factory default settings, press Menu | Reset To Default on the Profiles screen.

The Automatic profile switches the profile that is in use between Normal and Meeting depending on whether there is an appointment on the Calendar. For example, if the Automatic profile is in effect and you receive a call during the time of an appointment on the Calendar, the phone will vibrate. When you receive a call after the meeting is over, the phone will ring.

Profile	Ring Type	Volume
Normal	Ring	Medium (3)
Silent	Silent	Off
Meeting	Vibrate	Off
Outdoor	Ring	Loud
Headset	Ring	Medium (3)
Car	Ring	Medium+ (4)
Speakerphone	Ring	Loud

TABLE 5-5   Smartphone Profiles

Change the Home Screen

The Home Screen is the most visible component on the Smartphone, and you can change the Home Screen layout to one of five that ship with the Smartphone. To change the Home Screen layout, select the Home Screen setting, select the Home Screen Layout field, and select one of the options on the screen.

Another way to change the Home Screen is to change the graphic that displays in the background. Use the Navigation button to select the Background Image field and select one of the images in the list. If your Smartphone has a camera, pictures that you take and store on the phone will appear in the list, as do pictures that synchronize with Outlook contacts.

The Smartphone display times out after a period of time to conserve battery life. To change the length of time before the display times out, select the Time Out field on the Home Screen settings screen.

Change the Date and Time

To change the date and time that displays on the Smartphone, select the Clock & Alarm setting, and then select Date And Time to open the screen shown here. Use the Navigation button to change the Time Zone, Date, and Time fields and press Done to save the changes.

You can use a Smartphone as an alarm clock by turning the alarm on or off when you press the Alarm option on the Clock & Alarm settings screen. Use the Navigation button to change the alarm time and to turn the alarm off. The alarm will continue to go off at the time specified until you turn it off using the Clock & Alarm setting.

The Sounds setting specifies what sound plays when the alarm goes off, and the current profile controls the alarm volume.

Change the Data Connections Settings

Smartphones are capable of infrared and Bluetooth connections with other devices, as well as Internet connections using the wireless data service of your mobile service provider. To configure these connections, select the Connections setting to display this screen.

The GPRS option specifies the data communications settings for mobile providers that use GSM. Your phone may have an option other than GPRS that corresponds to other data communications technologies. In most cases the data communications settings are entered by your mobile service provider, but if you bought your phone from a store not associated with a provider, you may need to enter the settings.

For example, if you have a GSM phone, select the GPRS option on the Connections settings screen, which may open a blank screen with Done and Menu assigned to the left and right softkeys. To add data settings, press Menu | Add to open the screen shown here. Enter a description for the data connection in the Description field.

Select the Connects To field to specify the type of network connection; in most cases you will select the Internet. Enter the access point name (APN), which you can get from your mobile provider, in the Access Point field. Enter a username, password, domain name server (DNS), and IP address information in the appropriate fields if required by your mobile service provider. Press Done to save the settings and return to the GPRS screen, and press Done again to return to the Connections settings screen.

Smartphones can connect to dial-up modems if your mobile service provider supports this capability, which is called Circuit-Switched Cellular. To configure the Smartphone to use a dial-up connection, select the Dial-Up option on the Connections settings screen, then press Menu | Add to enter the dial-up information. Enter the information on the Add Dialup screen and press Done to save the settings.

The Proxy and VPN options on the Connections settings screen are used to enter information about proxy servers and virtual private network gateways, which are used on corporate networks. Chapter 10 provides instructions for using these options to connect to corporate networks.

Most Smartphones have an infrared port that can be used to exchange information with other devices. If you don't use infrared to send and receive data, you can turn off the infrared port to conserve battery life. Select the Beam option on the Connections settings screen, and then clear the Receive Incoming Beam check box to turn off the port. To turn the infrared port back on, press the Receive Incoming Beam check box.

Pair Your Smartphone with Bluetooth Headsets

Bluetooth is wireless communications technology that you can use to connect devices like headsets, keyboards, and GPS receivers to Smartphones. If you use Bluetooth at all, it's most likely because you want to use a headset with your Smartphone. To use a Bluetooth headset with a Smartphone, you need to turn Bluetooth on and then configure the headset to work with the phone. The configuration process is called *pairing* or *bonding*.

You turn Bluetooth on or off using the Bluetooth option of the Connections settings screen. When you press Bluetooth on the Connections settings screen, you open a screen with one field that displays the current Bluetooth status. Press the field to open a screen of options, which include Off, On, and Discoverable. If you select Discoverable, other devices that use Bluetooth will be able to find your phone and try to establish communications with it; therefore, it is best to not turn on Discoverable mode unless you know exactly what devices are in range.

To turn on Bluetooth, you must select On from the Select An Item screen and then press Done twice to return to the Connections screen. After you turn on Bluetooth, the next step is to pair your headset with the phone.

TIP   *Most Smartphones display a blinking blue LED to indicate that Bluetooth is on.*

To pair the two, you need to perform steps on the headset and on your phone. First, you need to make the headset discoverable. Follow the instructions that came with your headset to put it in Discoverable mode. In most cases you press the On/Off button until a LED displays a solid blue. Also make note of the headset's passkey or PIN, which you will have to enter on the phone.

On the phone, open the Bluetooth settings screen, then press Menu | Devices, which will display all of the devices that are paired with your phone, but if you have not yet paired devices, this screen will be blank. Press Menu | New to scan for Bluetooth devices; once all the devices are found, they appear in a list as shown here:

Use the Navigation button to select the headset, and then enter the headset's Passkey and press Next. When the Smartphone has successfully paired with the headset, you will see the following screen.

Press Next, which provides an opportunity for you to enter a name for the headset, and then press Next a second time to display the Services screen. For headsets, you will only see one service listed, Headset, but other devices may have multiple services that you can select on this screen. Press Done to return to the Bluetooth Devices screen, where you will see the headset listed along with other devices that the phone is paired with, such as shown here:

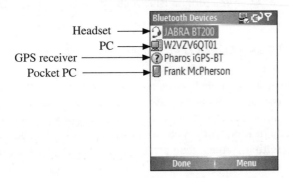

The icon next to the device name indicates the device type.

Once you pair a headset with a Smartphone, the audio for all calls automatically routes to the headset if Bluetooth is turned on and the headset is in range. Most headsets must be within 30 feet of the phone to work. Read the headset user manual for instructions on how to use the buttons on the headset to receive and end calls and to turn the volume up or down. In some cases you will be able to perform voice dialing if the software on the Smartphone is compatible with the headset.

Secure Your Phone

Most mobile phones have the capability to require a password before someone can use the phone to make phone calls, and most people do not use this feature. However, you may want to consider using the password feature, known as Phone Lock, on your Smartphone because it can store a larger amount of sensitive information than a regular mobile phone.

NOTE   *You do not need to enter the password to receive calls or to place emergency calls.*

Select the Security setting to display the different Smartphone security options. Select Enable Phone Lock to specify the time within which the phone is locked and requires a password, and then specify the password and press Done.

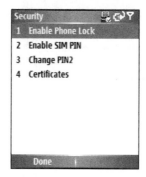

The SIM cards that come with Smartphones enable the phone to connect to the mobile network using your account. If your phone were stolen, the thief could put the SIM card in another phone and use your account. To prevent the SIM card from being used in other phones, press Enable SIM PIN and enter a PIN to secure the card. After you enable this feature, you will not be able to use the SIM card in another phone without entering the correct PIN.

SIM PIN2 secures some specific information, such as call barring and call forwarding, on the SIM card, but does not prevent you from using the SIM card in another phone. Press Change PIN2 to enable this security feature.

Digital certificates are sometimes used by web sites to prove the identity of devices. The device can also use a digital certificate to prove the identity of a server. Personal certificates provide identity information for Smartphones, while root certificates are used to confirm the identity of servers. If you need to add a personal or root certificate to the Smartphone, select Certificates on the Security settings screen.

Remove Programs

You can add functionality to your Smartphone by installing software. A number of different programs are available that you can install by following the instructions in Chapter 8. Be aware that while they may look similar, programs designed for Pocket PC Phone Editions will not run on Smartphones. To uninstall software from a Smartphone, select the Remove Programs setting, use the Navigation button to highlight the program you want to uninstall, then press Menu | Remove.

Some web sites provide the ability to install software directly on your Smartphone. Use Internet Explorer to open the web site, then select the link to the program's setup file. The file will download to the Smartphone and then automatically open, installing the program on the device.

Conserve Battery Power

Because the Smartphone's display consumes a significant amount of power when it is at full brightness, Windows Mobile provides settings to turn off the display to conserve power and increase battery life. To change the display timeout settings, select the Power Management setting, which opens the screen shown here.

The Smartphone backlight is either on or off, and the value of the Backlight Time Out On Battery field specifies how long the backlight stays on with no activity before it is turned off. Press the Navigation button on the field to select a different value, then press Done. The Backlight Time Out On AC field specifies how long the backlight stays on when the phone is plugged in.

When the backlight turns off, the display is still on, and you can still see information on the screen. The Display Time Out field specifies the length of time before the display is turned entirely off. Press the Navigation button on the field to select a different value, then press Done.

Some Smartphones have a light sensor that Windows Mobile uses to adjust the brightness of the display. If a sensor exists, you will find the Light Sensor Enable field on the Power Management settings screen; set this field to On to allow Windows Mobile to automatically adjust the display brightness.

Change the Font Size

There are a number of settings that control what you see on the screen or how you interact with the Smartphone. For example, to display larger characters on the Settings screen, select the Accessibility setting, select the System Font Size field, and select Large.

The Accessibility settings screen is as follows: Multipress Time Out specifies how long you must wait to enter a different letter on the same button on the keypad; Confirmation Time Out specifies how long the Smartphone waits for you to provide input to certain dialog boxes before it automatically closes the dialog box; and In-Call Alert Volume specifies how loud alerts, such as meeting reminders, sound when you are in a call.

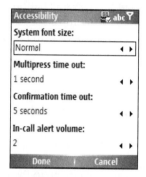

Change the Date and Time Format

The Regional Settings screen provides a Language field to specify what language is used for system dialog boxes, and a Locale field to specify the language of the location where you are using the phone. You also find on the Regional Settings screen fields for changing the format of dates, time, positive and negative numbers, and positive and negative currency.

Enter Owner Information

If you want to store information about yourself as the owner of your Smartphone, select the Owner Information settings screen, enter values for the Name, Telephone Number, E-mail Address, and Notes fields, and then press Done.

Find Out How Much Storage Is Available

The About settings screen displays a significant amount of information about the Smartphone, including what version and build of Windows Mobile is installed, the available storage, total storage, available memory, and total memory. To access this information, select the About setting.

Submit Error Reports to Microsoft

Unfortunately, there are times when Windows Mobile does not work as it should, and errors occur. It helps Microsoft to improve Windows Mobile if it receives information about the errors, so it has added a voluntary service called Error Reporting that sends information about the errors to Microsoft. The service is disabled by default, and it does not send personal information to Microsoft.

If you are willing to help Microsoft by transmitting error reports to it, select the Error Reporting setting and change the Error Reporting field from Disable to Enable.

Work with Applications

Hundreds of applications are available for Windows Mobile that you can download from the Internet and install on your Smartphone. In Chapter 8 you learn how to use ActiveSync to install applications on your Smartphone. The application icons install in the Start menu, which you access by pressing the Start button at the Home Screen.

As you would expect, Smartphone applications work in the same manner as all the other software on the phone. Most applications assign a menu to the right softkey, so you press Menu to execute the commands for most applications. The left softkey is usually assigned to the most frequently used commands.

If you have an application open and you want to return to the previous open application, press Back. Press the Home button to return to the Home Screen. Once an application starts, it continues to run, even when you switch to another application or the Home Screen. Windows Mobile for Smartphones does not include a built-in way for you to shut down running programs, though many Smartphone manufacturers include their own task manager program that you can use to shut down programs.

One popular third-party task manager for Smartphone is Resco System Toys, available at www.resco.net. System Toys has two tools. One tool displays the remaining battery life, available internal storage, and available space on storage cards. The second tool is Task Manager, which you use to shut down or switch between programs running on the Smartphone.

SP Task Manager, available at www.binarys.com, has the same functions as Resco System Toys, plus it has the ability to format storage cards.

Manage Files

Windows Mobile Smartphones name files and store them in folders like Windows desktops. However, they do not include a file manager program for you to move, copy, or delete files on the device. Programs such as Windows Media Player and Pictures & Videos include Copy and Delete commands for you to work with the files associated to those programs.

There are two ways that you can manage files on a Smartphone. One is to use ActiveSync and Windows Explorer to work with the files on the device. The second way is to install a third-party file manager on your Smartphone.

To use ActiveSync to manage files on your Smartphone, connect the Smartphone to a computer and then click Explore in ActiveSync on the desktop PC to open the program window shown here. You use your mouse and keyboard on the PC to browse and delete files on the Smartphone.

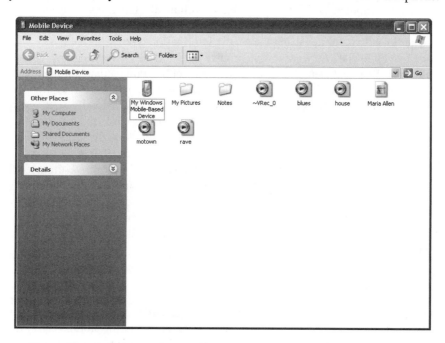

When a Smartphone is connected to a PC, you can also access the files on the device using Windows Explorer. Click the Mobile Device icon in the left window in Explorer to list the Smartphone files in the main window. With Windows Explorer, you can drag and drop files between folders on the PC and the Smartphone.

If you want to manage files on your Smartphone without connecting to a PC, you need one of the third-party file manager programs available for the device. Resco Explorer is one of the most popular Smartphone file manager programs. In addition to enabling you to manage files, it also provides the ability to compress or encrypt files. Resco Explorer also includes built-in file viewers and a Registry Editor. You will find this program at www.resco.net.

Increase Storage Space

Most Smartphones have a slot for miniSD storage cards, though you may have to remove the battery to insert a card into the slot. MiniSD, which is about three-quarters the size of Secure Digital cards, is one of the newest storage card sizes. You can purchase adapters to use a miniSD card in a Secure Digital card slot.

 **Synchronize Files with Smartphones**

As you will see in Chapter 7, ActiveSync has the ability to synchronize files between Windows desktop computers and Pocket PCs, but unfortunately, this file synchronization capability does not work with Smartphones. However, Chapter 7 does show how you can synchronize audio and video files using the Media information type in ActiveSync.

You have two options if you want to synchronize files between a Smartphone and desktop PC. One is Rubber Stamped Data Sync, found at www.rubberstampeddata.com, which is a program that runs on PCs and synchronizes files when you connect the Smartphone to the PC running ActiveSync. You can configure the program to automatically start and sync each time you connect the device and continuously sync changes while the Smartphone is connected. Despite the lack of information on the web site, I found that the program runs with ActiveSync 4.1 and Windows Mobile 5.

Another option is to use Pocket Controller Professional, available at www.soti.net. While this program is more expensive than Rubber Stamped Data Sync, it provides many more functions. With Pocket Controller you can remotely control a Windows Mobile Smartphone or Pocket PC from a desktop PC, where the device's display appears in a window on the screen. Pocket Controller also synchronizes files between Smartphones or Pocket PCs and PCs, and you can also use it to capture screen shots.

If you install a program on a Smartphone when a storage card is in the device, you will be prompted whether you want to install the program on the device or the storage card. Most Smartphone programs will run from storage cards, and therefore it is safe to install the programs on the cards. However, keep in mind that if you remove the card you will no longer be able to run the programs, and some system utilities should be installed on the device.

Wrapping Up

Windows Mobile Smartphone is easy to operate with one hand, and has many features that make it a powerful personal information appliance. You will learn in the remainder of this book how to take full advantage of the software that is available on the phone. One of the features that sets Windows Mobile Smartphone apart from regular mobile phones is the ability to synchronize data with Microsoft Outlook running on desktop PCs, or Microsoft Exchange running on a server. In the next chapter you will learn how to connect Smartphones and Pocket PCs to Windows PCs.

Part II

Connect with PCs

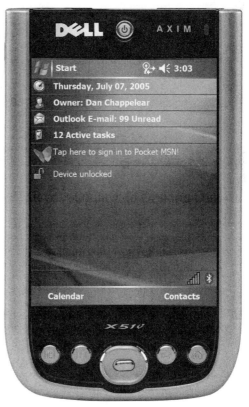

Chapter 6

Connect to Desktop Computers

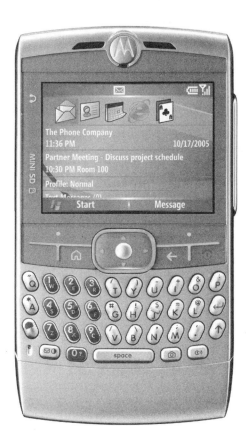
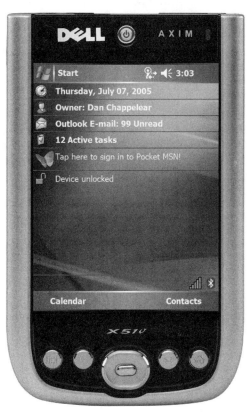

How to...

- Prepare to install Microsoft ActiveSync on a PC
- Install Microsoft ActiveSync
- Change ActiveSync connection settings
- Connect Windows Mobile devices to desktop computers by using infrared
- Connect Windows Mobile devices to desktop computers by using Bluetooth

Why did you buy your Windows Mobile device? One reason may be to carry information normally stored on desktop computers wherever you may go. You probably want to use your Windows Mobile device to update and add information, and then automatically copy those changes to your desktop computer at the next opportunity. Similarly, while you are away, changes may be made to the information on the desktop that you will want to copy to the Pocket PC or Smartphone automatically. This synchronization ensures that information is current on both your Windows Mobile device and desktop computer.

Your Windows Mobile device is designed to be a companion to your desktop computer— your PC away from your PC. Vital to this design is the desktop software called *ActiveSync,* which enables the communication between the device and personal computer. In this chapter, you'll learn how to install ActiveSync and how to connect your Windows Mobile device with desktop computers. Chapter 7 shows you how to configure ActiveSync to synchronize information between Microsoft Outlook and Outlook Mobile. In Chapter 8 you learn how to use ActiveSync to manage files and folders on your Pocket PC or Smartphone, and install or remove programs.

Introducing ActiveSync

ActiveSync has undergone several significant upgrades over the years. When Windows CE was first sold, the software was called H/PC Explorer (Handheld PC Explorer), then Windows CE Services, and finally ActiveSync.

The changes between the versions have been significant. At first, H/PC Explorer synchronized only with Microsoft Schedule+ and did not run on Windows NT. These issues were quickly resolved with Version 1.1 of the program, which supported Microsoft Outlook and Windows NT Version 4.0.

The next major release of the program came with the introduction of the Palm-size PC (P/PC). Because the name "H/PC Explorer" did not appropriately identify the software that now also worked with P/PCs, the name was changed to Windows CE Services. This version of the program included many significant features, such as the ability to synchronize with more than one desktop computer, continuous synchronization, file synchronization, e-mail synchronization, and an application manager. A later release, timed with the release of H/PC Professional, added support for synchronization of Pocket Access databases and made installation and performance improvements.

ActiveSync Version 4.1 is the most recent release of the desktop software, and it will be an important part of how you use your Pocket PC or Smartphone. The first steps to use ActiveSync are to install the software on a desktop computer and establish a connection between the device and the desktop. These two steps are the focus for this chapter.

ActiveSync Installation

Included with your Pocket PC or Smartphone is a copy of the ActiveSync software on a companion CD-ROM. Normally, you use that disc to install the software on your PC. However, before you install the software, check the Microsoft web site at www.microsoft.com/windowsmobile to verify that it is the current version. Your Pocket PC may not have the current version of ActiveSync, because a newer version may have been released after your version shipped from the factory.

Even if the version of ActiveSync on the CD-ROM is the same, you may still want to download the version from the Microsoft web site, because it may be a newer build of the same version. Microsoft often releases newer copies of ActiveSync as different builds that have the same version number. Save the program that you download to a directory on your PC, and remember its location because you will run that program to install ActiveSync.

Before you begin installing ActiveSync on your PC, verify that it meets the following minimum requirements:

- Microsoft Windows 2000 with Service Pack 4, Windows XP Professional or Home with Service Pack 1 or 2, Windows XP Tablet PC Edition 2005, Windows XP Media Center Edition 2005, or Windows Server 2003 with Service Pack 1
- Microsoft Outlook 98 or later
- Microsoft Internet Explorer 4.01 SP1 or later
- Hard disk with 12 to 65MB of available space, depending on the features that you select during installation
- Available 9- or 25-pin serial port, infrared port, or USB port
- One CD-ROM drive, if installing from CD-ROM
- VGA graphics card or a compatible graphics adapter at 256 colors or higher

You must install Microsoft Outlook on your PC before you install ActiveSync. You will find a copy of Outlook 2000 or 2002 on the companion CD-ROM that is packaged with Pocket PC devices. If you install ActiveSync before installing Outlook, you must reinstall ActiveSync after installing Outlook. Follow the instructions that come with Outlook to install it on your PC.

Pocket PCs and Smartphones connect to PCs by using a cable bundled with the device. Some manufacturers include a cradle in which you place the device to establish communication. Plug one end of the cable into the cradle and the other end into a USB or serial port on the PC, as described in the user manual that came with the device. If the device does not have a cradle, plug one end of the cable into the device.

If you connect a Pocket PC or Smartphone to a desktop computer with USB, do not connect the Pocket PC with the desktop until instructed to do so by the ActiveSync installation program.

Install ActiveSync on Desktop PCs

Even though you may download a newer version of ActiveSync from the Internet, you should first install the version on the CD that came with your device so that the drivers for the device install on your PC. After you install the CD version, you can install the new version that you downloaded.

This is particularly important if you are installing ActiveSync to work with older devices, because new versions of ActiveSync may not have the drivers needed to support communications with the device.

Insert the CD into the CD-ROM drive of your PC, and an opening screen loads with a picture of the device and four buttons on the right. Click Start Here to open the next screen, which provides the three first steps for setting up your Pocket PC.

As mentioned previously, before you install ActiveSync you must first install Outlook; if Outlook is not on your PC, click Install Outlook.

Click Install ActiveSync 4.1, and then click Install on the next screen to start the ActiveSync setup program. If Autorun is disabled on your PC, you can start the setup program by using Windows Explorer to open \MS\ACTSYNC\Main on the CD-ROM and run setup.exe. The setup program starts by opening the ActiveSync program window dialog box, as shown here.

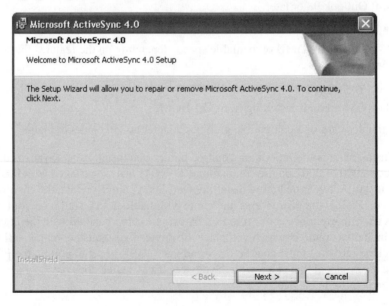

During setup, the ActiveSync program files copy to the PC and the software configures to connect with your device. At each step of the process, click Next to continue to the next step of the installation, click Back to go back one screen, or click Cancel to stop the installation. To display Online Help, click Help.

To begin the software installation, click Next in the program window. You will be prompted to accept the licensing agreement and enter some personal information. In the next program window, select the location where you want ActiveSync to be installed. Click Change to open a window in which you browse the folders on the PC hard drive to select the installation location. Once you select the location, click Next to begin installation.

After the program files copy to your PC, the Get Connected Wizard will start. Make sure that your device is connected to the USB or serial port of the PC so that the wizard will find it.

NOTE *Third-party firewall programs may interfere with communications and prevent ActiveSync from working. Check www.windowsmobile.com to see whether there are known issues with the firewall software that you are using.*

6

When you click Next, the wizard begins checking each serial and USB port on the PC to find the device. If the PC has an infrared port, it will be included among the ports the wizard checks. If you currently use the infrared port, you must start ActiveSync on the device before the Get Connected Wizard starts searching ports. The process for using ActiveSync via the infrared port is described in more detail later in this chapter, in the section "Connect with Desktop PCs by Using Infrared." When the device is found on a port, ActiveSync is configured to use that port for future communications.

The next step is to create a sync relationship between the PC and the device. A sync relationship defines how information synchronizes. Every Pocket PC or Smartphone can have relationships with only two different PCs, but a PC can have relationships with more than two devices.

TIP *ActiveSync Version 4 has problems if Outlook is not configured with an e-mail account. Even if you do not use Outlook as your e-mail client, you should configure Outlook with an e-mail account to keep from having problems with ActiveSync.*

For example, you can create a relationship between your Pocket PC and a PC at home and another at the office. Once the two relationships exist, the device cannot create a relationship with a third computer unless one of the previously created relationships is deleted. However, if everyone in a family of four has a Pocket PC, each one can create a relationship with the same PC at home.

NOTE *You can synchronize all information types with two PCs except Messaging. Messaging will synchronize with only one PC.*

Once ActiveSync configures the port, it will start the Synchronization Setup Wizard, shown on the following right page, which establishes a synchronization relationship between the PC and Windows Mobile device. (The title of the screen will change depending on whether you are

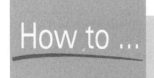

How to ... **Troubleshoot ActiveSync Connections**

One of the first things you should do when having problems with ActiveSync is to soft reset the device by pressing the reset button. If that does not fix the problem, try ActiveSync Online Help's troubleshooting wizard. You will also find an online ActiveSync troubleshooter at www.microsoft.com/windowsmobile/help/, and Chris De Herrera has a great *ActiveSync Troubleshooting Guide* at www.pocketpcfaq.com/faqs/t-shootactivesync.htm. The following are some troubleshooting tips:

- You may have problems connecting your Pocket PC with your desktop computer using a USB cable or cradle. This problem can be avoided by installing the latest version of ActiveSync, because it fixes bugs that existed in prior versions. Some USB hubs cause problems for ActiveSync, so it is best to plug the Pocket PC USB cable directly into the desktop computer.

- If the desktop computer does not detect that the Pocket PC is connected, click File | Connection Settings on the desktop and verify that the USB or serial connection options are selected.

- If you connect a Pocket PC with a desktop computer before installing ActiveSync, the PC may end up using the wrong USB drivers and ActiveSync will not be able to detect the Pocket PC. Start Device Manager on the desktop computer and remove the Windows CE USB devices. Then reinstall ActiveSync and connect the Pocket PC when instructed by the installation program.

- In some instances, the Get Connected Wizard may not find a device that is attached to a COM port. Typically, this happens because another program, such as a digital camera communications program, has the port locked for its use. Check to make sure that none of these programs is running.

- Another potential cause of the preceding problem is an interrupt conflict, which can happen if you are connecting the device to COM3 or COM4, and COM1 or COM2 is in use. COM1 shares an interrupt with COM3, while COM2 shares an interrupt with COM4. If this is a problem, try changing the interrupt of the port you are trying to use.

using a Pocket PC or a Smartphone.) If you click Cancel, the Windows Mobile device will connect to the PC as a guest. When you connect a Windows Mobile device to a PC as a guest, you cannot synchronize information between the two, but you can browse files and folders and install programs to the device. You can also use Desktop Pass Through to access the Internet or a LAN.

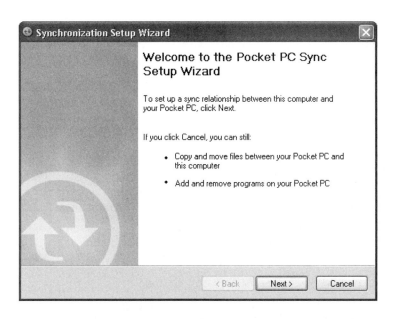

TIP *A Pocket PC or Smartphone can connect to any PC as a guest, regardless of how many partnerships the device has.*

If you click Next to create a relationship, the next step is to configure all of the possible synchronization settings between the device and the PC. These settings are described in more detail in Chapter 7. When you click Next, you see the Setup Complete program window. When you click Finish, ActiveSync will begin synchronization. Here, the horizontal bar indicates the synchronization progress; the window also displays how many items will synchronize and estimates the amount of time synchronization will take. When synchronization is complete, the bar will disappear and be replaced with the word *Connected*.

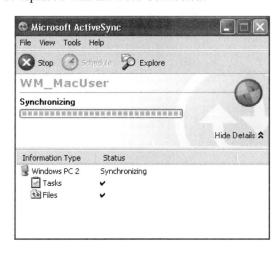

The ActiveSync installation program adds an icon to the System Tray. When a device connects, the System Tray icon turns green; otherwise, it is grayed out. Double-click the icon to start ActiveSync manually.

By default, ActiveSync is configured to start automatically whenever a Windows Mobile 5 device connects. If you have a device running older versions of Windows Mobile, you can configure ActiveSync from starting automatically by changing the synchronization mode, which is described in Chapter 7.

Start ActiveSync on Desktop PCs

Unless you have configured ActiveSync for manual synchronization, synchronization starts when you place the Pocket PC in its cradle. If you configure ActiveSync for manual synchronization, you will need to click the Sync toolbar button to start it.

To start ActiveSync without a connection, double-click the System Tray icon. The setup program also places a shortcut, as shown here, in the Start menu.

When you start ActiveSync while no device is connected, the program window looks like the image shown here. The name of the last device that synchronized with the PC is shown in the program window, along with the date and time of the synchronization.

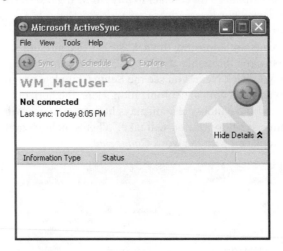

The partnership information is stored on the PC by the name of the device. ActiveSync 4.1 automatically creates a unique name for your device. If you want to create a specific name for your device, create it by following the instructions in Chapter 3. If you are using an older version of ActiveSync and synchronizing more than one device with the PC, be sure to give each device a unique name.

Most of what you can do with ActiveSync is not available unless you have a device connected, but you can delete relationships and configure connection settings without having a device connected. Instructions for configuring the synchronization options are provided later in this chapter.

Change Desktop ActiveSync Connection Settings

ActiveSync automatically loads when you connect a device to the PC. It first determines whether a relationship exists; if one does, synchronization begins. If no relationship is found, ActiveSync starts the Synchronization Setup Wizard, which is explained in "Install ActiveSync on Desktop PCs" section, earlier in the chapter.

Normally, the connection settings configure when you connect your device to the PC for the first time, and they don't need to be changed after that. However, on some occasions the connection settings may need to be changed or reset.

One such occasion is when you use the PC serial communications port to communicate with another device, such as a digital camera. If you connect a digital camera to the port, ActiveSync starts, determines that the connected device is not a Pocket PC or Smartphone, and then displays the Device Not Recognized dialog box. If you click Disconnect COM Port, ActiveSync disables communication to the port, and the next time you attempt to connect a device, ActiveSync will not start.

To restart communication via the COM port, first connect the Pocket PC or Smartphone, start ActiveSync, and choose File | Connection Settings to display the Connections Settings dialog box.

Serial communications is turned on or off by clicking the Allow Connections To One Of The Following check box. Specify which port to use by selecting one from the drop-down list. The dialog box displays the current status of the COM port. If you do not want the ActiveSync icon to display in the System Tray, clear the Show Status Icon In Taskbar check box.

If you are familiar with prior versions of ActiveSync, you may have noticed that ActiveSync Version 4.1's Connection Settings dialog box does not have an option for allowing Ethernet or Remote Access Service connections. Microsoft removed this functionality due to security concerns.

Connect with Desktop PCs by Using a Serial Connection

Smartphones do not support serial connections with desktop computers. By default, Pocket PCs are set up to use USB cables or cradles for synchronization, but they can be configured to use serial connections.

To switch to a serial connection on a Pocket PC 2002 device, start ActiveSync on the Pocket PC and tap Tools | Options. Select the serial port speed from the Enable Synchronization When Cradled Using drop-down list. The options are 115200 Default, 19200 Default, 38400 Default, and 57600 Default.

The fastest setting is Serial Port @ 115K. If you have difficulty establishing a connection using the 115K setting, try the Serial Port @ 57600 setting. Pocket PC 2002 defaults to USB connections.

To change the speed on Windows Mobile 2003, start ActiveSync and tap Tools | Options, and then tap the Options button on the PC tab. Select the serial port speed from the Enable PC Sync Using This Connection drop-down list. On Windows Mobile Version 5, start ActiveSync and tap Menu | Connections and select the serial port speed from the drop-down list.

Finally, make sure that ActiveSync 4.1 is set up for a serial connection on the correct COM port.

Connect with Desktop PCs by Using Infrared

Infrared is light beyond the color red in the spectrum that is not visible to the human eye. Data is sent between transmitters and receivers that are within a line of site, such as with television and stereo remote controls. Every Pocket PC and Smartphone includes an infrared port that can be used for wireless synchronization with desktop computers.

If you synchronize multiple devices with a PC, you will find yourself constantly unplugging and switching cables, because each device manufacturer uses a different cable. Infrared is wireless, making it easier to synchronize multiple devices with a PC by eliminating the need to switch cables.

To synchronize using infrared, you need software and an infrared port for your PC, but you do not need to install software on your device because each device is already configured for infrared communication. Windows 2000 and Windows XP have built-in infrared support.

Many notebook computers have built-in infrared ports, but most desktop computers do not. To add an infrared port to desktop computers, you must install an infrared serial or USB adapter, which you can find on the Internet by searching on "infrared adapters."

After you install an adapter on a PC, the next step is to configure ActiveSync to use the infrared port. Start ActiveSync and choose File | Connection Settings. Make sure the Allow Connections To One Of The Following check box is checked, select Infrared Port from the drop-down list, and then click OK.

To start synchronization, first line up the infrared port of the Pocket PC or Smartphone with the PC adapter, and then start ActiveSync on the device. Tap or click Menu | Connect Via IR, and line up the infrared port of the device with the PC port. The ActiveSync icon in the System Tray will turn green, indicating that the connection is established. To close the connection, tap or click Stop on the device.

Connect with Desktop PCs by Using Bluetooth

Bluetooth is a short-range, low-power wireless communications technology that replaces cables to connect mobile devices. There has been a significant amount of hype about Bluetooth for many years, but only recently have Bluetooth-capable devices become major players.

Pocket PCs and Smartphones are among the list of devices that now support Bluetooth, as several brands now come with built-in Bluetooth radios. You can add Bluetooth to other Pocket PCs by using a Bluetooth CompactFlash or Secure Digital card.

Windows Mobile 5.0 has built-in Bluetooth software that supports many profiles. Bluetooth profiles define the functions that utilize the wireless connection. For example, one of the profiles that Windows Mobile 5.0 supports is dial-up networking, so you can wirelessly connect a Pocket PC with a mobile phone and use the phone as a modem to connect to the Internet.

 You will find more information about using Bluetooth to connect to the Internet in Chapter 10.

To use Bluetooth to synchronize with a desktop computer, you need to add a Bluetooth radio to the PC. Several Bluetooth USB and PC Card adapters are available, such as D-Link's Bluetooth USB Adapter.

The key to making Bluetooth work with ActiveSync is that the Bluetooth software on the PC provides virtual serial ports, which ActiveSync can use for synchronization. You need to determine the Bluetooth serial host port, which will be something like COM4 or COM5, and configure ActiveSync to use that port. To configure ActiveSync, choose File | Connection Settings, and then select the serial host port number from the Allow Connections To One Of The Following drop-down list.

You will want to establish a Bluetooth binding, or pairing, between the device and desktop computer so that you don't have to enter security information on every connection. To bind a Pocket PC to another PC with Bluetooth, tap Start | Settings | Connections | Bluetooth | Devices, and then tap New Partnership. The Pocket PC will search for Bluetooth devices and list them. Select a device, tap Next, and then enter a PIN. You must enter the same PIN on the Pocket PC and desktop computer. Tap Next, enter the same PIN on the PC, and then tap Next. The Partnership Settings dialog box displays, listing the services available on the PC. Select Serial Port and then tap Finish.

The process of binding a Smartphone is slightly different from the process of binding a Pocket PC. On a Smartphone, press Start | Settings | Connections | Bluetooth | Menu | Devices, and then press Menu | New. The Smartphone will search for Bluetooth devices and list them. You then enter a PIN on the phone and PC as described previously for Pocket PCs.

You must start synchronization on the device. Start ActiveSync and tap or click Menu | Connect Via Bluetooth. If everything is configured correctly, a connection will be established and the device and PC will start synchronization.

Bluetooth provides wireless synchronization within 30 feet of your desktop PC and, unlike infrared, doesn't require line of sight. In the future, Bluetooth synchronization will be automatic, but for now you can enjoy the convenience Bluetooth provides even if it requires you to start the process manually.

One significant change with Windows Mobile 5 is that it no longer supports synchronization via wireless and Ethernet network connections. However, you can continue synchronizing older devices with ActiveSync 4.1 using these types of connections.

Wrapping Up

Microsoft ActiveSync supports three ways to connect Pocket PCs to desktop computers: serial/USB cable or cradle, infrared, and Bluetooth. The majority of the time, you will use a serial or USB connection, because the hardware needed for that connection is provided with the device. Infrared and Bluetooth provide flexibility either by supporting multiple brands of devices or by enabling you to synchronize while not being physically near the desktop computer.

The purpose for all of these connection types is to synchronize data between Windows Mobile devices and desktop computers. As you might guess, a variety of different settings in ActiveSync control what information is synchronized. In the next chapter, you'll learn how to change these synchronization settings.

Chapter 7

Synchronize Data with Desktop Computers

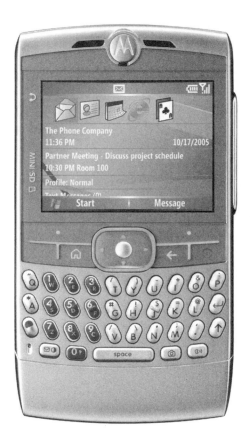
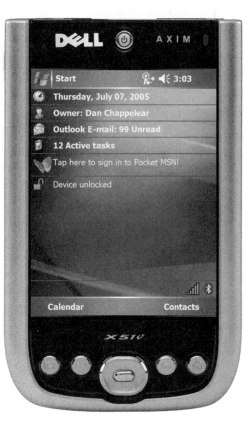

How to...

- Use the Synchronization Setup Wizard to create synchronization relationships between Windows Mobile devices and desktop computers
- Configure synchronization settings
- Resolve synchronization conflicts

Synchronization is the process of keeping information consistent on a Windows Mobile device and a desktop computer. What and how information is synchronized is stored in a *synchronization relationship* that is created between Windows Mobile devices and desktop computers by using the Sync Setup Wizard.

Whenever information changes on one side of the relationship, synchronization changes the information on the other side, too, so that it matches. For example, if you create a new task on your PC, that task is copied to your Pocket PC at the next synchronization. If you then mark the task complete on the Pocket PC, it will be marked complete on the PC after the next synchronization.

If the same piece of information is changed on both the PC and the device, ActiveSync identifies the conflict and determines which information it should keep. How ActiveSync resolves conflicts depends on how you configure conflict resolution.

ActiveSync matches each of the main sections in Outlook with corresponding programs on the Pocket PC and Smartphone: Calendar, Contacts, Messaging, Notes, and Tasks. Favorites corresponds with Internet Explorer, and Media corresponds to Windows Media Player. ActiveSync also synchronizes Contacts and Calendar with Microsoft Works.

In this chapter you'll learn how to use the Sync Setup Wizard to create and delete synchronization relationships between Windows Mobile devices and desktop computers. You'll also learn how to configure synchronization settings for all the information types that ActiveSync supports, change how synchronization starts, resolve synchronization conflicts, and change file conversion settings.

ActiveSync supports the synchronization of the Outlook primary Calendar, Contacts, and Tasks folders only. You cannot synchronize with any Calendar, Contacts, or Tasks subfolders unless you use a third-party synchronization program, such as Nokia's Intellisync. However, ActiveSync 4.1 does support synchronization of Messaging subfolders with Windows Mobile 2003 and Windows Mobile 5 devices.

Create a Synchronization Relationship

Synchronization relationships exist between Windows Mobile devices and desktop computers and contain all of the information that ActiveSync uses to synchronize data between the two. Normally, you create a synchronization relationship by using the Sync Setup Wizard the first time you connect the device to the PC.

When you connect a Pocket PC or Smartphone to a desktop computer for the first time, ActiveSync determines whether a synchronization relationship exists. If the relationship does

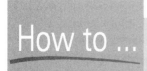

Synchronize with Programs Other than Microsoft Outlook

ActiveSync synchronizes only with Microsoft Works, Outlook, and Microsoft Exchange. If you want to synchronize your device with other desktop personal information manager programs, you must use a third-party synchronization program. Third-party synchronization programs include the following:

- Intellisync Handheld Edition from Nokia, www.intellisync.com
- XTNDConnect PC from Sybase's iAnywhere Solutions, www.ianywhere.com/esi/
- PDAsync from Laplink, www.laplink.com
- CompanionLink from CompanionLink Software, www.companionlink.com
- mNotes from CommonTime, www.commontime.com

7

not exist, the Sync Setup Wizard starts. If you do not want to create a relationship between the device and desktop computer, click Cancel. The device will then connect to the PC as a guest. Guest connections cannot synchronize data but can perform all the other functions provided by ActiveSync.

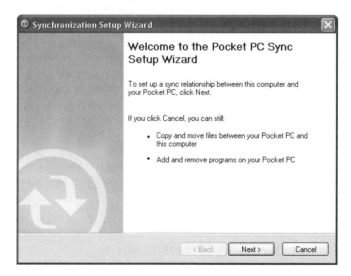

 *If you connect a device running Windows Mobile 2003SE or older to a PC running ActiveSync 4.1, you will first see a dialog box asking whether you want to create a Standard Partnership or Guest Partnership.*

Click Next to select the synchronization options, as shown here. Select which information you want to synchronize between the device and desktop computer by checking the boxes next to each information type. Select a type and click Settings to configure synchronization of each information type (listed in the Information Type column in this dialog box). The details for changing synchronization settings are provided later in this chapter in the sections "Configure Outlook Synchronization Settings" and "Configure Exchange Synchronization Settings." For now, select the information types and then click Next.

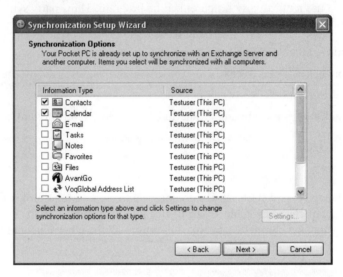

NOTE   *If you are connecting a device running Windows Mobile 2003SE or older, you will see a dialog box asking whether you want to synchronize with the desktop computer, or with a Microsoft Exchange server and/or the desktop computer. If you are setting up your Pocket PC at home, select the Synchronize With This Desktop Computer radio button. If you are at work and your company is running Exchange 2003 or Microsoft Mobile Information Server and you want to synchronize with Exchange, select the Synchronize With Microsoft Exchange Server radio button.*

The final dialog box of the Sync Setup Wizard tells you that it has all the information it needs to create the synchronization relationship. Click Back to return to the previous screens and make changes. Click Cancel to stop and not synchronize. Or click Finish to close the wizard and start synchronization.

Create Two Synchronization Relationships

A Pocket PC or Smartphone can be in a synchronization relationship with two PCs that have different names. This kind of relationship is commonly done to synchronize a device with a PC at home and another at work.

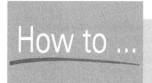

Synchronize with Macintoshes

Microsoft ActiveSync runs only on Windows desktop computers; there is no version for Macintoshes. You can synchronize a Pocket PC with a Macintosh running Virtual PC, but that does not provide synchronization with native Macintosh applications. Information Appliance Associates sells a native Macintosh synchronization program called PocketMac, and Mark/Space sells a program called The Missing Sync for Windows Mobile.

PocketMac comes in several versions that synchronize Pocket PCs and Smartphones with Microsoft Entourage, iCal, or Address Book on OS X. You can find more information about this program at www.pocketmac.net.

The Missing Sync for Windows Mobile also synchronizes Pocket PCs and Smartphones with Microsoft Entourage, iCal, or Address Book. It also transfers music from iTunes and photos in iPhoto to Windows Mobile devices. You can find more information about this program at www.markspace.com.

7

Before you decide to create a second relationship, you need to consider a number of issues:

■ You will not be able to synchronize e-mail information with two desktop computers. Messaging synchronization works only for the first partnership created between a device and a desktop computer.

■ If possible, both computers should use the same version of Microsoft Outlook. You can synchronize a device between two different versions of Outlook, but doing so may introduce synchronization problems.

■ Both computers should synchronize the same information and have the same synchronization settings.

■ All of the information in the device will synchronize to both PCs.

■ Synchronizing a device with two PCs can be complicated because it adds another place where information can change. Keep in mind that changes that you make at work and then synchronize to your Pocket PC or Smartphone will then appear on your home PC when you synchronize the device with it.

The process of creating a second synchronization relationship is much the same as creating the first one. You need a copy of ActiveSync installed on the second PC, along with Microsoft Outlook. Follow the steps for installing ActiveSync and using the Get Connected wizard described in Chapter 6.

When you connect the device to the second PC for the first time, the Sync Setup Wizard starts. After you click Next, the screen shown on the following page is displayed. This screen appears only if the device is already part of another relationship. ActiveSync stores the relationship information using the names of the computers that a device synchronizes with, so to create the relationship, either use the name provided or enter a name, and then click Next.

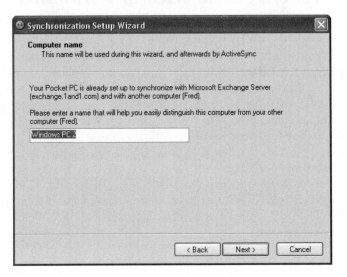

How to ... Synchronize and Keep Data Separate on Two Devices

Several Windows Mobile devices can synchronize with the same desktop computer. For example, I can synchronize my wife's Pocket PC and my Smartphone with our one desktop computer. However, unless we take steps to prevent it, our data will be combined in Outlook and end up on both of our devices. My wife's tasks will get mixed with my tasks on my Smartphone.

You can synchronize two devices with one desktop computer and still keep the data separate for both devices. To do so, you need to create separate Outlook profiles for each person or device.

The simplest way to create separate profiles is to use a different Windows logon ID for each person. Windows and Outlook automatically create separate profiles for each user. Each person then needs to log into Windows with his or her user ID prior to synchronizing the device.

Another way to create separate profiles in Outlook 2002 or 2003 is to open the Mail applet in Control Panel. Click Show Profiles, and then click Add to create a second profile. Finally, click the Prompt For A Profile To Be Used radio button so that you can select the profile that you want to use each time Outlook starts. In this case you need to shut down and restart Outlook prior to synchronization to keep data separate.

If you click Cancel in this screen, the device will connect to the PC in a Guest relationship, in which you can browse files and folders or install applications on the device.

If your device is already synchronizing with two computers and you attempt to create another relationship, the wizard displays the following screen. To create the new relationship, you must delete one of the two existing relationships listed here, or click Cancel to stop the wizard and connect to the computer as Guest.

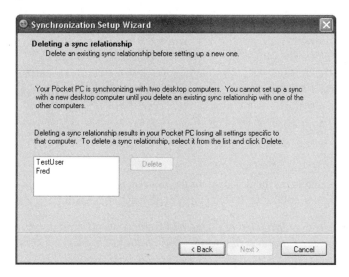

Sync Manager from KelBran Software provides a way to create partnerships with more than two desktop computers running ActiveSync 3.7 or older. You will find Sync Manager at www.pocketgear.com.

After you delete a relationship, click Next to continue through the same steps used when the first partnership was created and then start synchronization.

Managing Data with Two Synchronization Relationships

When you create a second synchronization relationship between a device and a desktop computer, there is a possibility that both will have data, and in some cases it may be the same data. During the initial synchronization, ActiveSync attempts to determine whether there is duplicate data, and if it finds the same data, it synchronizes one copy between the device and desktop computer.

However, if ActiveSync determines that the data is not the same, it may create a duplicate item in Outlook and on the device. For example, if you have contacts on a Pocket PC and desktop computer with the name of John Doe, but only one has a business phone number, after synchronization there will be two John Doe items in Contacts.

If ActiveSync finds items on the device and PC that have the same fields populated, but the data in one of the fields is different, it may treat the two items as a conflict and keep one copy using the conflict resolution setting for the relationship. By default, if ActiveSync finds

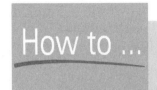

Handle Duplicate Data in Prior Versions of ActiveSync

Prior versions of ActiveSync and Windows Mobile handle the combination and duplication of data differently. If ActiveSync 3.7 or earlier finds information on both the PC and the device during synchronization, the Combine or Replace dialog box displays. Within this dialog box, indicate whether you want to combine the information found on both the PC and device, replace the information on the device with what is on the PC, or not synchronize any of the information. Select the option that you want and then click OK.

Earlier versions also display the Remove Duplicate Items dialog box when ActiveSync detects duplicate data. Select the duplicate items that you want to delete and click Remove Selected, or click Remove All to delete all of the items. If you want to keep the duplicates, click Keep All.

a conflict, it replaces the item on the device with the item on the desktop computer. Unfortunately, the behavior for whether or not duplicate data is created is not consistent.

Several add-ons exist for deleting duplicate Contacts and Calendar entries in Outlook. To find them, search the Internet for "deleting duplicate Outlook contacts or appointments."

Delete Synchronization Relationships

Normally you will delete a synchronization relationship when the Sync Setup Wizard detects that a device has more than two relationships. However, you can also delete a relationship manually within ActiveSync on the PC or the device.

On a PC, open ActiveSync and, if the name of the device for which you want to remove a relationship with displays, click File | Delete Mobile Device. You can delete only the open partnership in ActiveSync, indicated by the name of the device in the program window. If the PC has partnerships with more than one device and the one you want to delete is not displayed, open the partnership to be deleted by choosing File | Mobile Device and then choose the name of the device.

If file synchronization is included in the synchronization relationship, you will be asked whether you want to delete the Synchronized Files folder. Check the contents of the folder on the PC to determine whether you want to delete the files. Click Yes to delete the files from the PC, or click No if you do not want to delete the files.

With Windows Mobile 5 you can now delete synchronization relationships on the device as well as on a desktop computer. On a Pocket PC or Smartphone, select Start | Programs | ActiveSync, and then select Menu | Options. The following screen displays on a Pocket PC.

Prevent Accidental Deletion of All Information

Once you create a partnership between a device and a desktop computer, all changes, including deletions, will be synchronized. For example, if you delete a contact on a Pocket PC, it will be deleted from the PC during the next synchronization. If you delete all of the information from the PC, during the next synchronization, all of the information will be deleted from the Pocket PC.

It is always a good idea, despite the fact that a copy of the data exists on both the device and desktop, to back up your device. You can prevent ActiveSync from deleting all information by manually deleting the synchronization relationship. The PC will restore the information when you re-create the relationship and synchronize the device.

7

(A similar screen displays on Smartphones.) Select the name of the desktop computer with which you do not want the device to sync, and then click Delete.

You can configure synchronization settings on the device from this ActiveSync Options screen. Instructions for changing these settings are provided in the upcoming section.

Configure Outlook Synchronization Settings

Not only can you specify which information types to synchronize, but you can also control how much of the information to synchronize by changing the settings for each information type. To conserve storage space, some of the default settings limit the amount of information that synchronizes.

To change these settings in ActiveSync for a Windows Mobile 5 device, first connect the device to the computer and then either double-click the name of the information type while displaying details or choose Tools | Options to open the Options dialog box, shown here.

The dialog box lists the information types on the device that synchronize with Outlook running on a desktop computer. To change a setting for an information type, click the information type and then click Settings.

NOTE *You do not need to connect a device running Windows Mobile 2003SE or older to change its synchronization settings. Just click Tools | Options, or click the Options button on the toolbar in ActiveSync.*

If you are using a device running Windows Mobile 2003SE or older, the only way to change synchronization settings is with ActiveSync on a desktop computer. With Windows Mobile 5 or newer, you can also change synchronization settings on the device. On the device, start ActiveSync and then select Menu | Options, which opens the screen shown here. Each synchronization relationship is listed, along with all the possible information types that ActiveSync supports. Information types with a check next to them are those which synchronize in the relationship. Some check boxes are grayed out, indicating that you cannot make changes to the synchronization setting unless the device is connected to a PC.

To make changes to synchronization settings on the device, select the information type and then select Settings. For some information types, the Settings button is grayed out, indicating that there are no options for that setting.

The following sections provide instructions for changing settings for the basic information types.

Change Outlook Calendar Synchronization Settings

From the Calendar Synchronization Settings dialog box, shown here, you can specify the number of past appointments to synchronize by selecting an option from the drop-down list. This Calendar Synchronization Settings dialog box looks the same on the desktop computer and Windows Mobile device.

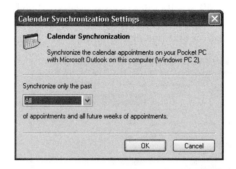

If you are synchronizing a device running Windows Mobile 2003SE or older, you will see different options, as shown next. To synchronize all Outlook appointments, select the Synchronize All Appointments radio button. If you want to synchronize only a select number of past and future appointments, select the Synchronize Only The radio button and then choose the number of past and future appointments from the drop-down lists. To synchronize appointments in specific categories, select Synchronize Only Those Appointments In The Following Selected Categories and then select the categories from the list. Then click OK to save the changes and close the dialog box.

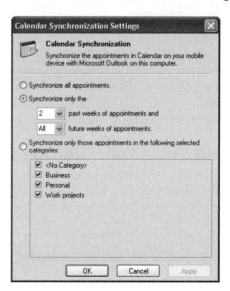

You cannot filter appointments by category from synchronizing to a Windows Mobile 5 device. Categories will not be listed unless the Windows Mobile 2003SE or older device is connected with the PC.

Change Outlook Contact Synchronization Settings

Windows Mobile 5 devices have no settings for synchronizing contacts. However, you can configure contact synchronization with Windows Mobile 2003SE or older devices from the ActiveSync Contact Synchronization Settings dialog box, shown here.

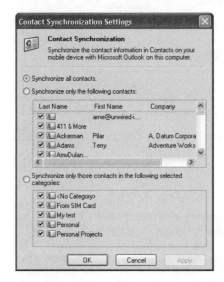

You can synchronize all contacts by selecting the top radio button. To synchronize only specific contacts, choose the Synchronize Only The Following Contacts radio button and then select the appropriate contacts from the list. If you want to synchronize contacts in specific categories, select the last radio button and then choose the categories from the list. Click OK to save the changes and close the dialog box.

Change Outlook E-mail Synchronization Settings

E-mail synchronization occurs between the Windows Mobile Messaging application and the Outlook Inbox. With these synchronization settings, you control the size and number of messages that synchronize and you select the Outlook Inbox subfolders that you want to synchronize with your Windows Mobile device.

You cannot synchronize Hotmail or IMAP4 e-mail to a Windows Mobile device.

ActiveSync does not synchronize the contents of Inbox subfolders, Deleted Items, Drafts, Outbox, or Sent Items folders. When you delete an e-mail, it is moved to Deleted Items, but

ActiveSync removes that e-mail from the Deleted Items folder and deletes the e-mail from the Outlook Inbox. ActiveSync moves new e-mail from the Outbox folder on the device to the Outlook Outbox folder. New e-mail messages that are written on your device and synchronized to Outlook are sent using the default e-mail service in Outlook.

To configure the e-mail synchronization settings for a Windows Mobile 5 device, click Tools | Options in ActiveSync on the PC, click the check box next to E-mail, then click Settings to open the dialog box shown here.

To specify the maximum size of Inbox messages, select a value from the Limit E-mail Size To drop-down list. Select a value from the Include The Previous drop-down list to specify how many days' worth of messages to synchronize. To include attachments, check the Include File Attachments box, and if you want to limit the attachment file size, check Only If Smaller Than and then enter a number in the KB field.

To specify what Inbox folders you want to synchronize to the device, click Select Folders and then click the folders that synchronize. While you can configure all other e-mail synchronization settings in ActiveSync on the Windows Mobile device, you can only select folders in ActiveSync on a PC.

When you open the ActiveSync Inbox information type for Windows Mobile 2003SE or older devices, the Mail Synchronization Settings dialog box displays. The Outlook Inbox mail folders display in the middle of the window, with subfolders indented beneath Inbox. Select the check box next to the subfolders that you want to synchronize with the Pocket PC.

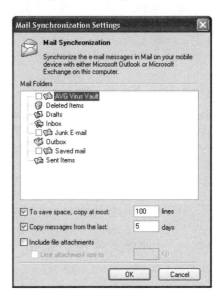

Change Task Synchronization Settings

Windows Mobile 5 does not have any synchronization settings for tasks. For Windows Mobile 2003SE or older devices, the Task Synchronization Settings dialog box, shown here, controls how tasks are synchronized between Outlook and Pocket Outlook.

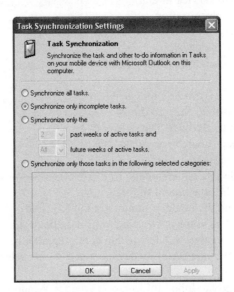

To synchronize complete and incomplete tasks, select Synchronize All Tasks. If you want to synchronize only incomplete tasks, select Synchronize Only Incomplete Tasks. You can control how active tasks synchronize by selecting the Synchronize Only The [ ] Past Weeks Of Active Tasks And [ ] Future Weeks Of Active Tasks radio button. Select the number of past and future weeks from the drop-down lists. To synchronize tasks in specific categories, select Synchronize Only Those Tasks In The Following Selected Categories radio button and then select the categories in the list. Click OK to save the changes and close the dialog box.

Change File Synchronization Settings

Smartphones do not support file synchronization, but Pocket PCs synchronize files between specific folders on the PC and the device. The PC files that synchronize with the device are stored in subfolders of My Documents. For example, a Pocket PC named *Sammy* synchronizes files stored in the \My Documents\Sammy My Documents folder.

To synchronize files to a Pocket PC, simply copy the file to the Synchronized Files folder on the PC. Using the preceding example, that folder is \My Documents\Sammy My Documents. Everything stored in the Pocket PC \My Documents folder synchronizes with desktop computers.

   *Only files located in internal storage on Pocket PCs synchronize with a PC.*

The File Synchronization Settings dialog box, shown here, displays the PC location of synchronized files for the Pocket PC. You cannot change this location from this dialog box, but you can add or remove files that are in the list of synchronized files.

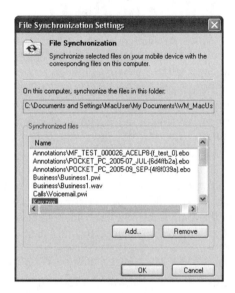

 *You can change file synchronization settings for Windows Mobile 5 devices only by using ActiveSync on a desktop computer.*

Click Add to browse a file and copy it to the Synchronized Files folder, or select a file in the list and then click Remove to delete the file from the Synchronized Files folder. If the device is connected, and continuous ActiveSync is enabled, the changes that you make will update immediately on the device. Otherwise, the changes will occur at the next synchronization.

Change Notes Synchronization Settings

Although you cannot make any settings changes for Notes synchronization, you can synchronize Notes with desktop computers in two ways. If you select the Notes information type in ActiveSync, the notes on your Windows Mobile device will synchronize with the main Notes folder in Outlook. If you do not select the Notes information type but select File Synchronization, notes on your Pocket PC will synchronize with the Synchronized Files folder on the PC.

 Notes synchronization does not support Outlook Notes subfolders or categories.

Change Favorites Synchronization Settings

The Favorites information type synchronizes your favorite web site addresses, known as Mobile Favorites, to your Pocket PC or Smartphone. To add a web site address to your Mobile Favorites,

7

Change the Synchronized Files Folder on the PC

When file synchronization is enabled, ActiveSync creates a folder for the synchronized files in the My Documents folder on the PC. The folder name is the combination of the Pocket PC name and My Documents (like this: *PCName* MyDocuments).

Editing the registry on the PC can change the location of the synchronized files on the PC. By following these steps, you can share one Synchronized Files folder on a PC with multiple devices running the same version of the Windows Mobile software. Do not attempt to combine the Synchronized Files folder for Windows Mobile 5 and Windows Mobile 2003SE or older.

Do not make any changes to the registry unless you are familiar with editing the registry. Any error in the registry can have disastrous effects, so it is wise to back up the PC before you make any changes. It's also a good idea to back up the device before you make this change, in case the content of the Synchronized Files folder is deleted.

Change the location for synchronized files by performing the following steps:

1. Run regedit on Windows 95/98/Me; run regedt32 on Windows NT/XP/2000.

2. Click HKEY_CURRENT_USER | Software | Microsoft | Windows CE Services | Partners | *[Partner ID]* | Services | Synchronization. The name of the *[Partner ID]* key is different for each device in a partnership with the PC. You'll find the device name in the DisplayName value of this key.

3. Double-click the Briefcase Path value of the Synchronization key and enter a backslash followed by a name for the folder followed by another backslash. For example, \Synchronized Files\. It is a good idea to write down the contents of this value before you change it. This must be a subfolder of the My Documents folder for the user currently logged in to the PC.

4. Close the registry editor.

During the next synchronization, the files will be written to the new location on the PC.

---

click Tools | Create Mobile Favorite in Internet Explorer on your desktop computer. If you have enabled the Favorites information type to synchronize with your device, the addresses you add will be added to Internet Explorer on your Pocket PC or Smartphone.

To remove a web site address from your device, clear the check box next to the corresponding page listed in the Favorite Synchronization Options dialog box. To stop synchronizing all addresses, click Clear All.

Change Media Synchronization Settings

Windows Media Player Version 10 for Windows and Windows Mobile devices includes synchronization of audio files and pictures between devices and desktop computers running the same version of the software. All Windows Mobile Version 5 devices come with Version 10 of Media Player, and some Windows Mobile 2003SE devices also have Version 10.

ActiveSync Version 4.1 has a Media information type, but you actually configure synchronization in Windows Media Player on your desktop computer. When you select Media in ActiveSync, you see the dialog box shown here. Media will only synchronize to a device via a USB connection, and it requires a storage card with at least 32MB of space.

To configure Media synchronization for a Windows Mobile 5 device, first connect the device to a PC, click Tools | Options, click Media, and then click OK. Next to Media, you will see a link titled Setup Must Be Completed, which you must click to start the process for setting up a partnership between the device and Windows Media Player on the PC.

If you have a device running Windows Mobile 2003SE, start Windows Media Player on the PC and then connect the device.

Next, click Yes to set up the partnership, which starts Windows Media Player and opens the Sync tab:

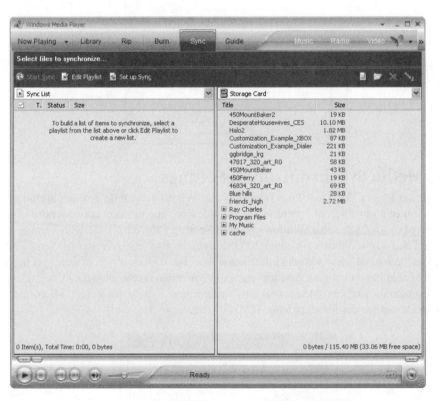

Click Set Up Sync, and then select Automatic if you want to automatically synchronize media files with your device each time that it connects, or select Manual to manually select items to synchronize. If you select Automatic, click Customize The Playlists That Will Be Synchronized to select the playlists on your PC that you want to synchronize with the device and then click Next. Click the check box next to the names of the playlists that you want to synchronize and then click Finish.

The files and playlist will then synchronize to the storage card in the device. When synchronization is complete, you will see a list of the music and playlists that have synchronized in the right side of the screen, as shown in the following image.

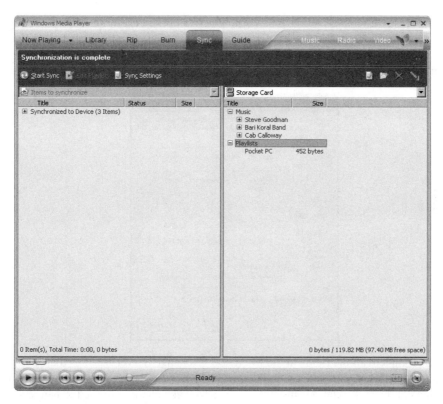

Chapter 18 includes instructions for managing the playlists and music that synchronize with your Pocket PC or Smartphone.

Configure Exchange Synchronization Settings

You can synchronize Calendar, Contacts, and Inbox information between your Windows Mobile device and an Exchange server running Exchange Server ActiveSync. Exchange 2003 includes Exchange Server ActiveSync, while you will need Microsoft Mobile Information Server to synchronize a device with Exchange 2002.

ActiveSync 4.1 provides Exchange Synchronization settings so that when you connect a device to the desktop it will synchronize with Exchange. You can configure a device to synchronize with Outlook and Exchange, but an information type can synchronize with only one location. For example, if you synchronize the Calendar with Outlook, you cannot then synchronize it with Exchange.

You can configure Exchange Server synchronization either on the device or from a desktop computer. To use a desktop computer, first connect your device to the computer, and then click Tools | Add Server Source to open the Microsoft Exchange Server Settings dialog box. Enter the server address, username, password, and domain name in the appropriate fields. Check Save

Password to store the Exchange server password, which is needed for automatic synchronization. If the connection to the Exchange server requires SSL, check This Server Requires An Encrypted (SSL) Connection check box. Finally, specify how you want ActiveSync to resolve conflicts by selecting an option from the If There Is A Conflict drop-down list.

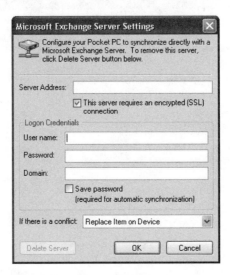

After you complete all the fields in the Microsoft Exchange Server Settings dialog box, click OK to open the Settings dialog box. On the Options tab, you see the Exchange Server settings and the settings of the sync relationship with the PC. To make changes to the Exchange server configuration, click Exchange Server and then click Settings. Select the check boxes next to the information types that you want to synchronize. To configure how the information synchronizes, click Settings. You cannot change the settings for Contacts.

The server synchronization settings are written to the Windows Mobile device—which is why it must be connected before you can make changes. To see the settings in ActiveSync on the device, select Menu | Options and you will see a screen that looks the same as on a desktop computer. To change either the Exchange server configuration or how Calendar or E-mail synchronizes with Exchange, select the appropriate option and then click Settings.

Change Exchange Server Connection Information

To change the Exchange server information in ActiveSync on a PC, first connect the device to the PC and then click Tools | Options to open the Settings dialog box. Click Exchange Server and then click Settings to change the Exchange server information. To change the way Calendar or E-mail synchronizes with Exchange, click either one and then click Settings.

You can also change the Exchange server connection information on a Windows Mobile device. For example, in ActiveSync on a Pocket PC, tap Menu | Options to open the screen shown here. Tap Exchange Server and then Settings to change the Exchange server information. Likewise, tap Calendar or E-mail and then Settings to change the synchronization settings for either one of these information types.

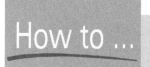
On a Smartphone, click Menu | Options, highlight an option, and click Menu | Settings.

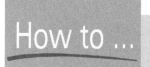
Synchronize Windows Mobile Directly with Exchange

Pocket PCs and Smartphones are capable of synchronizing directly with an Exchange server, so you do not need a desktop connection.

Direct synchronization works with any network connection that provides access to the Exchange server. You can use dial-up modems, Ethernet network connections, wireless Ethernet network connections, or wireless Internet connections. You may need to use virtual private networking (VPN) software to synchronize by using an Internet connection.

To synchronize a device directly with Exchange, start the ActiveSync program on the device and select Sync. You can configure the device to synchronize automatically at specified time intervals, and Exchange can even automatically synchronize (or push) new information with Windows Mobile 5.

To change the synchronization schedule with Exchange on the device, select Menu | Schedule.

Change the Synchronization Schedule

If you configure your Windows Mobile device to synchronize with Exchange via a wireless connection, you can schedule the synchronization to occur at regular intervals. To change the synchronization schedule from a desktop computer, first connect the device and then either click Schedule from the ActiveSync program window or choose Tools | Schedule in ActiveSync on the desktop to display the Settings dialog box with the Schedule tab selected, shown here. The changes you make on this screen define how often the Pocket PC or Smartphone directly synchronizes with an Exchange server over a network connection. If you use a wireless connection with different rates for peak and off-peak usage, you may want to control how often synchronization occurs to save money by selecting a time from the drop-down lists.

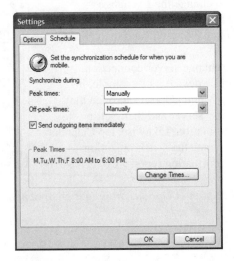

You can also specify whether you want the device to use the same synchronization schedule when you are roaming on another wireless network. Keep in mind that you may pay more for wireless data service when roaming on another network. To have e-mail sent immediately, click Send Outgoing Items Immediately.

To define the hours for peak times, click Change Times, and select the days of the week, start, and end times in this dialog box:

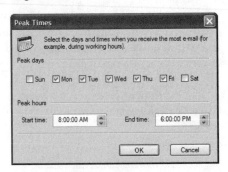

To change the synchronization schedule on your Windows Mobile device, select Menu | Schedule in ActiveSync. On a Pocket PC you will see this screen:

Select the time intervals for peak and off-peak synchronization from the appropriate drop-down lists, and tap Peak Times to change the days of the week, start, and end times for peak hours.

Resolve Synchronization Conflicts

With Windows Mobile 2003SE or older devices, when a conflict occurs during desktop synchronization, the affected item is marked as unresolved in ActiveSync and on the device, unless you tell ActiveSync how to handle conflicts. For Windows Mobile 5 synchronization, conflict resolution defaults to replacing the item on the device unless you change the conflict resolution setting.

To change the conflict resolution setting from a desktop computer, connect the device and then click Tools | Options, click the name of the sync relationship, and then click Settings to open the dialog box shown here. Select an option from the If There Is A Conflict drop-down list, and then click OK. Follow the same process to change the conflict resolution setting between a device and an Exchange server.

 **Fix Persistent Conflicts**

The approach that Windows Mobile 5 uses for conflict resolution fixes a problem with previous versions of persistent conflicts. Sometimes, one or more ActiveSync information types report conflicts that are not resolved, regardless of how conflict resolution is configured. This problem, along with other synchronization problems, is often caused by problems with the Outlook data file on the desktop computer.

The Inbox Repair Tool, of filename scanpst.exe, is installed on all PCs running Microsoft Outlook. If you have problems synchronizing data, you should use this tool to scan the Outlook data file, called outlook.pst. To use the repair tool, follow these steps:

1. Disconnect the Pocket PC from the desktop computer and exit Outlook.
2. Search your desktop computer for the filename outlook.pst, and make note of the file location.
3. Search your desktop computer for the filename scanpst.exe.
4. Start the repair tool by double-clicking scanpst.exe in the Search Results window.
5. Click Browse and select outlook.pst using the information provided in Step 1.
6. Click Start.

The Inbox Repair Tool will scan through the outlook.pst file and fix any problems that it finds. You may want to run the repair a second time if the first scan identified several problems.

As is the case with all other ActiveSync settings, you can change the conflict resolution setting directly on a Windows Mobile device. In ActiveSync on the device, select Menu | Options, select the name of the sync relationship, and then click Settings. To change the conflict resolution setting for an Exchange server, click Next after opening the Server Settings screen and then click Advanced.

The three settings for desktop synchronization are Leave The Item Unresolved, Always Replace The Item On The Device, or Always Replace The Item On The Computer. The settings for server synchronization are Always Replace The Item On The Device or Always Replace The Item On The Server. Select the setting you want and click OK.

Configure File Conversion Settings

ActiveSync converts files when they are copied, moved, or synchronized between the Windows Mobile device and desktop computer. To specify whether or not conversion is to take place and how files are converted, connect the device and then click Tools | Advanced Tools | Edit File

Conversion Settings. The File Conversion Properties dialog box, shown here, opens. Turn file conversion on by selecting the check box on the General tab. When the box is unchecked, file conversion is turned off.

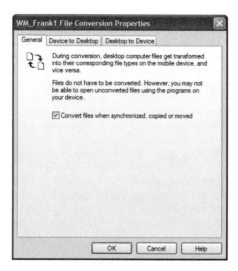

7

   You cannot change file conversion settings in ActiveSync on a Windows Mobile device.

Select the Device To Desktop tab of the File Conversion Properties dialog box to change conversion settings for files moved from the device to the PC. To make a change, select a file type from the list and then click Edit.

Select the desktop file type from the Type drop-down list in the Edit Conversion Settings dialog box and click OK. Then click OK on the File Conversion Properties dialog box to save the change.

The process for changing the file conversion settings of files moved from the desktop to the device is the same. First, select the Desktop To Device tab, select a file type, click Edit, select a new file type, and then click OK.

Wrapping Up

The primary reason for connecting Pocket PCs and Smartphones to desktop computers is to synchronize data with Microsoft Outlook or Microsoft Exchange. ActiveSync synchronizes data between the device's Calendar, Contacts, Tasks, Notes, and Messaging programs with their counterparts in Microsoft Outlook. You can synchronize Calendar, Contacts, and Inbox with Microsoft Exchange. ActiveSync also provides synchronization for Internet Explorer Favorites, as well as Windows Media. Software developers may also use ActiveSync to synchronize data between other Pocket PC applications and desktop counterparts.

Synchronization is not the only reason for connecting a Windows Mobile device to a desktop computer, however. As you will see in the next chapter, you can also use ActiveSync to manage files and folders on the device, to back up and restore data, and to install programs.

Chapter 8

Manage Your Windows Mobile Device from Your Desktop

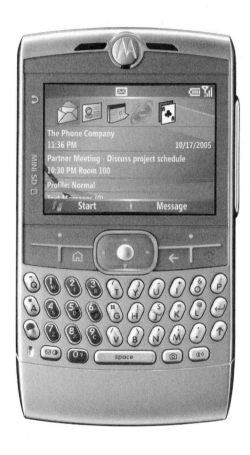
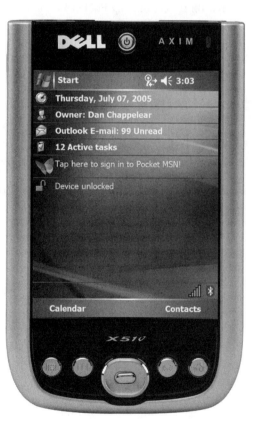

How to...

- Explore files and folders
- Copy, delete, and rename files and folders
- Install and remove programs
- Use Desktop Pass Through
- Back up and restore a Windows Mobile 2003 device

As you have seen in the previous two chapters, you can connect Windows Mobile devices with desktop computers and synchronize data in a variety of ways. Synchronization is not the only reason for connecting Pocket PCs and Smartphones with desktop computers, however. ActiveSync also provides help in managing devices, such as exploring files and folders, copying, deleting, and renaming files and folders, installing and removing programs, and connecting to networks. In this chapter, you will learn how to use ActiveSync to perform all of these functions.

Explore Files and Folders

All versions of ActiveSync enable the user to browse files and folders from a PC on a connected device. In fact, ActiveSync is the only way to browse Smartphones and older Palm-size PCs unless third-party software is installed on the device. Browsing with Handheld PC (H/PC) Explorer was done in a separate program window, but since the inclusion of Windows CE Services, device files and folders can be browsed from within Windows Explorer.

How to ... Protect Your Windows Mobile Device Against Viruses

Few viruses currently affect Pocket PCs or Smartphones, and so far there has been greater concern about devices spreading viruses to desktop computers than virus attacks on devices. If you are concerned about protecting your Pocket PC from viruses, you will find products from Trend Micro and F-Secure.

Virus scan programs that run on Pocket PCs include PC-cillin for Wireless from Trend Micro (www.trendmicro.com/en/products/desktop/pcc-wireless/evaluate/overview.htm) and F-Secure Mobile Anti-Virus (www.f-secure.com/products/mobileav/). For Pocket PC Phone Editions and Smartphones, there is Trend Micro Mobile Security (www.trendmicro.com/en/products/mobile/overview.htm).

Browse Files and Folders

You can browse files and folders on a connected device either within Windows Explorer or by using ActiveSync. As you can see in Figure 8-1, when ActiveSync is installed on the PC, a Mobile Device item is added to Windows Explorer.

If a Pocket PC or Smartphone is connected, double-clicking the Mobile Device icon in Windows Explorer displays the files and folders of the device. The process of browsing files and folders on a device is similar to browsing the hard drive of a PC. You open a folder by double-clicking its icon. But it differs from PCs in that double-clicking a filename opens a Properties dialog box rather than opening the file.

To use ActiveSync to browse a connected device, click the Explorer icon on the ActiveSync toolbar or choose Tools | Explore Pocket PC or Tools | Explore Smartphone. An Explorer

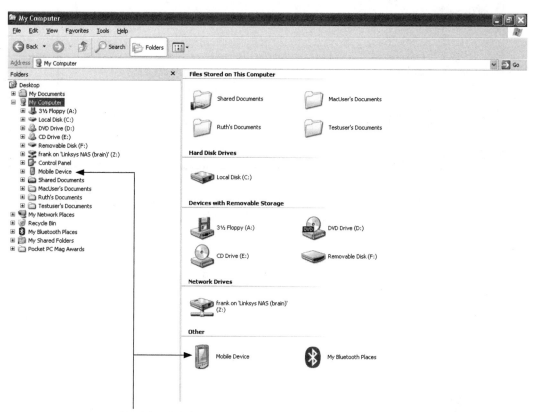

Double-click these to browse folders and files on the device.

FIGURE 8-1   With ActiveSync installed, a Mobile Device item is added to My Computer.

window, shown here, will open. To open a folder, double-click its icon. Double-click a filename to open a Properties dialog box.

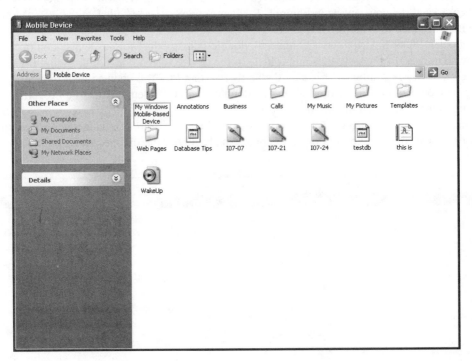

You first see the contents of the My Documents folder on the device when you explore the device on your desktop. To browse all the folders on the device, double-click My Windows Mobile-Based Device in the Explorer window.

Copy, Delete, and Rename Files and Folders

The processes for copying, deleting, and renaming files and folders on a Pocket PC or Smartphone using ActiveSync are the same as those on a PC. You can copy files and folders within locations on a device, such as between the My Documents folder and the Storage Card folder, and between the device and desktop computer.

To copy files or folders, use either the drag-and-drop method or copy and paste. ActiveSync will automatically convert files if file conversion is enabled. (See Chapter 7 for instructions on configuring file conversion.)

Use file synchronization to copy a file to a Pocket PC or desktop PC while the two are not connected. Move or copy the file to the Synchronized Files folder of either, and the file will be copied at the next synchronization. Unfortunately, Smartphones do not support file synchronization.

Delete a selected file or folder by simply pressing DELETE or by choosing File | Delete. Items deleted using ActiveSync are not backed up to a recycle bin prior to deletion. Rename a selected file or folder by choosing File | Rename or by right-clicking the item and then choosing Rename.

Back Up and Restore Files

ActiveSync Version 4.1 does not back up or restore files for Pocket PCs and Smartphones running Windows Mobile 5. Because these devices support persistent storage, your data will not be deleted even when the device loses complete power or is hard reset. However, Windows Mobile 2003SE or older devices can lose data when power is lost, and the only way to ensure that you can restore one of these devices to its current state is by running regular backups, which you can do with ActiveSync.

NOTE *ActiveSync does not back up files or folders that are on storage cards. If you want to back up data on storage cards, you need to use a third-party program, such as CF2Desktop from Information Appliance Associates, at www.pocketgear.com/software_ detail.asp?id=1557. If you want to synchronize files on a storage card, you can use MightySync, found at www.mydocsunlimited.com/html/mightysync.html.*

8

Automatic backups execute if you configure ActiveSync to back up whenever the device connects. To configure this option, connect the device to the desktop computer and then choose Tools | Backup/Restore to open the dialog box shown here. Check the Automatically Back Up Each Time The Device Connects check box and then click OK. The next time the device connects, a backup will run immediately after synchronization.

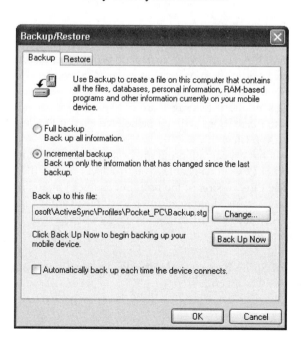

Backups can take a long time to run using older USB connections, so consider how long each backup will take before configuring it to occur every time you connect the device to the PC.

Automatic backups occur every time you connect a device, extending the time of synchronization. If you do not want backups to occur automatically, you can manually back up a device by connecting the device to the desktop PC and then choosing Tools | Backup/Restore. Click Back Up Now on the Backup tab, and the backup will start showing its progress as it works.

 Do not use the device until the backup is finished.

Define the Backup Type

ActiveSync will run either a full or an incremental backup. An incremental backup backs up only those changes that have occurred since the last backup, while a full backup backs up all information every time. Incremental backups are quicker than full backups and therefore work well with modem connections.

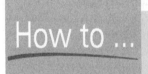 **Run a Local Backup**

Most Pocket PCs include a backup program that will back up the program files and data on the device to a storage card. You should find the backup program in the Program Files folder. These programs run faster backups than ActiveSync and are convenient to use while you're traveling away from desktop computers.

If your device provides an internal storage card in Flash ROM, consider storing backups to this area. Files written to Flash ROM will not be deleted even if the device loses power, so it is a safe location for backup files.

If your device does not have a backup program, or if you prefer a more robust program, try Sprite Backup for Pocket PC, which enables you to select specific files and folders to back up and restore. The Plus version of the program enables you to back up files to a desktop computer or network file share in addition to storage cards. You can schedule backups to run automatically at a specific time each day or once a week, and a battery-monitoring feature automatically backs up a Pocket PC or Smartphone when the battery reaches a defined threshold.

You can buy a copy of Sprite Backup for Pocket PC or download a trial version of the program from www.spritesoftware.com.

To define the backup type, choose Tools | Backup/Restore, select either the Full Backup or Incremental Backup radio button, and then click Back Up Now.

Define Where to Store the Backup

ActiveSync backups are written to the PC hard drive. By default, the filename is backup.stg and is stored in a folder with the name of the device stored in a subfolder of Documents and Settings. For example, for a user named Frank, the backup files may be in \Documents and Settings\Frank\ Application Data\Microsoft\ActiveSync\Profiles\Pocket_PC.

Two files that contain partnership information are also stored in the backup folder. These files have the names outstore.dat and repl.dat. If you want to back up the partnership information stored on the PC, back up these two files.

You may want to change the location of the backup file to a hard drive that has more storage space or to make it easier to back up on the PC. To change the location where the backup file is written, do the following:

1. Choose Tools | Backup/Restore.
2. Click Change.
3. Select a new location in the Select Backup Set dialog box.
4. Click Save to close the Select Backup Set dialog box.
5. Click OK to close the Backup/Restore dialog box.

You can also use this procedure for renaming backup files to something with the current date so that you can easily see when you ran the backup.

Restore from a Backup

ActiveSync restores data from the backup file on the PC to the device. During the process, all of the contents in the device are replaced by the items in the backup, and the recycle bin is emptied. Restore does not overwrite a device's password.

Before you perform a restore, you need to be aware of a few things:

■ If you change the country settings on the device prior to the backup, you must make sure the device is set to the same country settings before the restore; otherwise, the restore will not work.

■ The restore will replace everything within internal storage on the device. If files have been written on the device since the backup, you should copy them to a storage card or a PC before running Restore; otherwise, the files will be lost.

■ While you can back up a Pocket PC using a network connection, you must restore a Pocket PC using either a serial, USB, or infrared connection.

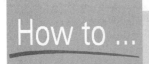 **Control Pocket PCs and Smartphones from Desktop Computers**

Some people find it awkward to work with Pocket PCs while they are docked in cradles and connected to PCs. Virtual CE from BitBank Software fixes this problem by enabling you to manipulate Pocket PCs from desktop computers while they are attached by cradles or over Ethernet networks. In addition to controlling Pocket PCs remotely, Virtual CE enables you to display Pocket PC screens on projectors and to capture various screen shots. You can download Virtual CE from www.bitbanksoftware.com/VirtualCE.html.

If you want to control a Smartphone from a desktop computer, you can use Pocket Controller Professional from SOTI Inc., available at www.soti.net.

To restore from a backup file, follow these steps:

1. Connect the device to the desktop computer. If the Partnership Wizard starts, follow the instructions to create the partnership.
2. Close any programs that may be running on the device.
3. Choose Tools | Backup/Restore and then choose the Restore tab.
4. Click Restore Now. Do not use the device while the restore runs.
5. After the restore completes, soft reset the device.

Install and Remove Programs

Most Pocket PC and Smartphone software includes a setup program that you run on a PC to install software to the device. Setup programs usually store copies of the device installation files on the PC and then run ActiveSync Add/Remove Programs to install the program on the device. With this process, ActiveSync tracks the software that has been installed, and it can be used to reinstall software without having to rerun the installation program.

To remove a program from a device, use either the Remove Programs setting on the device or the ActiveSync Add/Remove Programs dialog box. Chapter 4 provides the instructions for using the Remove Programs setting.

Use ActiveSync to Install Programs

To use ActiveSync to install software, you must first connect the Pocket PC or Smartphone to the desktop computer. The connection can be either in a synchronization relationship or as a guest.

After the connection is made, choose Tools | Add/Remove Programs. ActiveSync determines what programs are installed on the device and then displays the Add/Remove Programs dialog box.

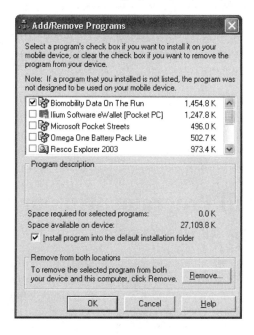

If the check box next to a program is grayed out, it means the program was installed on the device using a desktop computer other than the PC you are currently using.

The checked programs listed in the dialog box are installed on the Pocket PC or Smartphone, and those not checked are available for installation. To install one of these programs, select its check box and then click OK. If you are installing a program to a device running Windows Mobile 5, the setup files are copied to the device and you will then see prompts on the device confirming whether you want to install the program and where you want to install it.

If you are installing a program to a device running Windows Mobile 2003SE or earlier, the Install Program Into The Default Installation Folder check box is available. If the check box is checked, installation starts immediately; otherwise, the dialog box shown here displays, asking whether to install the program in main memory or on the storage card. (You will not see this dialog box when installing software on a Windows Mobile 5 device.) Select the location from the Save In drop-down list and then click OK.

As the software is installed, a dialog box indicates its progress, where you can click Cancel if you want to stop the installation. Once installation is complete, another dialog box displays, asking you to check your device to see if other steps are necessary to complete the installation.

Click OK to close the dialog box, and then check the device to see if instructions are displayed on the screen.

If you install programs to a Pocket PC running Windows Mobile 5 that are designed for previous versions of Windows Mobile, the Command bar menus will be different. Rather than the two-button Command bar that you see with Windows Mobile 5, you see a number of menu options on the Command bar. Even though the menu structure is different, most older programs should run on Windows Mobile 5.

Some very old applications were written to run on devices that had SH3 or MIPS processors, and they will not run on Windows Mobile 5 devices.

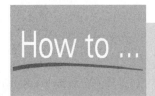 **Install Programs Without Using ActiveSync**

ActiveSync provides the easiest, but not the only, way to install programs on a Pocket PC or Smartphone. You can install programs onto Windows Mobile devices without using ActiveSync by manually copying a cabinet file to the device and then running it. Cabinet files contain compressed copies of program files and execute directly on the device.

The challenges with installing programs in this way are finding the cabinet file to copy to the device and ensuring that you copy the correct version of the cabinet file. The second challenge is an issue only for Pocket PC 2000 devices, because their processors require different versions of program files. All Pocket PC 2002 and older devices can run the same program files, so this is not an issue for these devices.

If a program has already been installed from a desktop computer, you will probably find the cabinet files for that program in the \Program Files\Microsoft ActiveSync folder on the desktop computer. Cabinet filenames use the extension *.cab*. The standard installation process that most programs follow creates a subfolder in the Microsoft ActiveSync folder on the PC and copies the device installation files to that folder. ActiveSync then copies those files to the Pocket PC or Smartphone and installs the program. If the installation files are not found in such a subfolder, you may find them elsewhere on the PC's hard drive, or they may be stored in a compressed file that you downloaded from the Internet.

Use Windows Explorer or ActiveSync Explorer to copy the cabinet file to the device. Then, use File Explorer on the device to browse to the file location, and tap the cabinet filename to install the program. Usually, after installation is complete, the cabinet file is deleted. If you don't want the cabinet file to be deleted, use Windows Explorer or ActiveSync Explorer to make the file read-only.

When you install a program by running a cabinet file, you cannot specify where it will install on the device. The freeware program CabInstl, available at www.freewareppc.com/utilities/cabinstl.shtml, enables you to specify the installation directory for programs in cabinet files.

Use ActiveSync to Remove Programs

To use ActiveSync to remove a program from a Pocket PC or Smartphone, connect it to the PC and then choose Tools | Add/Remove Programs. The Add/Remove Programs dialog box opens with the programs installed on the device checked.

The check indicates the program is installed.

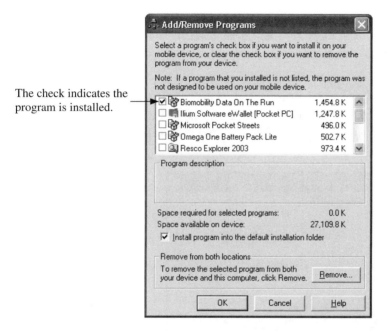

To remove a program from the device, clear the program's check box and then click OK. A message box will display, indicating that the program is being removed. When finished, the Add/Remove Programs dialog box closes.

If ActiveSync cannot uninstall an application because files are open, soft reset the device and then reconnect it to the desktop.

If you reopen the Add/Remove Programs dialog box, you will see that the removed program is still listed. It remains in the list because the installation files are still on the PC. If you want to remove the program from both the device and the desktop PC, clear the program check box and then click Remove.

Use Desktop Pass Through

Desktop Pass Through is a feature that enables the Pocket PC or Smartphone to access the Internet while it is connected with desktop computers. The feature works only with ActiveSync 3.5 and newer versions, and it is not available for Pocket PC 2000.

Any application that works with the Internet will work using Desktop Pass Through.

Pass Through uses the same Internet connection used by the desktop computer. If you access the Internet on the desktop using a modem, you need to establish a connection to the Internet before using Pass Through.

Desktop Pass Through works with ActiveSync Guest connections, so you can access the Internet via Pass Through from any desktop computer with ActiveSync installed on it.

Desktop Pass Through is always available, although you can change the configuration to specify whether to connect to the Internet or a LAN. To make this change, choose File | Connection Settings in ActiveSync on the desktop computer to open the dialog box shown here. Change the This Computer Is Connected To drop-down box to either Work Network or The Internet to connect to a LAN or the Internet, respectively.

Wrapping Up

Pocket PCs and Smartphones are designed to work as an extension of your desktop computer. ActiveSync enables the relationship between Windows Mobile devices and desktop computers by providing for data synchronization and device management. Now that you know how to connect your device with a desktop computer, it's time to learn how to use the Windows Mobile software.

Part III

Get Connected with Windows Mobile

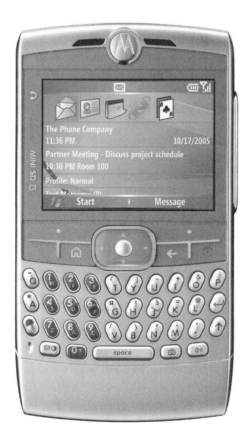

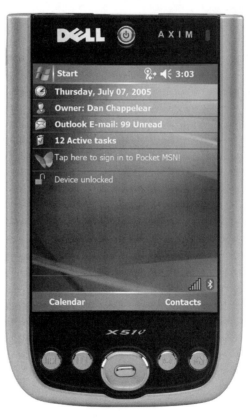

Chapter 9

Call a Friend

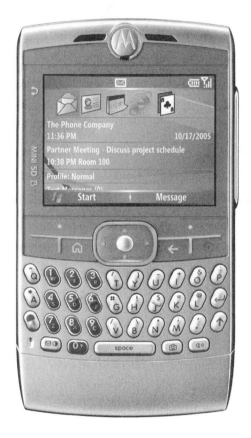

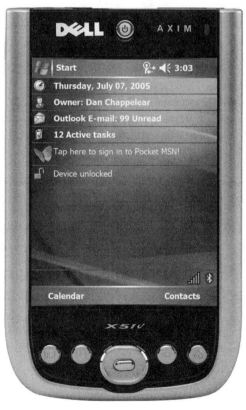

How to...

- Purchase a Pocket PC with mobile-phone capabilities
- Make and receive phone calls using Windows Mobile
- Manage phone call information
- Change phone, service, and network settings

Chances are, you own a mobile phone, and had one long before you even considered buying a Pocket PC. Today, a mobile phone is one of a growing number of gadgets that we consider essential and that must be carried with us at all times. A Pocket PC is also in that list of essential gadgets, but for many people, lugging around a mobile phone and a Pocket PC all day is one gadget too many. The answer, according to analysts and hardware manufacturers, is a device that integrates mobile phone and personal digital assistant (PDA) features.

Over the last several years, there has been considerable talk about integrated devices, which are often called *smart phones*. The popular Palm Treo, which works with the mobile services provided by Verizon, Sprint, Cingular, and T-Mobile, is called a smart phone, as are phones from Nokia and Sony-Ericsson. Microsoft Windows Mobile runs on two different types of devices that can be considered smart phones, Pocket PC Phone Editions and Smartphones.

Pocket PC Phone Edition is an extension to the Pocket PC software that supports mobile-phone hardware. Phone Editions are designed primarily to be handheld computers with wireless data communication that also can support voice communications. Pocket PC Phone Editions have touch screens and usually require two hands to operate.

Smartphone is a subset of the Pocket PC software, and is designed for easy one-hand operation of the device. Windows Mobile Smartphones look like mobile phones, and they do not have touch screens. Smartphones do not include the Mobile Office software.

In this chapter you will learn how to make phone calls using a Pocket PC Phone Edition or Smartphone, and how to use Windows Mobile to manage your voice communications.

Pick a Pocket PC or Smartphone

Several companies sell integrated devices, but the total number sold has not been nearly as high as the number of mobile phones or even handheld computers sold. The challenge is designing a device that is large enough to be useful as a handheld computer yet small enough to be carried around and used as a phone. With the trend of mobile phones becoming smaller, integrated devices feel and look like bricks in comparison.

The Microsoft solution to this dilemma recognizes that no one hardware design will be best for everyone. One part of the Microsoft solution is Windows Mobile software for Pocket PC Phone Edition and its mobile-phone capabilities, which is designed to be the best handheld computer capable of making phone calls. The second part of the Microsoft solution is the Windows Mobile software for Smartphone, which is designed to be the best mobile phone that also has some handheld computing capabilities.

The two Microsoft solutions are targeted at two different types of users. People who frequently use cell phones, or want to carry one small device, will prefer Smartphones because they are small and optimized for use in one hand. Those who do not frequently use cell phones, yet use handheld computers, will prefer Pocket PC Phone Edition because they won't have to carry multiple devices.

Trying to decide which Microsoft solution is right for you? First determine how frequently you make phone calls, and then determine whether you can live with the trade-offs of one solution over another. A Smartphone is smaller than a Pocket PC, but it does not have all of the features available on handheld computers. Pocket PC Phone Edition is larger than most mobile phones and can be awkward to hold up to your ear. You will most likely want to use a hands-free headset with any Pocket PC Phone Edition device.

Most Pocket PC Phone Editions are not sold in the same way as Pocket PCs. Rather than being sold directly by the device manufacturer, mobile service providers sell them. Instead of finding them at computer stores, you will find Pocket PC Phone Editions at mobile-phone stores, unless the computer store has a relationship with a mobile service provider. You will, however, find some Pocket PC Phone Editions from companies such as i-Mate that are sold online rather than directly by mobile service providers.

TIP   *Currently, all of the major mobile service providers in the United States sell Pocket PC Phone Edition devices. If you want to buy a Phone Edition device, first determine which provider provides the best service in your area, and then call them to find out what devices they sell, or go to the provider's web site.*

When you buy a Pocket PC Phone Edition or Smartphone from a mobile service provider, it will be configured to work with that provider's service. In most cases, all you need to do is dial a phone number to make a call or open a web site to connect to the Internet. If you have a problem using your device, you need to call the mobile service provider's support line.

Make and Receive Phone Calls

The mobile-phone features in Pocket PC are available only with integrated devices known as Pocket PC Phone Edition. You will not be able to obtain the Microsoft phone application unless you buy a Phone Edition or Smartphone. When you turn on Pocket PC Phone Edition or Smartphone, you will see a Phone Notifications icon. The phone searches for a connection, and when one is found it shows signal strength in the form of bars to the right of the icon.

On a Pocket PC turn the phone on or off by tapping the Phone Notifications icon. By default, the phone is always on, even when you have the Pocket PC turned off. To turn a Smartphone off, press and hold the power button until the device powers off. If you quickly press the power button, the Quick List, shown on the following page, displays. Select Power Off to turn the phone off.

Phone Notifications

If you want to turn the radio off but keep the Smartphone powered up so that you can use the other features that are available, select Flight Mode.

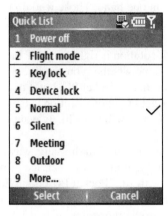

Make Phone Calls

You can make a phone call in one of several ways, depending on the number that you want to dial. One way to make a call is simply to dial a number using the Phone application, which you start on a Pocket PC by tapping Start | Phone. Tap the numbers on the keypad and then tap Talk. The screen here shows call dialing in progress. Tap End to complete the call and hang up.

 **Turn Off Your Pocket PC Phone Radio**

Whenever you take a plane trip, you are instructed to turn off mobile phones, which you cannot use for the duration of the flight. If you have a Pocket PC Phone Edition, you may want to use the other features of Windows Mobile, while complying with the flight attendant's instructions. To do so, you can switch the Pocket PC Phone Edition to Flight Mode. Tap the Phone Notifications icon and then tap Turn On Flight Mode. While the device is in Flight Mode, you cannot send or receive phone calls. To turn the phone back on, tap the Phone Notifications icon and then tap Turn Off Flight Mode.

Pocket PC Phone Edition also has dedicated hardware buttons for Talk and End, which are similar to the buttons on mobile phones. Press Talk while any application is open to open the Phone application.

Smartphones do not have a separate Phone application; simply press the numbers on the numeric keypad to dial a number, and then press Talk. As you dial a number, Smartphone searches your contacts and displays the contacts whose phone numbers match the numbers that you have entered so far, as shown here. The display is updated as you enter each number. Use the navigation button to select a contact to call.

Smartphones also attempt to match the name using a best guess based on the alphabetic characters on the keypad buttons. For example, pressing 223 will also match "Abe."

The Pocket PC Phone application supports speed dialing, which uses phone numbers that you program into storage locations associated with numbers on the keypad. To speed dial a number, tap-and-hold a number on the keypad, and the Phone application will dial the associated number. If the speed-dial location is a two-digit number, tap the first digit and then tap-and-hold the second digit. You can also tap Speed Dial on the keypad and then tap a number from the list that appears. To speed dial with a Smartphone, press and hold the keypad number that has a speed-dial number assigned.

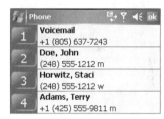

9

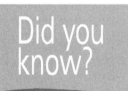

Mobile-Phone Technologies

GSM is widely used throughout Europe but is used much less in the United States. T-Mobile and Cingular Wireless provide the majority of GSM service in the United States. Verizon Wireless and Sprint use Code Division Multiple Access (CDMA), and these two companies provide the greatest mobile-phone coverage in the United States. You can also buy Pocket PC Phone Edition devices from both of these companies.

GSM and CDMA are voice communications technologies and both have data communications counterparts. General Packet Radio Service (GPRS) and Enhanced Data

(continued)

GSM Environment (EDGE) are the data counterparts to GSM, and Single Carrier Radio Transmission Technology (1xRTT) and Evolution Version Data Only (EVDO) are the data counterparts for CDMA. (1xRTT is also referred to as CDMA2000.) EDGE and EVDO provide the highest transmission speeds and are sometimes sold as wireless broadband.

GPRS, EDGE, 1xRTT, and EVDO provide data connectivity that is similar to local area networks (LANs). Rather than dialing a phone number, like a modem, they connect through access points that provide the device with an Internet Protocol (IP) address. Consequently, applications designed to work on IP-based networks will work on GPRS, EDGE, 1xRTT, and EVDO networks. Usually you will be charged for the amount of data that is sent to and received from the device.

While GSM is used throughout the world, it operates on different frequencies, so a device that you buy in the United States may not work in Europe, and vice versa. GSM devices operate on the 850 or 1900 band in North and South America and the 900 or 1800 band in Europe. Some Pocket PC Phone Editions will work on multiple bands.

An advantage for using GSM phones is Subscriber Identity Module (SIM) cards, which are smart cards that store mobile-phone service settings and user preferences. In some cases, SIM cards contain contact information that you can access as speed-dial numbers on Windows Mobile devices. You can also import contacts from SIM cards to Pocket PCs.

If you already subscribe to a GSM service, you should be able to use a Windows Mobile device with that service by simply transferring the SIM card from your phone to your device.

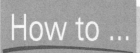 **Import SIM Contacts into a Pocket PC**

SIM cards used with GSM mobile service can store more than network information; they can also store contact names and phone numbers. If you use a mobile phone and then switch to a Pocket PC Phone Edition device, you may want to copy the contact information that you have been storing on the phone to the device. Windows Mobile 5 includes a utility called SIM Contacts that imports the contact information on SIM cards into Outlook Mobile Contacts.

Be aware that all of the contact information you import from a SIM card will synchronize with all PCs in a synchronization relationship with the Pocket PC. To start the program, tap Start | Programs | SIM Contacts. When all the contacts on the SIM card display, tap Copy Now to copy the contacts to Outlook Mobile Contacts. If a contact is found on the SIM card that is already on the Pocket PC, it will not be duplicated. Each contact from the SIM card is assigned to the From SIM Card category, which you can filter to display just the contacts obtained from the SIM card.

SIM contacts automatically display in Contacts on Smartphones. You will find SIM contacts at the end of the Contacts list on a Smartphone.

While speed dialing can be handy when making calls, you will most likely store all phone numbers in Contacts. The Contacts program on Smartphones and Pocket Phone Editions is enhanced to support dialing phone numbers. To dial a number from Pocket PC Contacts List view, tap-and-hold on the contact. On the pop-up menu, each contact method that is available will display. For example, if a contact has work and mobile telephone numbers, then Call Work and Call Mobile display in the pop-up menu.

Another enhancement to Contacts is that phone numbers, e-mail addresses, and text messaging addresses display with icons in the Contacts Summary view, shown here. To make a call, simply select any one of the phone numbers in the Summary view.

All the calls that you make or receive are tracked in the Call History. You can review and make calls from the Call History by tapping Call History on the Pocket PC Phone Edition keypad, or pressing Start | Call History on a Smartphone and then selecting a number or name on the list, as shown next. You also can filter the Call History to show missed calls, outgoing calls, incoming calls, or calls sorted by caller name by selecting Menu | Filter.

9

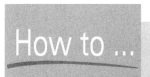

How to ...   Take Notes During Calls on Pocket PCs

If you want to take notes during a call, tap Call Status and then tap Note. The Pocket PC Notes application starts for you to write notes. Notes taken during a call are associated with the phone number, and you can open the note from within the Call Log. To take notes during a call, you need to use a hands-free microphone or the speakerphone functionality that may be available with integrated Pocket PCs.

Make Phone Calls Using Voice Command

One of the functions that you find with many high-end mobile phones is voice dialing, and Microsoft's Voice Command software provides this functionality for Pocket PCs. Voice Command is included in ROM of some Pocket PCs, or otherwise you can purchase it online at www.windowsmobile.com.

After you install the software, you will find a Voice Command icon on the Personal Settings tab of the Pocket PC. Tap the icon to enable Voice Command and configure its several options. After you install the software, you should follow these steps to optimize the program's performance:

1. Adjust the Pocket PC's microphone settings. Check to see if your Pocket PC has a Microsoft Automatic Gain Control (AGC) setting by tapping Start | Settings | System. If it does, turn off AGC and set the microphone gain to medium level. You may find specific microphone gain settings for your Pocket PC in the online help.

2. Set the Voice Command button. In order to activate Voice Command you need to press a hardware button. To assign a hardware button, tap Start | Settings | Buttons. Tap the button that you want to assign and select Voice Command in the Assign A Program drop-down list.

To use Voice Command, hold your Pocket PC about nine inches away from your mouth and press the hardware button that you assigned to Voice Command. You will see a *microphone icon* appear on the command bar. Clearly speak the command that you want to perform. For example, to call a person in your Contacts list, say **Call** *contact*, where *contact* is the first and last name of a contact on your Pocket PC. Voice Command will confirm your selection by repeating the name; if there are multiple phone numbers for the contact, it will ask which number you want to dial.

*You can specify which contact number to dial by saying **Call** contact **at** location. For example, Call Frank McPherson at work.*

To call a phone number that is not in your Contacts list, say **Dial** *number*. Additional commands are Callback, to return the last call received, and Redial, to repeat the last call made.

Receive Phone Calls

When the Pocket PC receives a call, a notification bubble appears on the screen with options for Answer and Ignore. Tap Ignore to silence the phone and transfer the call to voice mail, if it is included by the mobile-phone service, or tap Answer to receive the call. If the Phone application is running, you can also tap Talk to answer a call. Finally, if you use an integrated device that includes a Talk hardware button, press the button to receive the call just as you do with mobile phones.

If you receive a call on a Smartphone from someone in Contacts, the contact's name and picture, if it is included in Contacts, displays on the screen. Otherwise, you simply see the

Control Your Pocket PC with Your Voice

In addition to making phone calls, you can use Voice Command to control your Pocket PC in the following ways:

- **Show contacts** Say **Show *contact*** or **Lookup *contact*** to display a contact.

- **Read appointments** Say **What's my next appointment?** to hear the upcoming appointment. Say **What's my schedule today?** or **What's my schedule tomorrow?** to hear all your appointments for today or tomorrow.

- **Play music** Say **Play music** to have Voice Command guide you to select music. Say **Next track**, **Previous track**, **Play**, **Pause**, or **Stop** to control music playback.

- **Start programs** Say **Start *program*** to start or switch to a program.

- **Get status** Say **What time is it?** to hear the current time, or say **What day is it?** to hear the current day. To turn off all wireless radios on the Pocket PC, say **Turn flight mode on**, and to turn on all wireless radios, say **Turn flight mode off**.

- **Get help** To receive help using Voice Command, say **Help** or **What can I say?**

In addition to enabling you to control your Pocket PC, Voice Command also provides information. Voice Command will announce Calendar reminders, the current song that is playing, and incoming calls. You can turn off these announcements by tapping Start | Settings | Voice Command. For more instructions on using Voice Command, check the Online Help on your Pocket PC.

9

incoming phone number, unless the caller has caller ID blocked. Press the left or right softkey to answer or ignore the call. You can also press Talk to answer a call.

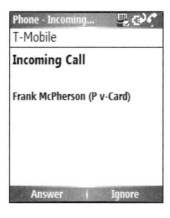

Many headsets, including some Bluetooth headsets, have buttons that you can press to answer a call.

Manage Calls

Every call that is made, received, or missed is entered in the Call History. To view the contents of the log, tap Call History on the Pocket PC keypad, or press Start | Call History on a Smartphone. You can filter the items in the Call History by selecting one of the following items from the Filter menu:

- ■ **All Calls**   Shows all the calls made, received, or missed in chronological order
- ■ **Missed**   Shows only those calls that were not answered
- ■ **Outgoing**   Shows only those calls made from the phone
- ■ **Incoming**   Shows only those calls made to the phone
- ■ **By Caller**   Shows only those calls associated with a single caller

If you create a note for a call, an icon appears next to the call entry in the log; tap-and-hold on the icon and tap View Note to open the note. Tapping within the white space of an entry in the log displays a tooltip showing the date, time, and duration of the call.

To delete all the items in the Call History on a Pocket PC, tap Menu | Delete All Calls. You can also delete individual entries from the Call History by tapping-and-holding on the entry and then tapping Delete. To automatically delete Call History items, tap Menu | Call Timers, and select an option from the Delete Call History Items Older Than drop-down list.

To display call statistics in the Call History screen on a Pocket PC, tap Menu | Call Timers. You can view the total time spent on all calls, the total number of calls, and the total time since the last time the Call History was reset. Tap Reset to reset the call statistics to zero.

There are more options in the Call History on Smartphones. To see the details of a call, use the navigation button to select the entry in the list and then press the navigation button. With the call information open, press Menu | Find Contact to open the contact information of the caller, press Menu | E-Mail to send an e-mail to the caller, press Menu | Delete to remove the information from Call History, or press Menu | Save To Contacts to add the caller name and phone number to Contacts.

You can also open a caller's contact information, send an e-mail to the caller, save the caller name and phone number to Contacts, or remove the call information by pressing Menu and selecting an option from the Call History menu.

To display all the Smartphone call statistics, such as those shown next, press Menu | View Timers in Call History. To reset the timers, press Menu | Reset Timers.

 *To delete all of the information, press Menu | Delete List in Call History on a Smartphone.*

Program Speed Dial

You can add a speed-dial number in three ways on a Pocket PC. To create a speed-dial number from a contact, tap-and-hold on the item in the Contacts List view, and then tap Add To Speed Dial to display the screen shown here. Select a phone number and location from the appropriate drop-down lists and then tap OK.

You can also create a speed-dial number by tapping Speed Dial on the keypad of the Phone application and then tapping Menu | New, which opens a Contacts list from which you can select a contact for a speed dial.

The final way to add a speed-dial number on a Pocket PC is also the only way that you can add a speed-dial number on a Smartphone. Open the Contact Summary view of the person for whom you want to create a speed-dial number, select Menu | Add To Speed Dial, and select the speed-dial location from the drop-down list.

Connect to the Internet

While Windows Mobile provides voice communications, it is particularly suited for providing wireless connections to the Internet. This part of the book provides instructions for connecting Windows Mobile devices to networks, sending and receiving e-mail, sending instant messages, and browsing the Web. Everything in this part applies to Pocket PC Phone Edition and Smartphone; however, this chapter covers Internet connectivity issues unique to these devices.

If you buy your Pocket PC Phone Edition or Smartphone from a mobile service provider, it should already be configured for wireless access to the Internet, if your mobile service provider includes wireless data access. Pocket PC's Internet connections are configured using Connection Manager, which is covered in Chapter 10. You use the Smartphone settings, covered in Chapter 5, to configure Internet connections on Smartphones. If you are having problems connecting to the Internet, you should call your mobile service provider for help.

The simplest way to connect to the Internet is to start Internet Explorer and open a web page. When the Pocket PC connects, you see a notification bubble. Tap Hide to close the bubble, and tap Cancel to disconnect from the Internet. You will also notice that the network icon at the top of the screen changes. You do not see this notification bubble on Smartphones. When you want to disconnect, press the End hardware button.

Tap here to display connection information.

Manage Your Mobile Data Bill

Most mobile service providers have separate rate plans for data communications that are based on the amount of data transmitted. Typically, these plans provide a set amount of data that you can transmit per month, and you are charged an additional amount per megabyte over your limit.

Unless you have a plan that allows you to transmit an unlimited amount of data for a set fee per month, you will want to monitor your data traffic each month. An application that monitors your data use is Spb Software House's Spb GPRS Monitor, which adds an icon to the top of the Pocket PC screen.

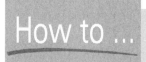

Make Phone Calls over the Internet

A growing number of people are using the Internet to make inexpensive or free phone calls to places all around the world. These people are taking advantage of a technology called Voice over Internet Protocol (VoIP). Skype (www.skype.com) is a popular program for making phone calls on the Internet, and you can download a free version of this program that runs on Pocket PCs.

Skype requires a high-speed connection to the Internet, so it works best with wireless LAN connections or 3G data connections from services such as Verizon, Sprint, and Cingular. If you use Skype on a Pocket PC that has built-in wireless networking, the Pocket PC needs at least a 300-MHz processor to run best. If you use an external wireless card, the Pocket PC's processor requirements increase to 400 MHz.

The GPRS icon provides a graphical indication of the data transmission speed, the amount of data transmitted per session, and battery strength. When you tap the icon, a notification bubble displays showing the amount of data transmitted that day and how much data is left in your plan.

 Spb GPRS Monitor is also available for Smartphone, and it has a Home Screen plug-in to show connection statistics.

You can download Spb GPRS Monitor from www.spbsoftwarehouse.com/. Another program that provides the same functionality is Ordina ALL-locations' GPRS Traffic Counter, which you will find at www.all-locations.com.

Configure the Pocket PC Phone

To change the phone settings, tap Menu | Options in the Phone application. Alternatively, you can choose Start | Settings | Phone on your PC. The Settings screen has at least three tabs: Phone, Services, and Network. Your Pocket PC Phone Edition may have more tabs depending on its features.

NOTE   *Chapter 5 provides instructions for configuring settings on Smartphones.*

Change the Phone Settings

The Phone tab, shown on the next page, displays the phone number, which is read from the SIM card. The Ring Type and Ring Tone settings configure how the Pocket PC reacts to an incoming call. Ring Type specifies the type of notification you receive for an incoming call. If you select a

Ring Type option, you can sample and select a Ring Tone option. You cannot select a Ring Tone option if you select the Vibrate Only ring type.

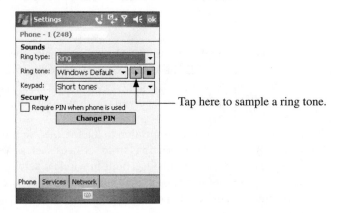

Tap here to sample a ring tone.

 TIP   *Windows Mobile 5 ring tone choices are WAV, Windows Media, and MIDI (including Polyphonic MIDI) files. Ring tones are stored in the \Windows\Rings folder.*

The Keypad field specifies what you hear when using the dialer. You can set the Keypad field to Short Tones or to Off so that it doesn't sound in public places. Select the Require PIN When Phone Is Used check box to prevent unauthorized use of the Pocket PC phone by requiring that a PIN be entered to use the phone. Tap Change PIN to change the PIN. Emergency 911 calls can be made at any time without first entering a PIN.

Change the Services Settings

You use the Services tab, shown here, to access and configure services provided by your mobile service provider. To configure a setting, select the service and then tap Get Settings.

The Caller ID setting controls whether or not your phone number displays to the person you call. You can prevent your number from being displayed by configuring this setting. Call Forwarding configures the service to forward calls made to the phone depending on the status of the phone. You can configure the following Call Forwarding options:

- **Unavailable**   Forwards calls if the phone is turned off or unreachable
- **Busy**   Forwards calls when the line is busy
- **No Answer**   Forwards calls if you do not answer the phone
- **All Incoming Calls**   Forwards all incoming calls

Forwarding calls from a mobile phone to another phone involves additional charges on each call.

Call Waiting allows you to receive a second call during a call. To turn call waiting off, tap Do Not Notify Me. Voice Mail And Text Messages configures the voice mail and text messaging access numbers.

TIP   *Speed dial location 1 is automatically configured for accessing voice mail.*

9

Change the Network Settings

The network settings allow you to select which mobile-phone network the Pocket PC phone will use. The selection remains active until you change it, lose the network signal, or change the SIM card. The currently registered network displays on the Network tab, shown here.

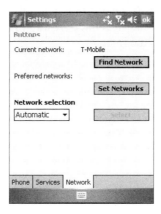

If your phone is not able to find a network, tap Find Network to start the network selection process. The phone will search for a network using the criteria that you specify in the Network

Selection drop-down list. If you select Automatic, the phone selects a network from those you specify as preferred networks. If you select Manual, the phone searches for all available networks and lists them. You can then select the network that you want to use from the list.

Tap Set Networks to specify the networks the phone should use and the order in which they should be accessed.

Change Device-Specific Settings

Your Pocket PC Phone Edition may have additional settings depending on the features provided by your mobile service provider. For example, GSM phones may have a Band tab that enables you to select wireless frequencies.

If you travel from North America to Europe, you will need to change bands because the European GSM network does not work on the 1900 band. Europe has two GSM bands, 900 and 1800, and therefore the phone may still not work if service is not available for the band you select.

Before you use a U.S.-based phone outside the country, check with your mobile service provider to determine whether roaming agreements are available at the locations you will visit and how much the service will cost.

Wrapping Up

Pocket PC Phone Edition is designed to be a great handheld computer that is also capable of making phone calls. Smartphones are mobile phones that include some of the software on Pocket PCs, and can be easily operated with one hand. Whether or not you want to use your Pocket PC as a phone, or use a Smartphone, depends on your mobile-phone needs. If you simply want a mobile phone that is capable of some personal information management, consider a Microsoft Smartphone.

In this chapter, you have seen how to connect to mobile-phone networks and to place a call. In the next chapter you will see how you can connect Windows Mobile devices to other types of wired and wireless networks to access the Internet.

Chapter 10

Connect to Networks

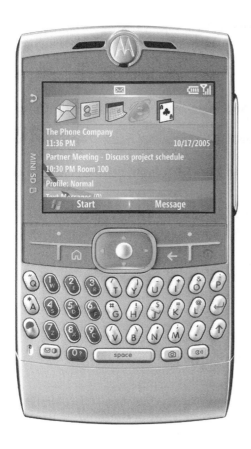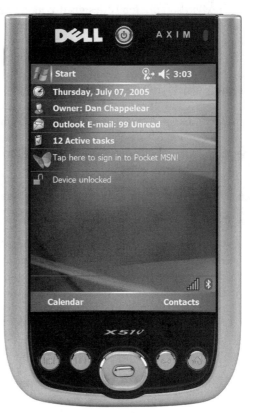

How to...

- ■ Use the Connection Manager to configure network connections
- ■ Select a wireless modem
- ■ Use ActiveSync Desktop Pass Through to connect to networks using serial cables
- ■ Connect to local area networks

By all accounts, the number of people who use the Internet has grown at a phenomenal rate. The majority of Internet connections are made using personal computers, but a variety of other devices, such as smart phones, TV/set-top boxes, and handheld computers, are starting to be used to connect to the Internet.

When Microsoft originally designed Windows Mobile, the company recognized the importance of connecting to the Internet; as a result, every Pocket PC and Smartphone has the ability to connect in a variety of different ways.

The modem and telephone line combination used to be the most widely used means of connecting to the Internet, but today two alternative methods are more popular. One is *wireless networking,* which provides a connection to the Internet using analog or digital cellular phones, special wireless modems, or wireless Ethernet cards. The second alternative method for Internet access is *broadband.* In the simplest terms, broadband is fast Internet access for consumers. Two implementations of broadband are popular: cable-modem service, using the same cable wire connected to your television set, and Digital Subscriber Line (DSL), which provides high-speed access using regular telephone lines.

Because broadband is associated with fast Internet access, some forms of wireless networking, such as 3G services, are marketed as broadband services.

Many of the latest Pocket PCs, and even some Smartphones, have built-in wireless Ethernet, or Wireless Fidelity (Wi-Fi), radios. For the majority of Pocket PC users, Wi-Fi will be the method used to connect to the Internet, and this chapter provides instructions for making the connection. Growing in popularity is wireless networking with cellular phones and wireless modems to connect to the Internet, and this type of connection is built into Pocket PC Phone Editions and Smartphones.

You'll find instructions for connecting to the Internet using all these forms of wireless connections in this chapter. You'll also learn how to use the device's USB cable and ActiveSync Desktop Pass Through to connect to the Internet.

NOTE *Windows Mobile 5 adds Wi-Fi networking to Smartphones. However, at the time this book is being written, no Smartphones with Wi-Fi are available for purchase. Consequently, this chapter will focus on networking with Pocket PCs.*

Network with Windows Mobile

Microsoft has designed Windows Mobile so that it is easy to connect Pocket PCs to computer networks and know the current status of the network connection. At the top of the screen you see a network status icon. Table 10-1 shows how the network status icon indicates the network

Connection Icon	Explanation
	The Pocket PC is not connected to the network. What appears in the notification bubble depends on what connections are configured. You will always see a Settings link that opens Connection Manager.
	The Pocket PC Phone Edition is connected to a GSM network that has GPRS data service. This icon does not appear on regular Pocket PCs, and may look different on Phone Editions that work with different network types.
	The Pocket PC is connected to a desktop PC.
	The arrows are moving in a circle, indicating that the Pocket PC is synchronizing with a desktop computer or server.
	The Pocket PC is connected to a wireless Ethernet network. When you tap the icon, a notification bubble displays the name of the network and the signal strength. To disconnect from the network, tap Turn Off Wi-Fi.

TABLE 10-1   Windows Mobile Connection Status Icons

connection status. When you tap the icon, a notification bubble displays, providing information about the connection and a link to open Connection Manager, which you use to change connection settings.

Tap here to open the notification bubble. ⎯⎯⎯⎯

Windows Mobile includes zero configuration support for Wi-Fi connections. If you have a wireless network card in your Pocket PC and its driver supports zero configuration, or your Pocket PC has built-in Wi-Fi, when the Pocket PC gets into the coverage area of a Wi-Fi network for the first time, a notification bubble appears asking if this network connects to the Internet or a Private/Corporate (Work) network. The selection that you make is stored in Connection Manager so that the next time the Pocket PC detects the same network, it is automatically configured to what you set it to earlier and you are not asked again.

 *If the network that you are connecting to uses encryption, you will be prompted to enter a password to connect to the network.*

Bluetooth provides wireless connections between devices. For example, instead of using a cable to connect a Pocket PC to a mobile phone, you can connect the two using a wireless Bluetooth connection. Windows Mobile has built-in support for Bluetooth and supports most Bluetooth capabilities, or what are called *profiles*. One of these profiles is dial-up networking, which enables you to use mobile phones with Bluetooth as wireless modems.

 *Unfortunately, some mobile service providers do not include the dial-up network profile with their phones, preventing them from being used as modems to connect PCs to the Internet.*

Manage Connections

Connection Manager controls all network connections for a Pocket PC. To start Connection Manager, tap Start | Settings | Connections | Connections to open the screen shown here. The Connection Manager has two tabs: Tasks and Advanced. On the Tasks tab you create and manage network connections. On the Advanced tab you configure how Connection Manager connects to networks and manages dialing rules.

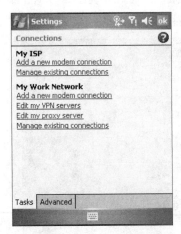

Connection Manager has two categories for network connections: My ISP and My Work Network. My ISP (or simply "ISP" hereafter) connections connect a Pocket PC to the Internet, and normally that is done by using a modem to connect to an Internet service provider (ISP), which is why Connection Manager lists these types of connections under My ISP.

My Work Network (or simply "Work" hereafter) connections define how a Pocket PC connects to LANs. Most corporations use LANs, which is why Connection Manager labels these as My Work Network connections. The same connection options available for ISP connections are also available for Work connections; however, two additional options are included for Work connections.

One option of Work connections is virtual private network (VPN) server connections. VPNs provide a secure connection to corporate networks by using encryption and public Internet connections. To use a VPN server connection, you first connect to the Internet, and then tap the connection status icon to open the notification bubble that provides a link to connect to the VPN server.

Another option for Work connections is a proxy server. Proxy servers provide a way to share an Internet connection with multiple PCs on a LAN. If your Work network has a proxy server, you must enter the information for the proxy server in Connection Manager or you will not be able to connect to the Internet while connected to the Work network.

Once you configure Connection Manager, it makes connections based on the type of information that you attempt to retrieve and the peripheral attached to the Pocket PC. Table 10-2 lists the applications that use network connections, along with the connection scenarios when using a modem. If a network interface card (NIC) is available instead of a modem, the applications will make a connection based on the NIC setting in Connection Manager.

If you want to synchronize Windows Mobile 2003SE and older Pocket PCs using a NIC, you must configure the card to connect to Work, and you must use ActiveSync 3.8 or older. You cannot synchronize devices with PCs running ActiveSync 4.1 via network connections.

Your Pocket PC can be connected to networks in a number of ways. It can use modems to connect with ISPs or with corporate remote access servers. The USB cable, infrared port, or Bluetooth radio that you use to connect a Pocket PC with a PC creates a small network between the two and can also be used by the Pocket PC to connect with the Internet.

LANs are common in offices today and are also sometimes installed in homes to enable two or more home computers to share resources and Internet connections. All Pocket PCs include the software necessary to connect to LANs by using either PC Card, CompactFlash, or Secure Digital Ethernet NICs. In the remaining sections of this chapter, you will see how you can use all of these connection types to connect either to the Internet or to Work networks.

Application	Internet	Work
Internet Explorer	Enter a URL in fully qualified domain name (FQDN) form, such as www.pocketpchow2.com.	Enter a one-word URL, such as fmcpherson.
Inbox	All Inbox services connect to the Internet by default.	Configure Inbox services to connect to Work.
MSN Messenger (Pocket MSN)	MSN Messenger is configured to use only a Passport account.	MSN Messenger works only with Internet-based messaging services.
Terminal Server Client	Does not directly make a network connection.	Does not directly make a network connection. If you use a modem, you must use Connection Manager.

TABLE 10-2   Scenarios for Which the Pocket PC Connects to the Internet or Work Using a Modem

Connect to Networks Using Modems

Many people still connect to the Internet by using a modem to dial in to an Internet service provider (ISP)—the company that provides connections to the Internet. Thousands of ISPs provide telephone numbers that you use either to connect directly to the Internet or, as is the case with America Online (AOL), to connect to a private network and then connect to the Internet. Pocket PCs work with the majority of ISPs that connect directly to the Internet, but you cannot use Windows Mobile's modem connections to connect to AOL.

TIP *If you want to connect to AOL, you can use the AOL for Pocket PC software, which you can buy at www.handango.com.*

You can also use modems to connect to Work networks, usually by dialing in to a remote access server (RAS). RAS provides secure access to LANs via modems. You will need the same information to create a modem connection to Work networks that you need for Internet connections.

Before you connect to the Internet or a Work network, you need to gather some information to configure the connections. If your ISP provides instructions for connecting to the Internet, what you need will be provided in those instructions. If your ISP does not provide instructions, you can find the information by opening the Properties of the connection in Windows. The system administrator of your Work network should be able to provide the information that you need to create the Work modem connection.

You need the following information to create Internet or Work modem connections on your Pocket PC:

- Do you provide a username and password in the Dial-Up Connection dialog box, or does a terminal window open after the number has been dialed (in which case you enter a username and password)? If a terminal window is used, you must configure the Pocket PC connection to open one, as explained in the "Create Modem Connections" section later in this chapter.

- Obtain the maximum baud rate for the connection and the settings for data bits, parity, stop bits, and flow control.

- Find out whether the connection uses Point-to-Point Protocol (PPP) or Serial Line Interface Protocol (SLIP). The most common in use is PPP.

- Does the network access server, or Windows 2003 remote access server, provide an IP address, or is one manually assigned? The most common configuration is server-assigned, but if it is manually assigned, you need the address provided by the ISP or the Work network.

- Does the connection use software compression and IP header compression? The most common configuration is to use both.

- Does the server assign addresses for name servers, or are they manually assigned? If they are manually assigned, you need the address for Primary DNS, Secondary DNS, Primary WINS, and Secondary WINS.

- Obtain the phone number to access the connecting server.

How to ...   Buy a Modem for Your Pocket PC

Many Pocket PCs only have a Secure Digital card slot. If your Pocket PC supports Secure Digital Input/Output (SDIO), it can use a modem. Socket Communications (www.socketcom .com) sells an SDIO 56K modem card, as does Pretec Electronics (www.pretec.com).

CompactFlash modems were once the most common modems for Pocket PCs, because most Pocket PCs had a CompactFlash slot. If you have a Pocket PC with a CompactFlash slot, you will find that all brands of CompactFlash modems work. You do want to make sure that if your Pocket PC has only a Type I CompactFlash slot, you buy a Type I CompactFlash modem. (Most Pocket PCs that have CompactFlash slots now have Type II slots. However, if you have an older HP Jornada Pocket PC, be aware that it has only a Type I slot.) Examples of Type I modems are CompactModem from Pretec; CF 56K Modem Card from Socket Communications, Inc.; and Pocket Modem from Targus (www.targus.com).

To connect infrared modems, such as the Wireless Infrared Modem available at www .pocketirmodem.com/, with the Pocket PC infrared port, select Generic IrDA from the Select A Modem drop-down list when you're creating modem connections. You can also connect Pocket PCs to standard external PC modems by using a serial ActiveSync cable, a null modem adapter, and an RS-232 cable. When using an external PC modem, select Hayes Compatible On COM1 from the Select A Modem drop-down list when creating a modem connection.

10

Create Modem Connections

Before you create a new modem connection, insert the modem into the Pocket PC. If the modem works in Pocket PCs, the drivers will be read from the card and loaded on the Pocket PC; otherwise, a message box displays saying that the card is not recognized. You will see the modem listed when you create the modem connection.

To create modem connections, tap Add A New Modem Connection under either the My ISP or My Work Network section on the Tasks tab in Connection Manager. You enter the connection information on three screens. On the first screen, shown on the following page, you enter a name for the connection and select the modem. The Select A Modem drop-down list contains modems that have been connected to the Pocket PC, along with Bluetooth, Generic IrDA, and Hayes Compatible On COM1 options. If you have a Pocket PC Phone Edition device, you also see options for Cellular Line and Cellular Line (GPRS).

The Bluetooth and Generic IrDA (infrared) options provide wireless connections to mobile phones, which you can use as modems. See the "Connect to Networks with Mobile Phones" section later in this chapter for instructions on using the Bluetooth and Generic IrDA options. You can also connect external modems using a serial ActiveSync cable, in which case you should select the Hayes Compatible On COM1 option.

If you select any modem type other than Cellular Line (GPRS), you enter a phone number for the connection on the second screen. You can enter the area code or extra numbers for outside lines or credit cards directly in the field on this screen. If you frequently change area codes because you're dialing in from various locations, use Dialing Rules. Dialing Rules store area codes, extra numbers, and instructions for when they should be dialed. Once you create the rules, you don't have to enter extra numbers for every connection. The "Create Dialing Rules" section later in this chapter provides instructions for creating dialing rules.

NOTE *After you turn on Dialing Rules, the second modem Connections screen changes to display separate fields for Country/Region Code, Area Code, and Phone Number.*

The Cellular Line (GPRS) option specifies the wireless data modem built into some Pocket PCs. If you select the Cellular Line (GPRS) modem type, you enter an Access Point Name (APN) on the second screen. Your mobile service provider should be able to provide you with the APN you need to use to connect to its wireless data network. Normally, the APN looks like a server name, such as apn.mobiledata.com.

NOTE *The names of the wireless data modem may be different depending on the type of wireless data network provided by your mobile service provider. For example, you may see Cellular Line (EDGE) or Cellular Line (EVDO) for data modems that connect to EDGE and EVDO data networks.*

The third screen has fields for entering the username, password, and domain that you provide to connect to the network. If the modem connection is to an ISP, you will probably leave the Domain field blank. If the modem connection is for a Work network, your system administrator can tell you what to enter in this field, or it can be left blank.

Normally, after you enter the information on the third screen, you tap Finish to complete the creation of the modem connection. However, if you need to change the modem baud rate, have a terminal window display, or change network addresses, tap Advanced. As you can see here, the Advanced modem connection Settings screen has four tabs.

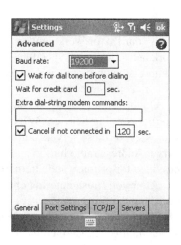

You specify on the General tab the speed of the modem connection and how the modem should dial the phone number. The Port Settings tab has fields to change the data bits, parity, stop bits, and flow control of the modem connection. All of these settings control how modems communicate, and you usually do not need to make changes to these fields. On this tab are also three check boxes for displaying a terminal window. The terminal window is a blank window in which you can enter modem commands. If you want to control the modem connection manually, you can select one of these check boxes.

Tap the Use Terminal Before Connecting check box to display the terminal window before the modem dials the phone number. Tap the Use Terminal Window After Connecting check box to display the terminal window after the modem dials the phone number and establishes a connection. You need to use this option if the ISP or Work network requires you to enter your username and password in a terminal window rather than from the information you enter on the third modem connection Settings screen. To enter the commands for the modem to dial the phone number manually, tap the Enter Dialing Commands Manually check box.

On the TCP/IP tab, you can specify how the Pocket PC obtains an Internet Protocol (IP) address and specify how network communication works. Most ISPs and Work networks provide server-assigned IP addresses, in which case you leave the Use Server-Assigned IP Address radio button selected. If you must use a specific IP address, which your ISP or Work network administrator provides, tap the Use Specific IP Address radio button and enter the address in the field.

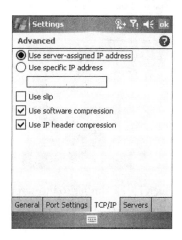

Serial Line Internet Protocol (SLIP) is an old method of connecting to networks using modems, and if your ISP or Work network requires this method, tap the Use Slip check box. If your ISP or Work network doesn't specify otherwise, leave the Use Software Compression and Use IP Header Compression check boxes selected. Most networks use these compression methods to speed up network communication.

On the Servers tab, you enter IP addresses for Domain Name Service (DNS) and Windows Internet Naming Service (WINS) servers. Normally, the ISP or Work network provides the addresses for these servers automatically, but if you need to specify them, tap the Use Specific Server Address radio button and enter the IP addresses in the fields on the screen. Fields are also provided for primary and alternative DNS and WINS servers.

After you finish entering changes to the Advanced modem settings, tap OK, and then tap Finish on the third modem setup screen. You then return to the Connection Manager Tasks tab.

You can enter more than one modem connection for ISP and Work network connections. When multiple modem connections are available, Connection Manager dials the number that has an area code matching the dialing location's area code, if Dialing Rules exist. The one exception is 800 numbers, which are always used even if local phone numbers are available.

Create Dialing Rules

Dialing Rules store area codes, extra numbers, and instructions for when they should be dialed. Once you create the rules, you don't have to enter extra numbers for every connection. To create new Dialing Rules, open the Advanced tab of Connection Manager and tap Dialing Rules, which opens the screen shown here. Tap the Use Dialing Rules check box, tap the radio button for either Home, Mobile, or Work to specify the location, and then tap Edit. Tap New to create a new dialing location.

Each specific dialing location screen looks similar to the screen shown next. In this screen, you configure information about the location from which you're dialing, including the local area code, the local country code, whether you use tone or pulse dialing, and whether or not you need to disable call waiting. You can also control dialing patterns, such as whether a 9 must be dialed to reach an outside line.

Dialing patterns are used to control how the modem will dial a phone number from the location you have selected. When you tap Dialing Patterns, you'll see the following screen. Here, you control how local, long-distance, and international calls are dialed. Placeholders—letters and punctuation marks—are used as a type of shorthand so that parts of the phone number that must be dialed each time can be merged into the dialing pattern. For example, suppose that the location you are dialing from requires that you dial a 9 to place a long-distance phone call. In the field For Long Distance Calls, Dial, you should enter **9,1FG**. If the number you are dialing is 248-555-1212, the modem will dial 9,12485551212 because your device will interpret the 9,1FG as dial 9, wait two seconds, and then dial 1, the area code (F), and the number (G). The characters you can use and their corollary interpretations are shown in Table 10-3.

10

To	Enter
Dial country code	E or e
Dial area code	F or f
Dial local number	G or g
Insert a pause (typically 2 seconds)	, (comma)
Wait for credit card tone	$
Wait for a second tone	W or w
Tone-dial the following numbers	T or t
Pulse-dial the following numbers	P or p
Transfer to another extension (0.5 seconds on hook, 0.5 seconds off hook, sometimes called *hook flash*)	!
Wait for *quiet answer* (typically indicated by 6.5 seconds of silence, followed by a ringing tone)	@
Use special controls on some systems (tone only)	ABCD or * or #

TABLE 10-3   Phone Call Dialing Characters Used by the Pocket PC

Manage Modem Connections

After you create a modem connection for ISP and Work networks, a Manage Existing Connections link appears on the Connection Manager Tasks tab. Tap the link to make changes to modem connections that you create. The screen shown here appears, listing all of the modem connects that exist. The radio buttons specify which modem connection Connection Manager will use to connect to a network. The Auto Pick option appears only when two or more modem connections are available, and it specifies that Connection Manager is to select automatically which connection to use based on the dialing location or device. You can force Connection Manager to use one of the other connections by tapping the radio button of the one you want to use.

To edit a connection, tap its radio button and then tap Edit. You can then go through each of the modem connection setup screens and make changes. To delete a connection, tap-and-hold on the connection and tap Delete on the pop-up menu. The pop-up menu also has a Connect option, which you can tap to initiate a call to the network manually. Tap New to create a new modem connection.

The screen that appears when you tap the Manage Existing Connections link has two tabs—General and Modem; the Modem tab opens by default. The General tab provides a field for you to change the name of the connection settings. For example, you can change the name from My ISP to Frank's Internet Connections. You may not have a need to change this name, but a company that provides Pocket PCs to its workers might want to change My Work Network to the company name.

Connect to Networks Using Virtual Private Networking

Virtual private networking (VPN) is a method for providing a secure connection to Work networks using the public Internet. All information is encrypted and sent to the VPN server, which then decrypts the information and passes it along to the corporate network.

Various methods can be used for implementing VPN, and Windows Mobile supports Microsoft's Point-to-Point Tunneling Protocol (PPTP) and IP Security Layer 2 Tunneling Protocol (IPSec/L2TP). You need to verify that the VPN server to which you need to connect uses these protocols, or you need a third-party VPN client for your Pocket PC.

To configure Windows Mobile to use VPN, tap Add A New VPN Server Connection under My Work Network. You need to complete two or three screens' worth of information, depending on which VPN type you use. On the first screen, you enter a name for the VPN connection and the host name or IP address of the VPN server, and then select the VPN type: IPSec/L2TP or PPTP. The Host Name (server name) or IP Address field must be completed. Tap Next to move to the next screen.

If you select the IPSec/L2TP VPN type, you see the screen shown here. Here, you specify how to authenticate the IPSec/ L2TP connection. If an IPSec/L2TP digital certificate has been installed on your device, usually by your company, select the first option. In most cases, you will select the second option, A Pre-Shared Key. You need to enter the shared key, usually a passphrase and not your VPN server username or password, into the field.

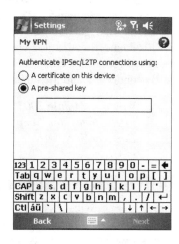

The third screen for the IPSec/L2TP VPN type is the same as the second (and final) screen for the PPTP VPN type. On this screen, you enter a username, password, and domain name for the VPN server in the fields provided. In most cases, after you enter this information, you can tap Finish; however, if you need to specify IP addresses for the VPN connection, DNS server, or WINS server, tap Advanced.

10

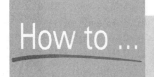 **Configure VPN Connections on Smartphones**

You can use VPN to connect to corporate networks using Windows Mobile Smartphones. To configure VPN, press Start | Settings | Connections | VPN, and to create a new VPN connection, press Menu | Add. Complete the Description, VPN Type, Server, User Name, Password, and Domain fields as described in this section.

Windows Mobile Smartphones have two additional fields not found on Pocket PCs. In the Connects From field, you select the type of network from which you are originating the VPN connection; in most cases this will be The Internet. The Connects To field specifies the type of network the VPN is connecting to, and in most cases this will be Work.

While Pocket PCs have a field for VPN Type, Smartphones have IPSec Authentication to specify the VPN type, and IPSec Pre-Shared Key for entering the preshared key if you are using preshared key authentication.

After you finish entering the VPN server information, the link under My Work Network changes to Edit My VPN Servers. When you tap this link, the screen shown here appears. To edit a connection, tap the connection's radio button and then tap Edit. Tap-and-hold on a connection to delete it.

Connection Manager automatically uses VPN connections whenever you try to access an item specified in the Work column of Table 10-2. For example, if you try to open a web site using a one-word address like http://fmcpherson, Connection Manager initiates the VPN connection to open that site.

To manually initiate a VPN connection, you have to open Connection Manager, tap Edit My VPN Servers, tap-and-hold the VPN connection that you want to use, and then tap Connect. Windows Mobile first connects to the Internet, if it is not already connected, and then initiates the VPN connection.

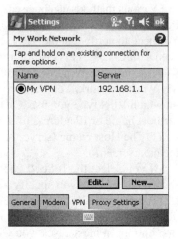

 *Windows Mobile 2003SE and earlier provides an easier way to manually initiate a VPN connection. Simply tap the network connection notification bubble and then tap Connect VPN.*

Configure Proxy Servers

Proxy servers provide access to the Internet from Work networks. To configure Windows Mobile to use a proxy server, tap Set Up My Proxy Server under My Work Network, which opens the screen shown next. Tap the two check boxes on the screen and enter the hostname or IP address of the proxy server in the Proxy Server field.

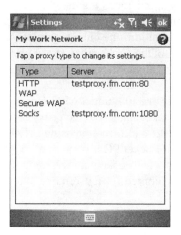

If you create a partnership between the Pocket PC and a desktop computer configured to use a proxy server, ActiveSync will use the information from the desktop to set up a proxy server automatically on your Pocket PC.

If you need to configure port or Socks settings for the proxy server, tap Advanced on the Proxy Settings tab to open the following screen. The table lists each type of proxy server that the Pocket PC can use. To edit a proxy server configuration, tap an entry in the table. You can specify a server name and port, in addition to username, password, and domain if they are needed to use the proxy server.

The HTTP proxy server is used by Internet Explorer when browsing the Web. The default port for HTTP is 80, and this usually shouldn't be changed unless specified by a network administrator.

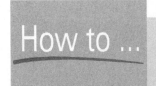

Configure Proxy Servers on Smartphones

If you connect a Smartphone to a Work network, you may need to configure a proxy server to connect to a web site on the public Internet. To configure your Smartphone to use a proxy server, press Start | Settings | Connections | Proxy | Menu | Add. Enter a name to describe the proxy server, and select the type of network connections the proxy server connects from and to in the appropriate drop-down lists.

In the Proxy field, enter the name of the proxy server, followed by a colon, and then the port number of the proxy server. For example, if you want to connect to an HTTP proxy server named testproxy.test.com, enter **testproxy.test.com:80** in the Proxy field.

Select the proxy server type from the Type drop-down list. If you are connecting to a web proxy server, select HTTP for the type. Finally, enter a username and password for the proxy server, if they are required. To save the proxy server configuration, press Done.

Wireless Access Protocol (WAP) settings are used to specify a proxy or gateway server and port that enable browsers using WAP to browse the Web. These settings are not commonly used and will be blank in most cases.

A Socks proxy server is used by applications that need to access application servers using TCP/IP. If you need to use Socks, enter the proxy server and port number. The default port number for Socks is 1080, and this usually shouldn't be changed unless you're instructed to do so by a network administrator. Two versions of the Socks proxy server protocol exist: Socks 4 and Socks 5. Socks 5 supports authentication, so if you tap the Socks 5 radio button, you must enter a user ID and password.

After you set up the proxy server, the link under My Work Network changes to Edit My Proxy Server, which you can tap to make changes to the proxy server settings. The proxy server is automatically used whenever you retrieve information using HTTP, WAP, or Socks protocols on a Work network. For example, if your Pocket PC is connected to a Work network and you open a page on the public Internet, such as www.pocketpchow2.com, the Pocket PC first connects to the proxy server, and you may be prompted for a username and password unless you already saved that information.

Connect Using Wireless Modems

Using a wireless modem, you can connect a Pocket PC to the Internet anywhere that the radio of the wireless modem can receive a signal. Wireless modems provide the convenience of not having to locate phone jacks and string phone cable to connect to the Internet.

Exclude Sites from Using a Proxy Server

Table 10-2 shows the various ways in which Windows Mobile determines how to connect to the Internet. One way is based on the format of the URL you open with Internet Explorer. If you enter an FQDN, for example www.pocketpchow2.com, Connection Manager determines that you need to connect to the Internet. If you enter a short name, for example pocketpchow2, Connection Manager determines you need to connect to a Work network.

This creates a problem for accessing web sites on a Work network that uses FQDNs. Connection Manager connects to the Internet when you want it to connect to a Work network. Windows Mobile offers a simple fix for this problem by providing a way for you to specify URLs that are associated with Work networks.

To enter URLs into the Work URL Exceptions list, open the Advanced tab in Connection Manager and then tap Exceptions. Tap Add New URL in the URL Exceptions list and enter the URL. You can use wildcards in the URL to cover entire domains; for example, enter ***.companyname.com** to add all pages with *companyname.com* in their URL to the URL Exceptions list.

When you enter a URL in Internet Explorer that is in the URL Exceptions list, Connection Manager connects to a Work network rather than to the Internet. The URLs you enter in the list are also not sent to proxy servers.

10

NOTE   *Smartphones and Pocket PC Phone Editions have built-in wireless modems that you can use to connect to the Internet. Usually, the connection settings are preconfigured by the mobile service provider that provides the device. If not, you can manually create a modem connection, as described in the earlier section "Create Modem Connections."*

Two types of wireless modems work with Pocket PCs. Some mobile phones have built-in modems, and these phones are usually classified as *data-capable*. To use the modems in these mobile phones with a Pocket PC, you connect the Pocket PC to the phone by using the infrared port, a serial cable, a CompactFlash card, or Bluetooth. You'll find a list of mobile phones that work with Pocket PCs at Chris De Herrera's Windows CE Website, www.pocketpcfaq.com/peripherals/cellular.htm.

The second type of wireless modem are PC Cards or CompactFlash cards that connect to Pocket PCs that have PC Card expansion sleeves (such as the Compaq PC Card Expansion Pack) or a CompactFlash slot.

Connect to Networks with Mobile Phones

Before you can use a mobile phone to connect to the Internet, you need to find out whether or not your mobile service provider supports data communications. Normally, you need to sign up for an additional service for data communications that may or may not use the minutes that are part of your regular plan. Contact your mobile service provider and ask whether you can connect to the Internet using its service.

TIP   *You can use Smartphones as a wireless modem for Pocket PCs by following the instructions in this section.*

The method that you use to connect your phone to a Pocket PC will depend on the capabilities of the phone. If the phone has an infrared port, you can create a modem connection that uses the Generic IrDA modem and align the infrared ports. Infrared is nice because it is available with all Pocket PCs, but because infrared ports must be lined up, it can be difficult to use.

Alternatives to infrared connections are serial cables and Bluetooth. Most mobile phones have unique ports that require special serial cables, which you can usually purchase from the phone manufacturer. To connect the cable to a Pocket PC, you need a null modem adapter and a serial ActiveSync cable for the Pocket PC. SupplyNet (www.thesupplynet.com) sells cables that connect some mobile phones directly with the HP iPAQ and Dell Axim Pocket PCs, eliminating the need for a null modem adapter or a serial ActiveSync cable.

Bluetooth is a specification for short-range radio links between PCs, mobile telephones, and other portable devices. Its purpose is to eliminate the need to carry and use cables to connect devices, which can multiply like rabbits when you use a lot of different peripherals. Bluetooth provides a function similar to the infrared ports on Pocket PCs, but it is better because it does not require a line of sight between devices and it promises to be supported by a wider range of devices.

To use Bluetooth to connect to the Internet, you need a mobile phone that has a Bluetooth radio, and the phone must be able to make connections to the Internet. Examples of phones that support Bluetooth are the Sony-Ericsson T68, T39, and R520 phones. Windows Mobile Smartphones, such as the Audiovox SMT5600 and the Motorola MPX220, also support Bluetooth.

You also need a Bluetooth radio for the Pocket PC. Some Pocket PCs have built-in Bluetooth radios, or you can add one using the CompactFlash or Secure Digital card slot. Socket Communications and Anycom sell Type I CompactFlash Bluetooth cards, and Toshiba and Socket Communications sell Secure Digital Bluetooth cards. The cards come with drivers that provide a Bluetooth modem option when creating modem connections.

TIP   *You can also use Bluetooth to connect Pocket PCs to printers and personal computers.*

Use Bluetooth to Connect to the Internet

Windows Mobile has built-in support for Bluetooth, so you may not need to install additional software to create a wireless connection with mobile phones. The first step to using Bluetooth is to create a modem connection (as described in the "Create Modem Connections" section earlier in this chapter) and select Bluetooth as the modem. You then see the following screen to create a partnership with a Bluetooth phone.

The process of creating a relationship between devices with Bluetooth is called *pairing*. Pairing is a security method for Bluetooth that establishes a relationship between two devices. Paired devices are given permission to communicate with each other, and this prevents any random device from being given access to a mobile phone to establish data connections.

To search for devices that support Bluetooth, tap New Partnership. Devices that are in Bluetooth Discoverable mode appear in the list. If the phone that you want to use does not appear, make sure that it is in Bluetooth Discoverable mode. Tap Refresh to perform another scan for Bluetooth devices.

TIP *To put Windows Mobile Smartphones into Discoverable mode, press Start | Settings | Connections | Bluetooth, select Discoverable in the drop-down list, and then press Done.*

Tap the name of your mobile phone and then tap Next, which opens the screen shown here, where you enter a PIN. The PIN is 1 to 16 characters long, and the same PIN must be entered on the mobile phone and Pocket PC. You first enter the PIN on the Pocket PC, and then you are prompted to enter the PIN on the mobile phone. If both PINs are entered correctly, the pairing completes and the name of the mobile phone is added to the list. Tap the name of the phone you just paired, and then tap Next.

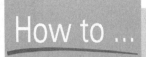 **Put Pocket PCs in Bluetooth Discoverable Mode**

If you have a problem pairing devices by initiating the pairing from the Pocket PC, try pairing from the mobile phone. First, you need to set up the Pocket PC so that it is discoverable. Tap Start | Settings | Connections | Bluetooth, and then tap the Make This Device Discoverable To Other Devices check box. When the mobile phone discovers the Pocket PC, you see this notification bubble. Tap Yes to continue and add the mobile phone to the Bonded Devices list. You then enter a PIN on both the mobile phone and the Pocket PC, and if the bonding succeeds, the mobile phone is added to the Bonded Devices list. To see the devices that are bonded with your Pocket PC, tap Start | Settings | Connections | Bluetooth and then tap the Devices tab.

The remaining screens are the same as described in the earlier "Create Modem Connections" section, but the information on these screens will be different from what you normally enter for modem connections.

You enter a special connection string on the phone number screen that tells the mobile phone to use GPRS or 1xRTT to connect to the Internet. The connection string is different for each service provider. An example string for connecting to T-Mobile's GPRS network is *99#. Your service provider should be able to provide this connection string.

GPRS and 1xRTT networks either don't require a username or password or use the username and password that you enter on the mobile phone. Therefore, you can leave the username and password fields blank on the third modem connection setup screen. If you do enter something in a field, it will usually be ignored.

After you create the modem connection, specifying Bluetooth as the modem, you can then use that connection to connect to the Internet just as you would via any other modem connection. When the Pocket PC connects to the Internet, it establishes a wireless connection with the mobile phone, which it uses as a modem to connect to the Internet. To use Bluetooth, the mobile phone must be on and within ten meters of your Pocket PC.

Manage Bluetooth Relationships

To rename or delete a device from the Paired Devices list, tap Start | Settings | Connections | Bluetooth, tap the Devices tab, tap-and-hold on the device name, and then tap Edit or Delete on the pop-up menu. If you delete a device from the list, you have to go through the entire pairing process to add it back to the list.

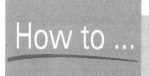

Pair Smartphones with Other Bluetooth Devices

To initiate Bluetooth pairing from a Windows Mobile Smartphone, press Start | Settings | Connections | Bluetooth | Menu | Devices, which displays a screen showing all of the devices paired to the Smartphone. To scan for discoverable Bluetooth devices, press Menu | New, select the device that you want to pair with, and press Next. Enter the passkeys on both devices, and when the pairing completes, you will see a screen to edit the name of the device. Press Done to save the information to the list of paired devices.

NOTE   *You might find the Bluetooth icon in the System tab (tap Start | Settings | Connections | System) instead of the Connections tab. A Bluetooth icon in the System tab is associated with different Bluetooth software than the software Microsoft includes with Windows Mobile. An example of this is the HP iPAQ 2215, which uses software provided by Widcomm, Inc. rather than software from Microsoft.*

Connect Using ActiveSync Desktop Pass Through

10

Desktop Pass Through, which is available in ActiveSync 4.1, provides network connection sharing between desktop computers and Windows Mobile devices. By using Desktop Pass Through, you can access the Internet or LANs from Pocket PCs while they are connected to desktops using serial, infrared, or USB connections.

Desktop Pass Through is available by default for all Windows Mobile devices, including Smartphones. Once you connect the device to the desktop, you can simply use Internet Explorer or Inbox to browse web sites or retrieve e-mail. Desktop Pass Through is always available, but you can control to what network type the device connects from within ActiveSync.

Manage Bluetooth Relationships on Smartphones

To manage Bluetooth relationships on Windows Mobile Smartphones, press Start | Settings | Connections | Bluetooth | Menu | Devices. Select the device you want to edit or delete, and press Menu | Edit or Menu | Delete.

First connect the device to the PC and, on the PC, click File | Connection Settings to display the screen shown here. Change the option of the This Computer Is Connected To drop-down list to specify whether the Desktop Pass Through connection is to the Internet or Work network.

 *Terminal Server Client, File Explorer network access, and VPN do not work with ActiveSync Desktop Pass Through.*

Connect to Local Area Networks

Once used only by corporations, LANs are being installed in homes, mainly to share a single high-speed Internet connection among two or more computers. The setup works something like this: You subscribe to a broadband service provider, which installs the cable or DSL data service in the home. To use the service with one PC, you install an Ethernet NIC in the PC and plug a cable into the card and either a cable or DSL modem.

 *You can also purchase for PCs DSL cards that eliminate the need to install an Ethernet NIC.*

Sharing a high-speed connection with other PCs on a LAN requires a cable modem or DSL router, which is sometimes called a *residential gateway*. Several manufacturers sell these devices; I use the Linksys EtherFast Cable/DSL router. You'll find information about the Linksys router at www.linksys.com. PracticallyNetworked.com provides a complete guide to many of the routers that are available, at www.practicallynetworked.com.

Any device that connects to a LAN either at work or home can access the Internet using the shared high-speed connection. The following section explains how to use network adapters with your Pocket PC to connect to LANs and to the Internet.

Select a Network Adapter

Many Pocket PCs have built-in wireless Ethernet adapters, but if your Pocket PC does not have built-in support for wireless Ethernet, you can add it. You can buy wired Ethernet adapters, which usually come in speeds of 10 Mbps or 100 Mbps, or wireless Ethernet adapters. Wireless Ethernet adapters support one of several wireless communication standards: 802.11b, 802.11g, or 802.11a. You need to take several factors into consideration when deciding which type of card to buy.

Did you know?

Wireless Ethernet Standards

Several wireless Ethernet standards can seem a bit like alphabet soup. The two key characteristics of the standards are the frequency and their maximum speeds. HomeRF, one of the oldest standards, uses the 2.4-GHz frequency and has a maximum speed of 2 Mbps. It also uses a unique method of transmitting data, so it does not work with any of the other wireless Ethernet standards.

> **TIP** *Cordless phones and microwave ovens also use the 2.4-GHz frequency, and they may interfere with wireless LANs using the same frequency. If you experience intermittent communication problems on a wireless LAN, check whether these devices are in use near the LAN.*

802.11b is currently the most popular standard; it uses the 2.4-GHz frequency and has a maximum speed of 11 Mbps. The 802.11g standard also uses the 2.4-GHz frequency and has a maximum speed of 54 Mbps. Since 801.11b and 802.11g use the same frequency and method of transmitting data, devices using the two standards can communicate with each other.

802.11a is a newer standard that uses the 5-GHz frequency and has a maximum speed of 54 Mbps. Since it uses a different frequency, it does not work with the other wireless Ethernet standards. Some manufacturers that make 802.11a access points and cards add a 802.11b or 802.11g radio so that they work with both types of wireless networks.

10

The first decision that you need to make is whether you want to buy a wired or wireless Ethernet adapter. Unfortunately, you cannot buy a wired Ethernet adapter in the Secure Digital card format, so if your Pocket PC only has a Secure Digital slot, you can only connect it to wireless Ethernet networks.

> **TIP** *Socket Communications is the only company that sells a wireless Ethernet card in the Secure Digital format. You will find more information about this card at www .socketcom.com.*

Wireless Ethernet adapters have radios that communicate with access points or other wireless adapters. The type of adapter that you need to buy is dictated by the standard used by the access point or wireless adapter that you want to communicate with. If the access point or adapter uses 802.11b, you must buy an 802.11b card; likewise for 802.11a or HomeRF.

> **TIP** *If your Pocket PC has a built-in wireless Ethernet adapter, you can turn the radio on or off using a program provided by the Pocket PC manufacturer. Consult the user manual of your Pocket PC to learn how to turn the radio on and off.*

The 802.11g standard is backward compatible with 802.11b, so you can use 802.11g cards with 802.11b access points. 802.11g access points work with 802.11b and 802.11g cards. Some manufacturers are selling cards that have multiple radios to work with various access points. 802.11b is currently the most popular wireless Ethernet standard, but the new 802.11g standard will probably become more popular within a few years because it is faster and backward compatible with 802.11b.

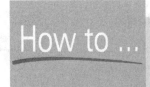

Most 802.11g access points can be configured to support both 802.11b and 802.11g, just 802.11g, or just 802.11b. If you have an 802.11b card that cannot connect to an 802.11g access point, make sure the access point is configured to support 802.11b.

To buy a wired Ethernet adapter, you need to know the network speed and the type of network cabling that is being used. You can buy adapters that support only 10 Mbps or 100 Mbps, and you can buy adapters that support both speeds. However, if the network speed is only 10 Mbps, you may want to buy a 10-Mbps adapter because they are cheaper. The most common network cable is Category 5 (CAT5) Unshielded Twisted-Pair (UTP), which has an RJ-45 connector. Most Ethernet adapters work with CAT5 UTP.

How to ... Use Wireless Ethernet to Connect to Home Networks

Wireless networking is becoming a popular way to connect computers to home networks where it is difficult to install network cable. You can use wireless Ethernet adapters to connect a Pocket PC to a home network in two ways. One way is to use access points in what is usually referred to as *Infrastructure mode*. The second way is to create a point-to-point connection between two wireless Ethernet adapters in what is called *Ad Hoc mode*.

Access points support multiple wireless Ethernet adapters and can be easier to set up than point-to-point connections. You connect an access point to an existing LAN by running a network cable from the access point to an Ethernet hub. This connection allows computers connected to the network with cables to communicate with computers connected to the network with wireless Ethernet adapters. If a cable or DSL modem is connected to the hub, you can access the Internet using the wireless Ethernet adapter.

Wireless Ethernet adapters cost less than access points, so if you want to connect a Pocket PC only to one computer, a point-to-point connection may be desirable. If the computer is connected to a wired network and supports network connection sharing, the Pocket PC can access the wired network. The downside of point-to-point connections is that when a wireless Ethernet adapter is configured for Ad Hoc mode, it cannot communicate with access points or other adapters.

Type of Ethernet Adapter	Web Site
Wired PC card	www.pocketpcfaq.com/peripherals/pccardethernet.htm
Wired CompactFlash card	www.pocketpcfaq.com/peripherals/cfethernet.htm
Wireless PC card	www.pocketpcfaq.com/peripherals/pccardwirelesslan.htm
Wireless CompactFlash card	www.pocketpcfaq.com/peripherals/cfwirelesslan.htm
Wireless Secure Digital card	www.pocketpcfaq.com/peripherals/sdiowirelesslan.htm

TABLE 10-4   Web Sites that List Pocket PC Ethernet Adapters

Several companies sell CompactFlash wired Ethernet adapters, and you can find them by using the link in Table 10-4 (above). When buying an Ethernet adapter to use in a Pocket PC, you need to consider whether or not a Pocket PC driver that works with the adapter is available. The card will not work without a driver. Wireless Ethernet adapters require specific Pocket PC drivers, but some wired Ethernet adapters will work with the built-in NE2000 Compatible Ethernet Driver that is available on all Pocket PCs. Table 10-4 provides addresses to web sites that list Pocket PC–compatible Ethernet adapters.

TIP *You can also use CompactFlash Ethernet adapters in laptop computers that have only PC Card slots by inserting the CompactFlash card into a PC Card adapter.*

10

Configure Network Interface Adapters

If you purchase a network adapter that has a Pocket PC driver, you must install the driver on your device by following the manufacturer instructions. To see the network drivers installed on your Pocket PC, tap Start | Settings | Connections | Network Cards, and the installed network adapter drivers are listed on the following screen.

Any number of adapter drivers may be installed on a Pocket PC. Most Pocket PCs include at least the NE2000 Compatible Ethernet Driver, which is a generic driver that can work with any NE2000-compatible card. Beyond that, each Pocket PC vendor may include additional drivers on its device to support a variety of types of network cards.

Regardless of whether you add an adapter or your Pocket PC has a built-in wireless Ethernet adapter, you need to configure it to connect to a LAN. With Windows Mobile, it is easy to set up and use network adapters. Windows Mobile automatically configures the card and, if it detects a network connection, displays a notification bubble. If you plan to access only the Internet, select The Internet and tap OK. If you plan to access files or folders on the LAN or synchronize the Pocket PC with a desktop computer using the network, tap the Work radio button and then tap OK.

If no server on the network provides network addresses, or the network adapter's driver is not designed for Windows Mobile, you need to configure the properties of the driver so that they work in your network environment. The configuration screens and process are the same for every driver type, so the following instructions are the same for every brand of network adapter.

To configure wired network adapters manually in Windows Mobile, do the following:

1. Tap Start | Settings | Connections | Network Cards.

2. Tap the adapter that you want to configure, which opens this screen:

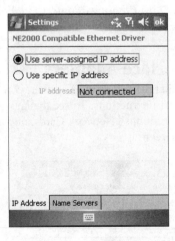

 NOTE *The settings that you configure in the IP Address and Name Servers tabs are specific to your network. Many residential gateways and cable or DSL routers automatically assign IP addresses; if that is the case for your network, you can select Use Server-Assigned IP Address and tap OK.*

3. If you need to use a specific IP address with the adapter, select Use Specific IP Address, and complete the IP Address, Subnet Mask, and Default Gateway fields, which appear when you select Use Specific IP Address.

4. If you need to enter addresses for DNS or WINS servers, tap the Name Servers tab and enter the addresses.

5. Tap OK.

Configure Wireless Ethernet Adapters

Network adapter settings are the same for wired and wireless Ethernet adapters, but wireless adapters have additional settings for the wireless portion of the network. The items that you must configure for all wireless Ethernet adapters are described in Table 10-5.

Some brands of wireless Ethernet adapters have additional settings found only on that adapter. An example of such a setting is a *Power-Saving mode,* which specifies how power is supplied to the adapter to save battery strength. Read the user manual of your adapter to determine how to change any settings that are unique to the adapter.

Like wired adapters, Windows Mobile automatically configures wireless Ethernet adapters if you are within range of an access point. First, install the drivers for the card and then soft reset the Pocket PC. Insert the adapter into the Pocket PC, or turn on Wi-Fi if it is built into your Pocket PC, and a notification bubble displays. All of the available networks are listed, shown by SSID. Tap the radio button of the network to which you want to connect, and tap OK. A second notification bubble, shown here, displays asking to specify whether you are connecting to the Internet or a Work network; tap the appropriate radio button and then tap Connect. If you tap Dismiss, you can tap the radio tower icon at the top of the screen to open the notification bubble.

10

Item	Description
Extended Service Set Identifier (ESSID) or Service Set Identifier (SSID)	The ESSID has up to 32 characters and provides a unique identifier for the wireless network. The ESSID assigned to the adapter must be the same as is assigned to all access points or other wireless adapters on the network. Some adapters display this setting as SSID.
Operating Mode	If the wireless adapter communicates with an access point, it must be set to an *Infrastructure* operating mode. If the wireless adapter communicates with another wireless adapter, the operating mode must be set to *Ad Hoc.* If you use an Ad Hoc operating mode, you need to specify a channel number, which must be the same for both wireless adapters.
Wireless Equivalent Privacy (WEP) or Encryption	WEP is a special form of encryption designed for wireless Ethernet adapters. The appropriate version of WEP depends on the size of the key that the encryption uses. Most adapters support 40- and 128-bit encryption. Some adapter drivers use ASCII characters for keys, while others use hex characters. The WEP key that you enter for the adapter must match the key used by the access point or wireless adapter that the card communicates with.

TABLE 10-5   Common Wireless Ethernet Adapter Settings

Wi-Fi Protected Access

WEP's small encryption key and method for sharing keys enable people to break into wireless networks that implement only WEP for security. While corporations have turned to stronger security methods such as VPN, these methods are not practical for home users. Fortunately, a better version of WEP, called Wi-Fi Protected Access (WPA), has been developed and should now be available for all Wi-Fi products. Windows Mobile 5 supports both WEP and WPA security.

If the network you are connecting to uses WEP or WPA security, you see the notification bubble shown here. Enter the key or password that is needed to access the network, or if your device has a digital certificate, you can leave the Key field blank and tap Connect. If you entered the correct key, your Windows Mobile device displays the Wi-Fi connect icon at the top of the screen, as shown in Table 10-1.

If no server on the network provides network addresses, or the adapter's driver is not designed for Windows Mobile, you need to configure the properties of the driver so that they

work in your network environment. Use the steps provided in the "Configure Network Interface Adapters" section of this chapter, but include one more step, because additional properties are required for the wireless network. When you tap the Network Cards button on the Connect tab of Settings with a wireless adapter turned on in the Pocket PC, you see the screen shown here. The Wireless tab displays the settings for the wireless network, and the Network Adapters tab, which is the same as described in the "Configure Network Interface Adapters" section, has settings for the Ethernet network.

NOTE *You will not see the Wireless tab if a wireless adapter is not in the Pocket PC or if the adapter's driver is not designed for Windows Mobile.*

On the screen, you see a list of wireless networks, and a status indicator. You can connect a Pocket PC only to one wireless network at a time, and other networks in range are listed as Available. Unavailable networks are those networks that the Pocket PC previously connected to but now are not within range. Wireless adapters can communicate only with networks that are within 100 meters.

 *To connect manually to an available wireless network, tap-and-hold on the network name and tap Connect on the pop-up menu. To remove a network, tap Remove Settings.*

For Connection Manager to configure the adapter for wireless networks automatically, the access points on the network must broadcast its SSID. For security reasons, some networks may be configured not to broadcast the SSID, in which case you must manually enter the information to connect to the wireless network.

To add settings manually for a wireless network, tap Add New to open the screen shown next. Enter the SSID or ESSID in the Network Name field. Select which type of network, The Internet or Work, the network connects to, and then tap the check box if you are connecting directly to a PC instead of to an access point. (See Table 10-5 for an explanation of these settings.)

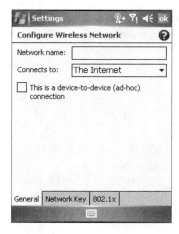

Tap the Network Key tab to open the following screen, where you configure the adapter for the network's security settings. Select an option in the Authentication drop-down list to specify the type of network authentication that is used.

10

If you are using WEP, you should leave Authentication to Open, but if you are using WPA, select either WPA or WPA-PSK in the drop-down list. If you are using WPA for a home network, select WPA-PSK for the Authentication type. The PSK portion of WPA-PSK stands for Pre-Shared Key, which means a key is provided by an access point rather than an 802.1X authentication server. When you set up an access point to use WPA on your home network, you enter a key, which is the same key that you must enter on the Pocket PC. WPA authentication requires an 802.1X authentication server, which corporations often use to authenticate devices requesting to connect to their wireless networks.

If the network uses WEP, select it in the Data Encryption drop-down list. If you select WPA or WPA-PSK in the Authentication drop-down list, the Data Encryption options include WEP and TKIP. Temporal Key Integrity Protocol (TKIP) dynamically changes keys as the wireless communication occurs, while WEP uses the same key that can be discovered by network tools after capturing enough network traffic. To take full advantage of the extra security WPA provides, select TKIP for the Data Encryption.

NOTE   *Some wireless access points, such as Linksys's, require TKIP if WPA is enabled.*

If you use WEP data encryption, and the wireless network provides the encryption key, keep the The Key Is Automatically Provided check box selected. If you use WPA-PSK authentication, or the network does not provide the encryption key for WEP, clear the check box and enter the key in the Network Key field. WEP supports four different network keys, so be sure to select the correct one that you are using in the Key Index field.

Some wireless networks, such as those using WPA authentication, use an enhanced mode of security called IEEE 802.1X, which uses the Extensible Authentication Protocol (EAP). Windows Mobile supports two types of EAP: Transport Layer Security (TLS) and Protected EAP (PEAP). The 802.1X security uses a server to authenticate users on a wireless network, and this is the method used by some companies to secure their networks.

If you are accessing a wireless network that uses 802.1X security, you need to obtain a personal certificate, which is used to identify who you are and enable the security on your Pocket PC. Personal certificates are encrypted files that contain information about you and are stored in the Windows folder on your Pocket PC. You can see what certificates are on a Pocket PC by tapping Start | Settings | System | Certificates.

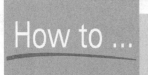

How to ... Troubleshoot Network Connections

One of the most important network troubleshooting tools for your Pocket PC is a free program called vxUtil from Cambridge Computer Corporation. You can download this program from www.cam.com/vxutil.html. If you have problems connecting to a network, use the Info utility in vxUtil to review the IP address settings of the Pocket PC and make sure they are correct. Use the Ping utility to test network communication between the Pocket PC and a destination computer.

To enable 802.1X security, tap the Use IEEE 802.1X Network Access Control check box on the 802.1X tab, and then select the EAP type in use on the network. Tap Properties to see the information associated with your personal certificate.

Use Zero Configuration Wi-Fi

If you use a wireless Ethernet adapter and connect to many different networks, such as at home, work, and a Wi-Fi hotspot, you will appreciate the Wi-Fi zero configuration feature. Windows Mobile automatically changes the wireless card settings when you move between networks.

 *Wi-Fi hotspots are public locations that provide wireless access to the Internet using Wi-Fi. Some hotspots provide free access, while others charge a fee. To find a hotspot in your area, see www.hotspotlist.com.*

Because each network may have different SSID settings, you have to specify which settings the adapter should use. In some cases, you have to change the information in several fields each time you want to connect to a different network. The software for some Wi-Fi cards simplifies this by storing all the settings in a profile; you select which profile to use, and all the fields change automatically.

Windows Mobile takes this one step further by automatically switching profiles. All you do is plug the card into the Pocket PC or turn on the Wi-Fi radio if it is built into the Pocket PC, and if you previously connected to the network, Connection Manager automatically selects the network settings. If Connection Manager does not find the network information, it displays a notification bubble for you to provide the settings. After you configure the wireless network settings for Windows Mobile, you may never need to change the wireless settings again.

Wrapping Up

Pocket PCs are capable of connecting to the Internet and LANs in a variety of ways. You use Connection Manager to configure all modem connections, and it automatically connects to the appropriate network based on the type of information you enter. Connection Manager also specifies whether network cards connect to the Internet or Work networks.

Wireless modems and network adapters are becoming the hottest accessories for Pocket PCs. With these accessories, you can use your Pocket PC to connect to the Internet from any location at any time.

Once you get connected to the Internet, you can send and receive e-mail using Messaging on the Pocket PC or Smartphone. In the next chapter, you will learn how to use Messaging to send and receive e-mail using Internet e-mail servers.

Chapter 11

Send and Receive E-mail, Text Messages, and Instant Messages

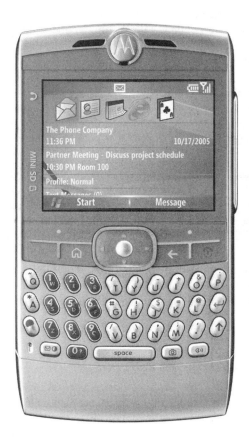

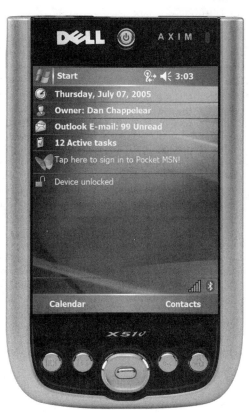

How to . . .

- Create e-mail accounts that work with POP3 and IMAP4 servers
- Synchronize e-mail messages with Microsoft Outlook
- Compose, edit, and send new e-mail messages
- Receive e-mail messages and reply to or forward messages
- Manage file attachments
- Send and receive text messages
- Send and receive instant messages

Back in 1992, people did not know much about the Internet unless they were in college, in the military, or computer geeks. My, how things have changed! Today, many people, even people who don't consider themselves "into computers," not only know what the Internet is but use it on a regular basis.

How do you use the Internet? Chances are good that you use e-mail to send messages to friends and loved ones around the world. You probably surf the Web to listen to music, check stock prices or sports scores, buy CDs or books, and follow the news. Perhaps you make friends by interacting with them in an online forum, or you keep in touch with other friends by using instant messaging.

Regardless of how you use it, chances are also good that the Internet is becoming increasingly important to you. E-mail might be the only way you communicate with coworkers, or perhaps you make a living building web sites for companies. As access to the Internet becomes more important, many people are seeking ways to stay connected, wherever they may be.

For that task, Windows Mobile devices are well suited. The combination of their small size, software, and communications hardware makes it easy to get connected. Included with every device is Messaging, a program that works with Internet e-mail servers, and Microsoft Outlook. If you have a Pocket PC Phone Edition or Smartphone, you can also use Messaging to send and receive text messages. In this chapter, you learn how to use Messaging to send and receive e-mail and text messages.

Use Messaging to Work with E-mail

One of the first acts of the new United States Congress in 1789 was to authorize a postal service, creating 75 local post offices covering 1875 miles. The fact that one of the first acts of a new nation was the establishment of a postal service highlights the importance of mail delivery at that time. As the nation grew, mail became more important for communication. For example, the Pony Express is credited with keeping California in the Union by providing rapid communication between the two coasts.

In 1861, the Pony Express gave way to the telegraph, introducing technology as a means of speeding communication. Ever since then, technology—from telephones to satellites—has been used to speed communication around the world. In the 1990s, e-mail came into widespread use, reducing the time it took to deliver messages around the world from days to seconds. Today we are accustomed to writing a message, clicking a button, and expecting it to end up around the world as soon as the button is released.

As e-mail becomes more important, methods for sending and receiving e-mail, no matter where we may be, also become more important. Combined with the right communications equipment, small Pocket PCs and Smartphones can be used to send and receive e-mail from your living room or the back seat of a taxi.

One of the reasons why you bought your device might have been to send and receive e-mail. In this chapter, I show you how to use Messaging to work with your e-mail. You will learn how to set up Messaging to access Internet mail servers and then retrieve e-mail from those servers. You'll also learn how to compose and send a message and how to handle file attachments.

Messaging has multiple roles: as a client to Microsoft Outlook, as an Internet e-mail client, and as a tool to send and receive text messages. Unfortunately, while these roles provide flexibility, they also add complexity. I will clarify these roles so that you can choose the best method for working with your e-mail.

NOTE   *Your device may also include Multimedia Messaging Service (MMS) support, which works the same way as text messaging and is described in this chapter.*

E-mail and traditional mail share a few common aspects. To receive mail, the post office needs to know your address. When someone sends you a card, he or she writes your address, which includes a postal code, on the envelope. In the United States, the postal, or ZIP, code on the card is used to route it to your state, city, and, finally, post office. Once at the post office, a person determines its final location by using the street address or post office box number.

The equivalent of a post office for e-mail is a mail server, which has a name that looks something like this: mail.acme.com. Just as you must register your address with the post office to receive mail, you need a mailbox registered at a mail server to receive e-mail. Usually, a mailbox is associated with a user ID, such as frank.

Internet e-mail addresses have a defined format, interpreted the same way by all mail servers. The address starts with the user ID, followed by the *at* (@) sign, and then followed by a domain name—for example, frank@acme.com. Each of these parts is used by mail servers to send and receive e-mail.

NOTE   *Conceptually, corporate e-mail addresses are similar to Internet e-mail addresses, but they may use a different format.*

Most post offices have a front and back entrance, with the front being where mail enters the office and the back being where mail leaves the office. E-mail is similar because two servers are involved in the process: one receives e-mail and the other sends e-mail.

The servers that receive e-mail are called POP3 (Post Office Protocol 3) or IMAP4 (Internet Message Access Protocol 4) hosts because of the protocols that they use. Because mailboxes reside on these servers, they are often simply referred to as mail servers. Servers that send e-mail are called SMTP (Simple Mail Transfer Protocol) hosts—because they use the SMTP protocol.

11

E-mail clients, such as Windows Mobile Messaging, are designed to work with both servers. When you send an e-mail message using Messaging, it transfers the message to an SMTP host. The SMTP host first uses the domain name portion of the e-mail address to contact a Domain Name System (DNS) server and obtain the TCP/IP address of the mail server. Once the SMTP host has the TCP/IP address, it contacts the mail server and tells it that it has a message for the user ID. The mail server determines whether a mailbox exists for the user ID, and if it does, it then accepts the message. If a mailbox does not exist, the SMTP server returns the message to the sender's mail server.

Messaging receives e-mail by logging in to the mail server and downloading the messages to the device. As you will see later in this section, Messaging can be configured to download only message headers or entire messages. Downloading message headers provides you with enough information to determine whether you want to download the entire message to your device. With that information, you can decide to skip certain messages that you don't want to read, saving the time it would otherwise take to download the entire contents of that message.

Start Messaging

The process for starting Messaging on a Pocket PC depends on how the Start menu is configured. By default, you start Messaging by tapping Start | Messaging. However, if the menu has been changed, Messaging may be under Programs, in which case you tap Start | Programs | Messaging. To start Messaging on a Smartphone, press Start | Messaging, which shows a list of the accounts, as shown here. Select one of the accounts to display the messaging window.

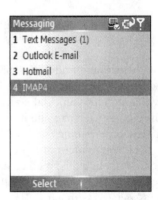

When Messaging starts on a Pocket PC, you see a message list such as shown below.

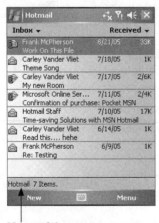

Name of the current account

A similar screen appears on Smartphones after you select an account. At the bottom of the window is the Command bar, with two options associated to the left and right softkeys. Above the Command bar on Pocket PCs is a status bar that displays the name of the account, the total number of items in the folder, and the number of unread items in the folder.

In the middle of the screen is the list of messages stored in a folder. Use the Show drop-down list in the upper-left corner of Pocket PCs, shown next, to select the account and folder that you want to display. The name of the open folder displays at the top. To change accounts on a Smartphone, press Menu | Switch Accounts, and to select a different folder, press Menu | Folders and then select the folder that you want to view.

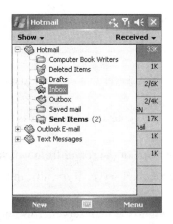

TIP   *One of the new features of Windows Mobile 5 is support for Microsoft Hotmail.*

To change the order of the message list on a Pocket PC, expand the drop-down list in the upper-right corner. The items can be sorted on From, Received Date, or Subject, and the field currently used for the sort is displayed at the top. To switch between ascending and descending order, repeat the selection of the sort field. For example, the message list shown here is sorted by From in descending order. To sort the message list in ascending order, select From in the Sort drop-down list a second time.

NOTE   *You cannot change the order of the message list on Smartphones.*

Add Internet E-mail Accounts

To send and receive e-mail, Messaging must communicate with POP3 or IMAP4 servers and SMTP servers, and to do that you must provide Messaging with information about those servers. That information is stored in an *account*.

One of the first things that you need to do to use Messaging is add an account. To do that, you need the following information about your mail servers, which your Internet service provider (ISP) can provide:

- **Account type** The type of mail server that you use to receive e-mail, either IMAP4 or POP3.

- **Connection** Used to connect to your ISP. The process for creating a connection on Pocket PCs is explained in Chapter 10.

- **Host or server name** The name of the server from which you receive e-mail.

- **User ID** Used to log in to the mail server. Typically, this is the same user ID that you use to connect to your ISP.

- **Password** Also used to log in to the mail server. This may also be the same password that you use to connect to your ISP.

- **Domain** Necessary only if you are connecting to a network that uses Windows 2000/2003 domain security. You do not need this for most Internet accounts.

- **SMTP host or server name** The name of the server used to send e-mail. You may also need a username and password for your SMTP host if it uses SMTP authentication.

- **Your e-mail address** Looks similar to this: taz@acme.com.

TIP *Another source for information about mail servers is Chris De Herrera's ISP Settings page at www.pocketpcfaq.com/wce/isp.htm.*

After you gather this information, you are ready to start Messaging, create an account, and start sending and receiving e-mail.

Add Messaging Accounts to Pocket PCs

To add an account on a Pocket PC, tap Menu | Tools | New Account. The first E-mail Setup screen displays. You use five screens for setting up an e-mail account. On the first screen, enter your e-mail address and tap Next.

On the next screen, you see a feature of Messaging called Auto configuration. Auto configuration connects to the Internet and then uses the e-mail address you enter to try to retrieve mail server names. The Pocket PC first checks a database on Microsoft's servers for the information; if there is no match, it attempts to retrieve the information from the e-mail service provider.

NOTE *Your Pocket PC needs to connect to the Internet for Auto configuration to work. Therefore, if you connect by modem, plug in the modem before executing this step. If you forget to attach the modem before accessing this screen, you can tap Back to return to the previous screen, attach the modem, and then tap Next.*

When Auto configuration completes, the status changes to Completed, and you can tap Next to go to the next step. On the third E-mail Setup screen, shown next, enter the name you want displayed on the messages you send, along with your mail server user ID and password.

Connect to Multiple E-mail Services with One Call

When you connect to an ISP from within Messaging, you can connect with only one mail server at a time. If you have multiple e-mail accounts and want to check e-mail on all of them using Messaging, you must disconnect and end the call before connecting to another account, even if the second account is configured to use the same dial-up connection.

This can be expensive when you are charged for each call that you make. Fortunately, there is a workaround for this problem. The trick is not to use Messaging to connect with the ISP, and instead connect using Connection Manager. Chapter 10 has instructions for creating modem connections in Connection Manager.

After the connection is established, switch to Messaging and tap Menu | Send And Receive to connect to the mail server and retrieve e-mail. Select the second e-mail account and then tap Menu | Send And Receive. If you see a dialog box asking if you can access the mail server using the current connection, tap Yes, and Messaging will then connect to the account and retrieve the e-mail.

While this process works for receiving e-mail, you may experience problems sending e-mail. Some ISPs do not allow you to use their SMTP servers unless you connect to their service. If that is the case, you will need to connect to the ISP to send e-mail, or find an SMTP server that can be accessed from any ISP.

11

Outlook E-mail
E-mail Setup (3/5)

User information

Your name: Frank McPherson

User name:

Password:

☐ Save password

Back   Next

Tap the Save Password check box if you want Messaging not to prompt you to enter your password each time you retrieve e-mail. Be careful with this feature; if you save the password, anyone who has access to your Pocket PC may be able to send and receive your e-mail. If you choose to save the password, you might consider password-protecting the Pocket PC by using the Password setting, as described in Chapter 3.

On the fourth E-mail Setup screen, select the type of mail server that you will use to receive e-mail in the Account Type drop-down list. The options are POP3 or IMAP4. Enter a name in the Name field and tap Next.

The fifth and final E-mail Setup screen, shown here, provides fields for entering the names of the incoming (POP3 or IMAP4) mail server and outgoing (SMTP) mail server. These fields may already be populated if Auto configuration found a match when it connected to the Internet. Otherwise, enter the names for the mail servers in the fields on the screen. If you are connecting to a network that uses Windows 2000/2003 domain security, enter the domain name in the Domain field. Normally you will leave this field blank.

TIP   *If you are using MSN's e-mail servers, you must enter **MSN** in the Domain field.*

Tap the Options button to configure additional settings that control how the e-mail service communicates with the mail server. Three Options screens appear. On the first Options screen, shown here, you can specify how often Messaging checks for new mail and whether the account connects to the Internet or a Work network. You should leave the Connection field set to The Internet, unless the e-mail account is for a corporate e-mail server, in which case you want to change the field to Work.

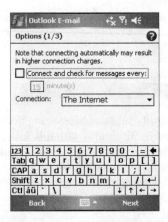

TIP
If you are using MSN's e-mail servers, you must check the Outgoing E-mail Server Requires Authentication check box in the second Options screen.

On the second Options screen, you can specify whether the outgoing (SMTP) e-mail server requires authentication, whether a Secure Sockets Layer (SSL) connection is required, and how many days of messages Messaging should display. While several different methods of SMTP authentication are available, Messaging uses only the POP server username and password. If your SMTP server requires a different username and password, you need to use a third-party e-mail program.

On the third and final Options screen, you specify whether Messaging retrieves only message headers or entire messages. If you select message headers, you can specify how much of the message the service retrieves along with the headers. If you are creating an IMAP4 e-mail account, you see an additional setting on this screen to specify whether the service downloads attachments when getting full copies of messages. You can specify the maximum-size attachment the service will download. Tap Finish to save the e-mail service.

Add Messaging Accounts on Smartphones

To add a new Messaging account on Smartphones, press Menu | Options | New Account to begin the new account wizard, the first screen of which is shown here. Enter the name you want displayed in your messages and the return e-mail address and then press Next.

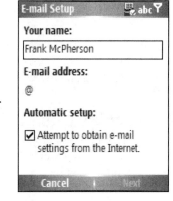

The wizard attempts to automatically find information about your e-mail servers based on the e-mail address, and then displays a screen for entering your username and password. After you enter this information press Next.

Select the e-mail server type from the Server Type drop-down list, enter an account name, and select the type of connection to use to retrieve your e-mail in the Network drop-down list. Normally, you select The Internet for the Network option, to retrieve e-mail from servers on the Internet.

Press Next and enter the incoming and outgoing e-mail server names. If the servers require SSL or authentication, select the appropriate check boxes and then click Next to move to the next wizard screen.

On the next screen, you specify the number of days' worth of messages to download, and how much of each message to download. Because of the limited storage space on Smartphones, you want to limit the number of messages you download.

Press Next to open the next wizard screen and specify whether you want Messaging to automatically connect and retrieve your e-mail at set time intervals, or to never automatically connect. If you select Never, you have to press Menu | Send/Receive in Messaging to retrieve e-mail. This is the last screen of the new account wizard; press Finish to save the information that you entered. You are asked whether you want to download e-mail to the new account; press Yes or No.

11

Edit and Remove Accounts

To change an account on a Pocket PC that has already been created, tap Menu | Tools | Options to display the Options dialog box, shown here. Tap a name in the Accounts list to open the E-mail Setup screen. To delete an account, tap-and-hold a name in the Accounts list and select Delete from the pop-up menu.

To change an account on a Smartphone, press Menu | Options | Account Options, and select a name in the Accounts list.

Synchronize E-mail with Outlook

You may have noticed that one of the Messaging accounts is Outlook E-mail. It is not listed as an account when you tap Menu | Tools | Options, but it is visible in the Accounts drop-down list of the Messaging List view. This account is built into Messaging and cannot be removed, but you can control whether it is used.

One of the purposes of the Outlook E-mail account is to synchronize e-mail messages between the Inbox folder in Outlook and Windows Mobile Messaging. With this feature, you can download e-mail to your device and then take it with you to read. You can reply to messages offline or create new messages, which will then synchronize to Outlook during the next ActiveSync session. Once in Outlook, the messages are sent using Outlook's e-mail connectivity.

Another purpose of the Outlook E-mail account is to synchronize e-mail messages with a Microsoft Exchange server. If you set up e-mail synchronization with an Exchange server, you cannot synchronize the Outlook E-mail account on a Windows Mobile device with Outlook running on a PC. See the "Configure Exchange Synchronization Settings" section of Chapter 7 for instructions on setting up synchronization with Microsoft Exchange.

E-mail synchronization with PCs has one significant limitation: you can synchronize e-mail only with the first synchronization relationship you create with the Pocket PC. If you have already created a relationship between the Pocket PC and a desktop computer, and you want to synchronize e-mail with a different desktop, you have to delete the first relationship.

How to ... Use Hotmail

Windows Mobile 5 includes Pocket MSN with Hotmail and MSN Messenger. This is the first time that Microsoft has included support for its Hotmail e-mail service in Windows Mobile. The Pocket PC Today screen for Windows Mobile 5 includes a Pocket MSN option that initially says Tap Here To Sign In To Pocket MSN. When you tap the option, a wizard prompts you to enter your MSN account information, which is used to set up Hotmail and MSN Messenger.

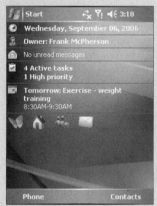

After you configure Pocket MSN, the Today screen displays four icons. Tap the envelope icon to open the Hotmail account in Messaging. Alternately, you can start Pocket MSN by tapping Start | Programs | Pocket MSN. You can tap Menu | Send/Receive to download your Hotmail e-mail to the Pocket PC. While you can perform all of the e-mail functions described in this chapter, you cannot make changes to the Hotmail e-mail account by tapping Menu | Tools | Options. To change the Hotmail account information, tap Start | Settings | MSN Options, select the Switch User tab, and tap the Switch User button.

To run Pocket MSN on a Smartphone, press Start | More | Pocket MSN, and then select MSN Hotmail to open your Hotmail e-mail.

Messaging synchronization works with any ActiveSync connection. See the "Change Outlook E-mail Synchronization Settings" section of Chapter 7 for instructions on setting up e-mail synchronization in ActiveSync.

Messaging synchronization works the same way it does for Calendar, Contacts, and Tasks. When you connect a Pocket PC or Smartphone to the desktop computer, as described in Chapter 7, ActiveSync compares the contents of the device and PC and synchronizes the changes. In the end, both have the same items. Of course, if you configure ActiveSync to synchronize only a limited number of messages, Messaging will not contain everything in Outlook.

Only Outlook's Inbox root folder and subfolders synchronize. E-mail messages that you write and send before synchronizing appear in the Outbox but are moved to Outlook during synchronization and then removed from the Outbox. Deleted items work in the same way. During synchronization, messages are removed from the Deleted Items folder on the device and the message is deleted from Outlook. The contents of the Drafts and Sent Items folders on the device do not synchronize with Outlook.

 **Synchronize with Outlook Express**

Many people have asked me how to synchronize their Pocket PC or Smartphone with Microsoft Outlook Express. Most are amazed to learn that ActiveSync does not support this Microsoft product. If you want to synchronize Messaging with Outlook Express, you need SyncExpress from Syncdata, which you can find at www.syncdata.it. SyncExpress adds an Outlook Express information type to ActiveSync and synchronizes e-mail and addresses. Outlook Express's Address Book synchronizes with Contacts on the device.

NOTE
Messaging synchronization does not control the number of messages that appear in subfolders. All messages in Outlook Inbox subfolders synchronize with the device, regardless of the setting for the root Inbox folder.

All Outlook Messaging subfolders appear on the device, but you must specify which of those folders synchronize by configuring the ActiveSync options on the desktop computer. Messages that you move to synchronizing subfolders appear on both the device and the desktop computer. However, if you move a message on the device to a subfolder that is not synchronizing, the message will be moved to the subfolder on the desktop computer but will not appear in that subfolder on the device.

The process of composing, reading, and responding to e-mail is the same for the ActiveSync service as it is for Internet mail services, which is described in the rest of this section.

Send and Receive E-mail

While you can send and receive e-mail using Messaging synchronization, the only way to update your e-mail is to connect the device with a desktop computer, unless you synchronize with an Exchange server. Although synchronization works, it may not be very functional. On the other hand, you can use an Internet e-mail service anywhere by using a modem or wireless connection.

Before you send and receive e-mail, you must create an Internet e-mail account, as described earlier in this chapter. If you have more than one Internet e-mail account, select the one you want to use from the Accounts drop-down list on a Pocket PC, or the Accounts list when you start Messaging on Smartphones.

You can send and receive e-mail by using any Internet connection. If you are using a modem connection on a Pocket PC, connect the device to the modem and plug in a phone line. For a network connection, insert a wired or wireless Ethernet adapter. Next, start Messaging and tap Menu | Send/Receive.

If you are using a modem connection on a Pocket PC, Messaging displays the Network Logon dialog box for the connection that you assigned to the service. Enter a username and password if they are not already provided, and tap OK. The modem then dials the number of the connection

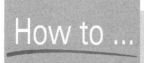

Have E-mail Pushed to Your Pocket PC or Smartphone

The feature that makes Research In Motion's Blackberry devices popular is push e-mail, which sends e-mail to the devices nearly the instant that it is received on an e-mail server. The e-mail synchronization that you read about in this chapter is based on Windows Mobile exchanging e-mail with servers at a time interval. In this case, e-mail may wait on a server for a period of time before it appears on a device.

Microsoft is making changes to its Exchange e-mail server software and Windows Mobile 5 to provide push e-mail capability to Pocket PCs and Smartphones. To get push e-mail, you will need Windows Mobile 5 and the Messaging and Security Feature Pack (MSFP) installed on the device. The Exchange server you use must run Exchange 2003 Service Pack 2. Microsoft has released Exchange 2003 Service Pack 2 and will provide MSFP to mobile service providers. Unfortunately, not all providers have committed to providing MSFP.

and logs on to the network. The Network Logon dialog box will close and you will start to see messages displayed on the status bar.

> **TIP**   *If you use a wired or wireless network connection, Messaging uses it to communicate with the mail servers and does not open the Network Logon dialog box.*

First, Messaging opens a transmit port with the SMTP host to send e-mail, and then it opens a receive port with the POP3 or IMAP4 host to receive e-mail. Once these ports are established, Messaging sends any e-mail waiting to be sent, and then starts downloading messages.

While the messages download, the status bar shows how many messages are on the server and how many have download to the device. In a process similar to ActiveSync, Messaging synchronizes messages with the mail server so that they both contain the same items. If a message has already been downloaded, it will not be downloaded again; if a message on the device is no longer on the server, it is removed on the device.

By default, Messaging does not automatically delete e-mail from the server. When you delete a message in Messaging, the message moves to the Deleted Items folder. You can open the Deleted Items folder, select the messages, and delete them again, and the messages will then be deleted from the server.

> **NOTE**   *When you delete e-mail from POP3 or IMAP4 accounts on Smartphones, they are not deleted from the server.*

You can simplify this manual deletion process by configuring Messaging to delete messages automatically. On Pocket PCs, tap Menu | Tools | Options and then tap the Storage tab, shown next. Change the selection of the Empty Deleted Items field to On Connect/Disconnect or Immediately.

11

You can download a fresh copy of all messages from a server by clearing them from the Pocket PC. To do so, tap Menu | Tools | Clear *account name* (where *account name* is the account name on the status bar) and then tap the Send And Receive button.

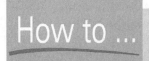
Smartphones do not provide a way to clear all messages from an account.

After all of the messages download, the status bar displays the folder name (Messaging) and the total number of items and unread items. If you are using a modem connection, Messaging disconnects the call if you configured the service to do so; otherwise, it remains connected.

How to ... Send and Receive E-mail Using Other Programs

Messaging is a functional e-mail program, but you may find that it does not meet your needs—or maybe you would prefer to use a different program. Two other e-mail programs work with POP mail servers and run on Pocket PCs. One is nPOP by Tomoaki Nakashima and the other is FlexMail 2006 from Web Information Solutions, Inc.

Unlike Messaging, nPOP supports multiple e-mail accounts on a single Internet connection, and it supports signatures. Messaging on Pocket PC 2002 and Windows Mobile 2003 does not support SMTP authentication, so nPOP is a workaround because it supports SMTP authentication and POP after SMTP. Unfortunately, nPOP does not work with Contacts, so you have to enter e-mail addresses in a separate address book. You can download English and Japanese versions of this program at www.nakka.com/soft/npop/index_eng.html.

Web Information Solutions' FlexMail 2006 can display HTML e-mail, provides e-mail signatures for each account, and supports SMTP authentication. If you use Pocket PC 2002 or Windows Mobile 2003, you will find that FlexMail adds many of the features of Windows Mobile 5 messaging. You can download FlexMail 2006 from www.pocketinformant.com.

If a new message arrives while the device is connected, Messaging notifies you. You see a notification bubble or hear a sound, unless notification sounds are turned off. If while connected you want to force Messaging to check for messages, tap the Send And Receive button.

Compose a New E-mail Message

An e-mail message can be written at any time, even if the device is not connected to the Internet. When the device is not online, the message is stored in the Outbox folder—where it will stay until the next time you connect with a mail server. Messaging retrieves the e-mail addresses that are stored in Contacts and makes them available for use when creating a message.

To create a new message on a Windows Mobile device, select New to open the following screen on a Pocket PC (shown at left). On a Smartphone the screen looks like the one shown at right.

The cursor is in the To field, ready for you to enter the e-mail address of the person receiving the message. E-mail addresses stored in Contacts can be retrieved for use in this field either by selecting the address or by searching for the address.

TIP

You can also create new e-mail messages directly from Contacts. On a Pocket PC, tap-and-hold an item in the Contacts List view and then tap Send E-mail on the pop-up menu. You can also select a contact's e-mail address in the Contact Summary view on either a Pocket PC or Smartphone.

To select an address from Contacts, select Menu | Add Recipient to display a list of all contacts with e-mail addresses. To search for an address, enter the first few letters of the person's name in the search box. As you enter letters, the list is filtered to display only the contacts containing the letters you type. Select the address you want, and it will be entered in the To field. If you select multiple addresses, each will be entered in the field, separated by a semicolon.

NOTE

Windows Mobile allows only semicolons as separators in e-mail addresses. Pocket PC 2002 allows both semicolons and commas.

11

Enter a subject for the message in the Subject field. To send a carbon copy or a blind carbon copy to another person, scroll the message up to display the BCC and CC fields. Enter an e-mail address in either the CC or BCC field by using one of the methods described previously in this section.

The body of the message is immediately below the Subject line. To compose the message, tap the empty middle pane of the window and begin entering text. The My Text menu provides a way to insert text quickly into a message. When you select Menu | My Text, a menu displays with nine messages. Select a message to insert the text into the e-mail.

The My Text menu contains the same entries for Messaging and MSN Messenger. If you change a My Text menu item in Messaging, that change is available in MSN Messenger.

You can change the phrases that are in the My Text menu on a Pocket PC by tapping Menu | My Text | Edit My Text Messages, to open the screen shown here. Tap a message in the list and edit it in the field at the bottom of the screen.

To edit My Text phrases in Messaging on a Smartphone, press Menu | My Text | Menu | Edit My Text.

How to ...   **Use E-mail Signatures**

Windows Mobile 5 Messaging supports e-mail signatures, which are predefined lines of text, such as your name, that are automatically inserted at the end of each e-mail that you write. To create a signature, tap Menu | Tools | Options on a Pocket PC and then tap the Signatures button. On a Smartphone, press Menu | Options | Signatures. You can create different signatures for each account. First, select the account from the drop-down list, tap the Use Signature With This Account check box, and then enter the signature text.

Signatures will be inserted only in new e-mail messages unless you select the Use When Replying And Forwarding check box.

To copy, cut, paste, clear, and select all text in a message on a Pocket PC, tap-and-hold on the text of a message and select an option in the pop-up menu. To check the spelling of an e-mail message on a Pocket PC, tap Menu | Spell Check. These options are not available on Smartphones.

To confirm e-mail addresses, select Menu | Check Names. Check Names will verify e-mail addresses using Contacts and the mail servers that you specify when creating accounts. You can specify additional servers for verifying addresses on Pocket PCs by tapping Menu | Tools | Options | Address when the message list displays.

If you want to add an attachment to the message, select Menu | Insert, which displays a menu on Pocket PCs containing Picture, Voice Note, and File options. On Smartphones the menu does not have a File option. Tap File to open the Open dialog box. Listed in the dialog box are all the files stored in the My Documents folder. Use the Folder drop-down list to switch to a different folder. While the Type drop-down list is shown in the dialog box, you cannot select anything but All Files. Tap the name of the file to attach and it will be added to the message, as shown here:

11

When you select Insert | Picture, an Insert Picture screen appears, showing thumbnails of all the pictures on the device.

You might find it quicker to send a voice message than to type or write a reply. To add a voice recording to an e-mail, tap Menu | Insert | Voice Note, which displays the recording toolbar on Pocket PCs:

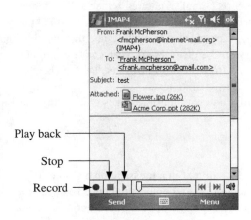

Tap the Record button on the toolbar and begin speaking, and tap the Stop button when you are finished. The recording file appears as a file attachment, and the message recipient will be able to play back the recording using a media player on their desktop computer.

When you press Menu | Insert | Voice Note on Smartphones, you see a screen with Record assigned to the left softkey. Press the left softkey to start recording a message, and a screen like the following appears, with a timer showing the length of the recording:

If you want to save the message, select Menu | Save To Drafts. If you want to cancel and delete the message, select Menu | Cancel Message. When you are ready to send the message, select Send, and the message will be placed in the Outbox folder.

TIP   *You can also save a message in the Drafts folder on a Pocket PC by tapping OK.*

To send a message, select Send, and the message will be sent and removed from the Outbox folder the next time you use the account to send and receive e-mail. If the message is composed for the ActiveSync service, during the next synchronization it will be moved from the Outbox folder on the device to the Outbox folder in Outlook. From there, how the message will be sent depends on how Outlook is configured.

Read and Respond to E-mail

New mail is written to the account's Inbox folder and appears in the message list. Messages that have not been read are in boldface, and messages that have been read are in a normal typeface. To open a message, select its entry in the message list, and the message will open, as shown here.

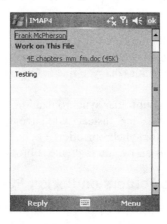

Windows Mobile 5 Messaging displays a sender's picture when an e-mail address matches a contact that has a picture. Select the sender's name to display the contact information for that contact. If you tap the name of a sender that is not in your Contacts list, Windows Mobile will ask you if you wish to create a new contact.

To move to the preceding message in the list, press the Navigation button to the left; press the Navigation button to the right to move to the next message. If the current message is at the top or bottom of the list, you return to the message list. Select Menu | Delete to delete the message that is currently open, and the next message will display. Other options under Menu include Reply, Reply All, Forward, and Mark As Unread.

When you tap Reply, a new message is created with the To field already filled with the e-mail address of the person who sent you the original message. The contents of the original message are inserted into the new message and the cursor is placed at the top. Enter the text of the reply and tap the Send button.

Reply All also creates a new message and fills the To field with the e-mail address of the person who sent the original message. However, if the original message contained any carbon copies or other recipients, the additional addresses are added to the CC line of the reply.

11

You can configure Messaging so that it does not insert the original message in replies. On a Pocket PC, tap Menu | Tools | Options, and then open the Message tab. To stop inserting the text, clear the When Replying To E-mail, Include Body check box. This option does not affect message forwarding, which always includes the contents of the original message.

To configure Messaging on Smartphones to not insert the original message in replies, press Menu | Options | Sending, and then clear the Include Copy Of Original Message When Replying To E-mail check box.

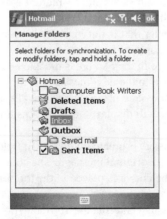

Manage Messages

Folders are valuable for organizing and storing many messages, and you can create folders for all e-mail accounts except ActiveSync. Unfortunately, Messaging does not have the message filter capabilities that you find in Outlook, but you can create folders and manually store messages in them.

While Windows Mobile supports subfolder synchronization, it does not allow you to create subfolders for Outlook E-mail on the device. Instead, you have to create subfolders on a desktop computer and then set up that folder for synchronization. Pocket PC 2000 does not support subfolder synchronization, but it does allow you to create subfolders for the ActiveSync service.

Create, Rename, and Delete Folders on Pocket PCs

To create, rename, or delete folders on Pocket PCs, tap Menu | Tools | Manage Folders to open this screen:

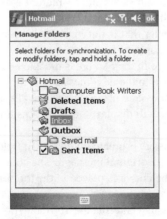

You can only create, rename, and delete folders for POP3 or IMAP4 accounts on Pocket PCs.

To create a folder, tap-and-hold a location within the folder hierarchy on the screen and then tap New Folder. Enter a name for the new folder and tap OK.

The folders that you see on the Manage Folders screen are for the active e-mail account.

To rename a folder, tap-and-hold it in the folder hierarchy, tap Rename, and then enter a new name in the Rename Folder dialog box. Delete a selected folder by tapping the Delete option on the tap-and-hold pop-up menu. The folder and its contents will be deleted.

You cannot create, rename, or delete folders on Smartphones.

Move and Copy Messages

Because Messaging does not provide filtering capabilities, you must manually move or copy messages from the main message list to a folder. When you move a message to a subfolder in the Outlook E-mail account, the message appears in the destination subfolder in Outlook. If the destination subfolder is set up for synchronization, you see the message at both locations. However, if the subfolder does not synchronize, it appears only on the desktop computer. When you move messages associated with Internet services, they are not deleted from mail servers.

To move a message that is in the message list or while a message is open, select Menu | Move and then select the destination folder.

Download a Full Copy of a Message

One of the Messaging preferences is to download only message headers and a specified number of lines. You may decide while reading a truncated message that you want to retrieve a full copy. You can tell Messaging to download a full copy of the message during the next connection with the mail server.

To download a full copy of an open message, select Menu | Download Message. On a Pocket PC you can also tap-and-hold on a message, and then tap Download Message on the pop-up menu.

If you later decide not to download the entire message, select Menu | Do Not Download.

Manage Attachments

Attachments are listed in the message header, as shown here:

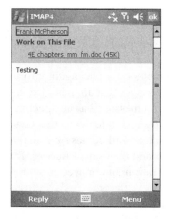

Select the filename of the attachment to have the device download it the next time it connects to the Internet and receives e-mail. E-mail messages that have attachments pending to download appear in the message list with the following icon:

After a message's attachments download, you see an icon display next to the filename in the message header. Tap the filename, and the attachment will open using the appropriate program, or you will be prompted to save the file to your device.

Messaging automatically converts Word, Excel, and PowerPoint documents to the mobile formats for display on Pocket PCs. You can purchase Westtek's ClearVue Office, which is available from www.westtek.com/smartphone/, to open Word, Excel, and PowerPoint attachments on Smartphones.

One of the problems with file attachments is their size, and if you download many messages with attachments, the internal storage space on your Pocket PC can be quickly used up. Fortunately, you can configure Messaging to put attachments on a storage card. To configure a Pocket PC to write attachments to a storage card, tap Menu | Tools | Options, tap the Storage tab, and select the Store Attachments On Storage Card check box.

While Smartphones support storage cards, you cannot configure Messaging to automatically store attachments on them.

Receive Meeting Requests

Outlook Mobile treats appointments, meetings, and events differently. Appointments are activities that you schedule in Calendar that don't involve inviting people. A meeting is an appointment to which you invite someone, and an event is an activity that lasts 24 hours or longer. Sending and receiving meeting requests involves integration between the Calendar and Messaging programs. The process for sending a meeting request is covered in "Schedule Appointments Using Calendar" in Chapter 13.

If you synchronize messages with Outlook, you automatically receive meeting requests. To receive meeting requests using an Internet service, the mail server must be running Microsoft Exchange Server. The Exchange server must use Rich Text Format and Transport Neutral Encapsulation Format (TNEF).

TNEF is a Microsoft proprietary method for packaging information to send across the Internet. If it is enabled, you will not receive messages that are included in other messages as attachments, and you will not be able to tell whether a message has an attachment until you get the full copy.

Meeting requests appear on Windows Mobile devices as attachments, and therefore you must either manually or automatically download full copies of e-mail to open them. When you receive a meeting request, select Appointment and then select Accept, Tentative, or Decline. The response will be sent during the next synchronization, or connection with mail servers, and the appointment is' added to Calendar.

Find Messages

As described earlier, Messaging folders are useful for separating and storing e-mail messages. Unfortunately, Messaging does not provide a way to move messages to folders automatically, which would make the process for finding messages easier. However, you can search for messages, and if you search on the same sending address, they all appear in one list.

To search for a message on a Pocket PC, use the Search utility, which is used to search for any information on the device. Tap Start | Programs | Search; enter a name, e-mail address, or phrase in the Find field; select Messaging from the Type drop-down list; and then tap Search. The results are displayed in the dialog box. To open a message, tap it in the list.

Smartphone does not have search capabilities built-in, but you can find third-party programs that add search capabilities at www.smartphone.net.

Send and Receive Text Messages

Text messaging provides a simple way to send and receive messages on mobile phones. It works like e-mail but does not require an Internet connection. Text messaging on GSM networks is called Short Message Service (SMS). The maximum size of an SMS message is 160 characters. On CDMA networks, this feature is called text messaging.

Pocket PC Phone Editions and Smartphones can send and receive text messages at any time while connected to the mobile network. When you receive a text message, a notification bubble displays on Pocket PCs. Tap the message to open it in Messaging, tap Reply to reply to the message, or tap Menu to delete or save the message, dismiss the notification bubble, or place a phone call to the sender.

11

When you receive a text message on Smartphones, you may hear a notification, depending on which profile you are using. If you are using the Windows default Home Screen, you also see the number of unread text messages on the Home Screen.

You use Messaging to read, reply to, write, and send text messages. To read and write text messages, select the Text Messages account when you start Messaging on Smartphones, or tap Menu | Switch Accounts | Text Messages on Pocket PCs.

Some mobile service providers include customized applications for working with text messages. Check the user manual of your device for instructions on how to use this application.

All you need to send a text message is a person's mobile-phone number. Simply enter the phone number in the To field of the message. To send a message to someone in your Contacts list, begin entering the contact's name and then select it from the pop-up list that appears.

You can also send a message from Contacts. Tap-and-hold on a contact name in the Contacts List view on Pocket PCs and then tap Send Text Message. From the Contact Summary view, select Send Text Message. Messaging starts with a new Inbox message that has the contact's mobile phone number in the To field.

SMS was originally designed for sending messages between phones. However, many wireless services provide SMS-to-e-mail gateways so that you can send messages to e-mail addresses. Usually, you can also receive e-mail messages. Check with your service provider to find out whether it provides an e-mail gateway and instructions for how to use it.

Send and Receive Instant Messages

The Microsoft Network (MSN) Instant Messenger client is included with Pocket MSN that comes with Windows Mobile 5. In prior versions of Windows Mobile, the client appears as a separate program. When you first use Pocket MSN, you are prompted to provide your account information, for which you can either use a Hotmail or Passport account. To create a new Hotmail account, go to www.hotmail.com; to create a new Passport account, go to www.passport.com.

To use MSN Messenger, you must connect your device to the Internet. On Pocket PCs, MSN Messenger automatically uses the default Internet connection that you set up in Connection Manager, or it uses a network card if one is available. Chapter 10 provides the instructions for creating connections in Connection Manager.

MSN Messenger also works with ActiveSync Desktop Pass Through, which is described in Chapter 10.

Tap the MSN Messenger icon on the Pocket PC Today screen, or tap Start | Programs | Pocket MSN | MSN Messenger. On a Smartphone, select Start | More | Pocket MSN. When you start MSN Messenger, you see the opening screen. Select Sign In to sign in to the MSN Messenger server.

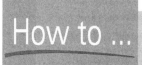

Add a MSN Messenger Icon to Programs on Pocket PCs

Pocket PCs running Windows Mobile 2003SE or older have an MSN Messenger icon in Programs, so you tap Start | Programs | MSN Messenger to run the program. Windows Mobile 5 does not have this icon by default, but you can add it by following these steps on your Pocket PC:

1. Start File Explorer.
2. Use File Explorer to open the Windows folder.
3. Scroll through the Windows folder until you find instmsgr.
4. Tap-and-hold on instmsgr and tap Copy.
5. Scroll to the top of the Windows folder, tap the Start Menu folder, and then tap the Programs folder.
6. Tap Menu | Edit | Paste Shortcut.
7. Tap-and-hold on the icon named Shortcut To Instmsgr and then tap Rename.
8. Enter **MSN Messenger**.

To confirm that you successfully added the icon, tap Start | Programs and scroll the program window until you find the icon.

11

All of your MSN Messenger contacts are stored on the Messenger server, and you see all of your contacts that are online or not online in the main program window, as shown here:

This contact is away from her desk.

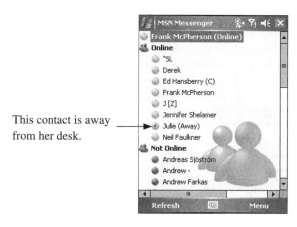

To send a message to a contact that is online, tap the contact name, enter a message, and tap Send. The message that you enter moves to the top of the screen, which is where you also see any replies from the person you are chatting with.

You can also tap-and-hold on the contact name and then tap Send An Instant Message on the pop-up list. To send an e-mail message, tap-and-hold on the contact name and tap Send Mail on the pop-up list. You can send e-mail to online and offline contacts.

You can chat with more than one person by selecting Menu | Chats to switch among people. However, each chat is in a separate window, and you cannot participate in conference chats. If you receive a message from a person with whom you are not chatting, or for whom you don't have the chat window open, the message appears in a notification bubble. The notification bubble displays for about 30 seconds, and if it closes before being acknowledged, an indicator appears at the top of the Pocket PC screen.

Message indicator

The notification bubble and indicator also appear if you have another program open on your Pocket PC while MSN Messenger is running. When you tap Chat on the notification bubble while another program is running, the Pocket PC switches programs so that you can enter a response.

If you do not want to chat, tap Ignore on the notification bubble. To change your status to indicate that you do not want to chat, select Menu | My Status.

Writing long messages can be tedious, so MSN Messenger provides a way to send predefined messages, which are listed in the My Text menu. Tap the text that you want inserted in the message, and then either add more text or tap Send.

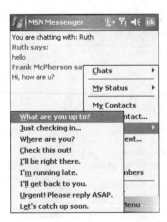

Manage Contacts

MSN Messenger Contacts is not the same as Pocket Outlook Contacts; MSN Messenger Contacts is stored on the MSN Messenger server. Because the contacts in MSN Messenger are on the server, the same contacts appear in versions of MSN Messenger running on desktop PCs or Windows Mobile devices. Before you can add a contact, you must be online with the MSN Messenger server.

To add a contact using a Pocket PC, tap Menu | Add A Contact, and enter the contact's MSN Messenger sign-in name in the Sign-in Name field. Tap Next, and if the sign-in name is found on the server, you see a message indicating that the contact has been added to your list. If the sign-in name is not found, you see a message saying that the operation has failed, and you return to the Add A Contact screen.

To delete a contact, tap-and-hold on its entry on the MSN Messenger screen and tap Delete Contact on the pop-up list. A message box appears in which you confirm whether or not you want to delete the contact. Tap Yes to delete or No to cancel.

If you want to prevent a contact from ever sending a message to you, tap-and-hold on its entry on the MSN Messenger screen and tap Block on the pop-up menu. When you block a contact, you'll always appear offline to that person. Blocked contacts show a cross-out indicator in the button next to the name on the MSN Messenger screen, as shown here. To unblock a contact, tap-and-hold on its entry and tap Unblock on the pop-up menu.

11

Wrapping Up

Your Windows Mobile device has all the tools you need for sending and receiving e-mail to family, friends, and coworkers. Messaging works with standard POP3 and IMAP4 e-mail servers and synchronizes with Microsoft Outlook. Perhaps the second most popular use of the Internet is to browse web sites, which you can do using Internet Explorer on your Pocket PC. In the next chapter you will learn how to use Internet Explorer.

Chapter 12

Browse the Web

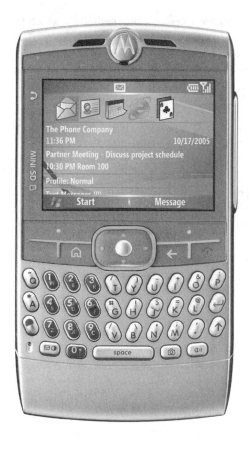

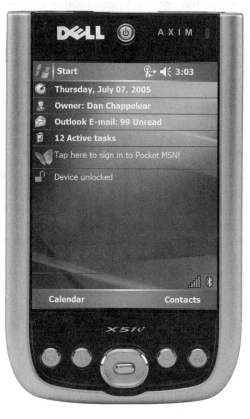

How to...

- Browse web sites using Internet Explorer Mobile
- Save shortcuts to your favorite web sites
- Download RSS feeds to your Windows Mobile device

In 1989, the World Wide Web was nothing more than a project for British physicist and computer scientist Timothy Berners-Lee. In 1993, when the first major browser, Mosaic, was developed, the Web was still not used for much more than research. All of that has changed dramatically, to the point where today numerous companies exist with nothing more than a web page as their storefront.

The Web has become the graphical user interface for the Internet—the method by which the majority of people use it. When you access the Internet to check stock quotes, buy a book, find a phone number, or read a magazine, you probably do so on the Web with a web browser.

Because of the importance of the Web, a web browser is now perhaps the most important program on your computer. Go to any computer store, look at any computer, and you'll find a web browser installed. Windows Mobile devices are no different; they, too, have a web browser installed, called Internet Explorer Mobile.

NOTE   *Previous versions of Internet Explorer on Pocket PCs were known as Pocket Internet Explorer.*

Like all the Windows Mobile applications, Internet Explorer Mobile is not designed to be your full-time browser. However, it provides enough functionality to perform the majority of tasks necessary when you don't have access to a browser on a desktop computer. In fact, the combination of a Smartphone, Internet Explorer Mobile, and wireless networking may represent the future of the Internet, a future in which the Internet is used for communication wherever one may be—at home, at the grocery store, or traveling.

The version of Internet Explorer Mobile with Windows Mobile 5 is based on the desktop version of Internet Explorer but does not support all of its features. The following is a summary of the features that are *not* supported:

- Java applets designed to run within a web browser
- Asynchronous JavaScript and XML (AJAX)
- Microsoft Visual Basic Script (VBScript)
- Several multimedia file formats, such as AVI and MPEG
- The HTML tags `APPLET`, `BLINK`, `ISINDEX`, `LINK`, `MARQUEE`, and `OBJECT`

Internet Explorer Mobile supports all the basic security types, including the 128-bit encryption used by some web sites.

Start Internet Explorer Mobile

To start Internet Explorer Mobile on a Pocket PC, tap Start |
Internet Explorer or tap Start | Programs | Internet Explorer,
depending on how the Start menu is configured. The program
window looks like the image shown here. The Address bar is at
the top of the program window, and the Command bar menu
options and buttons are at the bottom. A new feature of Internet
Explorer Mobile is a download progress bar at the bottom of the
screen that shows how much of the page has been downloaded to
the Pocket PC.

To start Internet Explorer Mobile on a Smartphone, press
Start | Internet Explorer, which displays your favorite web sites,
as shown in the following image (left). Use the navigation button
to scroll to the favorite that you want to open and then press the
Go button to select. The web site will appear in the browser, as
shown (right).

 *If Internet Explorer is already running on a Smartphone, you will see the last web site
that you opened when switching to the program rather than Favorites.*

Browse Web Sites

The process for browsing web sites in Internet Explorer Mobile is the same as with Internet Explorer.
First, you must connect to the Internet; Chapter 10 provides the instructions for configuring Internet
connections. Windows Mobile automatically connects to the Internet based on how it is configured
and the URL (Uniform Resource Locator—the web site address) you request in Internet Explorer.

 *You can also browse web sites while your Windows Mobile device is in its cradle by
using ActiveSync Desktop Pass Through. You will find more information about Desktop
Pass Through in Chapter 10.*

12

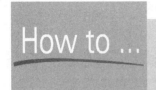

How to ...   Use a Proxy Server

Proxy servers are often used when connecting to the Internet through a LAN, such as that used by a corporate network. They allow multiple users to share the same connection to the Internet and provide added security by masking the TCP/IP address of the client PC.

On Pocket PC 2000 devices, Pocket Internet Explorer must be configured to access the Internet via a proxy server. Tap Tools | Options and then open the Connections tab. Select Use Proxy Server, and enter an address in the Proxy Server HTTP field and a number in the Port field. Ask your network administrator for the address and port number of the proxy server, if you do not know them. If you also access an intranet web site, you must select Bypass Proxy For Local Addresses so that the browser does not try to use the proxy server to access intranet sites.

Pocket PC 2002 moves the proxy server settings from Pocket Internet Explorer to the Work Settings portion of Connection Manager. To configure the proxy server, start Connection Manager by tapping Start | Settings | Connections | Connections. Tap Modify in the Work Settings portion of the screen, and then tap the Proxy Settings tab. Tap the two check boxes on the screen and enter the hostname or IP address of the proxy server on the screen. You will find more instructions for using Connection Manager in Chapter 10.

Windows Mobile 2003 and later changes the proxy server settings slightly and adds an Exceptions list. To configure proxy server settings on Pocket PCs, tap Start | Settings | Connections | Connections, and then tap Set Up My Proxy Server under My Work Network. To add items to the Exceptions list, which lists web site addresses that are not to be retrieved by a proxy server, open the Advanced tab in Connection Manager and tap Exceptions.

You will probably not use a proxy server with Smartphones, because they normally connect to the Internet using your mobile-phone service, which does not use proxy servers. However, you can configure Smartphones to use a proxy server by pressing Start | Settings | Connections | Proxy. To add proxy server information, press Menu | Add, enter the proxy server information, and then press Done.

Use the Address Bar and History

Access a web site by using the Address bar or Favorites. To use the Address bar on a Pocket PC, enter an address in the bar, and then tap the button with the curved arrow to the right of the Address bar.

The Pocket PC Address bar keeps a history of the web sites that you visit. The most recent sites are available from the drop-down list, as shown here.

To open one of these web sites, select the address, and Internet Explorer Mobile will load the page.

The Address bar does not display on Smartphones, so to enter an address for a web site, press Menu | Address Bar and the address of the current web site displays. Use the Back button to delete the contents of the Address bar, and then enter the address of the site that you want to open.

Internet Explorer Mobile also keeps a history of each web page that you visit, which you can use later to return to a page. To view the web page history, tap Menu | History to open the following Pocket PC screen. Tap the arrow next to Page Title to display the page titles or addresses. A similar screen appears on Smartphones, and you open a page by selecting an entry in the list.

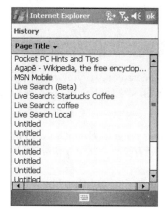

Use Favorites

The second way to access a web page is by selecting a shortcut in Favorites. To access a web page by using its Favorites shortcut, select Menu | Favorites and then select a shortcut listed in the Favorites dialog box.

TIP *On Smartphones the left softkey is assigned to Favorites, so to open a web site, you can simply press Favorites and then select the shortcut of the site you want to open.*

Keep Track of Your Favorite Pages

Web addresses can be difficult to remember and tedious to enter, particularly on a Windows Mobile device. Internet Explorer Mobile solves these problems by providing a place to store the addresses of your favorite web sites. Whenever you want to return to a site, all you need to do is select the site name from the Favorites menu, as described in the preceding section.

Add to Favorites

The first step to store a favorite site on either device is to open the web site in Internet Explorer Mobile. To store a favorite web site, select Menu | Add To Favorites to open this screen:

The web site's information is on the screen, so you can simply select Add to store the site. If you want to change the name of the web site, delete the contents of the Name field and enter the new name before selecting Add.

A quick way to add the current page to Favorites on Pocket PCs is to tap-and-hold on the page and then tap the Add To Favorites option in the pop-up list.

You can group your favorite shortcuts into folders, but you must create the folders first. To create a folder, follow these steps:

1. Select Menu | Favorites.
2. Tap the Add/Delete tab and then New Folder on Pocket PCs; press Menu | Add Folder on Smartphones.
3. Enter a name for the folder.
4. Select Add.

Shortcuts cannot be moved to folders, but if you synchronize Favorites, you can move the shortcuts into folders on a desktop PC and then synchronize those changes back to the device.

Synchronize Favorites

If Microsoft Internet Explorer 4 or later is installed on your desktop computer, you can synchronize favorite links. When you install ActiveSync on your PC, it will add a Mobile Favorites folder to Favorites in Internet Explorer.

To synchronize the links, you must enable the Favorites information type in ActiveSync. Start ActiveSync, connect your device, choose Tools | Options, and then select the box next to Favorites in the list of information types on the Options tab.

During the next synchronization, the contents of the Mobile Favorites folder in Internet Explorer will synchronize with Favorites on the Pocket PC. You can then add a link to either the desktop computer or the device; when you synchronize, the link will appear on both.

Configure Security Options

Internet Explorer Mobile supports the security protocols used by secure sites. To determine whether a web page is secure on Pocket PCs, look for the padlock icon to the left of the Address bar. An open padlock indicates that the page is not secure; a closed padlock, as shown in this image, indicates that the page is secure. The padlock displays at the top of the screen on Smartphones.

12

The Internet Explorer Mobile security settings are not sophisticated. It supports all of the standard security protocols, but does not provide you with the option for turning them on or off. A warning message will display when Internet Explorer Mobile moves from a secure page to an insecure page. To turn on or off that message on Pocket PCs, tap Menu | Tools | Options, select the Security tab, and check the box adjacent to Warn When Changing To A Page That Is Not Secure.

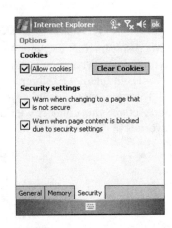

To turn off the security message on Smartphones, press Menu | Tools | Options | General and clear the Warn When Changing To An Unsecure Page check box.

Control Cookies

Cookies are files stored on the device that contain information about your identity and preferences. They are written by a web page and retrieved the next time you open the web page so that information can be tailored to your needs.

To prevent Internet Explorer Mobile on Pocket PCs from accepting cookies, tap Menu | Tools | Options, and then select the Security tab; clear the Allow Cookies check box and tap OK. To clear the cookies already on a Pocket PC, tap Clear Cookies. On Smartphones, press Menu | Tools | Options | General and then clear the Allow Cookies check box.

Change the Display

Unfortunately, the small screen size of Windows Mobile devices affects the way Internet Explorer Mobile displays a web page. Another problem is that the browser does not support as many colors as desktop computers; therefore, graphics may not look the same. Fortunately, you can make changes to help compensate for these problems.

While Internet Explorer Mobile does a good job of displaying web pages so that they are visible on the small Pocket PC and Smartphone screens, it is not perfect. Because of this, you may want to view only sites that are designed for display on the small screen. Todd Ogasawara maintains a directory of such sites at http://ogasawalrus.com/mobileviews/mobileaware/HomePage.

Control How Pages Display

Changing the font size of text on a web page enables more text to appear in the program window. To change the font size, select Menu | Zoom and select a size.

Web pages designed for higher-resolution screens may require horizontal scrolling unless Internet Explorer Mobile changes the display so that it fits completely in the program window. The default view for Internet Explorer Mobile does its best to make the page fit to the screen, but to force all of the web page content to display in one column so that there is no horizontal scrolling, select Menu | View | One Column.

If you need to see a web page as it displays on a desktop computer, select Menu | View | Desktop.

A new feature in Internet Explorer Mobile is Full Screen, which removes most of the components of Internet Explorer so that all you see is the web page, as shown here:

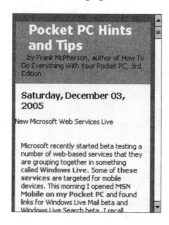

To turn on Full Screen mode, select Menu | View | Full Screen, and to turn off Full Screen mode, press the right softkey and then select Menu | View | Full Screen.

To quickly turn Full Screen mode on or off on a Pocket PC, tap-and-hold on the web page and then tap Full Screen.

While graphics make web pages visually appealing, they can take a long time to download to your device. Often, the words on the web page are all you need. To prevent Internet Explorer Mobile from downloading graphics, select Menu | View | Show Pictures. Pocket PC 2002 has a Command bar button that you can tap to turn images on and off.

When graphics are turned off, you see the locations on the page where they would appear. To select individual images for display, tap-and-hold on the location and tap Show Picture in the pop-up menu.

People all around the world create web pages, and some use alphabets other than the Roman alphabet (which Internet Explorer Mobile calls the Western Alphabet) used in many countries around the world. To display characters of other alphabets, tap Menu | Tools | Options and select an alphabet from the Default Character Set drop-down list on Pocket PCs. On Smartphones, press Menu | Tools | Options | General and then select an alphabet from the Encoding drop-down list.

Change the Home Page

The home page is the web page that opens whenever you start Internet Explorer Mobile on Pocket PCs. At first, this will be set to the default page, which is stored on the device. You may prefer a different home page to open whenever you start the browser.

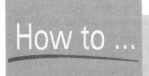

Add Tabbed Browsing to Internet Explorer Mobile

Tabbed browsing makes it easy to move between open web pages and is available in desktop web browsers such as Firefox, but it is not available for Internet Explorer Mobile. If you would like to be able to keep multiple web pages open on your Pocket PC, you can install either Spb Pocket Plus (www.spbsoftwarehouse.com) or MultiIE (www.southwaycorp.net). Both programs enhance Internet Explorer Mobile by providing ways to keep multiple web pages open at the same time.

NOTE   *Internet Explorer Mobile on Smartphones does not have a home page.*

To change the home page, open the new page in Internet Explorer Mobile, tap Menu | Tools | Options, and then tap Use Current to set the new home page. If you later decide to reset the home page to the default, open the Options screen and tap Use Default.

TIP   *As you open web pages on your Pocket PC, they are written to internal storage, and over time they can take up a significant amount of storage space. You can free-up space by tapping Delete Files on the Memory tab of Internet Explorer Mobile options.*

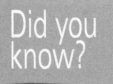

Use Alternative Web Browsers

Internet Explorer Mobile is not the only web browser you can use on your Pocket PC. Several third-party developers have written browsers to provide better performance or more features on Pocket PCs than Internet Explorer Mobile provides. One of these browsers is NetFront from ACCESS, available at www.access-us-inc.com. NetFront has built-in multiwindow browsing and zoom capabilities. Bitstream's ThunderHawk browser (www.bitstream.com) displays web pages in landscape view, so pages appear as originally designed. Finally, ftxPBrowser also provides multiwindow browsing and is free to download from http://park15 .wakwak.com/~ftx/ftxp3e/.

Two popular desktop browsers have Windows Mobile counterparts under development. One is Minimo, which is a port of the Mozilla browser to Pocket PCs. You can find Minimo at www.mozilla.org/projects/minimo/. Another is Opera, which you can find information about at www.opera.com.

Read Web Content Offline

Back in 1996 when Microsoft first released software for handheld computers, it was not easy or inexpensive to connect to the Internet. To enable users to read web content on their devices while disconnected from the Internet, Microsoft created Mobile Channels to synchronize web pages to devices for reading offline.

While it is easier and cheaper today to keep a Pocket PC connected to the Internet, there may still be times when you prefer to read web content offline, such as when you are flying in an airplane. *Really Simple Syndication (RSS)* is a file format that has emerged as a popular way to distribute web content. Since RSS only contains the information you see on a web page, and nothing about how the information appears on the screen, it is easy for programs to legibly display RSS on smaller screens.

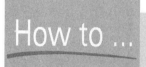 **Write a Weblog Using a Pocket PC**

Today RSS is used to distribute all different types of web content created by professionals, but RSS gained most of its popularity from hobbyists who use it to distribute their content written in weblogs. *Weblogs,* often called *blogs,* are web sites that contain frequently updated information in a reverse chronological order, with the most recent entry appearing at the top of the page. Weblog software makes it easy to publish writing to the Internet, and therefore weblogs have become very popular for personal web sites.

Several different web sites such as Blogger (www.blogger.com) and TypePad (www.typepad .com) provide the software and storage so that you can write and maintain your own weblog. While most weblogs are written from desktop computers, it has become popular to upload pictures and articles from mobile devices and publish them directly on weblogs.

Most weblog sites provide a way to use e-mail to publish articles and pictures to a weblog. Typically, that involves using a special e-mail address that you send the information to, and the software monitors the address and publishes anything that it receives directly to the weblog. In most cases, you can provide a keyword in the subject or body of a message that the software looks for to prevent spam from being published.

A few programs are available for Pocket PCs that you can use to write articles and publish them to a weblog. These programs can only communicate with certain weblog sites that provide ways for programs to communicate with the site. Therefore, before you can use one of these programs with your weblog, you need to find out whether it supports your site's weblog software.

Diarist is a Pocket PC blogging program that works with the .Text, Community Server, Blogger, Blogosphere, dasBlog, and BlogX weblogging software programs. You can download Diarist from www.kevdaly.co.nz/Software/Blogging/Diarist.aspx. Pocket SharpMT works with MovableType and TypePad and is available at www.randyrants.com/sharpmt/.

12

The programs you use to view an RSS file are called *RSS readers,* and they are also called *news readers* or *RSS aggregators.* RSS includes a date and time stamp for each item that is added to the file, and RSS readers use that information to display only new items that you have not yet read. By displaying only new information, RSS readers act in a manner similar to newspapers. The files are called RSS feeds, analogous to the wire feeds newspapers use to receive articles from around the world, and you subscribe to an RSS feed by adding the feed's URL to an RSS reader.

You will find two types of RSS readers: web sites and programs. Both are available for desktop computers and Windows Mobile devices. When you use RSS reader web sites, servers retrieve the RSS feed and display it on a web page, and you use Internet Explorer Mobile to view the page on a Pocket PC or Smartphone. To use an RSS reader web site, you need to connect to the Internet, which appears to defeat the purpose of using RSS. However, you can use the same RSS reader web site on desktop computers and Windows Mobile devices, making it easier to keep track of the feeds that you have already read.

Bloglines (www.bloglines.com) is a very popular web site RSS reader that works well on desktop computers and devices. Another web site that works well in Internet Explorer Mobile is NewsMob (http://mobile.newsmob.com).

RSS reader programs install on Windows Mobile devices and download subscriptions so that you can read them while not connected to the Internet. To download the subscriptions, the device needs to connect to the Internet, either via an ActiveSync connection or a direct connection to the Internet. One RSS reader program, RSS Sync, adds an information type to ActiveSync so that it synchronizes RSS subscriptions to Pocket PCs in the same way that Contacts and Calendar synchronize. Table 12-1 lists the RSS reader programs that you can download and install on your Pocket PC or Smartphone.

XML   Many web sites display an orange XML icon indicating that they provide an RSS feed. Normally, when you click the icon, the RSS feed loads in the web browser, and while the feed doesn't appear to provide useful information, you need the URL of the feed to add it to the subscriptions in an RSS reader. Typically, all you need to do is copy the URL from the browser Address bar and paste it into the RSS reader.

Name	URL
BeetzStream SmartRss	www.beetzstream.com
A4Pocket Newsreader	www.a4pocket.com
pRSSreader	http://pda.jasnapaka.com/prssr/
RSS Sync	www.viksoe.dk/code/rsssync.htm
NewsBreak	www.iliumsoft.com/site/nw/newsbreak.htm
PocketFeed	www.furrygoat.com/Misc/Software.html
Egress	www.garishkernels.net

TABLE 12-1   RSS Reader Programs for Windows Mobile

Download Podcasts to Your Windows Mobile Device

Podcasts are audio file recordings distributed to computers using RSS. People who listen to podcasts normally use software called a *podcatcher* that automatically downloads podcasts to a PC and then synchronizes them to media players such as the Apple iPod. You can then listen to the podcast at your leisure.

There are several methods for downloading podcasts to a device. You can use Doppler to download podcasts, and import them into Windows Media Player. Once the podcasts are in Windows Media Player, you can synchronize them to a device by following the instructions in Chapter 7. You can download Doppler from www.dopplerradio.net/.

BeetzStream SmartRss, available at www.beetzstream.com, is an RSS reader program that can also automatically download podcasts. Smartfeed is a podcatcher designed specifically for the Windows Mobile platform. It runs on Pocket PCs and Smartphones, and you can download it from www.smartfeed.org.

Since podcasts are distributed using RSS, the method of subscribing to podcasts is similar to subscribing to RSS feeds. If you are interested in listening to podcasts, you will find a large directory of them at www.ipodder.org.

Some RSS reader programs provide a wizard that makes it easy to subscribe to feeds. You will also find some web sites that provide lists of RSS feeds that you can subscribe to, such as Syndic8 at www.syndic8.com.

Wrapping Up

Internet Explorer Mobile enables you to access web sites when you are away from a desktop computer. It has most of the features that you use to view web pages while connected to the Internet, and you can download RSS feeds to a Windows Mobile device to read when it is not connected to the Internet.

Now that you have seen how you can connect your Windows Mobile Pocket PC or Smartphone to networks to send and receive e-mail and browse web sites, it's time for you to learn how Windows Mobile can help you stay organized. In the next chapter, you will learn how to use Outlook Mobile to keep track of appointments, addresses, and tasks.

12

Part IV

Make the Most Out of Windows Mobile

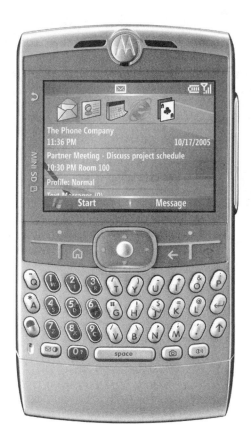

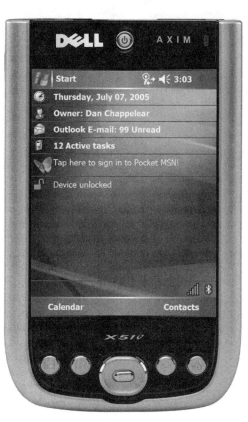

Chapter 13 Get Organized

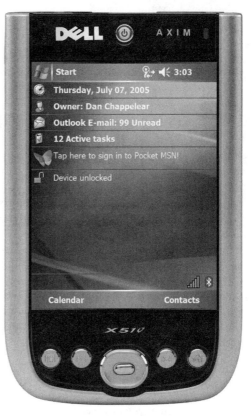

How to...

- Schedule appointments
- Store addresses
- Track tasks
- Search for appointments, addresses, and tasks

Today's fast pace and hectic schedules have made time management an important skill. The fundamental tools of managing time include a calendar for appointments, an address book for contact information, and a task list to keep track of what needs to be done. Despite all of the capabilities that Windows Mobile provides, you probably bought your device primarily to help manage these three things.

In this chapter, you learn how to use the programs included in Outlook Mobile: Calendar, Contacts, and Tasks on Pocket PCs and Smartphones. You will probably use each of these programs frequently throughout the day to enter and look up information. With Calendar's recurrence scheduling capability, creating an appointment that occurs on the same day and time every month is as easy as completing one screen, eliminating the need to write the appointment on multiple entries in a day planner.

Calendar and Contacts are integrated with Messaging, the e-mail program on your device that is covered in Chapter 11. From Calendar, you can schedule a meeting with people by retrieving their e-mail addresses from Contacts and e-mailing a meeting request. From Contacts, you can send an e-mail simply by selecting an entry in the Contacts list and tapping a button.

Appointments, addresses, and tasks can be sent to other devices by using the infrared port, making it easy to share information with other people. Perhaps even more important, as you read in Chapter 7, the information in these three programs can be synchronized with your desktop computer, enabling you to work with the same information whether you are sitting at your desk or in a taxi cab.

Of all the programs on your Windows Mobile device, Calendar, Contacts, and Tasks may be the ones that you use most frequently. Each program contains information that you use constantly throughout the day. Need to schedule an appointment? Start Calendar. Need to look up an address? Start Contacts. Been given another assignment? Start Tasks.

You will want to retrieve the information stored in these three programs quickly, and Windows Mobile is designed to help you achieve that goal. By default, shortcuts for Calendar, Contacts, and Tasks are placed in the Pocket PC Start menu. If the shortcuts are not in the Start menu, you will find them in Programs, which you open by tapping Start | Programs.

Each program may also be assigned to a Pocket PC hardware button, except on Pocket PC Phone Editions, which typically assign just Calendar and Contacts to hardware buttons, with two other buttons assigned to operate the phone. You can use the button settings program on the Pocket PC to change the assignment of all the hardware buttons.

If you assign Calendar, Contacts, and Tasks to hardware buttons, consider removing these programs' shortcuts from the Start menu. By doing so, you make space to add other programs to the Start menu for quicker access.

The instructions for starting Calendar, Contacts, and Tasks in this section use the Start menu.

Schedule Appointments Using Calendar

The Calendar program in Outlook Mobile is the Windows Mobile companion to the Calendar folder in Microsoft Outlook. ActiveSync synchronizes appointments that you enter in Calendar on Windows Mobile devices with the Calendar folder in Outlook or Exchange, as explained in Chapter 7. To enter an appointment, first start Calendar by tapping Start | Calendar, which opens the program window shown in Figure 13-1.

View Your Schedule in Calendar

You can view your schedule by day, week, month, and year. Calendar also provides an Agenda view that summarizes your appointments for each day.

Smartphones do not have a Day view, so you must use the Agenda view to see one day's worth of appointments.

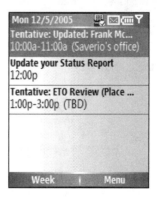

FIGURE 13-1   Calendar on a Pocket PC (left) and on a Smartphone (right)

Switching Views

The method for switching among Calendar views is different for Windows Mobile 2003 and Windows Mobile 5. In each release, pressing the Calendar hardware button cycles through views, but Windows Mobile 2003 also has the following five buttons on the Command bar:

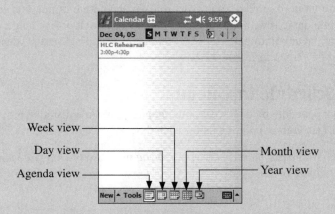

Week view

Day view

Agenda view

Month view

Year view

The left softkey is assigned to the different Calendar views in Windows Mobile 5. Press or tap the left softkey button to switch between views. The button name changes to show the name of the next Calendar view that will display when you press the button.

Each Pocket PC view has buttons, as shown here, used for moving forward and backward and for returning to the current date:

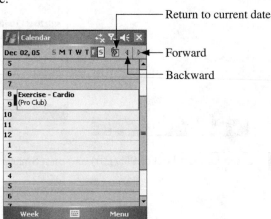

Return to current date

Forward

Backward

You will not find these buttons on Smartphones. Instead, press the navigation button left or right to move forward and backward by a day through the calendar.

You can press the navigation button left or right to move forward and backward by a day through the calendar in the Day and Week view. Press the navigation button up or down to scroll the screen up and down.

View a Daily Agenda

The Agenda view lists all of the appointments that you have for the day in a list, and it is the only view that shows a day's worth of appointments on Smartphones. To display the Agenda view, press or tap the left softkey until you see the following:

On Pocket PCs, you can switch directly to the Agenda view by tapping Menu | View | Agenda. When the Agenda view is showing, the left softkey on Pocket PCs shows that the Day view will display when you press the button. On Smartphones, it shows that the Week view will display.

The subject, start and end times, and location of each appointment appear in the list. Select an appointment to view more of the appointment details.

View One Day of Appointments on Pocket PCs

To display your schedule in the Day view, press or tap the left softkey until you see the following:

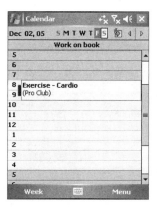

13

You can switch directly to the Day view by tapping Menu | View | Day. When the Day view is showing, the left softkey shows that the Week view will display when you press the button.

All-day events, which are items that you associate with a day but are not scheduled for a time, appear at the top of the screen. An example of an all-day event is an anniversary or holiday, or as shown in the previous illustration, Work on book.

Appointments are displayed in the middle of the screen, and by default are listed in one-hour slots. The slot sizes can be changed to 30-minute increments by tapping Menu | Options and then tapping the Show Half Hour Slots check box. More space is taken up on the screen when you use half-hour slots. Tap the date at the top of the screen to display a date picker, which you can use to select a different date to be displayed.

NOTE *Remember that you can use the buttons on the screen to return to the current date or move backward and forward through the dates.*

The left edge of the appointment shows a bar indicating its status. An appointment shown as free time by a white bar means that another appointment could be scheduled in that time slot. Appointments can be labeled Free, Tentative, Busy, or Out Of Office, as explained later in the chapter, and each is shown with a different color bar.

Icons are used to provide information about an appointment, such as whether a reminder is set or whether the appointment recurs. By default, the icons are turned off, and they can be turned on by tapping Menu | Options | Appointments to display the Appointments tab of the Options dialog box. Tap each of the icons that you want to be displayed so that the icon turns dark, as shown here, and then tap OK.

The icons then appear with the appointment in the Day view:

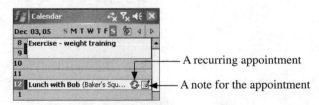

A recurring appointment

A note for the appointment

Each appointment can include more information than is displayed in the Day view. To see more details, tap the appointment to open it in Summary view, as shown here:

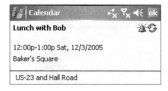

Summary view provides all the information about the appointment on one easy-to-read screen. Tap OK to close the Summary view.

View a Week of Appointments

The Week view displays appointments for the workweek, with each day displayed as a column:

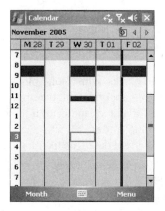

To switch to this view, tap Menu | View | Week, or press the left softkey until the Week view displays. Appointments appear as blocks in different colors, indicating statuses of Free, Busy, Tentative, and Out Of Office. All-day events are indicated by a bar running down the column. To display the appointment information, tap a block to show the information at the top of the screen.

You can change the number of days displayed in the Week view by tapping Menu | Options and then selecting either 5-Day Week, 6-Day Week, or 7-Day Week in the Week View drop-down list. Tap OK to save the changes and close the Options dialog box.

To move to a different week in the year on a Pocket PC, tap the month at the top of the screen to display a date picker, which you use to select a different date to be displayed. Switch years by tapping the year at the top of the screen, and select a year from the drop-down list that is displayed. Tap the column head of a day in the Week view to switch to the Day view for that day.

To move to a different week in the year on a Smartphone, press Menu | Go To Date, enter a date, and press Done. Use the navigation button to move to a date in the week, and press the navigation button to display the appointments for that day.

13

View a Month of Appointments

To display the calendar one month at a time, tap Menu | View | Month or press the left softkey until the Month view displays:

Morning and afternoon appointments and an all-day event

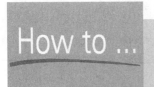

Current date

Morning and afternoon appointments

Morning appointment

All-day event

Afternoon appointment

Appointments are displayed as filled blocks, with a solid block indicating morning and afternoon appointments. If a day has only a morning appointment, the upper-left corner of the filled block is displayed. A filled-in lower-right corner of a block indicates afternoon appointments. All-day events are indicated by an empty block with a blue border.

A black box on a date indicates the current date. Tap the month at the top of the screen to display a drop-down list that you can use to select a different month to be displayed. Change the year by tapping the year at the top of the screen and selecting a different year from the drop-down list. To switch the display to the Day view for a specific date in a month, tap the date on the calendar. On a Smartphone, use the navigation button to select a date that you want to view.

How to ... Display Week Numbers in Month View

Windows Mobile has the ability to display week numbers in the Month view. To turn on week numbers, tap Menu | Options, tap the Show Week Numbers check box, and tap OK. In Week view, the number displays at the top right of the screen, and in Month view, the week numbers are displayed along the left edge of the screen.

European users who use a Julian-type week number scheme will notice a bug in the week numbers that causes the last week of the year to use the wrong numbers. For example, the last week of 2008 shows as week 1, while the last week of 2004 shows as week 53.

View a Year of Appointments on Pocket PCs

The Year view displays every month of a year. To switch to the Year view, tap Menu | View | Year or press the left softkey until the display changes to look like the following:

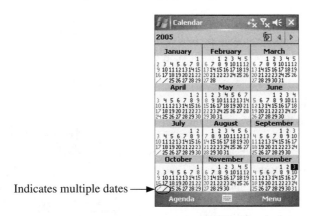

Indicates multiple dates ⟶

The current day is indicated by a black square. Each month in the Year view is limited to five lines, so a sixth line of dates is indicated by a slash (/).

To display a different year, tap the year at the top of the screen and select another year in the drop-down list. To switch the display to the Month view for a specific month in the calendar, tap the name of the month. You can switch to the Day view for a specific date by tapping a date in the Year view.

Create an Appointment in Calendar

To create an appointment in Calendar, select Menu | New Appointment, or on a Pocket PC, tap-and-hold anywhere on the screen and then tap New Appointment to open the Appointment dialog box, shown here. When the dialog box opens, the Subject field is selected, and the Pocket PC Software Input Panel is open and ready for you to enter a description for the appointment. Select each field on the dialog box that you want to complete, and enter information where appropriate.

 Although you can create appointments on Smartphones, a faster way to add appointments to Smartphones is by synchronization with a desktop PC or Exchange server.

Enter a description of the appointment in the Subject field, and enter a location for the appointment in the Location field. On Pocket PCs, the Location drop-down list contains locations that were previously entered. If the new appointment is at a location that you already entered, you can select it from this list.

The Subject field is also a drop-down list that contains words commonly used in appointments. Unfortunately, the list doesn't change, and there is no way to add words to the drop-down list. Press the navigation button in the Subject field on Smartphones to open the list of words.

On Pocket PCs, dates are entered in the Starts and Ends fields by tapping the date that is displayed to open the date picker, shown here. Tap a date on the calendar to select it for either field. You can use the arrows at the top of the calendar to move backward and forward a month at a time, or tap the month to jump to another month that appears in a pop-up menu. The starting date that you select automatically appears in the Ends field, though you can change the date by tapping the field.

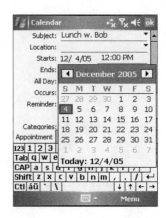

Starting and ending times are displayed in drop-down lists on Pocket PCs, which contain times in half-hour increments. Tap the values in the drop-down lists to set the starting and ending times for the appointment. If you opened the dialog box from within the Day view, the Starts and Ends fields contain the date and time selected in the Day view.

A quick way to enter the starting and ending times from the Day view is to select a group of time slots and then tap New. The dialog box opens with the Starts and Ends fields populated with the starting and ending times that you selected in the Day view.

On Smartphones, appointment dates and times are entered directly in each field. Use the navigation button to move to each field. When you enter a date field, it contains the current date, which you change by simply entering numbers from the keypad. Press the navigation button left or right to move the cursor in the date field, and press the navigation button up or down to move from field to field.

By default, Calendar creates appointments that have starting and ending times, but all-day events do not have these times. To create an all-day event on Pocket PCs, tap the All Day field and select Yes from the drop-down list that appears. The times in the Starts and Ends fields will be removed. On Smartphones, simply press the navigation button to put a check in the All Day Event checkbox.

You can schedule an appointment for multiple dates by selecting a recurrence pattern. The default setting is for each appointment to occur once, as indicated by the value in the Occurs field. To schedule the appointment for multiple dates, select the Occurs field to display the items shown here. (The items that appear in this menu vary according to the day of the week, day of the month, and date that you select.)

The appointment shown in the preceding illustration is being scheduled for Sunday, December 4, 2005. Select Every Sunday to schedule the appointment at the same time on every Sunday. Select Day 4 Of Every Month to schedule the appointment for the fourth day of each month. If you want to schedule the appointment for that specific date—in this case, December 4—every year, select Every December 4.

If none of the items in the drop-down list meets your requirements, tap <Edit Pattern...> to start the Recurrence wizard. The <Edit Pattern...> option is not available on Smartphones. The Recurrence wizard has three dialog boxes, the first of which is shown here. In this dialog box, you set the starting and ending times for the appointment. Typically, the times that you originally set appear here, and they are the times you likely want to use. If the starting time is correct, you can change the ending time by expanding the Duration drop-down list and tapping a value in the list. Tap Remove Recurrence to close the dialog box and delete the recurrence.

You can change the times in the dialog box by tapping them to open another dialog box; clocks and times on the left side show the starting time, and the clock and time on the right is the ending time. You can change the times by tapping the clock faces to move the hands or tapping the up and down arrows on the digital display. Tap OK to save the times that you select.

Tap Next to open the second dialog box of the Recurrence wizard, and tap the buttons along the top of the dialog box to define a recurrence time. When you tap Daily, two radio buttons appear. Tap the Every Weekday radio button to schedule the appointment on every weekday. To schedule the appointment for multiple days, tap Every and then select a number from the Day(s) drop-down list.

Tapping Weekly changes the dialog box, as shown next. Tap the days in the week that you want to schedule the appointment; you can select more than one day. Choose a value from the Week(s) drop-down list to schedule the appointment for several weeks on the days that you select.

13

Tap Monthly to define a monthly recurrence pattern, as shown next. The pattern can be defined for a specific date in a month (such as the twenty-first), for a select number of months, or for a day in a week (such as the third Monday) for a select number of months. Tap the radio button of the option you want, and select the values from the drop-down lists.

Tap Yearly to define a yearly recurrence pattern, as shown next. The yearly pattern is similar to the monthly pattern. Your options are to schedule the appointment for the same date each year, or for the day in a week of the month that you select. Tap the radio button of the option that you want, and select the values from the drop-down lists.

Tap Next to define the starting and ending dates of the recurrence pattern. Select the starting date by using the The Pattern Starts drop-down list. Three options are available for defining the end date: the recurrence pattern does not end, it ends on a date that you select, or it ends after a select number of occurrences. Tap the radio button of the option that you want and select the appropriate values from the drop-down lists.

After you select the starting and ending dates of the recurring appointment, tap Finish to return to the Appointment dialog box. The Occurs field will contain <Edit Pattern...> to indicate that a customized recurrence pattern has been created for the appointment.

The Reminder field on the dialog box sets the time when you will be notified about the upcoming appointment. Turn the reminder notification on or off by tapping the field and selecting either None or Remind Me from the drop-down list. The Reminder field on Smartphones contains one line; press the navigation button to open a screen of reminder options, shown here. Select None to turn off the reminder, or select one of the times in the list and then press Done.

On Pocket PCs, the second line of the Reminder field shows the amount of time prior to the appointment that notification occurs. For example, a reminder can be set for one day or 15 minutes before the appointment. Tap the number in the field to set the amount of time, and tap the minutes portion to select either minutes, hours, days, or weeks.

13

TIP   *To change the default time for reminders, tap Menu | Options | Appointments and select values from the Set Reminders drop-down lists.*

Appointments assigned to categories can be filtered in any of Calendar's views by tapping Menu | Filter. To filter appointments, you must first assign them to a category, which you do by setting a value for the Categories field in the Appointment dialog box. Tap the field to display a list of categories, and then tap the check box next to each category that you want assigned to the appointment.

NOTE   *Smartphones do not have Categories or Attendees fields.*

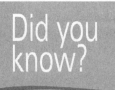

Time Zones Affect Appointments

If you change the time zone on your Windows Mobile device, you also change the times for appointments, because every appointment time considers the current time zone setting. For example, if you are creating an appointment in the Eastern time zone for 10 A.M., changing the Clock to the Central time zone causes the appointment time to change to 9 A.M.

Unfortunately, the way Windows Mobile treats time zones means that you have to keep in mind where you will be on the day of your appointment. If, for example, you are in New York today, and you are going to be in Chicago tomorrow for a 10 A.M. appointment, you can choose to not change the clock when you are in Chicago or you can create the appointment for 11 A.M. Eastern Time.

As you can tell, appointment times can become difficult to manage for those who travel. Web Information Solutions provides a Pocket PC program called WebIS Toolbox, which resets appointments to their original times after you change the Pocket PC Clock. WebIS Toolbox can be downloaded from www.webis.net.

The Attendees field is used to create a meeting and is explained in the next section. The Status field is a drop-down list containing Free, Tentative, Busy, or Out Of Office. The item that you select from the list changes the color of the bar on the left side of the appointment in the Day view, and it is used to indicate how the time should be treated when scheduling other appointments.

Selecting the Sensitivity field displays a drop-down list containing Normal, Personal, Private, and Confidential. If you select Private, the appointment will be private in Outlook and Exchange after it is synchronized with a desktop computer. Other Outlook and Exchange users may view Normal appointments.

Enter Notes for Appointments

Appointment notes can contain text, drawings, recordings, or writing in digital ink. To enter a note, tap the Notes tab on Pocket PCs or press the Notes field on Smartphones to display the portion of the Appointment dialog box that functions in a manner similar to the Notes program explained in Chapter 14.

To make a recording, press and hold the Hardware Record button. Your device will beep and begin recording. Stop the recording by releasing the button. Once the recording is finished, an icon is inserted into the note, which you tap to play back the recording.

NOTE   *You cannot attach recordings to appointments on Smartphones.*

Schedule a Meeting Using Calendar

In Calendar, meetings are appointments that include people. When you create a meeting in Calendar, an e-mail containing the meeting request is sent to the people that you select in the Appointment dialog box. To send the e-mail, Messaging must be configured with an e-mail account, as outlined in Chapter 11.

NOTE *You cannot schedule meetings on Smartphones.*

The process of creating a meeting is the same as creating an appointment, but with one additional step: you select participants in the Attendees field. Create a new appointment and complete the fields in the dialog box as needed. Tap the Attendees field to display the following dialog box, which lists names and e-mail addresses:

The names listed in the dialog box are entries in Contacts that contain an e-mail address. A name may appear in the list more than once if it has more than one e-mail address. Tap the name of the person to select him or her as a meeting participant. To add another name, tap Add and then tap the name of the second person to attend the meeting. When you are done adding names, tap OK.

Complete the fields on the Appointment dialog box and tap OK to create the meeting. The meeting is displayed in the Calendar Day view just like an appointment, but it contains a graphic to indicate that it is a meeting, as shown here:

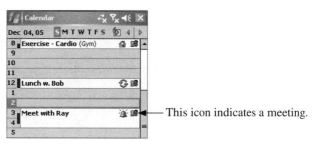

This icon indicates a meeting.

13

If you do not see the icon, tap Menu | Options | Appointments and check to see that the meeting icon is selected.

An e-mail message of the meeting request is placed in the Outbox of the e-mail service that you select in Calendar. To select the e-mail service in Calendar, tap Menu | Options | Appointments and select the service in the Send Meeting Requests Via field. The e-mail message will be sent the next time you use Inbox to send and receive e-mail, unless you select ActiveSync for the e-mail service. If ActiveSync is selected, the request will move to Outlook during the next synchronization.

Edit the Appointment Category List

Appointments can be filtered on categories so that only appointments belonging to a category are displayed. You assign categories in the Appointment dialog box while creating the appointment. The Category list contains several default items and is shared by Calendar, Contacts, and Tasks.

Smartphones do not support appointment categories.

You add items to the Category list, shown here, when you are creating an appointment or editing an existing appointment. Tap the Categories field on the Appointment dialog box to open the Categories dialog box. Tap New, enter the new category item in the box, and tap Done. While there isn't an option to directly delete a category, they are automatically deleted when all appointments, contacts, and tasks assigned to them are removed from the device.

Filter Appointments by Categories

Filters help you focus on specific groups of appointments by displaying only those entries that belong to a particular category that you select. To use filters, you must have assigned appointments to categories.

Smartphones do not support appointment filters.

To filter appointments on a category, tap Menu | Filter and then tap the name of the category that you want to display. If you want to display more than one category, tap Menu | Filter | More, tap the check boxes of the categories you want, and then tap Done.

A category does not appear in the Filter menu if no appointments are assigned to the category.

Clear the filter and display all appointments by tapping Menu | Filter | All Appointments.

Edit and Delete Appointments

Select appointments listed in the Day and Agenda views to display the appointment in Summary view. You can also open the Summary view from the Week view by selecting the appointment block.

To edit the appointment, select the Edit command at the bottom of the screen. The Appointment dialog box opens for you to make any changes by either selecting the fields or tapping the Notes tab on Pocket PCs. Tap OK or press Done to save the changes.

Appointments listed in Day, Week, or Agenda view on Pocket PCs can be copied, moved, or deleted by tapping-and-holding. Tap-and-hold the stylus on the appointment that you want to edit, and then tap Cut, Copy, or Delete Appointment from the pop-up menu. When you tap Delete Appointment, a confirmation dialog box asks whether you want to delete the appointment.

To paste an appointment that you cut or copied, tap-and-hold the stylus on an open time slot in either Day, Week, or Agenda view, and then tap Paste in the pop-up menu that appears.

Find Appointments in Calendar

To search for appointments in Calendar on Pocket PCs, tap Start | Programs | Search to open the following dialog box:

Enter the word or phrase that you are searching for in the Search For field, expand the Type field drop-down list, tap Calendar, and then tap Search.

Search will search through all appointments and list the entries containing the word or phrase in the Results portion of the dialog box. Tap an entry in the list to open the Summary view of the appointment; when you tap OK on the Summary View dialog box, you return to the Search dialog box.

You can search for entries in other Outlook Mobile programs by tapping their entry in the Type drop-down list or by tapping the Outlook Mobile entry to search across all the programs. The procedure for searching and viewing each type is the same.

13

Smartphones do not have a built-in ability to search for items, but you can add this functionality by installing SmartphoneFind, available from Syncdata at www.syncdata.it.

Send and Receive Appointments via Infrared

Any appointment in Calendar can be sent to another Pocket PC or Smartphone using the infrared port on the device. To send and receive appointments with infrared, follow these steps:

1. Start Calendar and select the appointment that you want to send, and then select Menu | Beam or Menu | Beam Appointment on Smartphones.

2. Line up the infrared ports of the two devices.

If for some reason the receiving device is not receiving the appointment, tap Start | Settings | Connections | Beam and make sure the Pocket PC is set to receive incoming beams. If you use an external keyboard, it may also interfere with receiving infrared beams, so check the keyboard software.

Once the connection is established, the appointment is transferred and the sending device displays the following dialog box:

The receiving device displays a notification that a device is sending you an appointment and asks you whether you want to add it to Calendar. Select Yes to add the appointment to Calendar or No to not add the appointment.

Configure Calendar Options

Several Calendar options can be set by tapping Menu | Options to open the Options dialog box.

By default, the first day of the week is Sunday, but you can change the default by selecting a day from the 1st Day Of Week drop-down list. To set the default number of weeks in the Week view, expand the drop-down list and tap 5-Day Week, 6-Day Week, or 7-Day Week.

To have Calendar show half-hour slots or week numbers, tap the check boxes for each in the dialog box. To have Calendar automatically set reminders for new appointments, tap the Set Reminders For New Items check box on the Appointments tab. Select the default time for the reminder notification by tapping the appropriate drop-down lists.

Tap the information icons on the Appointments tab that you want to be displayed on appointments in the Day view. The dark icons will be displayed on the appointment. Meeting announcements are sent using the Inbox e-mail service that you select in the Send Meeting Requests Via drop-down list on the Appointments tab.

The Options screen on Smartphones does not have an Appointments tab, nor do Smartphones support Category icons or the ability to send meeting requests.

Store and Retrieve Addresses Using Contacts

13

The Contacts program is the Windows Mobile companion to the Contacts folder in Microsoft Outlook. ActiveSync synchronizes addresses that you enter in Contacts on the device with the Contacts folder in Outlook or Exchange, as explained in Chapter 7. To enter an address, first start Contacts by tapping Start | Contacts, which opens the program window shown in Figure 13-2.

If you are at the Pocket PC Today screen or the Home Screen on a Smartphone, the right softkey is assigned to Contacts, which you can press to start the Contacts program.

View Addresses in Contacts

Your contacts are listed in alphabetical order by last name in the program window. At the top of the Pocket PC program window shown in Figure 13-2 are the alphabetical tabs, which you tap to move through the list. Tapping a tab multiple times moves through contacts by jumping to entries that start with each letter on a tab. Smartphones do not have these alphabetical tabs.

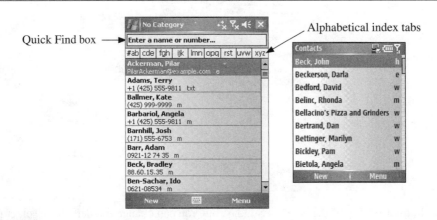

Quick Find box

Alphabetical index tabs

FIGURE 13-2   Contacts List view on a Pocket PC (left) and on a Smartphone (right)

TIP

Press-and-hold the navigation button, and after a brief pause the alphabet will scroll in large letters. Release the button to scroll to the first contact matching the letter displayed on the screen.

The Quick Find box above the alphabetical tabs on Pocket PCs is used to find names in the list. Tap the box and start entering a name. As you enter letters, the display scrolls and eventually shows the name that you are entering. A similar function exists on Smartphones; start pressing the numeric keys containing the letters of a contact's name and, as you do, contacts containing those letters display, as shown here:

Each contact in the list is displayed with the last name and first name, unless it is a business, in which case the business name is displayed. Also included with each contact on Pocket PCs is a phone number or e-mail address, indicated by a letter to the right of the contact information.

If a contact has multiple telephone numbers and e-mail addresses, the work telephone number is displayed by default. To change what is included with the contact in the list, press the navigation button left or right until the desired phone number or e-mail address displays.

To view the address information for a contact, tap its entry in the Contacts list to display the Contacts Summary view:

Tap OK to close the Summary view and return to the Contacts list. The Summary view displays only information that has been entered for a contact.

New Features in Contacts for Windows Mobile 5

Outlook Mobile Contacts has some of the most notable new features in Windows Mobile 5. It supports the Picture field available in Outlook 2003, and ActiveSync will synchronize pictures that you assign to a contact in Outlook 2003 to Pocket PCs and Smartphones. Pocket PC Phone Editions and Smartphones display a contact's picture when you receive a call from the contact, and the picture displays in the Phone application when you make a call to the contact.

You can assign unique ring tones to your contacts by selecting an option in a contact's Ring Tone field. When a Pocket PC Phone Edition or Smartphone receives a call from the contact, it plays the ring tone that you assigned to the contact, which helps you determine who is calling.

In addition to the Picture and Ring Tone fields, Contacts now supports all of the fields available to Outlook 2003 Contacts. For example, you can enter up to three instant messaging IDs. When you view a contact in Summary view, each mode of contact, such as mobile phone or home phone, has a different icon to easily differentiate each one.

13

Change the Contact List View

To view your contacts by company, select Menu | View By | Company to change the List view, as shown here. Each company name is listed alphabetically with a number to the right indicating the number of contacts you have included for that company. Tap the company name to display the contacts. Tap the company name a second time to collapse the Contacts List view.

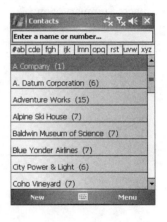

Tapping Menu | View By | Name switches the List view back to the default listing. Outlook's File As setting defines the default listing. Unfortunately, to change the default view, you have to edit each of your contacts in Outlook. If you wish to make this change in Outlook, do the following:

1. Start Outlook.

2. Open the contact that you want to change.

3. Click the File As drop-down field:

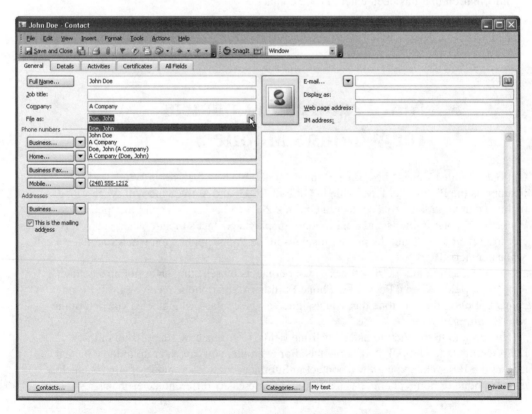

4. Select the option that you want, and click the Save And Close button. The next time you synchronize your device, the contact will be listed using the option you selected.

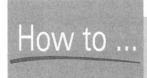

Have More Power over Contacts

While some will find By Company view in Contacts useful, others will find that it still does not provide the power they want over how contacts are listed. Fortunately, third-party programs address this shortcoming.

Pocket Informant by Web Information Solutions is a popular Pocket PC alternative to all the Outlook Mobile programs. It can display contacts by first name, last name, and company name. This program also provides an Agenda view that lists appointments and tasks for each day, and more informative week and month views. You can also link appointments, contacts, and tasks to each other and to files on your Pocket PC. More information and a trial version of the program are available at www.pocketinformant.com.

Another popular Pocket PC program is Agenda Fusion from Developer One. It also can display contacts by first name, last name, or company name. You can find out more about Agenda Fusion at www.developerone.com.

Create New Contacts

To create a new contact, select New to open the Contacts dialog box:

As you can see, the Pocket PC dialog box has two tabs: Details and Notes. The Details tab contains all of the fields available for a contact. Tap each field that you want to complete and then enter the information. The Notes field can contain text, drawings, recordings, or writing in digital ink.

NOTE *All Contacts fields display in one screen on Smartphones. The fields are also ordered differently, with Phone Number fields immediately following the Name field.*

The Name and Address fields in the Details tab each have a details indicator (a black triangle at the end of the field) that you can tap to display the different parts of the field. You can enter the information directly in the field, or tap the details indicator and enter the various parts of the field separately, as shown here:

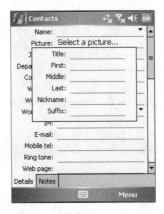

The Name field on Smartphones is slightly different and provides separate fields for First and Last names. Likewise, separate fields are provided on Smartphones for the different parts of an address.

Telephone numbers on the dialog box automatically include the area code that you define in the Contacts Options dialog box. To change the area code, tap Menu | Options, enter the number in the Area Code field, and tap OK.

 Contacts on Smartphones does not have an Options menu item.

Tap the Categories field on Pocket PCs to display the Category list. Assign the contact to one or more categories by tapping the check box next to the items in the list. If the category that you want to use is not available in the list, tap New, enter a category in the empty box, and tap Done.

To enter a contact note, tap the Notes tab to display the portion of the Contacts dialog box that functions in a manner similar to the Notes program explained in Chapter 14.

 Windows Mobile 2003SE and earlier supported the ability to attach voice recordings to contacts, but this is no longer supported in Windows Mobile 5. If you have an older device, press and hold the Hardware Record button. Your device will beep and begin recording. Stop the recording by releasing the button. Once the recording is finished, an icon is inserted into the note.

When you have finished entering all the information for the contact, tap OK and the contact will be added to the Contacts list.

Edit and Delete Contacts

To edit a contact, first select its entry in the Contacts list to open the Summary view. Then select Edit. Tap the Notes tab on Pocket PCs to edit the contact's notes.

When you tap some fields on Pocket PCs, such as the contact name or address, in the Summary view, the Edit view opens with the field highlighted.

To copy or delete a selected contact, select Menu | Copy Contact or Menu | Delete Contact. When you create a copy of a contact that you selected, it is inserted into the Contacts list. You can then edit the entry that was added to the Contacts list.

Entries in the Contacts list on Pocket PCs can be copied or deleted by tapping-and-holding. Tap-and-hold the stylus on the contact that you want to edit, and then tap Copy Contact or Delete Contact from the pop-up menu.

Filter Contacts by Categories

Filters help you focus on specific groups of contacts by displaying only entries belonging to a category that you select. For filters to be useful, you must assign contacts to categories.

To filter contacts on a category, tap Menu | Filter and then select the category that you want to display. If the category is not in the menu, select More, select the check box next to the

 **Create a Contact Template**

You might find yourself creating many contacts with the same information, such as contacts for people who work for the same company. One trick you can use to help speed up entering these types of contacts is to create a template that contains all of the duplicate information. By using the template, you save yourself the time spent entering the same information repeatedly. Here is what you do:

1. Select New to create a new contact.
2. Enter the company name as the first name of the contact, and enter **_Template** for the last name. By using an underscore for the first character of the last name, you ensure that the template appears at the top of the Contacts list.
3. Complete the remaining details, such as the work address and category that are shared by all the contacts.
4. Tap OK to add the template to the Contacts list.

The template contact appears at the top of the list. To create a new contact using the template, copy the template. Select the new copy that was added to the list, and edit the fields as needed for the new contact you are creating.

13

categories that you want to display, and then select Done. The name of the filter displays on the Navigation bar, such as Personal shown in the image here:

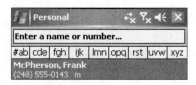

Clear the filter and display all contacts by tapping Menu | Filter | All Contacts, and the category name on the Navigation bar changes to Contacts.

Tap the Recently Viewed entry in the Filter menu to display the contacts you have recently added, edited, or viewed.

Find Contacts

To search for entries in Contacts, tap Start | Programs| Search to open the Search dialog box. Enter the word or phrase that you are searching for in the Search For field, expand the Type field drop-down list, tap Contacts, and then tap Search.

Unlike other Mobile Office applications, you can search directly within Contacts on Pocket PCs. As you enter characters in the Search box in Contacts, items that contain those letters display on the screen.

Search will search through all contacts and list the entries containing the word or phrase in the Results portion of the dialog box. Tap an entry in the list to open the contact, and tap OK in the Contacts dialog box to return to the Search dialog box.

You can search for an entry in other Outlook Mobile programs by tapping it in the Type drop-down list, and the procedure for searching and viewing each type is the same.

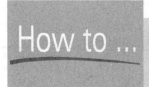 **Display Contacts Not Assigned to a Category**

A problem on Pocket PC 2000 devices is that you cannot display contacts that are not assigned to a category, which means that if you use categories, you might not find an uncategorized contact because it won't display. A No Categories option is available in the Windows Mobile Filter menu. When you select this option, only the contacts that have not been assigned to a category display.

Smartphones do not have a built-in way to search for contacts. However, if you are at the Smartphone Home Screen, press the number keys containing the letters of a name, and the names corresponding to those letters appear:

Once the name you want appears, use the navigation button to select the name, and the contact information will display.

Send E-mail to a Contact

To send e-mail to a person from Contacts, open the contact and select Send E-mail. Messaging will start, ask which e-mail account you want to use, and then create a new e-mail message using the contact's e-mail address.

On Pocket PCs, tap-and-hold on the person's entry in the Contacts list, and then tap Send E-mail on the pop-up menu. On Pocket PC Phone Editions, the tap-and-hold menu also provides options for calling work, home, and mobile phone numbers and sending text messages if they are available for a contact.

Complete the message, select Send, and you will return to Messaging. Return to Contacts by pressing the hardware button or tapping Start | Contacts.

Send and Receive Contacts via Infrared

Any entry in Contacts can be sent to another Windows Mobile device using the infrared port on the device. To send and receive contacts with infrared, follow these steps:

1. Start Contacts on the device sending the contact, select the contact that you want to send, and then select Menu | Beam Contact.

2. Line up the infrared ports of the two devices.

Once the connection is established, the contact transfers and the sending device indicates that the contact has been received. A notification appears on the receiving device asking whether you want to add what it received to Contacts. Select Yes to add the contact, or No to not add the contact.

TIP   *On Pocket PCs you can beam a contact from the Contacts List view by tapping-and-holding on a contact and then tapping Beam Contact on the pop-up menu.*

13

Configure Contact Options

You can set several options in Contacts by tapping Menu | Options to open the Options dialog box. Tap the check box next to Show Alphabetical Index or Show Contact Names Only to change how the Contacts list is displayed. Enter the default area code for new contacts by entering a value in the Area Code field. Tap OK to save the changes that you make and close the dialog box.

 Smartphones do not have Contact Options.

Manage Your Tasks

The Tasks program is the Windows Mobile companion to the Tasks folder in Microsoft Outlook. ActiveSync synchronizes tasks that you enter in Tasks on the device with the Tasks folder in Outlook, as explained in Chapter 7. To enter a task, select Start | Tasks, which opens the program window shown in Figure 13-3.

 *Tasks may not be on the Start menu, in which case you can tap Start | Programs | Tasks to launch the program.*

View Your Tasks

Tasks are displayed in the main program window in one complete list. To the left of each task is a check box that you tap to mark a task complete. Immediately to the right of the check box is the Priority column, which displays exclamation marks for high-priority tasks, an arrow pointing down for low-priority tasks, and nothing for normal tasks. The description of the task takes up the remaining space for each item.

FIGURE 13-3   Tasks on a Pocket PC (left) and on a Smartphone (right)

You can sort the Tasks list by Status, Priority, Subject, Start Date, and Due Date. A task has either an active or a complete status, and when the list is sorted by Status, active tasks appear before complete tasks. To change the sort order of the Tasks list, select Menu | Sort By and then select an option on the menu.

Task start and due dates do not appear in the Tasks list unless you enable them on a Pocket PC. To display start and due dates, tap Menu | Options and then tap the Show Start And Due Dates check box. When the dates are enabled, each task occupies two lines in the Tasks list, as shown in Figure 13-3. Past-due tasks are displayed in red in the Tasks list. You cannot display start and due dates in the Tasks list on Smartphones.

Each task can include more information than is displayed in the Tasks list. To see the details, tap the task to open it in Summary view:

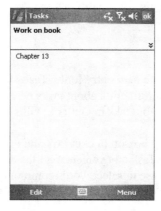

Summary view provides all the information about the task on one easy-to-read screen. By default the top part of the screen displays the task description and if more details are available you will see down arrows. Tapping the down arrows displays the task's start and due dates and category assignments. The bottom part of the screen displays notes. Tap the OK button in the upper right corner to close Summary view.

Create New Tasks

To create a new task on Smartphones, use the navigation button to move the cursor to the field at the top of the screen:

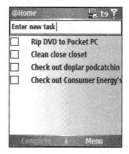

Beef Up Tasks on Smartphones

The Tasks program on Smartphones is noticeably under-powered in comparison to the same program on Pocket PCs. Fortunately, several third-party programs are available that provide more functionality than the Tasks program that comes with Smartphones.

Oxios's ToDo List adds all the basic functionality to Smartphones that you find on Pocket PCs, and more. For example, you can add call history and contact information to tasks. You will find this program at www.oxios.com.

You will find other tasks programs for Smartphones at www.smartphone.net by searching on tasks.

Press the navigation button to save the new entry to the Tasks list. Unlike on Pocket PCs, you cannot enter due dates or other information about tasks other than the subject. However, additional information that you enter for tasks in Outlook will synchronize to Smartphones and display in the Tasks Summary view.

Tap New to open the Tasks dialog box on Pocket PCs and create a new task. The dialog box has two tabs: Task and Notes. On the Task tab, you enter all the details about the task. The Subject field is a drop-down list that you can use to select words commonly used in task subjects. By using the drop-down list, you can speed up data entry, but unfortunately the list does not change and you cannot add words.

You enter dates in the Starts and Due fields by tapping the field to open the date picker. Tap a date on the calendar to select it for either field. You can use the arrows at the top of the calendar to move backward and forward one month at a time, or tap the month to jump to another month that appears in a pop-up menu. The Starts date that you select automatically appears in the Due field.

 *A task cannot be assigned a start date without a corresponding due date, but a due date can be assigned without a corresponding start date.*

You can schedule a task for multiple dates by selecting a recurrence pattern. The default setting is for each task to occur once, as indicated by the value of the Occurs field. To make the task appear multiple times, tap the Occurs field to display the items shown next. (The items will vary depending on the day of the week, day of the month, and date on which the task is to be created.)

The task shown in the illustration is being created on Sunday, December 4, 2005. Select Every Sunday to add the task to the Tasks list on every Sunday. Select Day 4 Of Every Month to add the task on the fourth of each month. If you want to add the task on the specific date—in this case, December 4—every year, select Every December 4.

If none of the items in the drop-down list meets your requirements, tap <Edit Pattern...> to start the Recurrence wizard. The Recurrence wizard has three dialog boxes. In the first dialog box, you set the start and due dates for the task. Typically, these have been entered already prior to creating the recurrence pattern. If the start date is correct, you can change the due date by expanding the Duration drop-down list and tapping a value in the list. Tapping Remove Recurrence closes the dialog box and deletes the recurrence.

Tap Next to open the second dialog box of the Recurrence wizard. Tap these buttons along the top of the dialog box to define a recurrence time:

- **Daily**   When you tap Daily, two radio buttons appear. Tap the Every Weekday radio button to create the task on every weekday. To create the task on multiple days, tap the Every radio button and select a number from the Day(s) drop-down list.

- **Weekly**   Tap the days in the week for which you want to create the task; you can select more than one day. Select a value from the Week(s) drop-down list to create the task for several weeks on the days that you select.

- **Monthly**   The monthly recurrence pattern can be defined for a specific date in a month (such as the nineteenth), for a select number of months, or for a day in a week (such as the third Saturday) for a select number of months. Tap the radio button of the option you want, and select the values from the drop-down lists.

- **Yearly**   The yearly recurrence pattern is similar to the monthly pattern. Your options are to create the task on the same date and month each year or for the day in a week of the month that you select. Tap the radio button of the option that you want, and select the values from the drop-down lists.

Tap Next to define the starting and ending dates of the recurrence pattern in the third dialog box of the wizard. Select the starting date by using the The Pattern Starts drop-down list. Three options are available for defining the end date: the recurrence pattern does not end, it ends on a date that you select, or it ends after a select number of occurrences. Tap the radio button of the option that you want and select the appropriate values from the drop-down lists.

After you select the start and end dates of the recurring task, tap Finish to return to the Tasks dialog box. The Occurs field contains <Edit Pattern...> to indicate that a customized recurrence pattern has been created for the task.

13

You may have problems synchronizing recurring tasks between your Pocket PC and Outlook. If you create a recurring task, edit it only on the Pocket PC; otherwise, the task may not be re-created for each occurrence.

The Reminder field on the Tasks dialog box sets the date on which you will be notified about the upcoming task. Turn the reminder notification on or off by tapping the field and selecting either None or Remind Me from the drop-down list. The second line of the Reminder field defines the date for the notification. Tap the date on the second line to display the date picker, and tap the date on the calendar on which you want the reminder notification to occur.

Long-time Pocket PC users will be happy to see that you can now assign a time for a task reminder, which has not been possible prior to Windows Mobile 5.

Tasks assigned to categories can be filtered in the Tasks list by using the Filter menu. To filter tasks, you must first assign them to a category, which you do by setting a value for the Categories field. Tap the field to display a list of categories, and then tap the check box next to each category that you want assigned to the task.

Enter Notes for Tasks

Task notes can contain text, drawings, recordings, or writing in digital ink. To enter a note, tap the Notes tab to display the portion of the Tasks dialog box that functions in a manner similar to the Notes program, explained in Chapter 14.

To make a recording, press and hold the Hardware Record button. Your device will beep and begin recording. Stop the recording by releasing the button. Once the recording is finished, an icon is inserted into the note, which you tap to play back the record.

Use the Tasks Entry Bar

The Entry Bar

The Entry Bar, which is the only way you can enter tasks on Smartphones, provides a quick way to enter tasks. If the Entry Bar is not displaying on your Pocket PC, tap Menu | Options, tap the Show Tasks Entry Bar check box, and then tap OK. When the Entry Bar is enabled, an extra line is added beneath the Categories and Sort drop-down lists.

The Entry Bar includes two priority buttons and the task subject. Set the task priority to either high or low by tapping the exclamation mark or arrow. Create the subject by tapping Tap Here To Add A New Task on the bar and entering the task subject.

When you have finished entering values on the Entry Bar, tap ENTER on the Software Input Panel to add the new task to the Tasks list.

Edit and Delete Tasks

Select an item in the Tasks list to display the Tasks Summary view, and then tap Edit on Pocket PCs to open the task information. Edit the task notes by tapping the Notes tab. Make any necessary changes to the fields in the dialog box, and then tap OK to save the changes.

Tasks can be copied or deleted by tapping-and-holding. Tap-and-hold the stylus on the task that you want to edit, and then tap either Create Copy or Delete Task on the pop-up menu that appears. When you tap Delete, a confirmation dialog box asks whether you want to delete the appointment.

To delete tasks on Smartphones, first select the task and then press Menu | Delete Task.

Filter Tasks by Categories

Filters help you focus on specific groups of tasks by displaying only entries belonging to a category that you select. As usual, for filters to be useful, you must assign tasks to categories. You use the Filter menu to filter items quickly by the category that you select.

The title on the Navigation bar changes to indicate the category currently being displayed. To filter tasks on a category, select Menu | Filter and select the category that you want to display. If the category is not in the drop-down list, select More, press the check box next to the categories that you want to display, and then select Done.

Clear the filter and display all contacts by tapping Menu | Filter | All Tasks.

> **TIP** *Tap the Recent entry in the Categories drop-down list to display the tasks that you have recently added, edited, or viewed.*

The Filter menu has two items that are useful for looking at tasks. Select Active Tasks to list all tasks with a start date before and on the current date. Tasks not assigned a start date are always active. Select Completed Tasks to list all tasks marked complete.

> **TIP** *You can select a category and Active Tasks or Completed Tasks to display the active or completed tasks for a category.*

Find Tasks

To search for entries in Tasks, tap Start | Programs | Search to open the Search dialog box. Enter the word or phrase that you are searching for in the Search For field, expand the Type field drop-down list, tap Tasks, and then tap Search.

> **NOTE** *Smartphones do not have a search function.*

Search will search through all tasks and list the entries containing the word or phrase in the Results portion of the dialog box. Tap an entry in the list to open the task, and tap OK in the Tasks dialog box to return to the Search dialog box.

How to ... Display Tasks Not Assigned to a Category

On Pocket PC 2000 devices, you cannot display tasks that are not assigned to a category, which means that if you use categories, you might miss an uncategorized task because it won't display. A No Categories option is available in the Filter menu of Windows Mobile 5. When you select this option, only the tasks that have not been assigned to a category will display.

You can search for entries in other Outlook Mobile programs by tapping their entry in the Type drop-down list, and the procedure for searching and viewing each type is the same.

Send and Receive Tasks via Infrared

Any entry in Tasks can be sent to another Windows Mobile device using the infrared port on the device. To send and receive tasks with infrared, follow these steps:

1. Start Tasks on the device sending the task, select the task that you want to send, and then select Menu | Beam Task.

2. Line up the infrared ports of the two devices.

Once the connection is established, the task transfers and the sending device indicates that the task has been received. A notification appears on the receiving device asking you whether you want to save the item to Tasks. Select Yes to add the item to the Tasks list, or No to not add the item.

Configure Task Options

Three options can be set by tapping Menu | Options on Pocket PCs to open the dialog box shown here:

Tap the Set Reminders For New Items check box to have reminders automatically created for new tasks. Add the start and due dates to the Tasks list by tapping the Show Start And Due Dates check box. Tap the Show Tasks Entry Bar check box to display the Tasks Entry Bar at the top of the Task List view.

Tap OK to save the changes that you make and close the Options dialog box.

 There are no options to configure in Tasks on Smartphones.

Wrapping Up

Outlook Mobile provides the tools that help you manage your time. Recurring appointments are easy to schedule in Calendar because you have to enter the appointment information only once, and your Pocket PC automatically enters that appointment on all the other days.

The Tasks program provides the same functionality, reminding you of tasks that you must complete at regular intervals. All of your addresses are stored in Contacts, which makes it easy to retrieve a phone number or e-mail address.

Now that you have learned how to use your Windows Mobile device to stay organized, it's time for you to learn how you can use a Pocket PC to write letters or reports. In Chapter 14 you will learn how to use Word Mobile to create and edit documents on a Pocket PC.

Create Documents and Take Notes

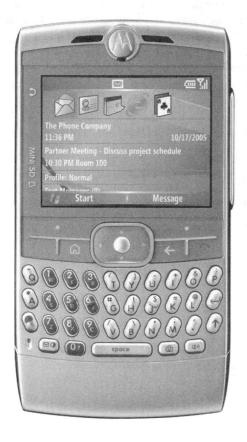

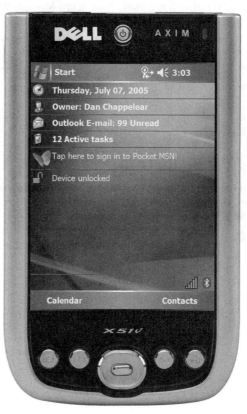

How to...

- Create and save documents
- Edit and format documents
- Send documents via e-mail
- Beam documents using infrared
- Create notes in digital ink or text
- Make voice recordings

Word Mobile enables you to use your device for more than just storing personal information and retrieving e-mail. With Word Mobile, you can create letters, memos, or notes wherever the need arises. Word Mobile is similar to Microsoft Word, but its purpose is to complement the desktop software rather than replace it. Because of this, Word Mobile does not have many of the formatting features—such as tables and footnotes—that you find in Microsoft Word. With Word Mobile, though, you can instantly write documents wherever you are, and then transfer the documents to a desktop computer for further editing and final formatting.

NOTE *This application was called Pocket Word in prior versions of Windows Mobile.*

Use Word Mobile on Your Pocket PC

Unlike the desktop version, Word Mobile cannot do any of the following:

- Password-protect documents
- Print documents
- Create tables
- Create headers or footers

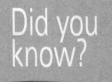

Improved Round-Tripping

Unlike prior versions of Windows Mobile, when you synchronize documents that contain tables, headers, and footers to a Windows Mobile Version 5 device, the tables, headers, and footers stay in the document. When you synchronize and edit documents on devices running prior versions of the software, tables, headers, and footers are removed from the document when it synchronizes to a PC, or when you e-mail the document.

You will not see headers or footers in Word Mobile, but you can edit table contents.

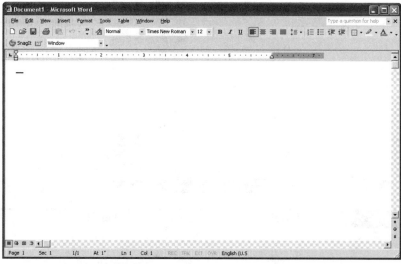

FIGURE 14-1 Word Mobile program window with Windows Mobile for Pocket PC (left) and Microsoft Word program window (right)

 Word Mobile is not available on Smartphones, so this chapter focuses on Pocket PCs. You can view Word documents on Smartphones using Westtek's ClearVue, which you can find at www.westtek.com/smartphone/.

Figure 14-1 (above) shows the differences between the Word Mobile program on the Pocket PC and Word on a desktop computer. At the bottom of the Word Mobile screen is the Command bar, which contains the Menu button on the right, and either the New or View buttons on the left.

 *Command bar is a term created by Microsoft to refer to the bar at the bottom of the screen on the Pocket PC.*

14

Create, Open, and Save Documents

To start Word Mobile, tap Start | Programs | Word Mobile, which opens to the File List view, shown in Figure 14-2. Tap New to create a blank document in the program window.

To create documents using a template, follow these steps in the File List view:

1. Tap Menu | Options.

2. Tap to expand the Default Template drop-down list.

3. Tap the name of the template you want to use.

4. Tap OK.

5. Tap New.

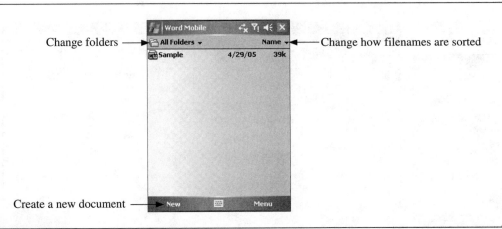

Change folders ——▶ All Folders ▾   Name ▾ ◀—— Change how filenames are sorted

Create a new document —— New   Menu

FIGURE 14-2   Word Mobile File List view on the Pocket PC

At this point all new documents are based on the template that you select. To revert to blank documents, repeat these steps and select Blank Document from the Default Template drop-down list.

Previous versions of Windows Mobile have the New pop-up menu, which displays Pocket Word templates and contains options for creating the following: Appointments, Contacts, E-mails, Excel Workbooks, Notes, and Tasks.

Use the File List view shown in Figure 14-2 to create new documents or to open, copy, delete, rename, or move existing documents. By default, all documents in the My Documents folder, and any subfolders, are displayed. If a My Documents folder exists on a storage card inserted in the device, its contents, along with the contents of its subfolders, will be merged into the list. Tap the down arrow next to All Folders to display the Folders drop-down list, shown here. Select a folder name from this list to display its contents. If you tap the Add/Delete item at the bottom of the drop-down list, you can create, rename, and delete subfolders.

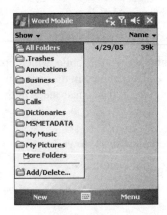

Pocket PCs look for only those documents stored in the My Documents folder. That's why, if you want to store your documents on a storage card, it is best to create a My Documents folder on the card and then store the documents in it.

In the File List view, the files are sorted alphabetically by name. To sort them by Date, Size, or Type, tap the arrow to the right of Name. Notice that the type of sort that you select displays on the top line.

To open a document, tap its filename. Tap-and-hold on a filename to display the pop-up menu shown here. Tap Create Copy, and another copy of the file using the same filename appears with a copy number added to the filename. For example, if you select Create Copy for the file named Foo, the filename Foo(1) will be added to the list. Tap Delete to delete the file that you selected, and tap Rename/Move to open a dialog box in which you can specify a new filename, folder, and storage location.

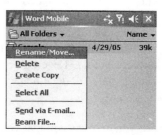

Edit Your Word Mobile Documents

Word Mobile provides all the tools you need for editing text in a document. With the commands available by tapping Menu, you can copy, delete, search for, and replace text.

To count the number of words in a document, tap Menu | Tools | Word Count.

Copy Text

To copy or move text within a document, follow these steps:

1. Select the text by tapping-and-holding at the beginning of the text to be selected, dragging to the end, and releasing.
2. Tap Menu | Copy to copy text, or Menu | Cut to move text.
3. Tap at the location where you want the text to be inserted.
4. Tap Menu | Paste.

A shortcut on the Pocket PC is to tap-and-hold on the selected text, and then choose Copy, Cut, or Paste from the pop-up menu. With the onscreen or built-in keyboard, you can also use CTRL-C to copy, CTRL-X to cut, and CTRL-V to paste.

Delete Text

To delete text from a document, select the text and then tap Menu | Edit | Clear. To select all of the text in a document, tap Menu | Edit | Select All.

14

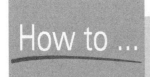

How to ... Revert to the Previously Saved Document

The Undo command recovers mistakes that you make, one at a time. For example, if you enter a line of text in a document, and then decide to remove it, tapping Menu | Undo removes the sentence. If you made a number of edits to a document, you might want to cancel them all, but unlike Word 2000, there is no Close menu command or button to close the file without saving. To cancel all the changes you made since you opened the document, tap Menu | File | Revert To Saved, and then tap Yes when Word Mobile asks whether you want to undo all document changes.

If you make an edit that you do not like, you can undo it by selecting Menu | Undo. If you performed multiple edits, continue to select Menu | Undo to remove each edit that you performed. The opposite is Menu | Redo, which restores each edit that was removed using Menu | Undo.

Search for a Text String

To search for a word or phrase in a document, tap Menu | Edit | Find/Replace to open the Find dialog box:

Enter the search text in the Find What field. If you want to search only for a whole word that you enter, and not search for words containing the letters you type, select Match Whole Words Only. If you want to search only for words using a specific case, select Match Case. After you have entered the text, tap Find. The first instance of the text in the document will be highlighted and a bar will appear above the Command bar that contains four buttons.

Tap Next to move to the next occurrence of the text in the document. Tap the Close button, which looks like an *X*, to stop searching for text.

Replacing text is a similar process. Tap Menu | Edit | Find/Replace, and then tap the Replace button. Enter the text to be replaced in the Find What field, and enter the new text in the Replace With field. If you want to match whole words, or case, be sure to select the appropriate check boxes and then tap Find. A bar appears with buttons for Next, Replace, Replace All, and Close; the first instance of the text to be replaced is highlighted. To skip the instance and move to the next, tap Next; to replace the text, tap Replace. The text is replaced and the search continues to the next occurrence of the text. If there are no more occurrences, a dialog box displays saying that Word Mobile has finished searching the document. Tap Replace All to replace all occurrences of the text without a prompt for direction from you.

Check the Spelling

To check the spelling in a document, tap Menu | Tools | Spelling. Each questionable word is highlighted in turn and a pop-up menu appears near the word, as shown here. Tap one of the recommended words at the top of the pop-up menu to replace the highlighted word. If the highlighted word is correct as is, tap Ignore, and the next questionable word will be highlighted. Tap Ignore All to skip the remaining instances of that word in the document. When you tap Add, the highlighted word is added to the Spell Check Dictionary so that the word will not be highlighted as questionable in the future.

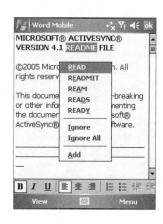

 **Edit the Spell Check Dictionary**

14

Words that you add to the Spell Check Dictionary are stored in a file named custom.dic. You can find this text file in the Windows folder on your Pocket PC. To edit the file, copy it to your desktop using ActiveSync Explorer, open the file, and add or remove words. Save the file and then copy it back to the Windows folder on your Pocket PC with ActiveSync Explorer. By default, the Pocket PC Windows folder is hidden in ActiveSync Explorer. To view the folder and its files on your PC, click Tools | Folder Options, click the View tab, and then click the Show Hidden Files And Folders radio button. Chapter 8 provides instructions for using ActiveSync Explorer to copy files between a Pocket PC and desktop computer.

Format Your Documents

Text displayed in a document can use different fonts and be aligned left, center, or right. Paragraphs can also be indented in a couple of different ways. To make these changes, use the Word Mobile Menu | Format option.

Apply formatting to existing text by selecting the text and then choosing the desired option. If you specify the formatting that you want before typing text, anything that you enter will display as specified. Most formats can be specified using the toolbar buttons as well as through menu selections. The Pocket PC pop-up menu that appears when you tap-and-hold on selected text includes the same Font and Paragraph menu options that are in the Format menu.

In the Font dialog box on the Pocket PC, shown next, you can select fonts and font sizes from the appropriate drop-down lists. Select font color from the Font Color drop-down list. In addition to the standard font styles, you can also select Highlight, which adds yellow highlighting over the text, and Strikethrough, which displays a line through selected text.

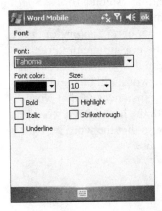

To specify paragraph formatting, tap Menu | Format | Paragraph, and the following Paragraph dialog box appears:

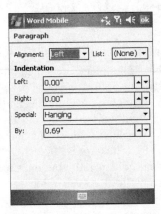

Align text left, center, or right by selecting the corresponding menu item from the Alignment drop-down list. To indent the margins, use the arrows in the Left and Right fields to select the indent value. If you want the first line of the paragraph to be indented, or you want a hanging indent, select it from the Special field; the size of the indent is specified in the By field directly beneath the Special field.

To create a bulleted or numbered list, select the desired option from the List drop-down list. You can create outlines from either a bulleted or numbered list by pressing the indent and outdent buttons on the toolbar:

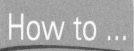 **Type Documents in Word Mobile**

The easiest way to write large documents on a Pocket PC is to use a keyboard. A variety of keyboards are available for most Pocket PCs. One popular keyboard is Think Outside's Stowaway, a full-sized keyboard that folds up to about the same size as a Pocket PC. Information about the Stowaway keyboard is available at www.thinkoutside.com.

Some versions of the Stowaway keyboard connect to the Pocket PC accessory port, which varies according to Pocket PC brands. However, Think Outside also sells infrared and Bluetooth versions of its keyboard. The infrared version works with any Pocket PC, while the Bluetooth version works with Pocket PCs and Smartphones that have Bluetooth radios.

Thumb keyboards, which are tiny keyboards that you type on using your thumbs, also attach to the accessory port. Some Pocket PCs, such as the i-mate PDA2K and the iPAQ hw6515, have thumb keyboards built-in.

If you use one of these keyboards, you will be glad to know that Windows Mobile includes some basic support for keyboard shortcuts in Word Mobile. For example, you can use CTRL-B for bold, CTRL-I for italics, and CTRL-U for underlined text.

Pocket PC 2002 doesn't support even these three basic shortcuts. To add more support for keyboard shortcuts on your Pocket PC, download and install WordCommands from www.lagorio.net/pocketpc/wordcommands/. WordCommands provides 26 different shortcuts that significantly speed up text entry by keyboard in Word Mobile.

14

Do Full-Featured Word Processing on Your Pocket PC

As you can tell by this chapter, Word Mobile does not provide many of the features available in desktop word processors. For example, you cannot create tables or footnotes, nor can you make changes to the layout of a document. If you need more word processing features, your only option is SoftMaker's TextMaker word processor.

TextMaker has just about every feature available on desktop word processors. Not only can you create tables, add footnotes, and change the document layout, but you can also work with embedded graphics and create borders and shades. TextMaker works directly with Microsoft Word files, which allows you to synchronize and edit Word files on your Pocket PC without worrying about losing formatting. SoftMaker also sells a desktop version of TextMaker that runs on Windows and Linux.

While TextMaker provides a ton of features, they come at a price. The program costs $39.95 and requires a little over 6MB of storage space and 3MB of program memory. You can find more information about this program at www.softmaker.com/english/.

Use the View Menu to Change the Screen Display

The View menu is used to control the screen display. To hide or show the toolbar, tap View | Toolbar. Turn Wrap To Window on or off by tapping View | Wrap To Window. Use View | Zoom to change the display size by selecting from one of the five settings in the menu.

Share Documents Easily with Other Users

Word Mobile makes it easy to share documents with other people by including the ability to send documents via infrared or e-mail. Use infrared to send a document to another Windows Powered device by following these steps from the File List view:

1. If the receiving device is running Pocket PC 2000, tap Start | Programs | Infrared Receive; otherwise, simply align the two devices' infrared ports.

2. On the sending device that has a document open in Word Mobile, tap Menu | Beam File, and line up the device infrared ports.

NOTE   *If the sending device is running Pocket PC 2000, tap Tools | Send Via Infrared.*

3. After the two devices recognize each other, the file transfers to the receiving device. When the transfer is complete, the sending device indicates that one file has been sent, and a Close button appears, which you tap to return to Word Mobile.

To send a document via e-mail, tap Menu | Send Via E-mail, and a new e-mail message opens with the document as an attachment. Enter an e-mail address, subject, and message, and then tap Send. Inbox will send the message the next time you connect to the Internet and retrieve e-mail.

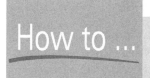 *You can also beam or e-mail documents by tapping-and-holding on the filename and tapping either Beam File or Send Via E-mail in the pop-up menu.*

Copy and Delete Documents

To create another copy of the document currently open in Word Mobile, tap Menu | File | Save Document As to open the Save As dialog box. Enter a new filename, select the location where you want the file to be stored, and tap OK. Tap Cancel to close the dialog box and not save the document.

Tap Menu | File | Delete and then tap Yes on the Confirmation dialog box to delete the currently open document. The document is deleted, and you are returned to the Word Mobile List view.

Create, Open, and Save Notes

If you need to write a quick note, what do you use? Before I started using my Pocket PC, I would write notes on pieces of paper and stick them somewhere easy to find. On my desk at work, notes were scattered everywhere, and over time my workspace would look cluttered. Inevitably, I would lose a note that had an important phone number or appointment, causing me either to lose time hunting for the phone number or to miss a meeting.

How to ...   Add Fonts to Your Pocket PC

14

Like Windows XP, Windows Mobile uses TrueType fonts, and each device comes with six different fonts. You can add fonts to your Pocket PC by copying the font file from your desktop computer to the device. On your desktop computer, the default location for your computer fonts is the \Windows\Fonts folder.

If you want to transfer a font from your desktop computer to your Pocket PC, use Windows Explorer and ActiveSync to copy a font file to the \Windows\Fonts folder on your Pocket PC. Once the font is copied, do a soft reset and then start Word Mobile. Check the Fonts drop-down list to verify that the font is now available.

See Chapter 8 for directions on how to copy files from your desktop computer to the Pocket PC using ActiveSync.

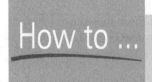

Write Text Notes on a Smartphone

Windows Mobile Smartphones do not include a text editor, so if you want to write text notes using a Smartphone, you need to add a third-party program. One such program is SmartphoneNotes, from Syncdata, which you can find at www.syncdata.it.

SmartphoneNotes enables you to create, edit, and manage text notes on your Smartphone. Best of all, it synchronizes notes with Outlook versions 2000, 2002, and 2003.

Now that I have my Pocket PC, I store phone numbers in Contacts and enter appointments in Calendar, and when I need to jot a quick note, I turn to the Notes application. Of course, I could use Word Mobile, but I have found Notes to be better suited for this task.

Tap Start | Programs | Notes to start the Notes application. The application opens in the List view, as shown in Figure 14-3. Simply tap a filename in the List view to open the note. Tap New to create a blank note page that is ready for handwriting, text, or recordings. Tap OK to save the note and return to the List view.

Write Notes

Writing notes is as simple as using a paper notepad. When you create a note by tapping New, the screen displays a ruled page that looks similar to a paper page. If you write directly on the screen, your handwriting appears as digital ink, as shown in Figure 14-4. By default, Notes is in

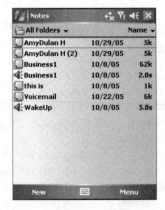

FIGURE 14-3   The Notes application in List view

FIGURE 14-4   Draw mode, in Notes

Draw mode; if you want to type text in Notes, tap Menu | Draw, which clears the check next to Draw in the menu. Select the same commands to switch back to Draw mode.

If you want to always have your handwriting be translated to text instead of appearing as digital ink, you can change the default Draw mode by tapping Menu | Options from the List view, and then select Typing from the Default Mode drop-down list.

If you tap Menu | Tools | Recognize, all handwriting in the note converts to text. You may also narrow the conversion down to a portion of the handwriting by first selecting the portion and then tapping Menu | Tools | Recognize. To make corrections to the conversion, tap-and-hold the stylus on the incorrect word and tap Alternates. Tap the correct word from the list that appears. Undo the conversion by tapping Menu | Undo.

Although you can make drawings in Notes, you may have problems viewing the drawings after you synchronize the file to a desktop PC. If you tap Menu | Tools | Recognize to convert an entire document to text, Notes converts the drawing to text as well, generating some strange results.

14

Edit Notes

You can use the standard edit functions (Cut, Copy, and Paste) to edit Notes. Select these functions from either the Notes menu or the pop-up menu. To select writing, tap the stylus on the screen until the cursor appears, drag the stylus across the writing, and then lift the stylus. When selecting text, just drag the stylus across the words that you want to select and lift the stylus. Embedded recordings are also selected in this manner. Tap-and-hold the stylus on the selection to open the pop-up menu and tap Cut, Copy, Paste, or Clear. These same functions are also available in the menu.

To select the entire note, tap Menu | Edit | Select All. You can undo any edit function by using the menu. The Undo options in the menu change according to the last edit that you performed. For example, if you just cut an item from the document, the Edit menu contains Undo Clear, which will replace the item cut (deleted) from the document.

TIP   *To insert the current date and time into a note, tap-and-hold the stylus on the screen until the pop-up menu appears, and then select Insert Date.*

Zoom Notes

Change the display size by selecting a zoom percentage from the Zoom menu; for example, to increase the display size to 200 percent, tap Menu | Zoom | 200%. You cannot customize the Zoom settings.

Make Voice Recordings

How often do you drive and use your computer at the same time? (Not often, I hope, or I would like to know what roads you travel on so that I can avoid them.) Yet, while you shouldn't be using your computer while driving, there probably have been times when you've had a thought that you would like to make sure you remember. For that, you could use a cassette recorder or your Pocket PC.

You make voice recordings with a Pocket PC the same way that you do with a cassette recorder, but once a recording is completed, the Pocket PC capabilities shine. You can label the recordings, giving each a name that you can easily identify for later retrieval, as well as date and time stamp each recording. Recordings can be grouped in folders and synchronized to a desktop computer. They can also be attached to e-mail and sent to anyone with an Internet e-mail address, and they can be beamed via infrared to any other Pocket PC.

The number of recordings you may store on your device is limited by the amount of storage space available. You can store recordings either in internal storage memory or on a storage card. Your Pocket PC creates files in the Waveform (WAV) audio format, and there are different types of WAV files. Depending on which format you select and its recording quality, a three-second recording can require 1KB to 28KB of storage. Approximately one hour of recordings can take up to 1MB of space.

Storage space is not your only consideration; using the microphone and other peripherals drains batteries fast, decreasing the amount of recording time. If you plan to make long recordings, make sure the battery is fully charged and remove any unnecessary peripherals.

TIP   *If you want to record audio to the MP3 format on a Pocket PC, or you want a voice recording program that provides more functions than Notes, check out VITO Technology's SoundExplorer at www.vitotechnology.com.*

Create Recordings

Your Pocket PC is designed to work like a tape recorder. To make a recording, press-and-hold the Record hardware button. The device will beep and begin recording. Stop the recording by

Make Recordings on Smartphones

One way to store quick notes on Smartphones is to use Voice Notes, which you start by pressing Start | More | Voice Notes. Once Voice Notes is running, press Record to start recording a note and press Stop to stop recording. To play back a recording, press the navigation button up or down and then press the navigation button to play. To rename or delete a recording, press Menu | Rename or Menu | Delete.

releasing the button. The recording is stored on your device and is included in the Notes List view with a default filename. To play a recording, tap its filename, and use the buttons on the Recording toolbar to control the playback.

You can also create recordings in Notes by selecting View Recording Toolbar from the Notes menu to open the Recording toolbar:

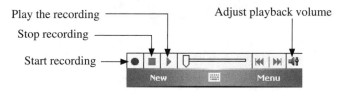

Tap the Record button on the toolbar to begin recording, and tap the Stop button to end recording.

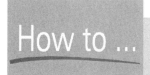

Create a Customized Alarm

14

Your Pocket PC comes with several different sounds that are used for reminders in Calendar and Tasks and as general alarms. You can record your own customized alarm by using Notes. First, create the recording that you want to use, and then tap-and-hold on the file and rename the file to something easy to remember. Then, start File Explorer and copy the file from the My Documents folder to the Windows folder. To use the recording for reminders, tap Start | Settings | Sounds & Notifications, and then tap the Notifications tab, select Reminders from the Event drop-down list, and select your recording from the Sound drop-down list. To create an alarm, tap Start | Settings | System | Clock & Alarms, and then tap the Alarms tab. Tap the Alarm button and select your recording from the Play Sound drop-down list.

 *The default filename for text notes and recordings is based on the folder name in which the item is stored. For example, if you select a folder named* Projects *in the Notes List view, notes and recordings will have the default filename of* Projects *and a number, such as* Projects1.

If you make a recording while a note is open, it will be embedded in the note. Once the recording is finished, an icon is inserted into the note, as shown in the following image. Play the recording by tapping the icon.

 *Speak directly into the microphone to create good recordings. Check the user manual of your Pocket PC to locate the microphone.*

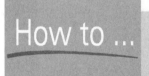 **Change the Format of Voice Recordings**

Recordings are created using one of several formats available on your Pocket PC. Which format you use depends on your personal preferences for sound quality, and how much you want to record. Higher-quality recordings require more storage space.

To change the recording format, tap Start | Settings | Input, and then tap the Options tab on the Input screen. Tap the Voice Recording Format drop-down list to expand the list of available formats, and then select the format you want to use. The Pulse Code Modulation (PCM) and Global System for Mobile Communications (GSM) 6.10 formats come standard on Pocket PCs. Pocket PC hardware manufacturers may add formats that are unique to their devices.

Of the standard formats, PCM provides the highest quality, and the drop-down list provides several different bit rates of this format in either mono or stereo, which you can select to balance between quality and storage space. GSM 6.10 provides medium-quality recordings, and both formats can be played on Windows desktop computers. If your Pocket PC has additional formats, make sure you select either PCM or GSM 6.10 as the format to use if you plan to e-mail recordings to people who can receive them only on Windows desktops.

Send Notes and Recordings via E-mail or Infrared

You may send notes and recordings to someone via e-mail, which the receiver opens using Microsoft Word or the default WAV file player. To e-mail a note, follow these steps:

1. If the note is already open, tap Menu | Tools | Send Via E-mail.

2. If the note or recording is displayed in the Notes List view, tap-and-hold on the filename and select Send Via E-mail from the pop-up menu.

3. Inbox starts with a new message and the note attached. Enter an e-mail address. (See Chapter 11 for instructions on how to use Inbox.)

4. Enter a subject.

5. Tap Send.

Depending on how you use Inbox, the e-mail will be sent the next time you connect with your Internet service provider (ISP) or the next time you synchronize with your desktop computer.

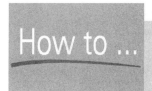 **Assign an Alarm to a Note**

There are many good reasons for taking notes; one of them is to remind yourself to do something in a couple of hours. You could create an appointment or task and set a reminder, but sometimes that is overkill when you just want to jot a quick note to yourself. Fortunately, three software developers have created solutions that sound an alarm and display a written note at a set time, or automatically play a voice recording at a set time.

RemindMe from Applian Technologies is available in English, German, French, and Spanish. RemindMe can display notes or play voice recordings either within a certain amount of time, say 15 minutes from now, or at a set time. You can find a trial version of this program along with more information at www.applianmobile.com/pocketpc/remindme/index.php.

BugMe from Electric Pocket is an award-winning Palm OS application that has also been written for the Pocket PC. It provides the same functions as RemindMe, plus it adds the ability to change note and ink colors and lock notes so they can't be accidentally deleted. A trial version of BugMe is available at www.electricpocket.com/bugme/.

If you already use Pocket Informant as an alternative to Pocket Outlook, you don't need to install RemindMe or BugMe, because their features are available as a Pocket Informant Alarm Note. By default, Pocket Informant assigns the Alarm Note feature to the Voice Record button on your Pocket PC. Pocket Informant provides many more features than described here, and more information and a trial version of the program are available at www.pocketinformant.com.

14

TIP   *If you e-mail a voice recording and the person who receives the recording cannot play it, check to make sure the recording is in either the PCM or GSM 6.10 format.*

Notes and recordings can be transferred between devices using the infrared port. To perform infrared transfers, follow these steps:

1. If the note is already open, tap Menu | Tools | Beam.

2. If the note or recording is displayed in the Notes List view, tap-and-hold on the filename and select Beam File from the pop-up menu.

3. Make sure the device receiving the transfer is set to Receive.

4. Line up the infrared ports of both devices. A sound indicates that a connection is made, and the note transfers.

5. The receiving device indicates that one file was received and the sending device indicates that one file was sent.

Manage Your Notes and Recordings

The best way to manage notes is by using the Notes List view. You can sort notes by Name, Date, Size, or Type.

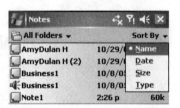

Notes are copied, deleted, renamed, or moved by using the pop-up menu that appears when you tap-and-hold the stylus on a note. Table 14-1 summarizes the pop-up menu options.

You can rename or move an open note by tapping Menu | Tools | Rename/Move. To delete a note while it is open, tap Menu | Tools | Delete Note.

Menu Option	Action
Create Copy	Places a copy of the selected note in the List view. The copy has the same name as the original with the addition of a number in parentheses—Note(1).
Delete	Opens a warning dialog box telling you that the selected item(s) will be permanently deleted. Tap Yes to delete or No to cancel.
Send Via E-mail	Starts Inbox and creates a new e-mail message with the note you select as an attachment.
Beam File	Initiates an infrared beam of the note that you select. After you tap Beam File, align the infrared ports of the sending and receiving Pocket PCs.
Rename/Move	Opens the Rename/Move dialog box. Enter a name in the Name field to rename the note. Move the note to a different folder by selecting it from the Folder drop-down list, or to a different storage location by selecting it from the Location drop-down list.

TABLE 14-1   Notes List View Pop-Up Menu Options

Note-Taking Alternatives

If Notes does not provide enough functionality for you, several alternative note-taking applications are available for the Pocket PC. Here is a list of some of these programs:

- **PhatNotes**   www.phatware.com
- **Forget Me Not** and **Journal Pro**   www.dsrtech.net
- **dNote**   www.derago.com/n/changelang-eng.htm

If you prefer to take notes in an outline format, you may prefer to use one of these outlining programs available for the Pocket PC:

- **TreNotes**   www.fannsoftware.com
- **Pocket Mindmap**   www.pocketmindmap.com
- **Streamliner**   www.kopsisengineering.com/streamliner
- **Pocket Outliner**   www.dsrtech.net

Configure Notes

Unlike all other Pocket PC applications, you can configure Notes only from the List view. You can set several options in the Options dialog box, which you open by tapping Menu | Options. Table 14-2 lists these options, what they do, and their possible values.

Option	What It Does	Possible Values
Default Mode	Specifies which mode Notes will be in when the application starts.	Writing Typing
Default Template	Specifies the template used to create new notes.	Blank Note Meeting Notes Memo Phone Memo To Do
Save To	Specifies the default storage location for new notes.	Main memory Storage card 1 (if available)
Record Button Action	Specifies what happens when you press the Hardware Record button.	Switch to Notes Stay in current program

TABLE 14-2   Notes Configuration Settings

14

 *Notes written to a storage card will not synchronize with your desktop computer.*

Wrapping Up

Now, whenever you need to write a quick note, reach for your Pocket PC rather than a scrap piece of paper. Anything that you need to write and throw away quickly you can write with digital ink in Notes, and a backup copy of your notes is stored in Outlook by ActiveSync.

Because Word Mobile does not have all the features of Microsoft Word, I use it primarily for creating text, and then I transfer documents to a PC for formatting. As you have seen in this chapter, Word Mobile has all the features you need for creating new documents, including spell check and word count capabilities.

Spreadsheets are important documents for people who analyze financial data. In the next chapter, you will learn how to use Pocket Excel to create and edit spreadsheets on your Pocket PC.

Chapter 15 Crunch Numbers

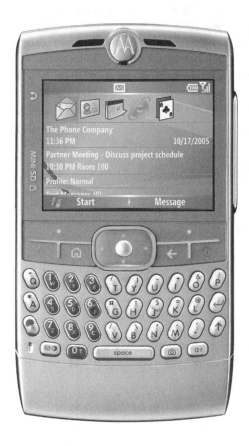

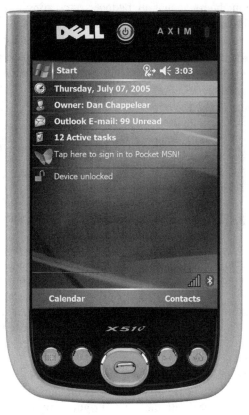

How to...

- Create Excel Mobile workbooks
- Add data and formulas to workbooks
- Edit and format workbooks
- Password-protect workbooks

Of all the types of software that have been written for personal computers, spreadsheets may have had the most impact. Indeed, it wasn't until VisiCalc and Lotus 1-2-3 were released that businesses began to use personal computers in earnest, perhaps launching the entire personal computer industry. The appeal of the spreadsheet is its tremendous versatility: it can be used for tracking hours, managing budgets, or creating *what if* scenarios.

Excel Mobile provides similar versatility for your Pocket PC. In this chapter, you'll learn how to use Excel Mobile to create workbooks that crunch numbers. You'll learn how these workbooks can be transferred to a desktop computer, beamed via infrared to other Windows Powered devices, or e-mailed to your friends and coworkers via the Internet. Because workbooks may contain sensitive information, you'll also learn how to protect your data by assigning a password to workbooks.

Excel Mobile is not available on Smartphones, so this chapter focuses on Pocket PCs. To view spreadsheets on Smartphones, use Westtek's ClearVue, available at www .westtek.com/smartphone/. To create and edit spreadsheets on Smartphones, try PTab Spreadsheet, available at www.z4soft.com.

Excel Mobile on the Pocket PC

Excel Mobile is similar to the version of Excel that you run on your desktop computer, except that you cannot print spreadsheets and it does not support macros or the Visual Basic for Applications programming language. Like Excel, Excel Mobile spreadsheets can have 256 columns, but only 16,384 rows—versus the 65,536 in PC Excel—can be used. Nonetheless, Excel Mobile features do allow you to create spreadsheets that will meet the majority of your needs.

In this section, you learn about Excel Mobile for the Pocket PC and how to use it to create and save workbooks, work with data, password-protect workbooks, and send workbooks via e-mail or infrared.

Figure 15-1 shows the differences between the Excel Mobile program window on the Pocket PC (left) and Excel on a desktop computer (right). At the bottom of the screen on the left is the Command bar, with the left and right softkey buttons for View and Menu. By default, the toolbar is not displayed. Tap View | Toolbar to display the toolbar, and tap again to hide the toolbar.

Command bar is a term created by Microsoft to refer to the bar at the bottom of the screen on the Pocket PC.

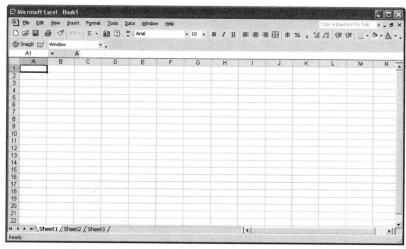

FIGURE 15-1	Excel Mobile program window on a Pocket PC (left) and Excel program window on a desktop computer

Start Excel Mobile

To start Excel Mobile, tap Start | Programs | Excel Mobile, which displays the List view window:

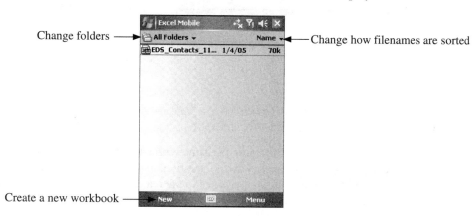

Change folders ⟶ ... Change how filenames are sorted

Create a new workbook ⟶

> NOTE *If you start Excel Mobile with no workbooks stored in the My Documents folder, the program automatically creates a blank workbook and skips the List view.*

Use the List view window to create new workbooks or to open, copy, delete, or move existing workbooks. By default, all workbooks in the My Documents folder, and any subfolders, display. If a My Documents folder exists on a storage card inserted in the device, its contents, and the contents of its subfolders, are merged into the list. Tap the down arrow next to All Folders to display the Folders drop-down list:

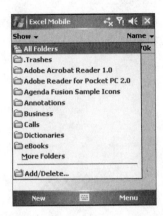

Select a folder name from this list to display its contents. If you tap the Add/Delete option from the drop-down list, you can create, rename, and delete subfolders.

Pocket PCs look only for documents stored in the My Documents folder. Therefore, if you want to store your documents on a storage card, it is best to create a My Documents folder on the card and store the documents in it.

To open a workbook, tap the filename in the list. Tap-and-hold on a filename to display the following pop-up menu:

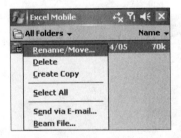

Tap Create Copy to copy the file using the same filename with a number appended. For example, if you select Create Copy for a file named Foo, the filename Foo(1) if added to the list. Tap Delete to delete a selected file, and tap Rename/Move to open a dialog box in which you can specify a new filename, folder, and storage location.

Create a New Workbook

Tap New on the Command bar in Excel Mobile to create a blank workbook, as shown in the following image.

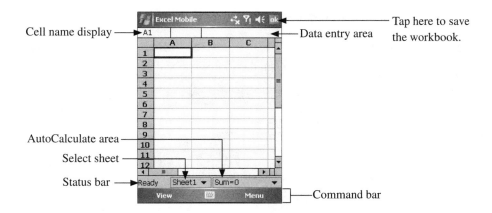

Cell name display → A1

Data entry area

Tap here to save the workbook.

AutoCalculate area

Select sheet

Status bar → Ready

Command bar

Save Workbooks

When you tap OK in Excel Mobile, the current workbook writes to the My Documents folder and is given a default filename, unless you are editing a previously saved workbook. To assign a filename to a workbook, tap Menu | File | Save As to open the Save As dialog box. Enter a filename, select a file type and storage location, and then tap OK.

When you tap OK in Excel Mobile, the List view replaces the application program window. To rename a workbook in the List view, tap-and-hold on a workbook name, select Rename/Move from the pop-up menu, and then enter a filename.

Move Around in Workbooks

Spreadsheets tend to grow in size as you add information, which can make it difficult to move through cells quickly. The Define Name command and the Go To command can help with this problem. By using the Define Name command, you can name a cell, and then use the Go To command to move the cursor to that cell.

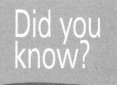

15

Password-Protecting Workbooks

Excel Mobile does not provide a way to password-protect workbooks, but you can password-protect Pocket Excel workbooks with Windows Mobile 2003SE or older. To create a password in a workbook on these devices, tap Edit | Password. Don't forget the password; without it, you will not be able to open the workbook, nor will you be able to synchronize the workbook with your desktop computer.

To assign a name to a cell, follow these steps:

1. Tap a cell to select it.

2. Tap Menu | Insert | Define Name to open the Define Name dialog box:

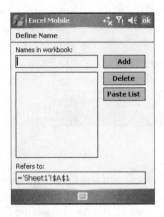

3. Enter a name in the Names In Workbook field.

4. Tap Add.

5. Tap OK to close the dialog box.

After the name is assigned, it appears in the cell name display area. If you want to assign a name to a range of cells, select the range in Step 1 and then enter the name in the Names In Workbook field.

A quick way to define a name for a cell is to tap in the cell name display area and enter a name.

To use the name with the Go To command, first tap Menu | Edit | Go To to open the Go To dialog box. Select the Cell Reference Or Name radio button, enter the name in the field, and then tap OK. The cursor moves to the cell, or range of cells, assigned to that name. Choosing the Current Region radio button selects the region of cells around the current cell. Cell references also work with the Go To command. For example, entering F18 in the dialog box moves the cursor to cell F18 in the spreadsheet.

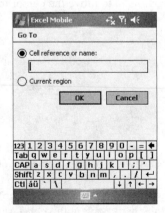

You can also use the cell name display area to move to cells within a sheet. Tap the display, enter the name or reference, and then tap ENTER on the Software Input Panel (SIP).

The Go To command works across all spreadsheets in a workbook. To use the Go To command to move to a cell reference in another sheet, enter the sheet name, an exclamation mark, and the cell reference in the Go To dialog box. For example, to move to cell A1 in Sheet1, enter **Sheet1!A1**.

A workbook may contain more than one sheet, and you can use the sheet selector in the Status bar to move between them. Tap the down arrow in the sheet selector to display a pop-up list of the sheet names, and then tap the name of the destination sheet.

Add Data and Formulas to Workbooks

Entering data into Excel Mobile is a simple process. First, select the cell in which you want to enter data, open the SIP, write the data, and then tap ENTER or move to another cell. If the cell is not visible on the screen, use the Go To command, as described in the preceding section.

Entering data on a Pocket PC is easier when using the keyboard buttons on the SIP. Chapter 3 contains information on how to use these buttons.

What you write appears in the data entry area, and three buttons appear to the left of that area for canceling the entry, entering the value in the cell, and opening the Insert Function dialog box:

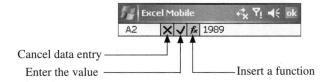

Cancel data entry ⎯⎯⎯⎯⎯

Enter the value ⎯⎯⎯⎯⎯⎯⎯⎯⎯⎯   ⎯⎯⎯⎯⎯⎯ Insert a function

Use Fill to Enter Data Quickly

To enter a series of data quickly in a range of cells, enter the first value in a cell, select the range, and then tap Menu | Edit | Fill to open the Fill dialog box:

To copy the value entered in all cells in the range, select an option in the Direction drop-down list, select Copy from the Fill Type drop-down list, and then tap OK. The value will be copied into all the cells in the range.

 *The fill direction is based on the range. If you select a column of cells, the direction is up or down; but if you select a row of cells, the direction is left or right.*

If you want the range to contain a series of data, such as the numbers one through ten, select Series from the Fill Type drop-down list, and then select one of the following options in the Series Type drop-down list:

- **AutoFill**   Creates a series based on the contents of the first cell. The first value must be a day of the week or month, or text followed by a number. For example, a range starting with Value1 will be filled with Value1, Value2, Value3, and so on.

- **Date**   Creates a series of dates. Specify which part of the date to increment by selecting Day, Month, or Year from the drop-down list. The series will increment by the amount entered in the Step Value field.

- **Number**   Creates a series of numbers that is incremented by the value entered in the Step Value field. For example, to create a series of even numbers, the first value must be even, with a Step Value of 2.

 *The starting value of a date series must contain at least a month and a date. Other values will generate unexpected results.*

Enter Formulas

Every formula begins with the equal sign (=) plus one or more of the following: values, cell references, name references, operators, and functions. The result of the formula displays in the cell in which it was entered. For example, if cell A1 contains the value 10, cell B1 the value 5, and C1 the formula =A1–B1, then the number 5 will display in cell C1.

To enter a formula, select the cell that you want to contain the result, enter the equal sign, enter a combination of one of the following, and then tap ENTER:

- **Values**   Otherwise known as constants, may be numbers, characters, text, or dates.

- **Cell references**   The two-character identifiers made by the intersection of the column and row headers. For example, G6 is the cell at the intersection of column G and row 6. An example of cell references in a formula is =A1+B1. To use cell references of multiple sheets in a formula, add the sheet name and an exclamation mark before the reference. For example, the formula =Sheet1!A1+Sheet2!A1 adds the values in the A1 cell of both sheets and places the result in the selected cell.

- **Name references**   Names that you assign to a cell using Tools | Define, as described earlier in this chapter. An example of a name reference in a formula is =Assets–Liability. Name references of multiple sheets can also be used in formulas, such as =Sheet1!Total+ Sheet2!Total.

- **Operators**   May be arithmetic, comparison, or reference. Arithmetic operators perform basic mathematical operations such as addition, subtraction, multiplication, and division. Comparison operators compare two values, the result of which is either true or false. Reference operators combine a range of cells for calculations.

■ **Functions** Predefined formulas that return a result, based on constants or references passed to them as arguments. For example, the formula =POWER(2,3) displays the value 8. If 2 were entered in cell A1, and 3 in cell B1, the formula =POWER(A1,B1) would also display the value 8.

Excel Mobile supports many functions, a list of which you can find in Online Help. If you have Excel on your desktop computer, you can find out more information about the functions in its Online Help.

Excel Mobile does not support all of the functions available in the desktop version of Excel.

Fortunately, the Insert Function dialog box is available to assist in adding functions to formulas. Tap Menu | Insert | Function to open the Insert Function dialog box:

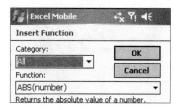

Another way to open the Insert Function dialog box is to tap Function in the data entry area.

The functions are listed in the middle of the dialog box; to narrow the list of options, select an item from the Category drop-down list. Tap a function to add it to the formula in the data entry area. When you add a function to a formula, it includes a template between the parentheses for its arguments—for example, POWER(*number,power*). The template items must be replaced with either a value or a reference—for example, POWER(2,3).

A description of each function displays in the Insert Function dialog box when you tap a function name in the list.

The most common function that you will use is Sum, and the AutoSum (Sigma) button on the toolbar provides a quick way to insert the sum of a range of cells into a spreadsheet. To use AutoSum, follow these steps:

1. Select the cell in which you want to insert the sum.

2. Tap AutoSum. AutoSum automatically selects a range of cells adjacent to the selected cell. The selection starts with the first cell above the selected cell and continues until it finds a blank cell. If the cell immediately above the selected cell is blank, AutoSum selects a range of adjacent cells to the right. However, if you wish, you can select a range and override what AutoSum automatically selects.

3. Press ENTER.

Change the View in Workbooks

Excel Mobile provides multiple ways to change the view of a workbook. These commands are particularly useful with the small display of the Pocket PC. The horizontal scrollbar, the vertical scrollbar, the Status bar, and row and column heads are turned on and off by selecting the appropriate command from the View menu. Turning off these elements allows more of the spreadsheet to display in the program window.

Split the Screen

By splitting the screen display horizontally or vertically, you can see different parts of the spreadsheet at the same time. To split the screen, tap View | Split, and the screen splits above and to the left of the selected cell:

If you want to split the screen horizontally, select a cell in column A, and then tap View | Split. To split the screen vertically, select a cell in row 1, and then tap View | Split. To remove the split, tap View | Remove Split.

Adjust the screen split by moving the horizontal and vertical bars. To make the adjustment, tap-and-hold the stylus on the bar, and then drag it in the direction you want it to move.

Freeze Panes

Freezing panes locks a column or row in place while you scroll through the rest of the spreadsheet. This is typically done to display column and row heads of data beyond the screen. To freeze panes on a spreadsheet, first select the cell where you want to freeze panes, and then tap View | Freeze Panes. All rows above the current cell, and all columns to the left of the current cell, are frozen. Lines appear above and to the left of the cell, indicating the location of the panes. To unfreeze panes, tap View | Unfreeze Panes.

Change the Screen Display

The Zoom command changes the display size of items in the spreadsheet, allowing more rows and columns to display. To zoom the display, tap View | Zoom, and then select the magnification. Create a custom zoom setting by tapping View |

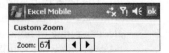

Zoom | Custom, and then enter a value in the Custom Zoom dialog box. Zoom settings apply to the entire workbook, and they are saved when you save the workbook.

To display even more columns and rows, tap View | Full Screen. All that appears are the cell reference and data entry areas, along with the spreadsheet rows and columns. To exit the Full Screen view, tap Restore.

Adjust Column Width and Row Height

Changing the size of columns and rows displays more or less of the data that they contain. To change the size of a column, tap-and-hold the stylus on the right edge of the column head, and then drag the stylus left or right. To adjust the row height, with a stylus, tap-and-hold on the bottom edge of the row head, and then drag the stylus up or down.

Automatically adjust the size of a column to the width of its longest value by double-tapping the right edge of the column head, or tap Menu | Format | Column | AutoFit. To size a row automatically, double-tap the bottom edge of the row head, or tap Format | Row | AutoFit.

Hide Rows or Columns

Hiding a row or column removes it from the display but does not delete the contents from the workbook. To hide a row or column, follow these steps:

1. Select a cell in the row or column to be hidden.
2. To hide a row, tap Menu | Format | Row | Hide.
3. To hide a column, tap Menu | Format | Column | Hide.

To display a hidden row or column, follow these steps:

1. Tap Menu | Edit | Go To.
2. Type a reference for a cell, such as E4, in the hidden row or column.
3. Tap OK.
4. To display the hidden row, tap Menu | Format | Row | Unhide.
5. To display the hidden column, tap Menu | Format | Column | Unhide.

Insert, Rename, Move, and Delete Sheets

By default, each new workbook contains three sheets. To insert another sheet into a workbook, tap Menu | Format | Modify Sheets. Tap Insert, enter a name for the sheet, and then tap OK. The Modify Sheets dialog box is also used to rename, delete, and move sheets.

Edit Data in Workbooks

As you select each cell, its contents display in the data entry area. To edit the contents, place the cursor in the area by tapping the area, and then use the SIP to edit the data. If you intend to replace the contents of a cell, just select it and begin writing and the contents are replaced.

TIP   *If you decide that you do not want the edit after you make it, you can restore the previous contents by using the Menu | Undo command.*

15

View Your Spreadsheet in Landscape

By now you have probably thought to yourself, "Wouldn't it be great to view a spreadsheet in landscape?" Indeed, by default, the Pocket PC portrait display shows only three columns in Excel Mobile, although spreadsheets tend to have many more columns.

Windows Mobile 2003SE and newer can switch the screen display to landscape. Tap Start | Settings | System | Screen and select one of the Landscape radio buttons. You can also assign a hardware button to rotate the screen by assigning the <Rotate Screen> action in the Buttons setting (tap Start | Settings | Buttons). Some Pocket PCs with built-in keyboards automatically switch to landscape display when you use the keyboard.

To copy, move, or delete the contents of a cell or a range of cells that you select, tap-and-hold and select either Cut, Copy, Paste, or Clear from the pop-up menu. You can also use tap-and-hold to insert, delete, or format cells.

TIP   *If you want to only paste formulas, values, formats, or everything except borders, select Menu | Edit | Paste Special.*

Find or Replace Cell Contents

To find or replace a number or text in a cell value or formula, tap Menu | Edit | Find/Replace to open the Find dialog box, shown here, and then follow the steps.

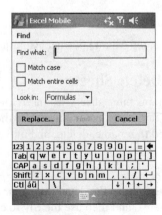

1. Enter a value in the Find What field.
2. Check the Match Case or Match Entire Cells boxes as needed.

3. Specify whether to look in the cell values or formulas from the Look In drop-down list.

4. Tap Find to search for the value you entered in Step 1.

5. To replace a value with another value, tap Replace, enter values in the Find What and Replace With fields, and then tap Find.

6. Tap OK.

The first instance of the value being searched for is highlighted, and a toolbar appears with buttons for Next, Replace, Replace All, and Close. Tap the appropriate button on the toolbar, or tap Close to stop the search.

Format Data in Workbooks

Excel Mobile provides a variety of ways to format the display of data in a workbook. Select a cell, or a range of cells, and then tap Menu | Format | Cells to open the Format Cells dialog box:

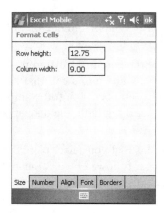

With this dialog box, you can change the cell size, and format the display of numbers, alignment, font, and borders (and fills) by making changes in the tabs and then tapping OK.

Tap a row or column head to select the entire row or column and then change the formatting for the entire selection.

Change the Cell Size

The Size tab, shown in the previous illustration, has fields for the row height and column width, in pixels. Changing the values of these fields changes the entire row or column of the current cell. The default row height is 12.75 pixels, and the default column width is 9.00 pixels.

You can also change the row height or column width from the spreadsheet. To change the row height, tap-and-hold on the line underneath the row number and drag up or down. To change the column width, tap-and-hold on the line to the right of the column letter and drag left or right.

Format Numbers

Ten predefined formats exist for numbers: Number, Currency, Accounting, Date, Time, Percentage, Fraction, Scientific, Text, and General. You can also customize the format of numbers. By default, every number in a spreadsheet has a general format.

To apply a format, first select a cell or range, select a format from the Category drop-down list, configure the format, and then tap OK. As you change the settings, a sample of the format displays in the dialog box. The following list summarizes each number format:

- **Number** Changes the display to show the number of decimal places specified. Negative numbers display based on the format selected from the Negative Numbers drop-down list. To include a 1,000 separator (a comma), check the Use 1000 Separator box.

- **Currency** Adds the currency symbol to the display when Use Currency Symbol is checked. The symbol is based on the settings that you define using the Regional Settings icon in Pocket PC Settings. This format also defines the number of decimal places and negative numbers.

- **Accounting** Adds the currency symbol and decimal places to the display. Negative numbers are formatted using parentheses and cannot be changed.

- **Date** Enables you to change the date in 11 different ways by selecting the format from the list. When you enter a value into a cell that contains a number followed by a forward slash and then another number (4/5, for example), Excel Mobile automatically assumes you are entering a date. By default, the date appears as specified in the Pocket PC Regional settings.

- **Time** Has six different formats that you select from the list. When you enter a value into a cell that contains a number followed by a colon and then another number (such as 12:05), Excel Mobile automatically assumes you are entering a time. The default format is specified in the Pocket PC Regional settings.

- **Percentage** Adds the percent symbol (%) at the end of a number, and you select the number of decimal places in the Decimal Places field.

- **Fraction** Changes the display of a calculated value, such as =1/4 from a decimal of 0.25 to a fraction. To specify the number of digits in the fraction, select it from the Type field. To enter a fraction in a cell, the fraction must be preceded by an equal sign; otherwise, the value is treated as a date.

- **Scientific** Displays the value in scientific notation, using the number of decimal places that you specify.

- **Text** Forces the contents of a cell to be formatted as text, even when a number is in the cell.

Create a Custom Format If none of the pre-existing formats meets your needs, you can create a custom format by creating a template using format codes. Excel Mobile includes several predefined templates that you can select and customize. The templates contain four sections of format codes, which are separated by semicolons. The sections define positive numbers, negative numbers, zero values, and text, in that order. If only two sections are specified, the first is used for positive numbers and zeros and the second for negative numbers and text. When only one section is specified, it is applied to all numbers. To skip a section, include the ending semicolon for that section. Excel Mobile uses the same format codes as Excel, and you can find the codes in the Excel Online Help.

Change Alignment

To align cell contents, first select the cells to be changed, open the Format Cells dialog box, and tap the Align tab. Options in the Horizontal drop-down list change the position of values left-to-right within the cell, and options in the Vertical drop-down list change the position of values top-to-bottom within the cell. You can also align cell contents by tapping the left, right, or center align buttons on the toolbar.

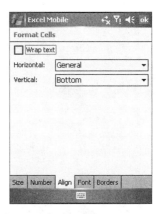

 *Unless you change the row height, you will not notice much change on the device screen after selecting Vertical alignment options.*

If you enter text that is longer than the cell width, it will not display completely within the cell. To see the complete text in the cell, check Wrap Text in the Align tab.

Change Font Settings

The Font tab of the Format Cells dialog box provides settings to change the display of text or numbers. Select the cells, tap Format | Cells, tap the Font tab, select the changes on the tab, and then tap OK. Change the font by selecting a font from the Font drop-down list. Selecting a value from the Size drop-down list changes the font size, and checking the appropriate box sets the font style to Bold, Italic, or Underline. To change font colors, select a color from the Color drop-down list.

Change Borders and Fills

To change the cell border or fill color, use the Borders tab of the Format Cells dialog box. Select the border color from the Borders drop-down list, and check the options in the Border group to select which sides of the border to change. To change cell fill colors, select a color from the Fills drop-down list.

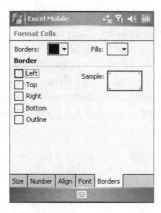

Work with Data in Workbooks

As your spreadsheets grow with data, you may want to hide some data so that you see only a subset, or you may want to change the order in which the data is entered so that similar values are grouped together. The Excel Mobile Sort and AutoFilter tools enable you to change the order of data and decrease the amount of data in the display.

Filter Data

A filter uses values in columns to decrease the number of rows that display below the point where the filter is created. Where the filter starts depends on how it is created. If only one cell is selected, the filter begins in row 2, but if a range of cells is selected, the filter begins in the row that contains the range. Figure 15-2 shows a filter that starts in row 2.
This filter will not change rows above row 2, but the rows below will change.

To filter data, follow these steps:

1. Select a cell, or a range of cells, in a row.
2. Tap Menu | Tools | AutoFilter.
3. Tap the arrow in one of the columns to open a drop-down list.
4. Select a value from the drop-down list.

Only the rows containing the value that you selected display below the location of the filter. For example, if you select the number *5* in the Filter drop-down list in Step 3, only the rows

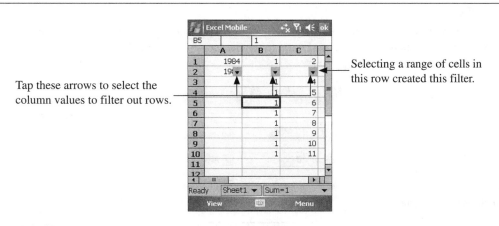

Tap these arrows to select the column values to filter out rows.

Selecting a range of cells in this row created this filter.

FIGURE 15-2   This filter affects rows below row 2.

below the filter that contain the number *5* continue to display. To remove the filter, tap Menu | Tools | AutoFilter.

Custom filters give you more control over what rows are displayed. To create a custom filter, select Custom from the Filter drop-down list to open the Custom AutoFilter dialog box:

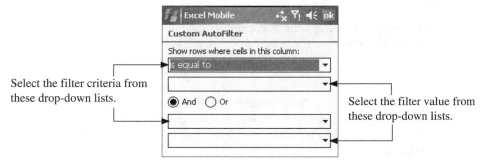

Select the filter criteria from these drop-down lists.

Select the filter value from these drop-down lists.

The two drop-down lists at the top of the Custom AutoFilter dialog box contain the filter criteria, such as Is Greater Than and Is Not Equal To. The two drop-down lists at the bottom of the dialog box contain the filter values that are in the column below the filter.

You can have your filters define two sets of criteria by selecting values in the second set of drop-down lists and selecting one of the middle radio buttons (And or Or). For example, you could create a filter that shows rows in which the column value is greater than 3 and less than 9.

In addition to the column values and the custom filter selection, you also see All and Top 10 in the Filter drop-down list. Selecting All clears the filter and displays all of the rows; selecting Top 10 displays rows that contain the top ten values in the column.

15

Sort Data

The Excel Mobile Sort command enables you to change the order of rows in a selected range of cells based on values in columns. To sort data, first select a range of cells, and then tap Menu | Tools | Sort to open the Sort dialog box:

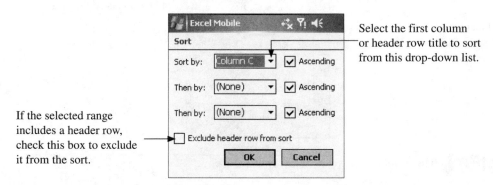

Select the first column or header row title to sort from this drop-down list.

If the selected range includes a header row, check this box to exclude it from the sort.

You can include up to three columns in a sort, which you select from the drop-down lists; these columns are sorted in order from top to bottom. By default, the sort is in ascending order. To change the sort to descending order, clear the Ascending check box for the column. If the range of cells includes a header row, and the Exclude Header Row From Sort box is checked, the header titles appear in the drop-down lists rather than the column references, and the row is not included in the sort.

TIP   *If you do not select a range of cells, the Sort command automatically selects all adjacent rows and columns of the selected cell for the sort.*

Insert Charts

Windows Mobile 5 introduces charting functions in Excel Mobile. Previous versions of Pocket Excel did not have any integrated charting functions. To add a chart to an Excel Mobile workbook, select the data you want in the chart, tap Menu | Insert | Chart to start the Chart wizard, and do the following.

1. Select a chart type and tap Next.

2. Confirm the data range and tap Next.

3. Chose a data layout and tap Next.

4. Select whether there are labels in the first row or column and tap Next.

5. Select whether to insert the chart in a new sheet or in the current sheet and tap Finish.

To edit a chart, tap-and-hold on the chart and select Format Chart to open the following dialog box. On the Titles tab you can create titles for the chart, X axis, and Y axis. Change the chart scale on the Scale tab, and select a different chart type on the Type tab. If you want to change the colors and line styles of the chart, tap Patterns on the Series tab.

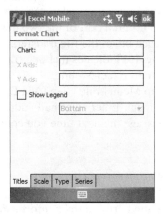

To delete a chart, tap-and-hold and select Delete Chart. To turn the chart legend on or off, tap Show Legend.

 **Graph Pocket Excel Data**

While Pocket Excel in Windows Mobile 2003SE or older does not create graphs, you can generate graphs on these Pocket PCs from Pocket Excel data by using AutoGraph from DeveloperOne. To create a graph with AutoGraph, first select and copy data in Pocket Excel and then paste it into AutoGraph. You can then create bar, column, descriptive bar, pie, *XY* scatter/line, line, and stock trend graphs. After you create a graph, you can save it to a bitmap file or copy it to the clipboard and paste it in Pocket Word or a graphics editor. More information and a trial version of AutoGraph are available at www.developerone.com.

SpreadCE from Bye Design Ltd. is a spreadsheet program that you can use instead of Pocket Excel. It provides the same functionality described in this chapter, but also includes macros and graphs. Unlike AutoGraph, the charts you create in SpreadCE stay within the spreadsheet, and they change as you update the data for the chart. You can open and save Pocket Excel files in SpreadCE, but you can save charts only in Excel 97 format, which is the default file format for the program. More information and a trial version of this program are available at www.byedesign.freeserve.co.uk. Another alternative to Excel Mobile that provides charting functions is SoftMaker's PlanMaker, available at www.softmaker.com.

15

Share Workbooks

Excel Mobile makes it easy to share workbooks with other people by including the ability to send workbooks via infrared or e-mail. To use infrared to send a workbook to another Pocket PC, tap Menu | File | Beam and line up the infrared port of the two devices.

After the two devices recognize each other, the file transfers to the receiving device. When the transfer is complete, the sending device indicates that one file has been sent and a Close button appears, which you tap to return to Excel Mobile.

To send a workbook via e-mail, tap Menu | File | Send Via E-mail, and a new e-mail message opens with the workbook as an attachment. Enter an e-mail address, subject, and message, and then tap Send. Inbox will send the message the next time you connect to the Internet and retrieve e-mail.

Wrapping Up

Excel Mobile enables you to analyze numbers and track information. You have now seen how Windows Mobile helps you create documents and spreadsheets that you may use at work. In the next chapter, you will learn more ways that Windows Mobile can help you be more productive at work.

Chapter 16

Be Productive at Work

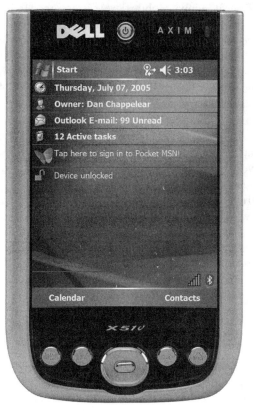

How to...

- Secure information
- View presentations
- Send and receive e-mail from Exchange
- Send and receive e-mail from Lotus Notes
- Access mainframe applications
- Access corporate databases
- Run Windows programs

Your Windows Mobile device is designed to help you organize your life and to have fun along the way. While at home, you may enjoy listening to music using the Windows Media Player or reading a book using Microsoft Reader. But many of you will most often use your device at work.

One of the reasons why you might have bought a Pocket PC or Smartphone is because a coworker has one. Personal digital assistants (PDAs), whether they are Pocket PCs, Palms, or Blackberries, are increasing in numbers at corporations. These devices are usually brought to work by employees who bought them with their own money or received them as a gift.

The extent to which you use your device at work will depend significantly on how the computers at work are used and supported. Before you connect your device to your desktop PC at work, you should find out whether your company has a policy for using PDAs. Some people will have no problem connecting their device to their desktop PC at work, while others may be restricted because of corporate policy. Unfortunately, in many cases, policies are defined without knowledge of how Windows Mobile devices work.

This chapter provides information for using your device at the office. You will find tips for connecting your device to your desktop at work and with the corporate network. Windows Mobile 5 includes PowerPoint Mobile, which you can use to view presentations created in PowerPoint on PCs. You will also learn ways to secure information and access your company's e-mail, and how to run Windows programs.

Bring Windows Mobile to Work

Many great features are built into your device to help you be more productive at work and, it is hoped, to gain more free time to enjoy life. Obviously, you can use your device to schedule appointments, track tasks, and store contact information, yet the Pocket PC Mobile Office applications enable you to create documents and spreadsheets as well.

You probably already knew about all these features before you bought your device, and you probably tried each soon after you took the device out of its box. Inevitably, the time will come when you pack your Pocket PC or Smartphone in your briefcase and head off to work, but once you are there, how will you use your device?

Connect to Your PC at Work

You will encounter few problems using your device at work, but you may face some hurdles connecting the device to your work computer. You need to resolve two issues:

- The physical connection between the device and computer
- Installing and running ActiveSync

Make the Connection

Every Windows Mobile device is capable of partnering with two PCs, but most devices include only one cable or cradle. Chances are good that you already use the cable or cradle with your home computer, so you might be faced with the prospect of carrying the cable back and forth between work and home. There are a few solutions to this problem.

First, check whether your work computer has an infrared port—some notebook computers have built-in infrared ports. If the port is available, it can be used to communicate with your device. Chapter 6 provides the instructions for using infrared ports with ActiveSync.

The second solution is to buy a second cable to use at work. All hardware manufacturers sell cables as accessories. Most of the cables sell for less than $25 and are available from the manufacturers or from any online store that sells Windows Mobile devices. If you upgrade within a brand, you might already have two cables, so be sure to check the manufacturer's web site.

Finally, you can use Bluetooth to make the connection between your device and the desktop PC. Many notebooks now have built-in Bluetooth support; otherwise, it is pretty easy to add Bluetooth to PCs by using a Universal Serial Bus (USB) adapter. Chapter 6 provides the instructions for using Bluetooth to connect Windows Mobile devices to PCs.

Install ActiveSync

After you determine how you will connect the device to your computer at work, the next step is to install ActiveSync. When installing ActiveSync on PCs running Windows NT 4, Windows 2000, or Windows XP, the user ID that you use to install ActiveSync must be a local administrator on the PC. Once installed under Windows NT 4, ActiveSync will run even if the ID is only in the local Users group.

The same is not true for Windows 2000 or XP, however. By default, to run ActiveSync, the ID must at least be for a user in the Power Users local group if ActiveSync is installed on a drive formatted with NTFS (NT File System). The reason is that the Windows 2000/XP default security on the Program Files folder and subfolders does not provide users with write access, and ActiveSync must be able to write files in the \Program Files\Microsoft ActiveSync folder. An alternative is to modify the NTFS permissions of the ActiveSync folder so that the users group has full control over the folder.

This problem does not occur if the Program Files folder is on a FAT (file allocation table) partition.

Many corporate PCs run firewall software that may interfere with ActiveSync. You might need to configure the firewall software to allow ports 5678, 5679, 990, 999, 26675, and 5721

16

in order for ActiveSync to function. If you are running the Microsoft firewall that comes with Service Pack 2 of Windows XP, it should be automatically configured for ActiveSync.

Sometimes antivirus, virtual private networking, and LAN configuration tools might conflict with ActiveSync. To enable synchronization between a Windows Mobile device and the PC, you might need to disable this software.

Work with Non-Microsoft Applications

Personal Information Managers (PIMs) for the desktop PC have been available for many years, but they have never caught on in a major way, probably because the data stored by PIMs is not as useful when anchored to a desk. Sure, when you sit at your desk, you could quickly search for a telephone number or an appointment, but what happens when you are in a meeting? The best solution is probably to print the information on paper and take it with you, but adding appointments and tasks is tedious because the device requires that you enter that information when you return to your desk.

The synchronization capabilities of PDAs make PIMs more useful because carrying and updating data is easier. Furthermore, the data is in electronic form, so it is much easier to share with others, and that has led to the group scheduling capabilities that make PIMs corporate tools.

Microsoft Outlook is a popular PIM, but it is certainly not the first, or only, one used by companies. Lotus Organizer has been available for much longer, and its user interface, which looks like a paper planner, is popular. Other programs store PIM data but specialize in contact management, such as ACT!, GoldMine, and Maximizer. Collaborative software such as Microsoft Exchange Server and Lotus Notes also store PIM data.

With all of these options, there is a chance that your company uses a program other than Microsoft Outlook. If that is the case, for your Windows Mobile device to be useful at work, you need to come up with a way to synchronize data with that program. The good news is that Windows Mobile can synchronize with programs other than Outlook. The bad news is that you may need to buy additional software, because ActiveSync communicates only with Outlook and Microsoft Works.

Synchronize Data with Non-Microsoft Applications

Four programs expand the Windows Mobile synchronization capabilities beyond Outlook to several different PIMs:

- **Intellisync Handheld Edition from Intellisync**   www.intellisync.com/
- **XTNDConnect PC from iAnywhere**   www.ianywhere.com/
- **CompanionLink Express or Professional from CompanionLink Software**
  www.companionlink.com/

These programs include features not found with ActiveSync that provide more control over synchronization and address shortcomings. For example, Intellisync and XTNDConnect PC support synchronization of Outlook subfolders, which is not possible with ActiveSync.

Each of these programs synchronizes Calendar, E-mail, Contacts, and Tasks. Both Intellisync and XTNDConnect PC give you the ability to match fields of data, providing flexibility not available with ActiveSync, which is optimized for Outlook. What may be appealing to companies is that both programs synchronize with Windows Mobile and Palm devices, enabling them to provide a standard method of synchronization with a standard PIM.

Manage Contacts

Contact managers are programs that store data in a manner similar to PIMs, but they are designed for the purpose of managing relationships with people. Usually, all of the data in a contact manager relates back to a person. For example, using a contact manager, you can quickly see all the appointments that you have scheduled with a particular person. Sales departments of companies commonly use these programs to help build relationships with people.

The four third-party synchronization programs described in the previous section support the synchronization of Outlook Mobile with popular desktop contact managers like ACT! and GoldMine. However, Outlook Mobile does not provide many of the features, such as linking contacts with appointments or tasks, that one expects of a contact manager. If you want these features on your device, you have to obtain a third-party application.

One of the most popular of these applications on Pocket PCs is Pocket Informant, available for download from www.pocketinformant.com. Pocket Informant enables you to link contacts with appointments, tasks, other contacts, or files. It also provides the ability to create appointments or tasks using the contact information, which is automatically linked to the contact.

Pocket Informant works with your Outlook Mobile data, so everything synchronizes with Outlook. On-Schedule version 6 for Pocket PC from Odyssey synchronizes with On-Schedule version 6 or Microsoft Outlook. Because of this, it is a good alternative to Outlook Mobile if you don't like Outlook.

Unlike Outlook Mobile, On-Schedule provides journaling capabilities to track contact information, and it supports multiple address books, calendars, and to-do lists. For people who find Outlook Mobile categories insufficient for separating data, On-Schedule may be a good alternative. You will find more information, and a trial version of the software, at www.odysseyinc.com.

Convert Files

Even though Microsoft Word and Excel are the most popular word processor and spreadsheet programs, they are not the only programs used by companies. At one time, WordPerfect and Lotus 1-2-3 were more popular, and they are still in use.

Unfortunately, no widely available file-conversion tools exist for Windows Mobile to enable you to open WordPerfect or Lotus 1-2-3 files in Word or Excel Mobile. In both cases, the best way to work with these files is to save them in Microsoft formats before downloading to your device. This also means that if someone wants to e-mail a WordPerfect document as an attachment, the file must first be converted to a Microsoft format.

Word Mobile and Excel Mobile on Windows Mobile 5 use the same file formats as Office 2003; however, prior versions of these programs use the Pocket Word and Pocket Excel formats. Chapter 7 explains how ActiveSync converts files as they move between a device and a desktop computer.

Inbox on Windows Mobile 2003 SE and earlier converts files so that you can easily send and receive Word and Word Mobile file attachments. But if you use any other method of transferring files, such as an FTP client or a network connection, you have to convert the file manually to a supported format.

You can use Westtek's ClearVue Suite to view native Microsoft Office 97, 2000, and XP PowerPoint, Excel, and Word files on Pocket PCs and Smartphones. More information about this software is available at www.westtek.com.

Pocket Word can save files in Rich Text format (RTF), plaintext, Word 97, and Word 6.0/95 formats. To save a document in these formats, tap Tools | Save Document As, expand the Type drop-down list, and select a format. Pocket Excel can save files in Excel 97, 5.0, and 95 workbook formats. To save a Pocket Excel workbook in one of these formats, tap Tools | Save Workbook As, expand the Type drop-down list, and select a format.

Word and Excel Mobile only support the native Word and Excel formats in the Save As dialog box.

Open Adobe Acrobat Files

The Adobe Portable Document Format (PDF) has become the de facto standard for distributing documents on the Internet. This is because Adobe distributes Acrobat Reader, which is required to view PDF files, for free on the Internet. PDF files look exactly the same as printed documents and are easy to create. For these reasons, many companies create documentation in PDF format and make it available from their web sites.

You can view PDF files with Acrobat Reader for Pocket PC, which is capable of viewing tagged and untagged Acrobat files. Tagged files are preferable for viewing on Pocket PCs because the Pocket PC allows Acrobat Reader to format the text for the size of the Pocket PC screen. When you install Acrobat Reader on your Pocket PC, it adds an Acrobat file converter to ActiveSync, which attempts to convert Acrobat files to the tagged format. If the PDF file cannot be converted to the tagged format, it is copied to the Pocket PC in the untagged format. You can find more information about Acrobat Reader at www.adobe.com/products/acrobat/readerforppc.html.

Before Adobe Acrobat Reader, PDF Viewer from Global Graphics was the only Acrobat Reader for Pocket PCs. PDF Viewer supports most PDF image formats, including bookmarks, hyperlinks, and Table of Contents. It provides magnification capabilities that are important for viewing documents designed for larger PC screens. More information and a 30-day trial version of this program is available at www.globalgraphics.com/products/editor/primer.html.

Adobe does not provide a version of Acrobat Reader for Smartphones, but if you need to view Acrobat files on a Smartphone, you can use Westtek's ClearVue PDF. You can find more information about this program at www.westtek.com/smartphone/pdf.

Access the Corporate Network

Chances are good that your computer at work is connected to a LAN so that it can access shared resources such as printers and e-mail servers. Windows Mobile includes the software to enable it to connect to these networks, either by using a modem and dial-up connection or directly with an Ethernet card. You can use this connectivity to send and receive e-mail from your company mail server or to access web pages on your corporate intranet.

Gather Dial-Up Information

Today, many companies provide dial-up access to their networks to enable employees to access resources from home or on the road. The dial-up access is probably expected to work with desktop computers, while few companies provide support for Pocket PCs. This does not mean that your Pocket PC will not work with a company dial-up access, but it does mean that you may have to gather more information and probably configure the device yourself.

If you can access a corporate network using standard Windows Dial-Up Networking, you should be able to connect using a Pocket PC. You need to gather some information before you can create a dial-up connection. If your company provides instructions for connecting using Windows, what you need is provided in those instructions. If the dial-up connection has already been created, you can find the information by opening the connection Properties window.

The following is the information that you need to create the dial-up connection on your Pocket PC:

- Find out whether you provide a username and password in the Dial-Up Connection dialog box, or whether a terminal window opens after the number has been dialed (in which you enter a username and password).

- Obtain the maximum baud rate for the connection as well as the settings for data bits, parity, stop bits, and flow control.

- Find out whether the connection uses Point-to-Point Protocol (PPP) or Serial Line Interface Protocol (SLIP). The most common in use is PPP.

- Determine whether the network access server, or Windows NT Remote Access Server, provides an IP address, or whether one is manually assigned. The most common configuration is server assigned, but if it is manually assigned, you need the address.

- Find out whether the connection uses software compression or IP header compression. The most common configuration is to use both.

- Learn whether addresses for name servers are server assigned or manually assigned. If they are manually assigned, you need the addresses for the primary DNS server, secondary DNS server, primary WINS server, and secondary WINS server.

- If a proxy server is used to access the Internet, you need the proxy server name. To find the proxy server name found in Internet Explorer on desktop computers, click Tools | Internet Options, and then click the Connections tab and the LAN Settings button.

- Determine whether you need to use virtual private networking (VPN) to connect to the corporate network. If you do, obtain the hostname or IP address of the VPN server.

- Obtain the phone number for accessing the corporate network, or if you use VPN, obtain the phone number for an Internet service provider (ISP).

16

Configure Pocket PC Connection Manager Work Settings

After you gather this information, you are ready to create the dial-up connection. To create a dial-up connection on Pocket PCs, you use Connection Manager, which simplifies the process.

Connection Manager, shown in the following image, has two sections: one for configuring ISP connection settings and another for configuring Work network settings.

To open Connection Manager on your Pocket PC, tap Start | Settings | Connections | Connections. To create a dial-up connection to a Work network, tap Add A New Modem Connection under My Work Network on the main Connection Manager screen. You then enter information on three screens to create a modem connection. On the first screen, enter a name for the connection, select the modem that you will use, and tap Next.

On the second screen, enter the phone number exactly as it should be dialed, including extra numbers such as an outside line or credit card, and then tap Next. If you travel or frequently change location (and thus area codes), configure the Pocket PC to use Dialing Rules.

Finally, on the third screen, enter the username and password you use to log onto your Work network. If you are connecting to a Microsoft Windows network, you may need to enter a domain name, which your network administrator can provide. Tap Advanced to change the modem baud rate or enter network addresses for the Pocket PC, DNS servers, or WINS servers. Tap OK to exit the Advanced Settings screen, and then tap Finish to exit from the third and final modem connection screen.

After you create a modem connection for a Work network, a new option called Manage Existing Connections appears on the Connection Manager screen. Tap this option to change the modem connection settings.

Most Work networks use Dynamic Host Configuration Protocol (DHCP) to configure network addresses automatically, and Pocket PCs use DHCP by default, so you should not need to enter network addresses. If you need to enter TCP/IP or name server information, or if you need to have a terminal window open after the modem connects so that you can log onto the network, tap Advanced on the third modem connection screen.

The Advanced Settings screen has several tabs, as shown here:

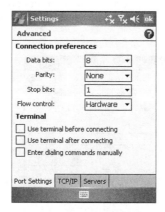

The Port Settings tab has check boxes to specify whether a terminal window displays. Tap the Use Terminal After Connecting check box if you need a terminal window for logging onto the network. Tap the Use Terminal Before Connecting or Enter Dialing Commands Manually check boxes if you need to enter modem commands prior to the call being made.

Tap the TCP/IP tab to enter the IP address that the Pocket PC should use when connecting to the network, and tap the Servers tab to enter IP addresses for DNS and WINS. Tap OK to close the Advanced Settings screen.

Windows Mobile 5 supports VPN solutions that use the Point-to-Point Tunneling Protocol (PPTP), IP Security (IPSec), or Layer Two Tunneling Protocol (L2TP). To configure your Pocket PC to use VPN, you need the hostname or IP address of the VPN connection. To configure Windows Mobile to use VPN, tap Add A New VPN Server Connection on the Tasks tab of Connection Manager.

Enter the hostname or IP address for the VPN server, which your network administrator can provide, and tap Next. Enter your VPN server username and password on the second VPN settings screen, and tap Finish.

Virtual Private Networking Provides Access to Corporate Networks

Virtual private networking (VPN) uses encryption to secure communication between a client and a server, and it is commonly used to enable one to use the public Internet to access servers on a private network. Typically, you first dial an ISP using dial-up networking. Then, you run a VPN client, which establishes a connection with the VPN server. After a VPN connection is made, you can run any application that requires a network connection.

16

The final work setting to configure is for the proxy servers. Proxy servers are typically used by web browsers to access pages on the Internet on computers connected to a corporate network. If you need to use a proxy server, tap Set Up My Proxy Server on the Connection Manager screen, which opens the following:

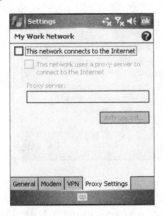

Tap the two check boxes on the screen to select them and enter the hostname or IP address of the proxy server in the Proxy Server field. Tap Advanced if you need to change the ports for the proxy server, enter a WAP (Wireless Application Protocol) proxy server, or configure the Socks proxy server.

WAP proxy servers provide access to web pages that are designed for display on mobile phones. Socks proxy servers enable clients and servers of client/server applications to communicate with each other by using the Internet.

Tap OK to return to the main Connection Manager screen. You now see an Edit My Proxy Server link under My Work Network, which you can tap if you need to make any changes to the proxy server settings.

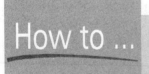 ## Configure Smartphones for Work Connections

Smartphones do not have a connection manager like Pocket PCs that distinguish between Internet and Work connections, but they do support VPN and proxy servers. To configure Smartphones to use VPN, press Start | Settings | Connections | VPN, and to configure Smartphones to use proxy servers, press Start | Settings | Connections | Proxy.

Smartphones do not support dial-up modems like Pocket PCs, but you can configure some Smartphones to use Circuit-Switch Cellular, which works like dial-up. If your mobile service supports Circuit-Switch Cellular data communications, you can configure your Smartphone to use it by pressing Start | Settings | Connections, and then pressing Menu | Add to create a dial-up connection.

Connect to the Corporate Network

The easiest way to make a dial-up connection to a Work network is directly from Messaging or Internet Explorer. Chapter 11 shows you how to configure an account in Messaging so that it uses the Work settings.

Internet Explorer does not have an option for you to specify whether to use an Internet or Work connection. Instead, the Connection Manager determines which type of connection to use based on the URL you enter in the Address bar or the URL you select in Favorites. If the address is a fully qualified domain name (FQDN), such as www.pocketpchow2.com, Connection Manager connects to the Internet. If the address is one word, such as pocketpchow2, Connection Manager connects to Work.

If you access to a corporate intranet that uses FQDNs, and you have a Pocket PC 2002 device, you have to either manually initiate the call using Connection Manager or configure the Internet connection to access the corporate network. Windows Mobile 2003 and newer fixes this by providing a way for you to enter intranet web addresses as exceptions, so that when you try to open them in Internet Explorer, Connection Manager will establish a connection to a Work network.

To add a URL to the Exceptions list on Windows Mobile, tap the Advanced tab on Connection Manager, and then tap Exceptions, which opens the Work URL Exceptions screen. Tap Add New URL and then enter the URL of the web sites on your intranet. You can use wildcards—for example, entering *.companyname.com matches any URL ending with companyname.com.

If your corporate network uses a proxy server to connect to the Internet, Internet Explorer Mobile does not use the proxy server to access web sites in the Exceptions list.

Use Ethernet Networking

Most Pocket PCs are capable of connecting to an Ethernet network, which is used by most companies that have LANs. You can use Internet Explorer Mobile to access intranet web sites, and you can even use a proxy server to access the public Internet. Furthermore, Messaging can also access e-mail servers that use standard Internet e-mail protocols. Before you connect your device to the network in your office, review the information in this section with your network administrator.

16

Before you can connect the Pocket PC to an Ethernet network, you must gather the following information so that you can configure the Ethernet card driver. Your network administrator can provide this information. Chapter 10 provides the instructions for using this information to configure the Ethernet card driver.

- Does the network provide IP addresses using DHCP, or are they manually assigned (static)?

- If the addresses are static, what are the address, the subnet mask, and the default gateway?

- If the network provides the addresses, are the DNS and WINS addresses also provided? If not, obtain the IP addresses for the primary and secondary DNS servers, and the primary and secondary WINS servers.

Connection Manager also has a role in how a Pocket PC uses network cards, because it specifies whether network cards connect to the Internet or Work networks. If the intranet you wish to connect to uses a proxy server, you must configure the network card to connect to a Work network. To specify how Windows Mobile uses network cards, tap Start | Settings | Connections | Network Cards to open this screen:

Select either The Internet or Work from the My Network Card Connects To drop-down list on the Configure Network Adapters screen.

If you specify that a network card connects to Work, and the Work settings are configured for a proxy server, you will not be able to access web sites on the Internet unless the proxy server is available. This means that if you connect to a home network that does not have a proxy server, you need to set the network card to the Internet to access web sites.

Use ActiveSync Desktop Pass Through

With Windows Mobile ActiveSync version 3.7 or greater, you can access the corporate network from a Pocket PC or Smartphone while the device is connected to a desktop computer. The feature is enabled by default in ActiveSync, and you can access Internet or intranet sites depending on the URL that you enter in Internet Explorer. If you are having problems using a proxy server to access an Internet site, click File | Connection Settings in ActiveSync on the desktop PC and select Work from the This Computer Is Connected To drop-down list.

View Presentations on Pocket PCs Using PowerPoint Mobile

Many business people rely on Microsoft PowerPoint every day as part of their job. For those people, if a Pocket PC is to replace notebook computers, they must include software that can view and display PowerPoint presentations. Windows Mobile 5 includes PowerPoint Mobile, which you can use to open and view presentations created on your PC. Previous versions of Windows Mobile do not include a Pocket PC version of PowerPoint, but several companies provide programs that can display PowerPoint presentations on a Pocket PC. Table 16-1 lists the programs that are available for Windows Mobile 2003SE and earlier.

PowerPoint Mobile displays presentations that are created using PowerPoint 97 or later. It supports most of the features of PowerPoint except for the following:

- You cannot view slide notes or notes pages.
- You cannot rearrange slides in presentation or edit slides.

Open and View Presentations

Start PowerPoint Mobile by tapping Start | Programs | PowerPoint Mobile, which opens the program file list, and tap the name of the presentation that you want to view. If you tap the filename of a PowerPoint file in an e-mail attachment, or with File Explorer, PowerPoint Mobile

Program	URL
CNetX Pocket SlideShow	www.cnetx.com
Conduits Pocket Slides	www.conduits.com
Westtek ClearVue Presentation	www.westtek.com
RepliGo	www.cerience.com

TABLE 16-1   PowerPoint File-Viewing Programs for the Pocket PC

16

starts and opens the presentation that you selected. The presentation displays in Slideshow mode, as shown here:

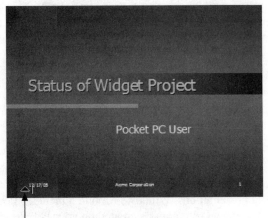

Tap here to open the Slideshow menu.

By default, presentations display in landscape, but you can change the display orientation by opening the Slideshow menu, tapping Show Options, and then tapping the orientation that you want. The Playback tab of the Options window provides a way for you to specify whether you want to override the settings specified in presentations. For example, you can specify that you do not want animations to play when they are in presentations.

Press the navigation button to move forward and backward through the slideshow, or open the Slideshow menu and tap Next or Previous. To jump to a specific slide, tap Go To Slide in the Slideshow menu, and then tap the name of the slide you want to jump to. Tap Zoom In or Zoom Out to enlarge or shrink the display of the slide. Tap End Show on the Slideshow menu to close the slideshow and return to the file list.

Secure Information

Because Windows Mobile devices are small, they are handy to carry around. Unfortunately, their size also makes them easy to steal. It is bad enough that your appointments, addresses, and tasks are at risk, but it is another thing entirely to expose confidential documents to outsiders. Fortunately, you can secure the information and data in a Windows Mobile device in several ways. This section reviews some of these methods, to help you determine which is the best for you.

Use the Pocket PC Power-On Password

Every Pocket PC can be assigned a password that you must enter whenever you turn on the device. The only way to access the device without the password is by performing a hard reset, which removes all information stored on the device. To assign a password to your device, follow the instructions provided in Chapter 3.

 *Windows Mobile supports strong passwords, which consist of alphabetic and numeric characters. Because strong passwords are more secure than the simple four-digit numeric PINs used with Pocket PC 2000, they are preferred by corporations.*

Assign PINs on Smartphones

There are several built-in ways to secure information on Smartphones. One way is to enable phone lock by pressing Start | Settings | Security | Enable Phone Lock. You can specify the amount of time of inactivity before the phone is locked, and the password. While the phone is locked you can still receive phone calls and make emergency phone calls, but to access information on the phone or make a phone call, you need to first enter the password.

The Smartphone security menu also includes options for enabling the SIM PIN, which secures information on the SIM cards that are used in some Smartphones, and changing PIN2. PIN2 is a second PIN code for SIM cards that unlocks certain features such as Fixed Dialing and Call Cost metering. Not all SIM cards use the PIN2 code.

Use Antivirus Software

Although few viruses have been reported on Windows Mobile devices, the release of "proof of concept" viruses indicates that virus writers are experimenting with the platform. The good news is that the popular script-based viruses that take advantage of Outlook do not work on Windows Mobile because it does not have the same scripting support as Outlook. Table 16-2 lists the virus-scan software that you can buy for Pocket PCs and Smartphones.

Store Sensitive Information in Secure Databases

It seems as though the Internet has dramatically increased the number of user IDs and passwords in our lives. Combined with account numbers and PINs, it can be too much information to keep track of. A Windows Mobile device is perfect for storing and retrieving this information, but how do you protect it?

Fortunately, several programs have been written to store and protect this type of information. One of these programs is FlexWallet from Two Peaks Software, which is an information manager that lets you store password and registration information in one encrypted database. You can

Product	URL
Airscanner Mobile AntiVirus Pro for Pocket PC	http://airscanner.com
Symantec AntiVirus for Handhelds Corporate Edition	www.symantec.com
Kaspersky Security for PDAs	www.kaspersky.com
SMobile VirusGuard	www.fb-4.com

TABLE 16-2   Windows Mobile Virus-Scan Software

16

use FlexWallet to store passwords, CD-ROM keys, and web site registration information. For information and an evaluation copy, go to www.twopeaks.com.

eWallet from Ilium Software has a graphical user interface (GUI) that takes the form of a *wallet*. In this wallet, you can store cards that resemble credit cards, calling cards, and cards that include PINs and registration numbers. Each card can be protected with a password and encryption. Ilium Software sells versions of eWallet for all Windows Mobile platforms, and a version is also available for desktop computers. For more information and an evaluation copy, go to www.iliumsoft.com/wallet.htm.

Encrypt Files

Encryption is the process of converting messages and data into a form that is unreadable by anyone except the intended recipient. People commonly use this method to secure data transferred across the Internet. For example, the Secure Sockets Layer (SSL) protocol developed by Netscape encrypts the contents of web pages before they are transmitted between the web server and the web browser.

Encryption can also be used to secure files so that they cannot be opened unless a password is provided. While encryption is effective for securing documents, there is a risk that if the password is lost or forgotten, the document cannot be opened. One way to protect against this risk is to store unencrypted copies of the files in a secure location. Two products, Sentry CE and PocketLock, provide encryption for Pocket PCs.

SoftWinter, Inc., sells Sentry 2020 Pocket PC, which is also available for Windows XP. Sentry 2020 creates an encrypted virtual volume on a Pocket PC that is compatible with its Windows XP product, which means that if the volume is on a storage card and your device fails, you still can gain access to the data. Encrypting a file is a simple matter of copying the file to the virtual volume and providing a password. The virtual volume can be created on a storage card, which you can then remove from the device and store for even more security. The virtual volume looks like a large file when viewed with File Explorer. You can find more information about Sentry 2020 at www.softwinter.com.

PocketLock from Applian provides simple encryption and decryption of files and folders located internally or on a storage card. It uses the Microsoft High Encryption Pack to provide eight encryption methods. To encrypt a file or folder, you simply select either using PocketLock and provide a numeric PIN. Encrypted files can be automatically decrypted from File Explorer, but they are not visible to Pocket Word or Excel. You can find more information about PocketLock at www.applianmobile.com.

While SmartPhones do not have programs such as Word and Excel Mobile to create documents or File Explorer to manage files on the device, they do store files like Pocket PCs and desktop computers. You might receive file attachments in e-mail, or transfer files to Smartphones using ActiveSync. To manage and encrypt files on a Smartphone, you can use Resco Explorer, which provides the ability to encrypt individual files on Smartphones, Pocket PCs, and desktop computers. You can find Resco Explorer at www.resco.net.

Encrypt All Device Contents

The programs presented in this section provide a way to encrypt files that you store on Windows Mobile devices, but they do not encrypt the data you have in Outlook Mobile or Messaging. A few programs exist that encrypt all data on Windows Mobile devices, but they are typically sold to corporations.

One affordable program is SureWave Mobile Defense from JP Mobile, which was previously known as PDA Defense. This program currently is only available for Pocket PCs, but a version is in development for Smartphones. You can find more information about this product at www.pdadefense.com.

Several corporations use Pointsec to encrypt data on desktop and notebook computers, and there are also versions available for Pocket PCs and Smartphones. The advantage of Pointsec for corporations is that it can be centrally managed, making it easier to support a high number of devices. More information about Pointsec for Pocket PC and Smartphone is available at www.pointsec.com.

Connect to Corporate E-mail Systems

You might expect Messaging to work with Microsoft Exchange Server. After all, they're both Microsoft products, so why wouldn't they work together? However, prior to Microsoft releasing Exchange 2003, you needed an intermediary program to synchronize e-mail with Exchange unless it was configured to support Internet protocols. Exchange Server 2003 includes Server ActiveSync (previously called Mobile Information Server), which supports synchronization with Pocket PCs.

Lotus Notes and Novell GroupWise are two other popular e-mail servers used by corporations, but both primarily support their own clients, which do not use the Internet e-mail protocols. Unless Internet protocol support is added to these servers, the only way to use Inbox with them is through an intermediary program. Inbox communicates with the intermediary program using the Internet protocols, and the intermediary program communicates with the e-mail server using the appropriate non-Internet protocols.

TIP   *Messaging supports SSL encryption for communicating with e-mail servers using Internet protocols. See Chapter 11 for instructions on how to use SSL with Inbox.*

The good news is that the intermediary program can run on a server and provide access to the corporate e-mail server for several clients. The bad news is that you must add a server to the corporate network, which may be beyond your capability.

16

You do have a couple of alternatives, however. One is to synchronize messages between Messaging and an e-mail client running on your PC. The process for synchronization between Messaging and Outlook, explained in Chapter 11, enables you to send and receive messages from Exchange when Outlook is used as an Exchange client. Intellisync and XTNDConnect PC, described earlier in this chapter, are both capable of synchronizing Messaging messages with Lotus Notes clients, and Intellisync can also sync with Novell GroupWise.

Send and Receive E-mail from Exchange

As explained in Chapter 11, Messaging is primarily an Internet e-mail client. While Exchange includes support for Internet protocols, many implementations have this feature disabled. If the Exchange server that you use does support either the POP3 or IMAP4 protocol, Messaging can be configured to work with the server. Follow the instructions provided in Chapter 11 for setting up an Internet service.

As previously mentioned, Microsoft Exchange Server 2003 includes Server ActiveSync, which supports direct synchronization of Windows Mobile devices with Exchange. Chapter 7 provides instructions for configuring your device for synchronization with Exchange.

A highly anticipated new feature of Windows Mobile 5 is the support of push e-mail. *Push e-mail* transfers e-mail messages to devices nearly the instant the messages are received by the e-mail server, and was made popular by Research In Motion's Blackberry software.

To enable push e-mail for Windows Mobile devices, you need to install Service Pack 2 (SP2) for Exchange Server 2003 and you need to install the Messaging and Security Feature Pack (MSFP) on Windows Mobile 5 devices. Unfortunately, while Microsoft has released SP2 for Exchange, MSFP will only be available from mobile carriers or device manufacturers, and no company has announced when it will make MSFP available for its devices. If you are interested in using push-email with your Windows Mobile 5 device, contact the device manufacturer and ask when it will make MSFP available.

Send and Receive E-mail from Lotus Notes

To say that Lotus Notes is commonly found among corporations around the world is an understatement. Recently, Lotus announced that it had reached 50 million users. The popularity of this program has created a whole new category of software, called *groupware*.

Companies use groupware to provide access to free-form information stored in databases. Several copies of the same database may be kept consistent throughout a company through a process called *replication*. Replication is similar to the synchronization process that you use to keep your device and Outlook consistent. The difference is that the databases may be countries apart, and they use networks and messaging to pass information back and forth.

At first, Lotus Notes consisted of e-mail messages and databases. Later, PIM features and group scheduling were added to the product. The product has also been divided in two, with Notes being the client and Domino being the server, but people often refer to the two as one and call it Lotus Notes.

Lotus Notes has many features and can be complicated. If you are trying to determine how to get a Windows Mobile device to work with Lotus Notes, things can get confusing. First, you need to ask yourself a few questions: Do you want to communicate with the Notes client or the Domino server? Do you want to synchronize E-mail, Calendar, Contacts, and Tasks, or do you want access to databases? Let's see if we can sort this out.

A number of the products already described enable synchronization of E-mail, Calendar, Contacts, and Tasks with the Lotus Notes client. Intellisync and XTNDConnect PC support Lotus Notes versions 4.5, 4.6, 5.0, and 6.0.

If you need access to Lotus Notes databases, you will want to look at mNotes from CommonTime Ltd. This product is the only one designed specifically for working with Lotus Notes databases, which CommonTime specializes in developing. If you are familiar with Lotus Notes, you will find that CommonTime products provide the most support for all of its features. More information is available at www.commontime.com/.

Run Windows Programs on Pocket PCs

You may be painfully aware by now that the Pocket Office applications included with Pocket PCs do not have the same functionality as those provided in Microsoft Office. If you travel frequently, you may have hoped that your device could replace that notebook computer you lug around, only to have those hopes dashed when you found out that you couldn't create tables in Pocket Word. Wouldn't it be great if you could run the full copy of Microsoft Word on your Pocket PC?

Well, you can, kind of. Actually, you can work with a display of Word on your Pocket PC while the program actually runs on another computer. The process for doing this is called *network computing,* and it is similar to the mainframe programs you access with a terminal emulator.

A terminal server client runs on your Pocket PC that accesses programs running on the server. The display of those programs appears on your Pocket PC, and it seems as if you are sitting at a regular desktop computer, but all of the processing happens back at the server. This software is becoming a popular way for companies to provide remote access to their systems, because it centralizes support. Programs are installed on one computer and made available to all who access it, rather than having to install programs on hundreds of notebook computers spread throughout the country.

While they work incredibly well, terminal server clients have one significant limitation: the client must be able to connect to the server to run applications. People who travel frequently on airplanes may find this limitation to be a problem when they want to run Microsoft Word or Excel. However, for users of Pocket PCs, these clients are the only way to run Windows programs.

Use Microsoft Mobile Terminal Services Client

The first step in using the Microsoft Mobile Terminal Services Client is to obtain access to the server. Your network administrator will create a username and password that you will use to log onto the server. The administrator also sets you up with the programs that you need to run on your Pocket PC. You also need to connect your Pocket PC to the corporate network, as described in the "Access the Corporate Network" section earlier in this chapter.

How to Do Everything with Windows Mobile

To start the Terminal Services Client, tap Start | Programs | Terminal Services Client. Enter a hostname or an IP address of the terminal server and tap Connect. After a connection is established, you see the standard Windows logon screen.

Along the bottom of the screen are five buttons that you can use to quickly move the display around the screen. If you limit the size of the server desktop to fit the Pocket PC screen, the buttons do not display.

The Pocket PC portrait orientation limits what you can see on the Windows desktop; to see more of the screen, switch to landscape mode by tapping Start | Settings | System | Screen and then tap one of the landscape buttons.

Use the stylus for mouse operations when running Windows programs, and tap-and-hold to open a drop-down menu (like the one that appears when you right-click with your PC mouse). You cannot use Transcriber with Terminal Services, so you need to use the keyboard, Letter Recognizer, or Block Recognizer to enter information. To end the terminal session, tap Start | Shut Down, select Logoff, and then tap OK.

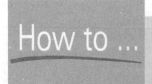

Turn On Remote Desktop in Windows XP

If you want to use the Terminal Services Client to access a Windows XP desktop, you need to enable Remote Desktop, which is turned off by default. On the desktop PC, click Start | Control Panel | System, then click the Remote tab, and check the Allow Users To Connect Remotely To This Computer check box. Only user accounts that have passwords on the PC will be allowed to connect.

The Pocket PC Close button does not shut down the Terminal Services Client. If you tap Close and then switch back to Terminal Services, you will find that your Pocket PC is still connected to the server.

Use Citrix WinFrame

Citrix pioneered the development of server-based computing when it created and sold WinFrame. The Independent Computing Architecture (ICA), also developed by Citrix, enables client devices running a variety of operating systems to access their terminal server. Included among those devices are Pocket PCs.

Because Citrix has been selling WinFrame for a number of years, a large number of corporations have it installed. If your company uses Citrix, you will be able to download and use the ICA client, which you can find at http://download.citrix.com/.

Use Other Remote-Control Applications

Remote-control software works like terminal servers because you run programs running on other computers. The difference is that the host program can support only one client session at a time. Perhaps the most popular use of these programs is to provide remote troubleshooting and help desk support for remote and mobile workers.

Virtual Network Computing (VNC) is a remote display system that allows you to view a desktop environment running on a machine from anywhere on the Internet. It is usually used to display an X Windows System that runs on Unix, but it will also run on Macintoshes and Windows. With VNC Viewer running on a Pocket PC, you can access desktops running on Unix, Macintosh, and Windows computers running the VNC server. Best of all, the software is free and available for download from the Internet. To download any one of the server programs, go to www.realvnc.com/. You can find a Pocket PC version of VNC Viewer at www.cs.utah.edu/ ~midgley/wince/vnc.html.

While the small screens on Smartphones make it hard to view a desktop computer, there is at least one version of a VNC viewer for Smartphones, .NET VNC Viewer, at http:// dotnetvnc.sourceforge.net/.

Wrapping Up

Windows Mobile devices are powerful productivity tools at the office. They connect to corporate networks and synchronize with Exchange servers, open Internet and intranet web sites, retrieve e-mail from corporate mail servers, and run Windows programs using the Terminal Services Client. A number of third-party applications are available to synchronize data with PIMs, such as ACT! and Lotus Organizer, and to view PDF files.

Just as Windows Mobile devices are useful at the office, they are even more useful when traveling. In the next chapter, you will learn how to take full advantage of your device while you are away from your home or office.

16

Chapter 17

Travel with Windows Mobile

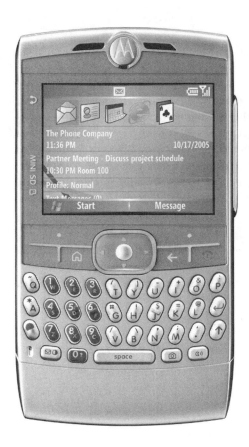

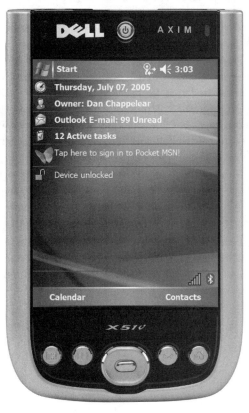

How to...

- Prepare to travel with your Windows Mobile device
- Extend battery life
- Get connected to the Internet while traveling
- Print to different types of printers
- Back up your device while traveling
- Connect a GPS receiver to your device
- Find maps to install on your device
- Find language translators for your device

Whether you choose to replace your notebook computer with a Windows Mobile device on your next business trip will depend on the amount of functionality that you need from software applications versus the convenience of less weight, longer battery life, and the "instant on" startup time provided by a device. If you need to retrieve your e-mail, give a presentation, write documents, and create spreadsheets, a Pocket PC will meet your needs, with much less weight and longer battery life than most notebook computers. However, if all you need to do is retrieve e-mail and make phone calls, you might be able to get by with a Smartphone. In this chapter, you'll find many tips on traveling with Windows Mobile devices, along with a handy checklist that you can use while packing for your trip.

Prepare to Travel

Murphy's Law seems to apply most often when you are on the road and away from any help. Preparation will either prevent problems or help you deal with them when they happen. Planning how you'll use your device on your trip will reduce stress and increase productivity. Four items that you should plan ahead for before embarking on your trip are power, connectivity, printing, and backup.

Keep Your Windows Mobile Device Running

Every computer ever made has at least one thing in common: it needs a power source to work. Batteries enable computers to be used in places where using a power cord is not possible. The longer the battery lasts, the more productivity you gain using the computer. A Windows Mobile device maximizes your productivity with its long battery life.

Unfortunately, no matter how long a battery can last, it will eventually need to be replaced or recharged. Because power is so important, you should take the time to plan how you will power your device and recharge its battery while traveling. Here are some tips for planning for your power needs:

- *Charge the battery before you leave.* Batteries tend to run out at the worst possible time, like halfway through a flight while you're writing a report that is due the next day. That would not be a good time to recall that the last time you charged the battery was last week. Don't let a depleted battery be the cause of not finishing that report; charge it the night before you leave.

- *Pack an extra battery.* If your device uses a removable battery, consider buying a spare battery that you can bring on long trips. Of course, make sure you also charge that extra battery before you leave on the trip.

- *Buy an external battery pack.* Some Pocket PCs do not have a replaceable battery but do have an external battery pack that connects to the power adapter port and recharges the internal battery. An example is the Socket Mobile Power Pack, which you can find at www.socketcom.com.

- *Buy an extra power adapter.* If you frequently travel to the same location, buy an extra power adapter and leave it at that location. It is also a good idea to keep adapters at your office and home. By doing this, you lighten your luggage and avoid forgetting to pack the adapter.

- *Buy a USB sync-and-charge cable.* This cable draws power from the USB port on a personal computer and also supports synchronization. By using this cable, you do not have to carry separate power adapters and synchronization cables or cradles. You can find sync-and-charge cables at retail and online computer stores that sell Pocket PC and Smartphone accessories.

- *Pack an extension cord.* Older hotel rooms tend to have too few power outlets, and the ones they do have always seem to be behind beds and dressers and placed as far from the desk or table as possible. An extension cord allows you to use your device wherever it is convenient.

- *Pack a portable surge suppressor.* Power surges can occur anywhere, creating the possibility of destroying your device. Most computer stores carry portable surge suppressors that have two outlets and possibly two or three phone jacks, all of which protect your device from power surges.

- *Get a power adapter for your car.* If you spend a lot of time traveling by car, consider getting an adapter that converts the car cigarette lighter socket into an outlet for the AC adapter of the device. Using this adapter, you can charge up your device while driving your car.

- *Remove cards.* Modem and network cards draw extra power from the device, even if they are not being used. Plug the cards into your device only when you are using them. As an extra precaution, use the card in your device only while it is using the AC adapter. Buy a case to house extra storage cards so they don't get lost.

17

■ *Be aware of international power differences.* Many countries have different power standards from those of the United States. AC adapters designed for the United States do not work in those countries, and vice versa. Check with the manufacturer of your device to find out whether its power adapter works in the country to which you plan to travel. You may need to purchase an international power adapter for your device, or you may find it easier to buy a power conversion kit.

■ *Know the power-saving features of your device.* Most devices include features designed for extending battery life. An example of this is settings that control the backlighting of the display. Learn how to use these features, and use them while you travel.

Plan How to Connect Your Pocket PC to the Internet

Next to battery life, the biggest challenge of using a Pocket PC on the road is Internet connectivity. Most of us have become dependent on Internet access to communicate via e-mail and to keep abreast of news on the Web. Determining how you will access the Internet, or your office network, before you leave on a trip will help tremendously when you finally make it to your hotel room.

NOTE   *Even though these tips are for access to the Internet, they also apply to accessing corporate networks. Chapter 16 has additional information on accessing corporate networks via the Internet using virtual private networking (VPN) software.*

Here are some tips to help you get connected on the road:

■ *Pick hotels with high-speed Internet access.* Many hotel chains today provide in-room Internet access, by providing wired or wireless Ethernet connections. Some chains provide access for free while others charge a daily fee. When making your hotel reservations, find out whether the hotel provides Internet access and how that access is provided. If the hotel provides only wired Internet access, be sure to pack an Ethernet adapter. Check whether you need an account to access the Internet, and be aware that you may have to set up the account from a PC before it will work on a mobile device.

■ *Check wireless coverage.* If you have a Pocket PC Phone Edition or a Smartphone, check the mobile service provider's web site to verify that it provides coverage for your destination. Most providers do not charge for roaming, but coverage may be limited to metropolitan areas. If your Pocket PC supports wireless Ethernet, check whether Wi-Fi hotspots are available where you are traveling (for example, search www.wi-fihotspotlist.com/).

■ *Get the local ISP phone numbers before you leave.* Most ISPs have pages on their web sites that list all their phone numbers, or they provide the numbers based on an area code and phone number that you enter. They may also have a toll-free number that you can call to obtain these numbers. Use the hotel phone number to determine what will be a local phone call. If your ISP provides a toll-free access number, find out what it is; while you may be charged more for using the number, it might be the only way to connect with the ISP at the destination.

■ *Test access numbers before you leave.* If being able to connect to the Internet at your destination is important, it may be worth the long-distance call to test the connection before you leave. Use remote networking to create a new dial-up connection using the access number. You will find it easier to get help while you are at home, and you can travel with the confidence that you will be able to connect to the Internet when you reach your destination.

■ *Know how to create and use dialing locations.* Most hotel and office phones require the entry of a number to access an outside line. The dialing locations of a Pocket PC make it easy to configure your modem to dial that number before making any call. Chapter 10 provides instructions for creating dialing locations on a Pocket PC.

■ *Use a calling card.* Your ISP may not have a local-access number or toll-free number that you can use at your destination. In these cases, you may want to use a phone company calling card. You can create dial-up connections that use calling cards by putting the appropriate codes in the telephone number field of the Dial-Up Connection dialog box. Chapter 10 provides instructions for creating dial-up connections.

■ *Research international requirements.* If you plan to travel to another country and want to use your device to connect to the Internet, you need to do some additional research. First, find out whether your ISP has access numbers outside the United States; many of them do not. Next, be aware that international numbers do not include a one (1) before the area code, but they may require country and city codes. This is best handled by using dialing locations and dialing patterns, as described in Chapter 10. The international dialing pattern is used when a dial-up connection of a country code is blank.

■ *Pack a phone line tester.* A few hotels and businesses use digital phone lines that can damage the modem. The tester has an indicator light that shows whether the line is digital, which should not be used, or analog, which is safe.

■ *Pack a long phone cord.* Phone jacks may be hidden behind beds and dressers, making them difficult to reach. A long phone cord can be useful for connecting your device to those phone jacks. Computer and electronics stores carry retractable phone lines that are easy to carry.

■ *Pack a one-to-two phone jack adapter.* Some hotel rooms have only one phone jack and a phone without a data port. In this case, the adapter enables you to connect your modem and the phone to the jack.

■ *Pack a phone line adapter for international travel.* The phone jacks in some countries may not match the jacks you use at home. Call ahead and find out whether you need a special adapter, or ask your travel agent. If you travel abroad, you may want to buy a travel kit, which is available at most computer stores. These kits contain many adapters and tools that you may need to connect to phone systems in other countries.

■ *Pack a line-noise filter.* Some hotels have phone systems that are not modem-friendly, and some European countries add a *tax tone* to monitor usage. The result is a reduction of signal clarity, making it difficult for modems to communicate with each other. A noise filter can reduce this problem.

17

Print on the Road with a Pocket PC

The Pocket PC does not have built-in support for printing, but you can add the ability to print Word Mobile documents, plain text, or e-mail using ActivePrint from Pocket Watch Software. ActivePrint uses ActiveSync to print documents, so while you are away from your desktop computer, your print jobs queue up on the device and print once you connect to a PC. You can find more information about ActivePrint at http://activeprint.pocketwatchsoftware.com.

If you have a Windows Mobile 2003SE or earlier device, you can use PrintPocketCE from FieldSoftware Products. The program prints to HP PCL3-compatible printers as well as various printers that have built-in infrared ports. A list of supported printers is available at www .fieldsoftware.com/PrintersSupported.htm, and you can find more information and a 30-day trial copy of PrintPocketCE at www.fieldsoftware.com.

Infrared provides the simplest way to connect a Pocket PC to a printer. When using PrintPocketCE, all you need to do is align the infrared ports and tap Start Printing. The FieldSoftware Products web site lists a number of printers that have infrared ports, or you can connect an infrared printer adapter to a printer parallel port. Such adapters are available from ACTiSYS Corporation, at www.actisys.com/actir100.html.

TIP   *Serial printers are harder to find, but still available. You can use a serial sync cable for your Pocket PC and a null modem adapter to connect with a printer serial cable. You cannot connect a Pocket PC to a printer using a USB cable.*

If you don't plan to do a lot of printing, you might not want to purchase extra software or cables. Yet you may find that, on occasion, you need to print a page or two. In these instances, a road-warrior trick comes in handy: fax the document from your device to a fax machine.

To send faxes from your Pocket PC, you need fax software. The following two fax programs are available: pocket PhoneTools (www.bvrp.com) from BVRP Software and KSE Truefax (www .ksesoftware.com) from KSE Software. Most hotels provide fax services for their customers, so call the front desk and get the fax number. Then start up either pocket Phone Tools or Truefax and send the document to that fax machine.

NOTE   *Pocket PhoneTools and Truefax may not work with Windows Mobile 5 devices. Check with the software vendor about compatibility before purchasing these programs to run on a Windows Mobile 5 device.*

If you decide that you need a printer, Pentax, Hewlett-Packard, Citizen, Canon, and Seiko Instruments all make portable printers. Be aware that these printers may require special paper, and they are not designed for high-volume printing. Some of these printers have built-in infrared ports, which eliminate the need for carrying and connecting extra cables.

Back Up Your Windows Mobile Device on the Road

If you consider the information in your Pocket PC or Smartphone to be critical, you ought to live by the motto "Back up early and often." Chances are good that when traveling, you will not have access to a desktop computer, yet the risk of losing data while traveling is great. Therefore, you need a way to back up your device without using a PC.

The best tool for backing up your device on the road is a storage card. If you already use a storage card, consider buying an extra card that you use only for backups. The extra card should be at least 128MB for Pocket PCs and 64MB for Smartphones so it can hold all of the files in internal storage memory.

You could copy files to the storage card, but many devices have a better method of backup. Included is software designed to back up the entire contents of internal storage to a storage card. Backing up this way is faster than using a serial cable, so you might want to use this as your main backup method. Consult the user manual of your device for instructions on using its backup software.

The backup software on most Pocket PCs is pretty basic in its functioning, and some Pocket PCs and Smartphones may not have built-in backup software. Sprite Software's Sprite Backup for Pocket PC has features such as automatic backup when the battery is low and scheduled backups. It also provides a way to select specific files and folders to back up and restore, and there are versions for Pocket PCs and Smartphones. You will find Sprite Backup at www.spritesoftware.com.

NOTE *Be aware that the backup file is written in a proprietary format. If the device is lost or stolen, you will need to obtain an identical device to restore the files.*

For an additional level of security, use a PC storage card reader to copy the backup file from the card to a computer hard drive. You will find this a better method for backing up your device to a desktop computer, but it has the additional cost of the card reader.

The Internet is also a useful tool for backing up files on your device. If you don't have a storage card and you want to back up a file, attach the file to an e-mail message and mail it to yourself. The e-mail message and the file will stay on the mail server until it is deleted. This has the added benefit of giving you access to the file from any computer that can read e-mail from the server.

TIP *Google, Yahoo, and MSN all provide free web-based e-mail services with large amounts of storage space. Create an account with one of these services and back up files by sending them as e-mail attachments to that account. An additional benefit of this approach is that you can access your backup files from any computer with Internet access.*

Secure Your Data

While traveling, your Pocket PC and the data it contains are at risk of being lost or stolen. Backing up your data to a storage card and then carrying that card separately from the device ensures that you have a secure copy of your data at all times. Other methods exist for securing the data even further, but they come with the cost of some inconvenience and the risk of rendering data inaccessible due to lost passwords.

Here are some tips for securing your data:

■ *Use password protection by using the Password icon in Settings on a Pocket PC or the Security settings on Smartphones.* With power-on protection enabled, a password must be entered every time the device is turned on. If you forget the password, the device will be inaccessible unless you perform a hard reset, which removes all installed applications and data from the device. Windows Mobile 5 devices that have the Messaging and Security Feature Pack (MSFP) installed support "remote kill," which enables system administrators to send a command to the device that deletes all of the data on that device.

17

■ *Use software that securely stores personal information such as bank account numbers and user IDs.* Programs that provide this function include CodeWallet Pro at www.developerone .com; eWallet at www.iliumsoft.com; and FlexWallet at www.twopeaks.com.

■ *Encrypt data stored either internally or on a storage card.* Data on storage cards is particularly vulnerable because the cards are easy to steal and use in other devices, including personal computers. Tools such as Sentry 2020 Pocket PC (www.softwinter .com/sentry_ce.html) can encrypt files that are on storage cards so that they are protected if the card is lost or stolen.

TIP   *Chapter 16 provides more information about securing your Windows Mobile device.*

Turn Your Windows Mobile Device into a Traveling Tool

Now that you have all of the preparations out of the way, you are ready to look at some additional hardware and software that turn your Windows Mobile device into a valuable travel tool. From time to time, we all get lost while traveling and we may end up looking to the skies for direction. With a global positioning system (GPS) receiver, a Pocket PC or Smartphone can show your exact location on a map. Even if you don't have a GPS receiver, several different mapping programs run on Windows Mobile devices, and with the software, you won't have to figure out how to refold the map.

TIP   *These GPS systems may not include maps for use outside the contiguous United States. You may want to check which systems provide maps for Alaska, Hawaii, or other countries.*

International travel presents additional challenges of overcoming language barriers. Several language translators exist that run on Windows Mobile devices, and using one can help you order a grilled cheese sandwich in France or Spain.

Know Where to Go and How to Get There

GPS has existed since 1973 and is operated by the United States Department of Defense. It determines a location by computing the difference between the time a signal is sent and the time it is received. The signals come from three different satellites floating over the earth. A GPS receiver uses the data to triangulate a location in latitude and longitude, which is then used to identify a spot on a map.

GPS hardware and software are popular Windows Mobile accessories. While you can buy a stand-alone GPS receiver, there are several advantages to using a receiver with a Windows Mobile device. For example, in a car, you can place the receiver wherever the signal strength is the greatest and hold the device in your hand. In addition, Pocket PCs are cheaper than many stand-alone GPS receivers that have high-resolution color displays. Finally, Windows Mobile GPS software is designed to work with storage cards, providing a significantly greater amount of space to store maps over stand-alone GPS receivers.

Several companies sell GPS receivers and software that work with Pocket PCs and Smartphones. Each product provides driving directions, voice prompts, route computation, and off-route warning. Maps are provided on CD-ROM and are downloaded either to internal storage on a device or onto a storage card. The following is a summary of the GPS solutions available for Windows Mobile.

- Pharos bundles its GPS receiver and software in a product called Pocket GPS Navigator, and versions are available for most Pocket PC brands. If your Pocket PC supports Bluetooth, you can use the wireless version of the GPS, which allows you to place the receiver anywhere in your car. You can find more information about this product at www.pharosgps.com.

- CoPilot Live Pocket PC 6 and CoPilot Live Smartphone 6 from ALK Technologies are the Windows Mobile versions of its popular CoPilot software for PCs. If you use this product with a device that has a wireless Internet connection, you can receive live updates on road conditions and accidents. Map data is downloaded to a device or storage card using desktop software. This product can be found at www.alk.com.

- TeleType GPS sells several receivers that work with Pocket PCs, including CompactFlash and Bluetooth versions that turn your Pocket PC into a portable GPS. The TeleType GPS software can be purchased separately and works with other GPS receivers that are compliant with the standards of the National Marine Electronics Association (NMEA). You can find these products at www.teletype.com.

- HandMap from Evolutionary Systems is a vector-based map viewer. The professional version of the software includes plug-ins that work with GPS receivers. A standard version is available as a free download from the company's web site, but it works only with maps provided by Evolutionary Systems. More information can be found at www.handmap.net.

- TomTom NAVIGATOR is a bundle that includes TomTom's popular Route Planner mapping software and a GPS receiver. You can buy a version of the bundle that uses either Bluetooth or a serial cable. You can find this product at www.tomtom.com.

Configure GPS on Pocket PCs

Windows Mobile 5 enables multiple applications to retrieve data from GPS receivers at the same time. To enable this functionality you need to configure the GPS system settings by tapping Start | Settings | System | GPS, which opens this screen.

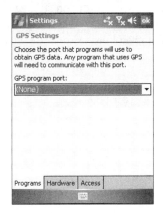

On the Programs tab, you specify what communications (COM) port the GPS software will use to communicate with GPS receivers. Select one of the COM port options from the GPS Program Port drop-down list.

Your Pocket PC may automatically detect the GPS receiver that you are using, and enter the settings on the Hardware tab. If not, you have to select the COM port that the GPS receiver uses to communicate with the Pocket PC, and the speed of the communications, by selecting the appropriate values from the drop-down lists on the tab. You will find this information in the user manual of the GPS receiver.

Windows Mobile 5 automatically manages access to the GPS receiver, allowing multiple programs to retrieve GPS data simultaneously. Some GPS programs may not be able to work with the automatic configuration, in which case you can shut it off by clearing the Manage GPS Automatically check box on the Access tab.

17

View a Customized Map with Microsoft Pocket Streets

Pocket Streets is a map-viewing program for Pocket PCs and Smartphones that displays maps created with Microsoft Streets & Trips 2005 or MapPoint 2004. It is included with these programs, or you can buy a stand-alone version at www.microsoft.com/pocketstreets.

Microsoft provides 318 U.S. and Canadian city maps and 277 European city maps on the setup CD-ROM, and you can also download these maps from www.microsoft.com/pocketstreets. To use these maps, copy the file to the device or storage card.

NOTE   *Pocket Streets will run a little slower if it loads maps from a storage card.*

To create your own maps using Streets & Trips, select a portion of the map on your desktop using the mouse, right-click within the selected area, and then click Export Map for Pocket Streets. Streets & Trips calculates the approximate amount of storage space the map will need on the device and then prompts you for a location on your desktop to store the files.

Two files are created: a map file that has an .mps extension and a pushpin file that has a .psp extension. Copy these two files to the My Documents folder on your device or on a storage card using ActiveSync Explorer, as described in Chapter 8.

TIP   *If you have a storage card reader connected to your desktop, you can export the map file directly to a storage card.*

When Pocket Streets starts on a Pocket PC, you may see the standard Pocket PC List view showing all the map files stored in the My Documents folder on your Pocket PC. If only one map is on your device, Pocket Streets automatically loads that map. Maps that you put in the My Documents folder on storage cards are also listed. If you do not see a map, make sure it is in the My Documents folder. Tap a map name to open the map, as shown here. Tap the buttons on the Command bar to zoom the map, and tap the buttons in the Navigation box to move the map.

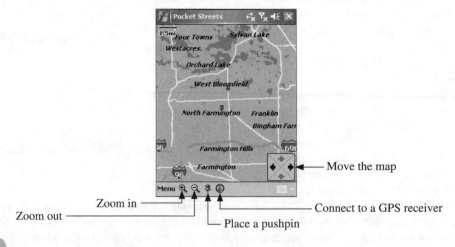

Move the map
Zoom in
Zoom out
Connect to a GPS receiver
Place a pushpin

TIP   *Another way to zoom in on a map is to select an area of the map using the stylus.*

Pocket Streets looks slightly different on Smartphones because it is designed to work with the left and right softkeys. When you load a map on a Smartphone, it looks like this:

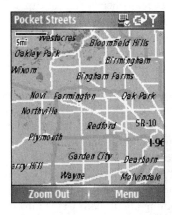

Press Zoom Out to zoom out the map, or press Menu to zoom in, find an address, or select points of interest to display on the map.

Pocket Streets 2005 works with GPS receivers to display the current location on the map, but it does not provide directions like other GPS navigation software. Tap the GPS button on the Pocket PC Command bar, or press Menu | GPS | Menu | Start GPS to connect to a GPS receiver.

Online services such as MSN Mobile (http://mobile.msn.com) and Yahoo Mobile (http://mobile.yahoo.com) provide maps or text directions that work with Windows Mobile devices. While they don't work with GPS receivers, they are useful for finding directions.

Translate Foreign Languages

English is a widely used language inside and outside of the United States. Americans who do not speak foreign languages, or those who are learning them, rely on either interpreters or language translators. Typically, these translators list English words and their foreign-language equivalents. Language translators are available for Windows Mobile and provide searching capabilities that make it easier to find the correct words to say. Here is an overview of some language translator software available for your device:

■ ECTACO's Talking Partner dictionaries provide word translation both in text and audio for English, Russian, Spanish, simplified Chinese, traditional Chinese, French, and German. ECTACO also sells text-only translation dictionaries for many more languages, as well as learning language software. You can find all of ECTACO's products at www.ectaco.com.

■ Translation Experts' PocketTran runs only on Pocket PCs, and does phrase-by-phrase and word-by-word translations for several languages. You can find PocketTran at www .tranexp.com.

■ LingvoSoft sells dictionaries, language-learning software, speech interpreters, flashcards, and dictionaries for travelers in several languages that run on Pocket PCs and Smartphones. You can find LingvoSoft's products at www.lingvosoft.com.

17

Hit the Road

Having read this far, you know how to plan ahead for your trip and how your device can help you get to your destination. Now it is time to put everything together, pack it up, and head off on your trip. Before you go, here are a few final preparations.

Make Final Preparations

If you plan to work in your hotel room, ask about accommodations for business travelers when you make the reservation. If the hotel does not provide in-room high-speed Internet access, ask whether computer modems can be used in the rooms. If not, and connecting to the Internet is important for you, you might want to stay at another hotel.

Some hotels have business centers that have personal computers and printers available for their patrons. Find out the manufacturers of their equipment and ask whether you can use their printers with your notebook computer. (Don't bother asking about Pocket PCs; chances are good the person you talk to will know nothing about them.) This information will help you decide what printer software should be installed on your device.

Make sure you download to your device or storage card all the data files that you will need. The wrong time to find out that you are missing a file is when you try to open it hundreds, or thousands, of miles away from home. The ActiveSync file synchronization capability helps with this, because as long as the file stays in the Synchronized Files folders, you know a copy is stored on the device. Chapter 7 has all the information you need on using file synchronization.

Don't put your Windows Mobile device, or important components, in checked luggage. Not only do you run the risk of the luggage, and your equipment, not showing up at your destination, but it can be stolen as well. Keep briefcases and computer bags with you at all times. Airports are popular locations for thieves.

What type of case do you use to carry your Pocket PC? If you use the case that it came with, it is probably too small to carry accessories, and it may not provide enough protection. Targus (www.targus.com) offers some nice cases, as does E&B Company (www.ebcases.com). Try to find a case that has enough padding to withstand normal travel abuses.

Todd Ogasawara keeps an extensive list of carrying-case vendors at http://to-tech.com/ windowsce/faqs/cases.htm.

Complete a Travel Checklist

Checklists are handy tools to help you remember what to pack and what to do as you prepare for a trip. Chapter 19 has information about Ilium Software's ListPro, a handy program designed for making and reusing lists. Unfortunately, a ListPro file cannot be attached to this book, so the next best thing is the travel checklist shown in Table 17-1.

☐ Charge all rechargeable batteries.

☐ Pack extra batteries or an external battery pack.

☐ Pack an AC power adapter.

☐ Pack a portable surge suppressor.

☐ Pack a phone line tester.

☐ Pack an extra phone cable.

☐ Pack a CompactFlash or PC Card modem.

☐ Pack a backup storage card.

☐ Find ISP access numbers for your destination.

☐ Determine whether you will need to print and, if so, how.

☐ Pack an extra storage card for backup.

☐ Download maps of the destination to your device.

If you are traveling outside the United States:

☐ Verify that your power adapter will work at the destination.

☐ Find out how phone calls are made at the destination.

☐ Pack an international phone line adapter.

☐ Pack a phone line noise filter.

TABLE 17-1   Windows Mobile travel checklist

Wrapping Up

Windows Mobile devices are made for traveling. With a little planning, you will have a happy and safe journey. When I travel, I enjoy taking along my Pocket PC and GPS receiver so that I know where I am and how much longer I have to travel. For anyone like me who gets anxious when they are lost, a GPS receiver can be a godsend.

In this section, you have learned how to get the most out of your Windows Mobile device, by using it to stay organized, create documents and spreadsheets, be productive at work, and take it with you on your travels. Pocket PCs and Smartphones are also great tools for relaxing and having fun, and in the next chapter you will learn how you can play games, listen to music, and read books using your Windows Mobile device.

Chapter 18

Have Fun with Games, Pictures, Music, Books, and Movies

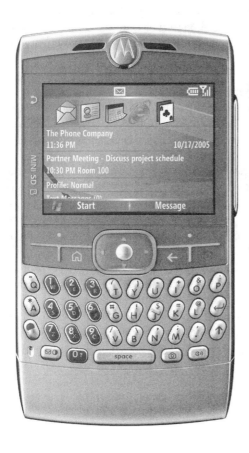

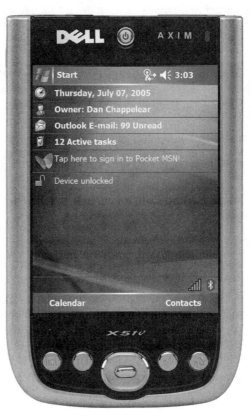

How to...

- ■ Pick the best Pocket PC for playing games
- ■ Find games to play on your Windows Mobile device
- ■ Read eBooks
- ■ Play music
- ■ Play movies and watch television shows
- ■ View pictures

Having read this far, you may think that a Pocket PC or Smartphone is for nothing more than managing time and creating documents. Nothing could be further from the truth. When it's time to kick back and relax, a Windows Mobile device can be a perfect companion. With your device you can play games, view pictures, listen to music or audio books, read a novel, or even watch a movie.

If you enjoy playing computer games, you'll be happy to find Windows Mobile programs for every game category. The speed, color screens, and sound capabilities of the latest Pocket PCs make them great portable game machines, and you might be surprised by what a Smartphone can do. Fortunately, many talented programmers have been hard at work writing games that exploit the capabilities of your Windows Mobile device.

If you don't find playing games to be relaxing, perhaps lounging on a couch listening to your favorite music is more to your liking. Here, too, your device is up to the task, thanks to Windows Media Player, which is capable of playing music stored in digital files that you can download to your device or put on storage cards.

Perhaps you find the complete audio and visual experience of a movie a great form of relaxation. No, you won't be able to play the latest box office hit, but several independent artists make their work available on the Internet so that you can download and play it using Windows Media Player.

Perhaps your favorite way to relax is to curl up in front of a warm fire and read a novel. You can purchase and download electronic books, or eBooks, from the Internet, and read them on your Pocket PC using software such as Microsoft Reader. Third-party eBook programs are available for Smartphones and Pocket PCs. You can also play audio books using Windows Media Player.

As you can see, Windows Mobile provides many tools to help you relax during a trip. It also lightens your load because you don't have to pack a half dozen CDs or a couple of books. Of course, you don't need to travel to enjoy all these features; anywhere your device goes, so goes your favorite music or books. Ready? Let's have some fun!

Play Games

If any one software category represents how well the Pocket PC has sold, it is games. When I wrote the first edition of this book in early 2000, few games were available, but today this is not the case. Right now, www.pocketgamer.org has 16 different categories of games listed, including action and arcade, board, role-playing, simulation, and strategy games.

Game software evokes a tremendous amount of passion from Pocket PC owners. Go to any online forum and ask which Pocket PC is the best for games, and you are certain to receive many replies promoting one brand over another. The debate over which brand of Pocket PC is best for games centers on three items: processors, screens, and buttons.

Of all the software available for Pocket PCs, games may be the most processor-intensive, particularly action and arcade games and simulations. Simply stated, many games run better on faster processors. If action and arcade games or simulations are what you like, you should consider buying the Pocket PC with the fastest processor; however, even slower processors are capable of playing card and board games.

Good computer games have great graphics, and the Pocket PC color screens set it above other handhelds for great-looking games. Graphics quality doesn't necessarily affect game play, so the differences have more to do with personal preference. If you want to see the best graphics in the games you play, pick a Pocket PC that has a *transreflective* display with the most colors.

Most current Pocket PC brands now use transreflective liquid crystal displays (LCDs). These screens reflect ambient light but also have a backlight to brighten the display in dark conditions. The combination provides a good display in a variety of lighting conditions. Older Pocket PCs had either *transmissive* screens, which had backlighting that worked better indoors than outdoors, or *reflective* screens, which had combined front-lighting and ambient light for good viewing outdoors but tended to look dark indoors.

Action games demand a lot not only from a processor, but also from a player in the form of input. While desktop computers can support a wide array of joysticks and game pads, the Pocket PC is limited to a few buttons. Casio pioneered the navigation button on its E-100 Palm-size PCs, and it has become the benchmark for game control on Pocket PCs because it provides complete cursor control.

Today most Pocket PCs have a navigation button, but some suffer from what many consider a flaw in not being able to process simultaneous button presses. If you press two buttons at once, one is ignored; this is unlike other Pocket PCs, which recognize both button presses. Consequently, you may find it difficult to play action games on these devices. If action games are important to you, ask the device manufacturer (or do research on the Web) whether its device can process simultaneous button presses.

 *Another source of information about the best Pocket PCs for playing games is PocketGamer's forums at www.pocketgamer.org.*

Download Games to Play

The best source of Windows Mobile games is the Internet, and Table 18-1 lists some of the web sites that provide games. Most of the download web sites described in Chapter 19 also have categories for games, where you can find many links for games that you can download and install on your device.

To install these games, first download the software to your desktop computer. If the software has been compressed, decompress it using one of the many desktop programs, such as WinZip, that are available for this task. Next, connect your device and run the setup program on the desktop computer.

18

Web Site	URL
PocketGamer.org	www.pocketgamer.org
Jimmy Software	www.jimmysoftware.com
Rapture Technologies	www.rapturetech.com
Ppcgaming.com	www.ppcgaming.com
ZIO Interactive	www.clubzio.com/eng/index.asp
PDAmill	www.pdamill.com
Clickgamer	www.clickgamer.com

TABLE 18-1   Windows Mobile Game Web Sites

Play Solitaire

It began as a tool to learn a new way to interact with a computer and quickly became a phenomenon. We all have probably seen people obsessed with clicking-and-dragging until they see cards drop all across their computer screen. Of course, I am talking about the great computer pastime—Solitaire.

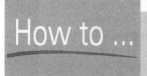 **Track Your Golf Game**

This chapter is about playing games on Windows Mobile devices, but your Pocket PC or Smartphone can also be used while you are playing games. By using a Smartphone, for example, you could take a couple of strokes off your golf game!

IntelliGolf Par Edition enables up to four players to score, analyze, and review statistics of their golf game. The software also enables players to place *on course* wagers. With this software, golfers can do the following:

- Automate golf scoring
- Calculate an approximate handicap
- Download courses from the Internet
- Capture round statistics to help improve their game

The Birdie Edition of IntelliGolf includes desktop software that will synchronize with the software on the device. By using the PC, golfers can review historical trends and evaluate their strengths using more than 60 categories of performance statistics. You will find more information about IntelliGolf at www.intelligolf.com.

Solitaire became part of the computer operating system when it was included with Windows Version 3.1. Since then, every Microsoft operating system, including Windows CE .NET, which is the Windows Mobile operating system, has included a version to help teach users how to click-and-drag with a mouse.

Windows Mobile users may not need to learn how to click-and-drag, but some people use Solitaire as a way to compare the speed and feel of different devices. It can also be a great way to kill a little free time.

To start Solitaire, on a Pocket PC tap Start | Programs | Games | Solitaire, and the game will load as shown in the following image at left. On a Smartphone, press Start | More | Games | Solitaire, and the game loads as shown in the image at right.

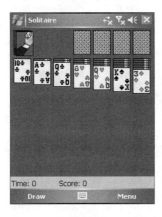

When you start Solitaire, the cards are dealt and displayed on the computer screen. Four spaces are marked at the top of the screen for building the foundation piles, and the hand is placed face down in the upper-left corner. Tap the top of the hand to turn over a packet of three cards into the stack. To turn over cards in the tableau piles, tap on them.

To move a card on a Pocket PC, tap-and-hold the stylus on the card, drag the card to a location on the screen, and then lift up the stylus. On a Smartphone, use the numeric keypad to move cards between locations on the screen. If the play is legal, the card stays on the pile; otherwise, the card returns to its original location.

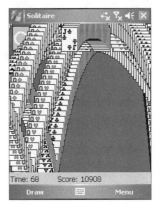

On a Pocket PC, double-tap a card to move it to a foundation pile, and the card will be placed in the correct pile.

Play continues until you win, exit the game, or deal a new set of cards. When you win, the cards cascade around the screen, as shown in this image.

Play Bubble Breaker

Bubble Breaker has been available for previous versions of Pocket PCs and is also called Bubblets and Jawbreaker. Microsoft made arrangements with the original software developer, Oopdreams Software, Inc., to include it with Windows Mobile 2003 and newer.

To start the game, on a Pocket PC tap Start | Programs | Games | Bubble Breaker, which opens the program window shown at left. On a Smartphone, press Start | More | Games | Bubble Breaker to open the program window shown at right.

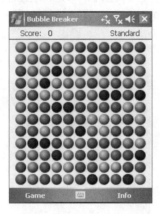
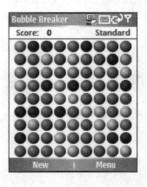

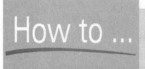 **Deal a Perfect Hand on a Pocket PC**

You might think I spent all night playing Solitaire to capture the screenshot of cascading cards. Actually, I didn't have to, because you can make Solitaire deal a winning hand every time. (You might want to stop reading the rest of this box if you don't want to know how to cheat at Solitaire.)

Here is what you need to do:

1. Start Solitaire.
2. Open the keyboard version of the Software Input Panel.
3. Tap CTL-SHIFT.
4. Tap Menu | New.

To start playing a new game, on a Pocket PC tap Game | New Game, and on a Smartphone press New. The objective is to align the same colored circles, or bubbles, to form large blocks before bursting them. The more bubbles in a block, the higher the number of points you earn when you burst the block.

On Smartphones, use the navigation button to move around the screen. As you move around the screen, the bubbles change size to show you which one is currently selected. To burst a bubble, click the navigation button. All of the connected bubbles are highlighted, and you see the number of points you earn if you burst them. To burst a block, click the navigation button.

To burst a bubble on a Pocket PC, tap one that is connected to the same color bubble. All of the connected bubbles are highlighted, and you see the number of points you earn if you burst them. To burst a block, tap a highlighted bubble. If you decide that you don't want to burst a highlighted block, simply select a different block of bubbles.

After you burst a block of bubbles, surrounding bubbles fill in the open space. The game continues until you have burst all the possible blocks of bubbles, and if less than five bubbles remain, you earn bonus points. The game ends if no more possible blocks exist for you to burst.

To set game-play options, tap Game | Options on Pocket PCs, or press Menu | Options on Smartphones. Bubble Breaker tracks game-play statistics, which you display by tapping Info | Statistics on Pocket PCs, or press Menu | Statistics on Smartphones. If you want to let someone else play the game without affecting the statistics, tap the Guest Mode check box on the Options screen.

Four different game styles are available, which you can select from the Game Style drop-down list on the Options screen. Standard is the default mode, in which a set number of bubbles is used and none are added during the game. If you select Continuous mode, an additional column of bubbles appears on the left as you burst a vertical block, and the remaining bubbles shift to the right. In Shifter mode, when you burst a block, the remaining bubbles to the top and left shift down and to the right. The MegaShift mode combines the Continuous and Shifter modes.

View Pictures

Twenty years ago, the only way you could see a photo right after it was taken was to use a Polaroid instant camera. After you shot the picture, the photo would pop out of the camera and the image would slowly appear on the paper after a couple of minutes. By today's standards, the old Polaroid is quaint compared to digital cameras, which enable you to see pictures at nearly the instant they are shot.

Digital photography not only enables us to see pictures instantly, but has also changed the way we store and transport pictures. While our parents and grandparents stored photos in albums, which lost color over time, you and I and our children are more likely to store our pictures on CD-ROMs or DVDs, and the pictures will be as vibrant in the future as they were on the day they were taken.

While you might still carry pictures of loved ones in a wallet or purse, it is also likely that you simply carry them on CD-ROM to display on a personal computer. You can even buy devices that are designed to display photos from CDs on TV screens. If you carry a Windows Mobile device, you can also view pictures anywhere by using one of the many picture-viewing programs.

18

To view pictures, you need to load them on the device, normally using a storage card. If you use a camera that stores pictures on CompactFlash or Secure Digital cards, you can simply remove the card from the camera and insert it into most Pocket PCs to view the pictures. All the picture-viewing programs display pictures from a folder as thumbnails, and you can select individual pictures to display or sort the pictures to display in a slide show.

Loading pictures on Smartphones can be more difficult because most Smartphones only support mini-Secure Digital (miniSD) cards, which are not used by most digital cameras. One option is to use a miniSD-to-Secure Digital card adapter to use the miniSD card in digital cameras that use SD cards. Otherwise, you need to use ActiveSync to transfer pictures to Smartphones by using the instructions in Chapter 8 for transferring files between PCs and devices.

TIP   *You can transfer pictures between Pocket PCs and Smartphones using infrared or Bluetooth communications.*

All the picture-viewing programs provide a way to rotate and zoom pictures. Most provide ways to annotate pictures with text and attach voice recordings to pictures. These extra features can be useful for recording information about the pictures when they are taken.

Microsoft did not include a picture-viewing program prior to Windows Mobile 2003. However, several manufacturers bundle these programs with Pocket PC 2002 and earlier devices. In some cases, they simply include third-party programs, but others provide their own picture-viewing programs. Table 18-2 provides an overview of the picture-viewing programs available for Windows Mobile. This section describes Microsoft Pictures & Videos, which is included with Windows Mobile 5.

Program	URL
PicturePerfect (Applian Mobile)	www.applianmobile.com/
Photo Explorer (Aidem Systems)	www.aidem.com.tw
Photo Viewer (Resco)	www.resco.net/homepage.asp
PocketPics (ScaryBear Software)	www.scarybearsoftware.com
Spb Imageer (Spb Software House)	www.spbsoftwarehouse.com/
Image Explorer (TangCode)	www.tang.btinternet.co.uk/tangcode/imgexp.html
Pocket QuickView (BitBank Software)	www.bitbanksoftware.com
Pocket Album (Conduits Technologies)	www.conduits.com
SplashPhoto (SplashData)	www.splashdata.com/splashphoto/
PocketSnapShots (stoutbytes.com)	www.stoutbytes.com

TABLE 18-2   Picture-Viewing Programs for Windows Mobile

View Pictures Using Microsoft Pictures & Videos

Microsoft Pictures & Videos enables Windows Mobile users to view and share digital pictures. You can also crop and rotate pictures and change their brightness and contrast. To start Pictures & Videos, on a Pocket PC tap Start | Programs | Pictures & Videos, which displays the program window shown at left. On a Smartphone press Start | More | Pictures & Videos, which displays the program window shown at right.

When Pictures & Videos starts, it scans the My Documents folder for image and video files and displays them as thumbnails along with the filenames. Pictures & Videos will also scan a Digital Camera Image (DCIM) folder that some digital cameras create on storage cards. On Pocket PCs, select an option from the Show drop-down list to switch between file locations:

Windows Mobile has a My Pictures folder inside My Documents. If you enable file synchronization, the pictures in this folder synchronize between the device and a desktop computer.

18

To change the file location on Smartphones, press Menu | My Device, which opens a screen showing the folders on your Smartphone:

Use the navigation button to move between the folders, and press the navigation button to select a folder.

 *To quickly switch back to the My Pictures folder on Smartphones, press Menu | My Pictures.*

By default, the thumbnail pictures are sorted by date, but you can change the sort order on Pocket PCs by selecting either Name, Date, or Size from the Sort drop-down list in the upper-right corner of the screen. You cannot change the sort order on Smartphones.

Select a picture thumbnail or select View to display a larger version of the picture on the screen. When you select a video thumbnail or select View, Windows Media Player launches and plays the video. Tap-and-hold a thumbnail on Pocket PCs to open a drop-down menu where you can choose to copy, delete, or rename the picture or video; send the picture or video as an e-mail attachment; beam the picture or video to another device; or select a picture as a Today screen background. Press the Menu button to perform similar functions on Smartphones.

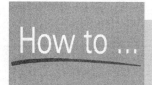 **Add Pictures to Contacts**

One of the new features of Windows Mobile 5 is photos in Contacts, which synchronize with Outlook 2003. If your Pocket PC or Smartphone has a built-in camera, you can use Pictures & Videos to associate pictures with contacts. Select a picture in thumbnail view, select Menu | Save To Contact, and then select the contact to associate with the picture. When you open the Summary view of the contact, you see the picture, and the next time you synchronize with Outlook 2003, the picture will synchronize to your PC.

If your device has a built-in camera, select the Camera icon thumbnail to take a picture. Most devices that have a built-in camera have a hardware button for taking pictures, which you can press to start Pictures & Videos in Camera mode. You then press the button a second time to take a picture.

When you display a picture, you can rotate, crop, or enhance it. First select Menu | Edit, and then, on a Pocket PC, tap the Rotate button to rotate the picture 90 degrees to the left. On a Smartphone, press Menu | Rotate. To crop a picture, do the following:

1. Select Menu | Crop.
2. Use the stylus to draw a box around the section of the picture that you want to keep. On a Smartphone, use the navigation button to draw the box.
3. Tap inside the box to remove everything in the picture except what is inside the box you drew. Once you select the second corner on Smartphones, the picture automatically crops.

If you decide after you crop the picture that you want to undo the change, select Menu | Undo, and the picture will be restored to its previous form. To change the picture's brightness or contrast, select Menu | Auto Correct, and brightness and contrast are automatically reset. Tap OK to return to the thumbnail view.

To display pictures in a slide show, select Menu | Play Slide Show, and the pictures automatically change after three seconds, or you can press the navigation button to move between pictures. Tap the screen or press Back to close the slide show. To display a picture across the entire screen, the slide show needs to display in landscape, which you can configure by selecting Menu | Options | Slide Show and then selecting the Landscape Pictures radio button on Pocket PCs:

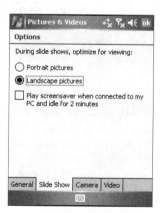

On a Smartphone, select Landscape Pictures from the Optimize For Viewing drop-down list. If you want your pictures to play as a screen saver, select the Play Screensaver When Connected To My PC And Idle For 2 Minutes check box.

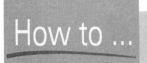

Moblog with Windows Mobile

Mobile blogging, or *moblogging,* is the posting of pictures to a web site in a reverse chronological order. Services such as Flickr (www.flickr.com) and TypePad (www.typepad .com/) provide web server software for posting your pictures and sharing them on the Internet. If you have a Pocket PC or Smartphone with a built-in camera, it is easy to use it for moblogging:

1. Take a picture, select the picture in thumbnail view, and press the navigation button to display the picture on the screen.

2. Select Send, which opens Messaging.

3. Select an e-mail account, enter the e-mail address for the Internet service that you are using, enter a subject, which will be the subject of the picture, and enter a description that you want to go with the picture in the body of the e-mail.

4. Select Send.

The picture is sent as an e-mail attachment to the service that you use and will then be posted to your web site.

Ilium Software's DockWare Pro displays pictures as a screen saver when docked on Pocket PC 2002, Windows Mobile 2003, and older devices. You can download DockWare Pro from www.iliumsoft.com.

Play Music and Videos

Recently, the Internet has become popular for distributing music, thanks to MPEG (Moving Picture Experts Group). MPEG is a family of standards for encoding audio-visual information in a compressed digital format. Part of the standard is the audio-coding format known as MP3, or MPEG Audio Layer 3.

Without compression technology, three minutes of CD-quality sound requires approximately 32MB of storage space, which is too large for distribution over the Internet. MP3 compresses this storage space to 3MB, making it possible to download sound files from the Internet.

Audio compression enables CD-quality music to be played on personal computers, portable music players such as the Apple iPod, and Windows Mobile devices. Windows Media Player on your Pocket PC or Smartphone plays music that you can download from thousands of web sites on the Internet. With your device and a storage card, you can listen to hours of music and not have to carry an extra CD player.

Audio File Formats

MP3 is one of several sound file types. Another type is WAV (waveform), which doesn't compress the size of the file and therefore requires a lot of storage space. It is, however, the simplest sound format and is typically used to create small files, such as the sounds available in Microsoft Themes. Pocket PCs create WAV files that vary in size based on the quality of the sound. Lower-quality sound, captured in kilobits per second (Kbps), creates smaller files than higher-quality sound. Windows CE, like all versions of Windows, has built-in support for playing WAV files.

Microsoft created the WMA (Windows Media Audio) format. It also compresses audio files but with half the size of MP3 and with better quality. The file format can be secured to protect sound files from being illegally distributed.

Play Music and Videos Using Windows Media Player

Windows Media Player Version 10 from Microsoft plays MP3 and WMA music files and Windows Media Video stored internally on a device or on a storage card. It can also play streaming media stored on a network. Windows Media Player is built-in on some devices; otherwise, it can be installed on the device. To start Windows Media Player on a Pocket PC, tap Start | Windows Media, which opens the Library screen shown at left. On a Smartphone, press Start | Windows Media to open the screen shown at right.

Tap here to select a library.

If you are playing music on a Pocket PC Phone Edition or Smartphone and receive a phone call, Windows Mobile automatically pauses the music playback while you are talking. When the call finishes, Windows Mobile automatically starts music playback.

18

When Windows Media Player starts, it searches internal storage and storage cards for audio and video content, and displays those files in the Library. You can browse the music files by selecting My Music, or select My Videos or My TV to browse video files. Music files display by artist, album, and genre, while video files display only by genre.

If Windows Media Player does not find new files that you copy to a device, you can manually update the library by selecting Menu | Update Library.

Libraries are created in every location where Windows Media Player finds files. For example, any files found in internal storage on your device are stored in the My Device library, while storage card files are in the Storage Card library. If you use multiple storage cards that contain media files, a library is created on each card and appears in the Library menu when the card is in the device.

You can arrange music in the order in which you want to hear it by adding songs to the Now Playing playlist. To add a song to Now Playing on a Pocket PC, tap-and-hold on the song title and then tap Queue Up. On a Smartphone, press Menu | Queue Up. To review what songs are in the Now Playing playlist, select Menu | Now Playing in the Library, or select Now Playing on the Command bar. You can then remove songs from the list or change the order in which they play.

While you can create playlists on devices that have Windows Media Player 9, you cannot create permanent playlists in Windows Media Player 10 on a device. However, you can create playlists using Windows Media Version 10 for Windows and synchronize those playlists to a device. See Chapter 7 for instructions on how to synchronize media files to a device using ActiveSync.

Any time that a media file or playlist is selected in the Library, the Play command is visible, which you can select to start playing the file or playlist. The music or video that you select starts playing:

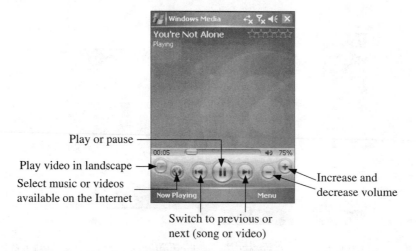

Play or pause

Play video in landscape

Select music or videos available on the Internet

Increase and decrease volume

Switch to previous or next (song or video)

Tap the buttons on the screen to control playback. If you have associated artwork with a song that you synchronize to a device, that artwork displays while the song is playing.

To play music or videos stored on the Internet, open the Library and select Menu | Open URL, enter the URL for where the music is located, and select OK. You can also play music or videos from Internet Explorer. When you select a link to the content on a web page, Windows Media Player automatically loads and starts playing the content.

Microsoft's WindowsMedia.com mobile web site provides media that you can play on your device. You will find a link to the web site in the Internet Explorer Favorites on your device. Alternately, on a Pocket PC you can tap the Internet button on Media Player to launch the web site.

Personalize Windows Media Player

Tape and CD players have buttons that control music playback. On a Smartphone you use the navigation button to control playback, while on a Pocket PC you can tap the onscreen buttons or use the navigation button, as listed in Table 18-3.

You can program the hardware buttons on your Pocket PC to perform different playback functions. Tap Menu | Options and then the Buttons tab to open the following screen:

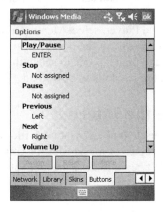

To map a button, double-tap a function such as Play/Pause and then press the hardware button that you want to use to perform that function. To remove a button mapping, tap the function name and tap None.

Function	Navigation Button Action
Play/Pause	Press
Next Song	Press Right
Previous Song	Press Left
Increase Volume	Press Up
Decrease Volume	Press Down

TABLE 18-3   Navigation Button Actions for Controlling Windows Media Player

18

The Toggle Screen function is unique to Pocket PCs; it turns the screen display on or off. Turning the display off saves battery life, which allows you to play more music. All of the button mappings that you program remain in effect while the screen is off so that you can easily adjust music playback.

Previous versions of Windows Media Player have a setting that you can configure to specify whether to unmap buttons when Media Player is running in the background. This is the default behavior for Windows Media Player 10, and there is no way to change it.

Windows Media Player supports *skins,* which you can change to tailor the user interface to your tastes. A Media Player skin consists of a number of bitmap image files and a text file. Files of each skin should be stored in a separate directory on the device. The skin directories can be stored anywhere on the device, but keep in mind that if a skin is on a storage card, the card needs to be in the device every time you run Media Player so that it can load the skin.

If Windows Media Player cannot find the skin it is configured to use, it automatically loads the Skin Chooser so that you can select another skin.

To change skins in Windows Media Player, select Menu | Options | Skins. The Skin Chooser dialog box displays with left and right arrows at the bottom of the box. Tap the arrows to scroll through the skins that are available, and then tap OK to select the skin. Table 18-4 lists web sites where you can find Windows Media Player skins to download.

Where to Find Music on the Internet

Of course, Windows Media Player is useless unless you have files to play. Fortunately, plenty of web sites on the Internet contain free copies of music files for you to download. In fact, so many MP3 web sites are available that I can't begin to describe them all. The simplest way to find them is to go to a large index web site, like Yahoo! or Excite, and perform a search for **MP3**. I assure you, you will find plenty of sites.

Be aware that you probably won't find legal copies of songs by popular artists in MP3 format, because the format does not have provisions to protect against piracy. Most of the music that you'll find at web sites like www.garageband.com is written and performed by relatively unknown bands and musicians from around the world. This, in itself, makes finding MP3s fun because it gives you a chance to discover music that you have never heard before.

Web Site	URL
SnoopSoft	www.snoopsoft.com/skins/other.html
PocketGear	www.pocketgear.com
Microsoft	www.microsoft.com/windows/windowsmedia/player/windowsmobile/ppcskins.aspx

TABLE 18-4 Web Sites of Windows Media Player Skins

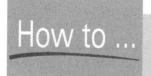

Play MPEG Video Files

MPEG is a more popular video file format than Windows Media Video, and you can play MPEG video files on a Windows Mobile device by using PocketTV. PocketTV is free for personal use and can be downloaded from www.pockettv.com. Another popular media player for Windows Mobile devices is Core Pocket Media Player, available at www .corecodec.org.

PocketTV is capable of playing streaming video files, and it can play video in both portrait and landscape view. It can improve video playback on certain devices, and has a Microdrive option that reduces the power used when playing videos from the Microdrives.

Encoders are programs that convert audio and video files from one format to another. Several encoders are available for making MPEG video files. You can use one of these encoders to create your own MPEG files from home videos. You can find several links to encoders at www.pockettv.com/encoding.html.

Finding WMA files is a little more challenging, because they are not as popular as MP3 files. The best site for WMA files is Microsoft's WindowsMedia.com at http://windowsmedia.com. At this web site, you'll find tracks from popular artists such as Green Day, Nickelback, and Martina McBride. The WMA format supports encryption to prevent music from being played unless it is purchased.

Alternative Music Players

Windows Media Player does not have an equalizer or other settings common to many music players. If you prefer to use a different music player, check out the players listed here:

Player	URL
Pocket Player 2 (Conduits)	www.conduits.com
PocketMusic (PocketMind)	www.pocketmind.com
iMusic (CITSoft)	www.citsoft.net
The Core Pocket Media Player (Gabor Kovacs)	http://tcpmp.corecodec.org/download

18

Microsoft Reader Digital Rights Management

Digital Rights Management (DRM) is technology that ensures that content, such as music and eBooks, is not pirated on the Internet. While the technology is implemented in a variety of ways, it typically involves encrypting the content to prevent it from being copied to multiple computers.

The Microsoft version of DRM has three levels: Sealed, Inscribed, and Owner Exclusive. Sealed eBooks are simply encrypted to ensure the authenticity of the content and can be distributed among multiple computers. Inscribed eBooks are Sealed and further encrypted to include the purchaser's name on the cover page. They can be distributed among multiple computers but will always display the purchaser's information to reinforce honest usage. Owner Exclusive eBooks include additional encryption that requires them to be read only on activated Reader clients. Activation uses the Microsoft Passport authentication, and you can activate only two computers using a Passport ID.

The Reader program that runs on Pocket PC 2000 devices does not support Owner Exclusive eBooks, or what has also been referred to as DRM Level 5. Microsoft does not intend to provide an upgrade for Pocket PC 2000 devices that will support Owner Exclusive eBooks. You can read Sealed (DRM Level 0) and Inscribed (DRM Level 3) eBooks on Pocket PC 2000 devices.

The Reader program that runs on Pocket PC 2002 and newer devices does support Owner Exclusive eBooks as well as Sealed and Inscribed eBooks. To read an Owner Exclusive eBook, you must activate the Reader client. The activation process is explained in an upcoming How To section.

Microsoft Reader's DRM may not work on Windows Mobile 5 devices. As this book is being written, DRM is not working with Windows Mobile 5, though you can expect Microsoft to fix this problem. Before you buy an eBook for Reader, check www.microsoft .com/reader to see whether this problem has been fixed.

Read eBooks

For many people, reading a book is the ultimate escape from computers and the Internet. Most people still read books printed on paper, but an increasing number of people prefer to have their favorite books available on their PC or PDA, which is the idea behind electronic books, or *eBooks*.

Read eBooks Using Microsoft Reader on Pocket PCs

Microsoft Reader is an eBook-viewing program for the Pocket PC. It uses a Microsoft-proprietary font-rendering technology called *ClearType* that is designed to make text easier to read on color LCD screens. With Microsoft Reader, you can read eBooks on your Pocket PC that you may have purchased and downloaded off the Internet.

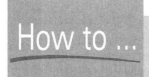

Activate Microsoft Reader on a Pocket PC

Premium eBooks are Owner Exclusive and can be read only using an activated Reader client. To activate Reader, you need a Passport ID, which you can get at www.passport.net. You also need at least ActiveSync Version 3.5 and Internet Explorer Version 4. (Reader cannot be activated on Pocket PC 2000 devices.) Your Pocket PC must be connected to a desktop running ActiveSync during activation and shouldn't have Reader running. You might have activated Reader the first time you synchronized; if not, follow these steps:

1. Connect your Pocket PC to the desktop.

2. Start Internet Explorer and open das.microsoft.com/activate/en-us/default.asp.

3. Log into the web site using your Passport ID.

4. Click Activate My Pocket PC.

The activation process associates your Passport ID with your Pocket PC. It also downloads files to your Pocket PC that are unique to you, along with an Activation Certificate, which is the key piece of information that enables you to read premium eBooks on your Pocket PC.

Microsoft Reader Help provides additional information about activation, and you can find an FAQ at the activation web site.

If Microsoft Reader is not on your Pocket PC, you can download it from www.microsoft .com/reader/downloads/ppc.asp, and then install it. To start Microsoft Reader on a Pocket PC, tap Start | Programs | Microsoft Reader, which opens the Microsoft Reader Library page. The Library lists all of the eBooks that are stored in the My Documents folder on the Pocket PC. Any eBooks stored in subfolders, or in a My Documents folder on a storage card, are also listed.

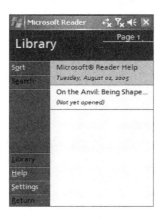

To open a book, tap its name on the Library page, and the cover page of the eBook will open, as shown here. Along the left side of the cover page are buttons you can tap to move to various parts of the eBook or the Reader program. Tap Go To to open a menu with options for moving to the Table of Contents, Most Recent Page, Begin Reading, Furthest Read, Annotations, About This Title, and Cover Image.

When you tap the Most Recent Page link, you return to the last page that was open in the eBook; when you tap Furthest Read, you return to the furthest page opened in the eBook. Tap Annotations to open a list of all the annotations added to the eBook. To move to an annotation quickly, tap its entry in the list.

The easiest way to read an eBook is to press the navigation button left or right on the Pocket PC to move back and forth between pages, or tap the arrows at the bottom of the page. When you tap the title of the eBook at the top of the page, a pop-up list appears:

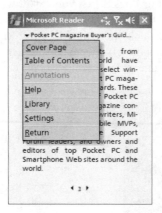

Tap Settings on the pop-up list to change how Reader displays an eBook. Three pages of settings are available: the first page is for turning the visual guides on or off, the second page controls annotations, and the third page controls the font size. To select a page, tap Go To, and

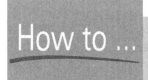

Read eBooks on Smartphones

The small screens that you find on Smartphones do not make them optimal for reading eBooks. Nevertheless, there are a few eBook programs available for Smartphones so that you can use them to read eBooks if you like. You can download Mobipocket Reader and purchase eBooks to read with it at www.mobipocket.com. Tiny eBook Reader from Golden Crater Software is available at www.goldencrater.com.

then tap the items on the page to turn them on or off. When you are done making setting changes, tap Return at the bottom of the screen.

You can annotate text on a page in an eBook by selecting the text using the stylus, which causes a pop-up list to appear:

Tap an entry in the menu to carry out its action. For example, to highlight the text that you selected, tap Add Highlight. When you tap Copy Text, the text is placed on the Pocket PC Clipboard and can be pasted into a Note or Word Mobile document. If you select a word and tap Find, Reader searches through the book for the next occurrence of that word.

Electronic notes can be attached to specific passages of text. To add notes, use the stylus to select text on a page and tap Add Text Note on the pop-up menu. A Note icon appears on the left margin and a notepad displays on the screen. When you are finished writing, tap outside the note to close it. To view notes, tap the Note icon in the left margin; to delete a note, tap-and-hold on the Note icon and tap Delete from the pop-up menu. To display a list of notes for an eBook from the cover page, tap Go To | Annotations.

For more information about how to use Microsoft Reader, open the Microsoft Reader Help eBook on your Pocket PC.

18

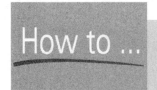

Create Your Own Reader eBook

Microsoft provides a free add-in for Word 2000 and Word 2003 that converts a document to the LIT format used by Reader. You can find the Read in Microsoft Reader (RMR) add-in at www.microsoft.com/ebooks/tools/default.asp. OverDrive ReaderWorks is another eBook-creation tool that converts HTML, text, and image files to the LIT format. ReaderWorks Standard is free; ReaderWorks Publisher costs $69 and enables you to add cover art and marketing data. You can download ReaderWorks from www.overdrive.com/readerworks.

Download Microsoft Reader eBooks

Many Internet web sites provide eBooks that you can download and read on your Pocket PC, some of which are listed in Table 18-5. To read these eBooks on your Pocket PC, copy them to the My Documents folder on your device, or copy them into a My Documents folder on a storage card.

Read eBooks Using Other Programs

Microsoft Reader isn't the only eBook program available for Pocket PCs. Most of the other eBook programs are available for Palm OS devices as well as Pocket PCs, and because of this fact, more eBooks are available. Table 18-6 lists the alternative eBook readers for the Pocket PC.

Listen to Books Using Audible Player

Audible, Inc., is a leading provider of Internet-delivered spoken content for playback on personal computers and Pocket PCs. The sound files can be purchased from the Audible web site at www .audible.com.

Web Site	URL
Pocket PC FAQ	www.pocketpcfaq.com
Elegant Solutions Software and Publishing Company	http://esspc-ebooks.com/default.htm
Pocket PC eBooks Watch	http://cebooks.blogspot.com
Baen Books	www.baen.com
University of Virginia	http://etext.virginia.edu/ebooks
Pocket PC Press	www.pocketpcpress.com
Blackmask Online	www.blackmask.com
Fictionwise	www.fictionwise.com
MemoWare	www.memoware.com

TABLE 18-5   Web Sites Offering Microsoft Reader eBooks for Download

Reader	URL
eReader	www.ereader.com
Mobipocket Reader	www.mobipocket.com/en/HomePage/default.asp
TomeRaider	www.tomeraider.com

TABLE 18-6   eBook Reader Programs for Pocket PCs

Much of the content available for you to buy is recordings of books, but you'll also find special broadcasts, such as *The Wall Street Journal Final & Analysis*. The process of downloading Audible files to a Pocket PC takes two steps. First, the Audible Manager, which is a program that runs on your desktop computer, logs on to the Audible web site and downloads the sound file to the PC. Second, you connect the Pocket PC to the desktop, and then you transfer the sound file to the Audible player.

For every hour of audio programming, you need 2MB of storage space. The recordings vary in length; for example, *The Wall Street Journal Final & Analysis* broadcast lasts 20 minutes, but you can also buy actor Gregory Peck's narration of the Bible that runs 19 hours and 45 minutes. Fortunately, you can specify where Audible will write the sound files when you download them to the Pocket PC.

The Audio Player software contains features optimized for playback of spoken content. You can skip back and forth to sections, which usually are chapters in books. If, during playback, you hear a particular segment to which you want to return, you can create a bookmark that the Audio Player is able to skip to during playback.

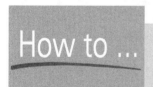 **Play Audible Content with Microsoft Reader**

When you install the Audible Manager, the installation program configures your Pocket PC, so it must be connected to the desktop. It installs the Audible Player on your Pocket PC, but you can also choose not to download the Audio Player and instead listen to books using Microsoft Reader, which is described earlier in the chapter. Microsoft Reader lists Audible content along with all other eBooks on the Library page. To play an Audible book, just tap its entry on the Library page. The Microsoft Reader playback features are not as robust as the Audible Player, but since Reader is already installed on your Pocket PC, you can save storage space by not installing another program that provides the same functionality.

18

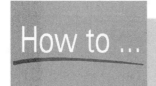
Listen to Podcasts

Podcasting is a new method of transferring audio files on the Internet, and it has become a very popular method for hobbyists and professional media organizations to make audio content available for download. Podcasts are usually recorded in MP3 format and therefore you can play them on Pocket PCs and Smartphones by using Windows Media Player.

One way to transfer a podcast to a Windows Mobile device is to download it to a PC and then synchronize the podcast files to the device. A popular Windows program that downloads podcasts is Doppler, available at www.dopplerradio.net.

Once you enter the RSS feed for the podcasts you want to listen to, Doppler downloads the podcast to your PC and adds it to a playlist in the Windows Media Player Library. You can then configure media synchronization, as described in Chapter 7, to synchronize the playlist to a Pocket PC or Smartphone. If you prefer to download podcasts directly to your device, check out DopplerMobile, which is also available at www.dopplerradio.net.

Wrapping Up

Windows Mobile is a great entertainer. It lets you play games, view pictures, store a library of eBooks, play music, and watch movies. All of these tasks take advantage of the Pocket PC and Smartphone multimedia features, which set it apart from the competition. As you now know, your Windows Mobile device helps you stay organized and is entertaining, but there is much more that your device can do, and you will learn about that in the next chapter.

Chapter 19

Do More with Windows Mobile

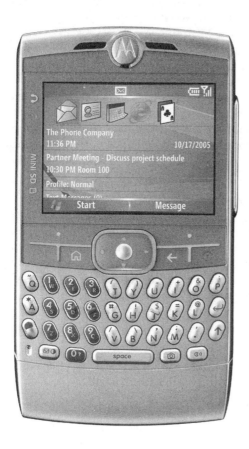

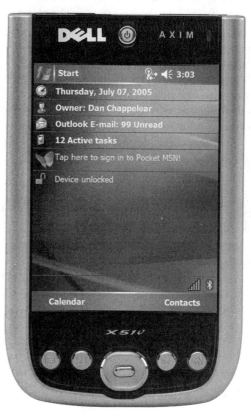

How to...

- Manage money
- Query and store data in databases
- Try some of the best Pocket PC and Smartphone software
- Expand your device with accessories

In the previous chapters, you have learned how to use the programs that come with your Windows Mobile device to manage personal information and edit Word and Excel documents. Many people use their device to perform just these functions, and possibly also to play music and read eBooks. However, there are many more ways for you to use your Pocket PC or Smartphone.

For example, you can use your device to track finances. Microsoft provides a Pocket PC version of Money 2006 so that you can track your spending while you are on the go and synchronize that information with your PC when you get back home. Finance-tracking programs are also available for Smartphones.

Many third-party programs are available that add functionality to your device. You can create and query databases, secure information, use your device as a travel assistant, and use your Pocket PC as a disk drive on your PC. These are but a sample of the many ways that you can do more with your Windows Mobile device with the help of thousands of programs that you can download from the Internet. This chapter describes some of the greatest programs that are available to help you do more with your Pocket PC or Smartphone.

Manage Your Money Using Microsoft Money

Microsoft Money (www.microsoft.com/money/) is a financial information management program that runs on Pocket PCs. With this program, you can track financial information such as checking accounts, savings accounts, credit card accounts, and investment accounts. If you run Microsoft Money on a desktop computer, all of your data can be synchronized between it and your device. Transactions that you enter on your Pocket PC automatically synchronize to your desktop and update account balances.

As this book is being written, Money 2006 does not synchronize with Windows Mobile 5 devices. I believe Microsoft is working to fix this problem, but I do not know a date for when the fix will be available.

Microsoft Money has five views: Account Manager, Account Register, Categories, Investments, and Payees. The current view is always displayed at the top of the screen, as shown in the following image of the Account Manager view. To switch between views, select a view from the View drop-down list, or tap one of the five Command bar buttons at the bottom of the screen.

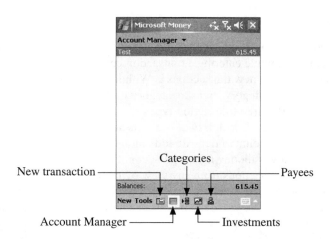

New transaction

Categories

Payees

Account Manager

Investments

Microsoft Money 2006 for Pocket PC runs on Windows Mobile 5, but does not support the Windows Mobile 5 softkeys.

Use Accounts and the Account Register

When you start Microsoft Money, the Account Manager view displays, which is the main view of the program. This view displays the name and balance for each account, as well as the total balance for all accounts. To see the transactions for an account, tap the account name in the Account Manager view. You can also switch to the Account Register view by expanding the View drop-down list and tapping Account Register, which opens the following program window on a Pocket PC:

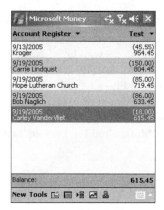

Notice that the current account displays in the upper-right corner. If you want to switch to another account, tap the drop-down list triangle next to the account name and tap an account name in the list.

19

Enter Transactions

Microsoft Money for Pocket PC is designed so that entering transactions is fast and easy. Many of the fields that you complete while entering a transaction contain default values; for instance, the default Type field entry for all new transactions is Withdrawal. AutoFill automatically enters the most recently used amount, category, and subcategory for the last transaction for a payee.

Microsoft Money supports three transaction types: withdrawal, deposit, and transfer. A withdrawal is a transaction that removes money from an account; a deposit adds money to an account; and a transfer moves money from one account to another. You can enter new transactions from any view by tapping the New Transaction button on the Command bar; or if you are in the Account Register view, tap New. When you create a new transaction, the screen shown here displays.

To enter a new transaction, do the following:

1. Select Withdrawal, Deposit, or Transfer from the Type drop-down list.

2. Select an account from the Account drop-down list.

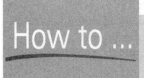 **Synchronize with Quicken**

LandWare is licensed by Intuit to develop and sell handheld versions of Quicken, which are called Pocket Quicken. The Pocket PC version of Pocket Quicken runs on Pocket PC 2000 through Windows Mobile 5 and synchronizes with Quicken Basic, Deluxe, Home & Business, and Premier versions 99 through 2006. Pocket Quicken also synchronizes with Quicken UK 2002 or later and Quicken 2004 Personal Plus Australian Version, while Microsoft Money synchronizes only with U.S. versions of Money. You can find more information about Pocket Quicken at www.landware.com/pocketquicken/ppc/index.html.

A few alternatives to Microsoft Money and Pocket Quicken include the following:

Program	URL
Mastersoft Money	www.mastersoftmobilesolutions.com/
Cash Organizer	www.inesoft.com/
PocketMoney	www.catamount.com/PocketMoney.html/
Money Manager	www.owlseeker.co.uk/
Spb Finance	www.spbsoftwarehouse.com/

3. Enter a payee in the Payee field, or select an entry from the drop-down list. AutoFill attempts to determine which payee you are entering and automatically displays one previously entered into the field based on the letters you enter.

4. Select a date from the Date pop-up menu.

5. Enter a value in the Amount field.

Smartphone Programs for Managing Money

Windows Mobile devices work well for tracking money because they are small enough to be carried everywhere, including places where you spend money. If you want to use your Smartphone to track your finances, check out one of the following programs:

Program	URL
XS Finance	www.xcitesoftware.com/
Keep Track	www.iliumsoft.com/
SmartMoney	www.mactiontech.com/english/

View Microsoft Access Databases

The Microsoft Access database application is not available for Pocket PC, and Microsoft does not provide a Pocket PC version of Access for you to install. Fortunately, several software developers have written Pocket PC database programs that you can download from the Internet. In this section, you'll learn how to use one of these programs to create databases to store and query information.

Windows Mobile 5 does not support Access database synchronization, but you can synchronize Access data with Pocket Access databases on Windows Mobile 2003SE and earlier devices. Synchronization between Pocket Access and Microsoft Access is not enabled by default. It has to be turned on by selecting the Pocket Access information type in ActiveSync.

As this book is being written, Access synchronization does not work with Windows Mobile 5; however, Microsoft may add an Access synchronization feature in a future release of ActiveSync.

While you can synchronize Microsoft Access data to a Pocket PC, you are limited in how much information you can synchronize. Only tables, fields, and indexes are synchronized between your device and PC. You can choose to synchronize only certain fields within a table or mark information as read-only on your device. Unfortunately, you cannot synchronize forms, queries, or reports. The Pocket PC database programs that work with Access data work with only one table of a database, and they don't provide the full functionality of a relational database.

NOTE   *Only 65,536 records can be synchronized from a host database to a Pocket PC database.*

To view or edit the data once it is on your Pocket PC, you need to download and install a third-party database program. Perhaps the easiest and least expensive of those programs is Data On The Run from Biomobility. A trial version of this program is available at www.biomobility.com.

Open a Database

When Data On The Run first loads, you see the following file list window. To open a database that is stored in the My Documents folder, either internally or on a storage card, tap the name of the database that you want to open. To create a new database, tap New.

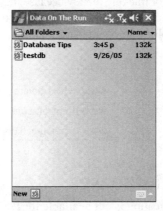

Access databases can contain several tables of records that store information. Only one table opens at a time in Data On The Run, so immediately after selecting a database, you are prompted to select the table to open from a drop-down list of tables in the database. To open another table in the database, tap the Tables tab, select a table, and then tap Open Selected Table.

View Data

The table that you select displays in the following Form view:

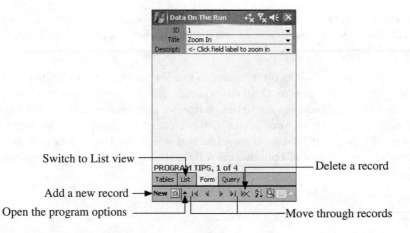

This Form view is automatically created by the program, and, unlike other database software available for Pocket PCs, Data On The Run does not allow you to create your own forms. You can configure Data On The Run to display the List view by tapping Use List View As Default View in the program's options.

The Command bar has buttons for moving through the records in the table. Above the Command bar are tabs for different parts of the database. Tap List to display all of the records in the table in a tabular view:

Tap here to move through records.

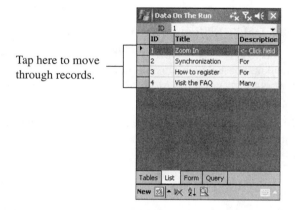

To resize a column, tap the stylus on the right edge of the column head and drag either left or right. Slide the scroll bar left or right to view more columns in the table.

Edit Data

You might choose to synchronize a Microsoft Access database so that you can edit the data when you are away from your desktop computer. Editing data using Data On The Run is easy. Simply tap the field that you want to change, make the changes, and then move to the next record to save the changes. To edit data in the List view, tap the field you want to change, which displays the field at the top of the screen, as shown here. Make the changes in the field at the top of the screen, and then tap another field to store the change.

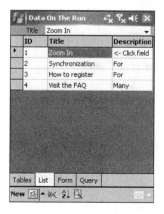

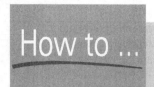

Synchronize Databases with Windows Mobile 5

While you may not be able to synchronize Microsoft Access databases with Windows Mobile 5 devices, there are three other databases that will synchronize with Windows Mobile 5:

- **Microsoft SQL Server 2005 Mobile Edition**   You can find information about this program at www.microsoft.com/sql/editions/sqlmobile/default.mspx.

- **Syware Visual CE**   A visual database development tool for Pocket PCs whose mEnable synchronization works with Windows Mobile 5. Find details at www .syware.com.

- **HanDBase**   A very popular database program for Pocket PCs that has a desktop equivalent and enables you to synchronize data between the two. You can find HanDBase at www.ddhsoftware.com/.

To add or delete data from either the Form or List view, tap either New or the Delete Record button on the Command bar. When you tap New while in List view, a new record is added, and you add data to the record by tapping the field and entering the data at the top of the screen.

One of the neat features that Data On The Run provides is the ability to define a drop-down list of data that is frequently entered into a database. Select Drop Down Wizard from the program menu to display the window shown here. Provide the information in the window and tap Next to either select a table to use for the drop-down values or manually enter the values for the drop-down menu.

A triangle to the right of a field indicates that a drop-down list contains information. When you add a record, tap the triangle to display the list, tap an item, and it will be inserted into the field.

Work with Databases on a Smartphone

A version of Data On The Run is not available for Smartphones, but you can view Microsoft Access databases, along with databases created using many other desktop PC database software, with Smartphone Database Viewer from Cellica Software Services. Smartphone Database Viewer has desktop and Smartphone components for creating an extract of a PC database that you then copy to a Smartphone and view. You can find more information about this program at www.cellica.com.

Other database software available for Smartphones includes:

Program	URL
FoneDB	www.syware.com
eSQL	http://vieka.com/

Top Ten Pocket PC Downloads

What you choose to install on your Pocket PC depends on your needs. You might want a better personal information manager than Pocket Outlook, or you may want to play games, view images, or play music. I have found a number of downloads to be valuable for use on my Pocket PC, and I've included a personal Top Ten list of favorites, although by no means am I suggesting that these programs are the best of what's out there. Rather, the applications presented here are a small sample of the type of software available for Pocket PCs and programs that I think will appeal to a wide variety of users.

Create Lists with ListPro

Do you find yourself making lists on all sorts of scrap paper? Many people create shopping lists to help them remember what they need to buy when they are at a store, or lists of Tasks to Do, Toys to Buy, Movies to Rent, and so on. Some lists are in numerical order, while others may be indented like an outline. The Pocket PC Tasks application is good for creating unordered lists, but it does not support numbered lists or indentation. To overcome these deficiencies, download ListPro from Ilium Software. With ListPro, you can create and reuse any type of list that you need.

You can find this program at any of the download web sites listed in this chapter and also at the Ilium Software web site at www.iliumsoft.com. A 30-day trial version is also available, which stops functioning after the trial period unless you purchase a registration code. You buy the code at the Ilium Software web site.

Versions of the program exist for Windows Mobile Pocket PCs and Smartphones. Ilium Software sells ListPro bundled with a Windows desktop version, or you can buy the two separately. Also, you need the Windows version if you want to synchronize lists between your device and a desktop computer.

Lists are stored in a single file and can be organized into folders. Once you create a file, you then create a list by defining how you want the list to work and what should display. By default, a list item displays a check box and description in columns. You can add columns to the display. Certain columns can be associated with special actions; for example, when you check an item, its color can change.

You can sort list items by any column and filter them so that only certain items display. If a list has an amount column, you can total those amounts at the tap of a button. Resetting a list clears all item check boxes, enabling you to reuse lists. If you find yourself writing the same shopping list over and over, create it using ListPro, and when you are done shopping, just reset the list to use it another day.

Read the Bible with PocketBible

Your Pocket PC is as handy as a book; wouldn't it be great to be able to read a book on it? Bible readers will appreciate PocketBible, a version of the Bible for Pocket PCs from Laridian Electronic Publishing. With this software, Bible verses are only a tap away. PocketBible consists of two parts: the reader program and any number of Bibles. Each piece is sold separately, and six different translations of the Bible are available, including the popular New International Version. A demo is available from Laridian at www.laridian.com/.

What makes this program particularly useful is its Go To Verse keypad. With a couple of taps of the keypad, you select the book, chapter, and verse to read. You can also search for verses using the PocketBible Find command and Boolean logic (AND, OR, NOT, and XOR). The Find dialog box even auto-completes popular search phrases.

Each Bible requires 2 to 3MB of storage space on the device, which can be on a storage card. If you store a Bible on a storage card, the software will run a little slower than if the file were stored internally. The PocketBible reader program can be stored internally, enabling you to store different translations on more than one storage card.

Test Network Connections with vxUtil

One of the more frustrating things about Pocket PCs is that while they provide a number of ways to connect to networks, they don't include the basic tools you need for troubleshooting network connectivity problems. For example, Pocket PCs do not have a way to display IP addresses. Pocket PCs also do not have a *Ping utility,* which you normally use to test network connectivity between two devices. Without these basic tools, it is impossible for you to determine what causes a network connectivity problem.

Fortunately, Cambridge Computer Corporation provides vxUtil, which is a free program that provides 14 network utilities. The program displays the current IP address of the Pocket PC and has a standard Ping utility. It also includes DNS Audit, DNS Lookup, Finger, Get HTML, IP Subnet Calculator, Password Generator, Port Scanner, Quote, Time Service, Trace Route, Wake On LAN, and Whois utilities.

If you connect your Pocket PC to a network, you should download and install vxUtil from www.cam.com/vxutil.html.

Create Outlines with Streamliner

When I write magazine articles or chapters for this book, I first create an outline using Outline View in Microsoft Word. I find that outlines help me to write about a subject thoroughly by identifying main points and related topics. While Word Mobile now supports outlines, Pocket Word, which is on Windows Mobile 2003SE and older devices, does not provide a way to create outlines. To create outlines on my Pocket PC, I use Streamliner from Kopsis, Inc., which you can download from http://kopsisengineering.com/streamliner/.

Streamliner provides all the basic functions for creating outlines, such as Expand, Collapse, and Indent. Outline items can include check boxes or progress indicators for tracking tasks. Streamliner is not integrated with Pocket Word, but you can export outlines to Rich Text Format, which you can open in Pocket Word.

Secure Information in eWallet

If you are like me, you probably use a number of user IDs and passwords to connect to web sites on the Internet. User IDs, passwords, and account numbers are the type of information that you want to keep secure. To store and secure all of this type of information on my Pocket PC, I use eWallet from Ilium Software.

With eWallet, you store information on cards with 30 different templates. For example, you can store credit card numbers on a card with a background that looks like a credit card. Information is organized in six categories: Accounts, Information, Internet, Memberships, Passwords, and Software Registration Codes. Each category can be protected with a password.

The eWallet data file is secured with RC4 128-bit encryption, and you can configure eWallet to prompt for a password before opening a file. You can also configure eWallet to lock and close after a set period of inactivity, as well as lock access for a period of time after a certain number of incorrect password attempts. A desktop version of eWallet lets you access information if your Pocket PC is lost or stolen.

eWallet is the most important program on my Pocket PC. You can download this program from www.iliumsoft.com.

Capture Screenshots with Screen Capture Utility

As you have read this book, you have seen a number of screenshots that I captured using Screen Capture Utility from ValkSoft. Screen Capture Utility creates bitmap image files (BMP) that are written to a folder you specify, which can be on a storage card. This program is available at www .valksoft.com/.

To use this program, you assign it to a hardware button and then press the button to capture a screenshot. The captured files are written to the My Documents folder on the device so that you can easily transfer them to a PC via ActiveSync file synchronization. You can use this program to capture QVGA and VGA Pocket PC displays.

19

Watch Live Television

Long before there were portable media players and video iPods, Pocket PCs were capable of playing audio and video content. As wireless networks become pervasive around the world, more streaming media will be available that you can play on Windows Mobile devices.

SmartVideo, one such streaming media service, provides live video from CNBC, MSNBC, and The Weather Channel, as well as video on demand from Court TV, E! Networks, and more. The service works with Smartphones, Pocket PC Phone Editions, and Pocket PCs with Internet access. There is a monthly subscription fee for SmartVideo. You can find more information about this service at www.smartvideo.com/.

View Flash Content

Flash is one of the most popular forms for multimedia content on the Internet. Web sites built with Flash appear and sound like programs that run on desktop computers. Macromedia sells the toolkits for making Flash content and provides Flash players for free from its web site. You can download Flash Player for Pocket PC from www.macromedia.com/software/flashplayer_pocketpc/.

Flash Player for Pocket PC is integrated with Internet Explorer Mobile, and you normally play Flash content by opening a web page on the Internet. However, Flash content can also be downloaded as individual files, which have the file extension .swf. You cannot open an SWF file on a Pocket PC; instead, you must open an HTML file that is designed to display the Flash file. To open the file, use File Explorer to locate the HTML file, and then tap to open the file in Pocket Internet Explorer.

Examples of the type of Flash content available for Pocket PCs include a Tetris game, a New York City subway map, and a Hewlett-Packard Scientific Calculator. You can find Flash files to download and play on your Pocket PC at http://flashdevices.net/.

Really Shut Down Applications

When you tap the X button in the upper-right corner of Pocket PC programs, the program disappears from the screen, but it does not shut down like in Windows. Spb Software House's Spb Pocket Plus, available at www.spbsoftwarehouse.com, changes what happens when you tap the X button so that programs shut down. If you tap-and-hold the X button, a menu appears that enables you to switch between running programs.

Spb Pocket Plus enhances many Pocket PC programs to make them more powerful and easier to use. It provides a Today screen plug-in that shows vital information about your Pocket PC, such as remaining battery life and storage space, and provides tabs of icons to launch programs.

Spb Pocket Plus improves alarms on your Pocket PC so that they repeat rather than play only once as they do by default on Pocket PCs. File Explorer gains ZIP file compression support, the ability to format storage cards, and a Folder Up button to jump to the parent folder. Internet Explorer Mobile gains multiple windows, which are similar to tabs that are popular in desktop web browsers, the ability to view HTML source code for the page that is currently displayed, and the ability to save web pages and pictures.

Use Your Pocket PC as a USB Flash Drive

USB flash drives have become popular for transporting files between computers. You plug in the drives, which are about the size of your thumb, to the USB port on your PC, and Windows treats it like a disk drive. Since Pocket PCs also use USB ports to connect to PCs, and support storage cards, many people wonder why their Pocket PC can't be treated like a USB drive.

Microsoft does not enable Pocket PCs to be USB drives, but you can add this feature with Softick Card Export II. The program adds an icon to the bottom of the Today screen to display a menu to switch between Card Export and ActiveSync modes. When you select Card Export and connect the Pocket PC to a PC, the PC recognizes the Pocket PC as a USB storage device and creates a disk drive. The disk drive maps to the storage card you have in the Pocket PC, and the program menu provides options for selecting which storage card you want to use if your Pocket PC has multiple storage card slots.

To synchronize the Pocket PC, select ActiveSync on Card Export II's menu. You do not need to install any software on the PC, and with the Pocket PC in Card Export mode, it can be connected to any computer running Windows, Linux, or Mac OS X. You can download this program from www .softick.com.

Top Ten Smartphone Downloads

Because I carry my Windows Mobile Smartphone everywhere, I seek out software that helps me the most when I am on the run. The software in this list stores information that I need when I travel or provides entertainment during small periods of downtime, such as waiting in line at the grocery store.

Customize the Home Screen

The Home Screen is the most prominent part of your Smartphone, but besides the five screens that come on the Smartphone, there appears to be little that you can do to change how your Smartphone looks. To change the look of your Home Screen, you can download one of the Home Screens (listed under Themes) available at Smartphone.net (www.smartphone.net) or Handango (www.handango.com), or you could create your own using Homescreen Designer.

With Homescreen Designer from RuttenSoft, you can graphically create your own Home Screens that support all of the standard Home Screen plug-ins, plus several third-party plug-ins. For more information about this program, go to www.ruttensoft.com.

Monitor the Weather

During a recent trip to visit family, we found ourselves racing against a snow storm as the storm made its way toward Michigan from Wisconsin, and we were traveling north. Radio updates of the storm's progress were spotty, so we relied on radar images on my Smartphone that I obtained from AccuWeather.com Wireless. A free version of AccuWeather Wireless is available at http://pda.accuweather.com, and it provides brief forecasts along with satellite and radar images.

One of the best weather programs that I have seen on any mobile device is WeatherBug Mobile, which is designed specifically for Windows Mobile Smartphones. With this program, you can see live, streaming weather conditions, detailed forecasts, local radar, and live cameras. The program costs $14.95, and you can download a trial version from either Handango (www.handango.com) or Smartphone.net (www.smartphone.net).

Find Travel Information

If you travel frequently, your Smartphone can be a useful tool for keeping track of your travel information, such as the weather conditions and the time zone at your destination. Fizz Traveler provides customized clocks for 58,000 cities around the world, along with weather information for those cities, and dialing codes. The program provides currency conversion and other conversion calculators, to-do lists, and alarms tailored to work when traveling through several time zones. You can find Fizz Traveler at www.fizzsoftware.com.

Secure Information

By now you know how I use eWallet to securely store information like passwords on my Pocket PC. While I carry my Pocket PC most everywhere, there are times when all I have is my Smartphone, so if I need information in my eWallet, I might be out of luck. Fortunately, Ilium Software also has a version of eWallet for Smartphones that can read the same file that is on my Pocket PC. You can download the Smartphone version of eWallet from www.iliumsoft.com.

Manage Lists

Just as I use eWallet on my Pocket PC to store information, and eWallet on my Smartphone to retrieve that information, I also use ListPro to create checklists on my Pocket PC, and a version of ListPro to use those checklists on my Smartphone. For example, this year I created a Christmas shopping list using ListPro on my Pocket PC, then I copied that list to my Smartphone, and while I was shopping I crossed items off my list on the Smartphone. You can find the Smartphone version of ListPro at www.iliumsoft.com.

Manage Files

While Smartphones store files in folders just as Pocket PCs and Windows desktops do, Smartphones don't come with a File Explorer program that you can use to copy or delete files on your device. With Resco Explorer, which is available at www.resco.net, you can manage the files on your Smartphone as well as encrypt and compress files. It also includes a file viewer to view text files and several of the common graphic file formats.

Send Instant Messages to AOL and Yahoo

Smartphones include MSN Messenger for sending instant messages to other people using MSN Messenger, but there are other instant messaging services such as AOL and Yahoo that your friends may use. Agile Messenger from Agilemobile.com supports instant messaging services from MSN, AOL, Yahoo, and ICQ, enabling you to use one program to keep in touch with all your friends that use these various services. You can find Agile Messenger at www.agilemobile.com.

Read RSS Feeds

Internet Explorer Mobile does a great job of formatting web pages for display on the small Smartphone screens, but some pages may not display well, or may take a long time to download. Really Simple Syndication (RSS) is a file format that many web sites use to provide content without information about the presentation, which means that Smartphone programs can display the content in the best way possible on the small screen.

NewsBreak from Ilium Software is one of the best RSS readers for Smartphones. You can configure it to automatically download RSS feeds, and it comes with a good built-in list of RSS feeds that you can subscribe to. NewsBreak is available at www.iliumsoft.com.

Play Mini Golf

If you really want to show off what your Smartphone can do, try one of the many games available for it, such as Pocket Mini Golf from Momentum Games. Up to six people can play the game, using golfers with different skills and playing on one of several different courses that come with the game. The game even includes weather effects, instant replays, and sound effects. Check out this game at www.momentumgames.com.

Rack 'Em Up with Virtual Pool

Another great game for Smartphones is Virtual Pool Mobile by Celeris, available at www.celeris .com. Virtual Pool Mobile is a 3-D pool simulation that has six different pool games and several different opponents. The interface is easy to use to aim, set the spin, and stroke the cue. Even though I am not a great pool player, I find the 3-D graphics of this program just stunning, and they should look remarkable on the QVGA screens of the newer Smartphones.

Accessorize Your Windows Mobile Device

As you have seen throughout this book, there are many ways to expand the functionality of Windows Mobile by installing software. Another way to expand functionality is with hardware accessories. For example, your Windows Mobile device becomes a navigation tool when combined with a global positioning system (GPS) receiver.

I have often been asked how one can increase memory in a device, or whether one can have their Pocket PC screen repaired, and I always refer people to PPC Techs at www.pocketpctechs .com. PPC Techs can repair the screens of many Smartphones and Pocket PCs for reasonable prices, and its RAM and ROM upgrades are the only way to increase internal program and storage memory on Pocket PCs. Over the years PPC Techs has expanded its offerings to include many popular accessories. In short, PPC Techs should be the first site you go to for repairing, upgrading, or accessorizing your Windows Mobile device.

Many companies sell accessories for Smartphones and Pocket PCs. Table 19-1 provides a sample of what is available to expand your device.

19

Cases	
Cases.com	www.cases.com/
Covertec	www.covertec.com/
EBCases	www.ebcases.com/
JAVOedge	www.javoedge.com/
RhinoSkin	www.saunders-usa.com/rhinoskin/
Storage Cards	
Kingston	www.kingston.com/
Lexar	www.lexar.com/
Pretec	www.pretec.com/
SanDisk	www.sandisk.com/
Keyboards	
Stowaway	www.thinkoutside.com/
JAVOKeyboard	www.javoedge.com/
Freedom Keyboard	www.freedominput.com/
FrogPad	www.frogpad.com/
Sync and Charge Cables	
JAVAOSync	www.javoedge.com/
miniSync	www.boxwave.com/
Styluses	
StylusCentral.com	www.styluscentral.com/
PDA Panache	www.pdapanache.com/
StyliSource.com	www.stylisource.com/
GPS Receivers	
TeleType GPS	www.teletype.com/
Pocket GPS Navigator	www.pharosgps.com/
WayPoint 200	www.mobilecrossing.com/
Pretec SDIO GPS and CompactGPS	www.pretec.com/
Car Mounts	
Arkon Resources	www.arkon.com/
Seidio	www.seidioonline.com/

TABLE 19-1   Windows Mobile Hardware Accessories

Screen Protectors	
ClearTouch	www.boxwave.com/
WriteSHIELD	www.pocketpctechs.com/
JAVAOScreen	www.javoedge.com/
Bluetooth Cards	
Bluetooth Connection Kits	www.socketcom.com/
Bluetooth PDA and PC Adapter Combo Card	www.belkin.com/
ANYCOM Blue CompactFlash Card	www.anycom.com/
Wired LAN Cards	
Socket Low Power and 10/100 Ethernet Cards	www.socketcom.com/
Wireless LAN Cards	
802.11b Wireless PDA Network Card	www.belkin.com/
Socket Go Wi-Fi E300	www.socketcom.com/
Pretec SDIO 802.11b Wireless Card	www.pretec.com/

TABLE 19-1   Windows Mobile Hardware Accessories (*continued*)

Wrapping Up

The success of any computing platform is measured by the amount of software and hardware available for that platform. Thousands of people have downloaded the free development tools that Microsoft provides, resulting in hundreds of programs that you can download and install on your device. The expansion capabilities of Windows Mobile ensure that you will be able to continue enjoying new software on your device for many years to come.

19

Index